Author's Preface

Dedicated to my precious wife, Charlotte, my parents, the dogs and animals who have touched my life, and all American veterans and those who are still POW-MIA.

As the author, I would like to thank you for choosing my book to learn about Demon carburetors. I feel grateful for the opportunity to create this text, and honored by the trust placed in me by S-A Design, Barry Grant, Inc., and you, the reader.

It is my intent for this book to be more than a learning tool about a carburetor. I hope that it becomes an inspiration, a catalyst that prompts someone to pursue an education in technology, engineering, or mathematics. As a nation, we are facing a severe problem due to the lack of enrollment in our colleges and universities to study the sciences. This will weaken our country from within and negatively impact the lives of every American citizen.

We can all do our part to inspire someone. I ask that when you are done with this book, instead of leaving it on the shelf, pass it on to another, and hopefully they will do the same. The impact of this small gesture can be monumental to our country and to the lives of those you may touch. May God bless our nation and all of you.

Ray T. Bohacz

About The Author

Ray T. Bohacz' interests have always revolved around mechanical apparatus, but his true love is engines; it matters little if it is a Detroit Diesel-powered irrigation pump in the middle of a corn field, or a nitro-burning Hemi. His passion for machinery was first displayed at age four, when he released the emergency brake of his parents' 1952 Dodge, with his grandmother in the rear seat. The car rolled backward, avoiding all but a few bushes.

Ray graduated high school by age 16 and was the youngest student on the college campus. Studying electrical engineering, the youthful mind of a hot-rodder became disenchanted when his professor could not explain how the then-new automotive electronic ignitions functioned.

Paying his tuition by working on his friends' hot rods, Ray became known as the "tune-up man." He took more pleasure in having a 100-horsepower engine that ran to perfection than a 400-horsepower engine performing at 80 percent. Ray left the hustle and bustle of New York City for the country life in rural New Jersey where he took a job as a training instructor for Allen Test Products, an emissions analyzer and oscilloscope manufacturer.

With the return of Detroit performance in 1985, Ray opened a speed shop that specialized in tuning and modifications. Some of the fastest street cars in the country wore his banner, and in 1993, he was the first to modify a fourth-generation Camaro. That car ran 11.70 @ 119 mph and took second place in the *Car Craft* Real Street Eliminator contest in 1994.

Disappointed that magazines were not giving readers any real technical information, he decided to try his hand at writing. His first byline appeared in 1995 in *Vette* magazine, and now you will find his work on a regular basis in *Hot Rod*, *Popular Hot Rodding*, *GM High Tech Performance*, *High Performance Pontiac*, *Corvette Fever*, *High Performance Mopar*, *Hemming's Rods and Performance*, *Muscle Car Review*, *Specialty Interest Auto*, and *Mustang Illustrated*, among others. He also created the ACCEL EMIC training manual and course curriculum taught at the University of Northwestern Ohio in Lima. Ray is a member of the Society of Automotive Engineers, the American Society of Materials, and the International Motoring Press Association.

When not writing or consulting to the automotive industry, he enjoys spending time with his wife and working on a fully restored 1940 Ford 9N farm tractor with the help of the family's dog, Sparky.

All text, photographs, drawings, and other artwork (hereafter referred to as information) contained in this publication is sold without any warranty as to its usability or performance. In all cases, original manufacturer's recommendations, procedures, and instructions supersede and take precedence over descriptions herein. Specific component design and mechanical procedures — and the qualifications of individual readers — are beyond the control of the publisher, therefore the publisher disclaims all liability, either expressed or implied, for use of the information in this publication. All risk for its use is entirely assumed by the purchaser/user. In no event will Cartech® Inc., or the author be liable for any indirect, special, or consequential damages, including but not limited to personal injury or any other damages, arising out of the use or misuse of any information in this publication.

This book is an independent publication, and the authors and/or publisher thereof are not in any way associated with, and are not authorized to act on behalf of any of the manufacturers included in this book. The publisher reserves the right to revise this publication or change its content from time to time without obligation to notify any persons of such revisions or changes.

HOW TO TUNE AND WIN WITH
DEMON CARBURETORS

By Ray T. Bohacz

Copyright © 2001, 2003 by Ray T. Bohacz. All rights reserved. Demon, along with the Demon Carburetion and Barry Grant, Inc. logos and their designs are trademarks of Barry Grant, Inc. and are used under license. It is unlawful to reproduce — or copy in any way — resell, or redistribute this information without the expressed written permission of the author. Printed in U.S.A.

OVERSEAS DISTRIBUTION BY:

BROOKLANDS BOOKS LTD.
P.O. Box 146, Cobham, Surrey, KT11 1LG, England
Telephone 01932 865051 • Fax 01932 868803

Brooklands Books Australia
3/37-39 Green Street, Banksmeadow, NSW 2019, Australia
Telephone 2 9695 7055 • Fax 2 9695 7355

Edited By

Monica Dwyer Abress

Production By

Tamara Baechtel

ISBN-13 978-1-61325-000-6

PART No. SA68P

CARTECH® INC., 39966 GRAND AVENUE, NORTH BRANCH, MN 55056

CONTENTS

- INTRODUCTION 4
- CHAPTER 1: BACK TO BASICS 6
  - HOW IT ALL STARTED 7
  - FOUR CYCLES OF AN ENGINE 9
  - STATIC AND DYNAMIC COMPRESSION 13
  - THE EFFECT OF COMPRESSION RATIO
    - ON OCTANE REQUIREMENTS 15
  - VOLUMETRIC EFFICIENCY 16
  - CARBURETOR 101 18
  - THE CARBURETOR NEEDS TO BE
    - MATCHED TO THE ENGINE 20
  - REVIEW QUESTIONS 21
- CHAPTER 2: THE CIRCUITS OF A CARBURETOR 24
  - CARBURETOR HISTORY 24
  - DEFINING VACUUM 26
  - HOW A CARBURETOR WORKS 27
    - Float System 28
    - Choke 29
    - Idle 29
    - Main Metering 30
    - Accelerator Pump 31
    - Power Enrichment 32
    - Secondary Barrels 33
    - Transfer Slots 34
    - Air Bleeds, Emulsion Holes, and Jets 34
  - PUTTING IT ALL TOGETHER 35
  - THE WORKINGS OF A DEMON 35
    - Air Entry 35
    - Float Circuit 36
    - Choke 38
    - Idle Circuit 38
    - Main Metering Circuit 39
    - Squirter Circuit 39
    - Power Valve Circuit 40
    - Secondary Circuit Control 40
    - Additional Features and Benefits 40
  - REVIEW QUESTIONS 41
- CHAPTER 3: CHOOSING THE PROPER CARB 42
  - UNDERSTANDING AIRFLOW RATINGS 42
  - VELOCITY vs. BOOSTER SIGNAL 46
  - BOOSTER VENTURI DESIGN 47
    - Straight 49
    - Down or Drop Leg 49
    - Annular Discharge 50
  - MECHANICAL vs. VACUUM SECONDARY 50
  - SQUIRTERS 53
  - EASE OF TUNING 53
  - REVIEW QUESTIONS 55
- CHAPTER 4: ROAD DEMON 56
  - WARM BLOODED 58
  - A GOOD ALL-AROUND CARBURETOR 60
  - REVIEW QUESTIONS 61
- CHAPTER 5: SPEED DEMON 62
  - REVIEW QUESTIONS 67
- CHAPTER 6: RACE DEMON 68
  - Drag Race Gas (DR) 68
  - Drag Race Gas Removable Sleeve (DR RS) 69
  - General Competition Gas (GC) 69
  - General Competition Gas Removable Sleeve (GC RS) . 70
  - Road Race Gas (RR) 70
  - Road Race Gas Removable Sleeve (RR RS) 70
  - Tunnel Ram Gas (TR) 71
  - Tunnel Ram Gas Removable Sleeve (TR RS) 71
  - Oval Track Gas (OT) 71
  - Oval Track Gas Removable Sleeve (OT RS) 71
  - Blower Calibration Removable Sleeve (BC RS) 71
  - 390 Removable Sleeve (390 RS) /
    - 750 Removable Sleeve Check Legal 72
  - ALCOHOL RACE DEMONS 72
    - Drag Race Alcohol (Alky DR) 72
    - Drag Race Alcohol Removable Sleeve (Alky DR RS) ... 72
    - Oval Track Alcohol (Alky OT) 72
    - Oval Track Alcohol Removable Sleeve (Alky OT RS) .. 73
  - REVIEW QUESTIONS 73
- CHAPTER 7: KING DEMON 82
  - General Competition Gasoline (GC) 82
  - Drag Race Removable Sleeve (DR RS) 83
  - Tunnel Ram Removable Sleeve (TR RS) 84
  - INTERMEDIATE CIRCUIT 84
  - REVIEW QUESTIONS 87
- CHAPTER 8: THE FUEL SYSTEM 88
  - PRESSURE AND FLOW 88
  - FUEL PUMP TYPES 90
  - HOW MUCH FLOW? 91
  - CHOOSING THE PROPER FUEL PUMP 92
  - PLUMBING AND INSTALLING YOUR FUEL SYSTEM 95
  - USING A FUEL PRESSURE REGULATOR
    - OR DIAPHRAGM BYPASS 97
  - UNDERSTANDING GASOLINE 97
    - Where oil comes from 97
    - What is Octane 101
    - What am I buying? 102
    - What does the engine want? 103
  - REVIEW QUESTIONS 105
- CHAPTER 9: TUNING FOR STREET/STRIP 106
  - THE HOW AND WHY OF SPARK ADVANCE 106
    - What does the engine really want? 108
  - UNDERSTANDING EMISSIONS 110
  - THE OFFENDERS 110
    - Hydrocarbons (HC) 110
    - Carbon Monoxide (CO) 111
    - Carbon Dioxide (CO_2) 111
    - Oxygen (O_2) 111
    - Oxides of Nitrogen (NOx) 111
  - THE CATALYTIC CONVERTER 112
  - DESIGNING AN EMISSIONS-FRIENDLY,
    - HIGH-OUTPUT ENGINE 113
  - PUTTING IT TO THE TEST 114
  - TUNING TIPS 114
    - Carburetor adjustment 114
    - Ignition 115
    - PCV 115
    - EGR 115
    - Air Pump 115
  - WHAT TO LOOK FOR 116
  - GENERAL TROUBLESHOOTING AND DIAGNOSING 116
  - TUNING THE DEMON CARBURETOR 117
  - CHECKING BASELINE ADJUSTMENTS 118
    - Throttle and Accelerator Pump Linkage 119
    - Closed Butterfly Position 119
    - Idle Mixture Screws 119
    - Bolting the Carburetor to
      - the Intake Manifold 119
    - Connecting Throttle Linkage 119
    - Connecting Fuel Lines 120
    - Connecting Vacuum Lines 120
    - Priming the Carburetor 120
    - Starting the Engine 120
    - Preliminary Float Adjustment 121
    - Curb Idle Speed and Mixture Adjustment 121
    - Achieving a Smooth Idle 123
    - Jet up or down? 123
    - Air Bleeds 124
    - Emulsion Bleeds 126
    - Float 126
    - Power Valve 126
    - Accelerator Pump 126
    - Vacuum Secondary 127
    - Spacers 129
    - Hood Scoops, Cowls, and Air Pans 129
  - REVIEW QUESTIONS 135
- CHAPTER 10: RACE TRACK PREPARATION 136
  - AIR DELIVERY 136
  - FLOAT ADJUSTMENT 137
  - IDLE MIXTURE SCREWS 137
  - JETTING 138
  - ACCELERATOR PUMP 139
  - POWER VALVE 141
  - THROTTLE LINKAGE 141
  - TUNING FOR CHANGING WEATHER CONDITIONS 141
  - SPACERS AND PLENUM DIVIDERS 142
  - CARBURETOR AND FUEL SYSTEM MAINTENANCE 142
  - TUNING EMULSION BLEEDS 142
  - THE BENEFIT OF DYNO TESTING 143
  - REVIEW QUESTIONS 144
- CHAPTER 11: GLOSSARY OF TERMS 145

How to Tune & Win with DEMON CARBURETORS

Introduction

To derive the most from this book, a few easy steps should be taken. The intent is to provide the reader not only a complete overview of the Demon carburetor line, but also an understanding of engine functions and how they affect the carburetor.

The text starts with a review of the basics and then progresses deeper into the subject matter. The end of every chapter includes review questions which are designed to firmly establish the concepts represented before the next topic is covered.

It is best to familiarize yourself with the book before getting started. Glance at that table of contents, randomly flip through the pages, and briefly read a few paragraphs. You will notice that there are numerous sidebars that add interesting points and help to round out the learning experience. Find a chapter that you have particular interest in and browse through it more thoroughly; this will give you an incentive to keep reading. After you feel familiar with the contents, read from the beginning at whatever rate you are comfortable. The average person should be able to finish the complete book in a week by devoting only about an hour a day.

You will notice that a modular approach is used, covering each model in the Demon line separately. This is done so material pertinent to the reader would be readily available. Wanting to have "form follow function," there is some repetition of photography and captions in Chapters 4, 5, 6, and 7. This occurs where a component such as a float bowl or accelerator pump cover is not application specific to one model. Do not consider the repetition an oversight.

Chapter 1 starts with a review of how the Demon carburetor line came into being and then quickly moves into the basics of combustion. A simple, easy-to-understand approach to the gas exchange process is taken and is meant to help the enthusiast, engine tuner, student, or entry-level engineer connect the events that allow an engine to function. With this established, the need to match the carburetor's design and size to the engine is explained. The chapter ends with a description of modular carburetor design.

The foundation of carburetor function is covered in Chapter 2, beginning with a generic description of circuitry and then moves into specific Demon internal features. Broken down into seven distinct categories, the reader is walked through the function of a carburetor from the basics to advanced circuit operation.

Chapter 3 is devoted to deciding which Demon carburetor is correct for your use. It begins by debunking the misconceptions related to choosing a carburetor size in cubic feet of air per minute. The chapter then looks in-depth at the options offered in booster design, secondary operation, and ease of tuneability.

As mentioned previously, Chapters 4, 5, 6, and 7 are each dedicated to a specific Demon model. This layout was used to separate the necessary information for each carburetor so there would be no confusion between the models. It is suggested that none of these chapters be skipped, especially if you have not yet purchased your carburetor. Many feel that it is necessary to only read the chapter that pertains to the model carburetor that they will use. The best tuners have a complete knowledge of all functions of a design and this helps them to obtain the greatest performance. As an example, understanding why a Road Demon uses different booster styles in both the primary and secondary sides can help adapt a more sophisticated design such as the Race Demon to a unique application. Each chapter includes interesting sidebars that can be applied beyond that particular model carburetor.

Often overlooked in carburetor books is any mention of the fuel system and gasoline, even though they are inherent components of carburetor function. Breaking from this mold, Chapter 8 covers fuel system design, installation, and choices. Basics such as when to use a fuel pressure regulator and how a fuel pump functions are discussed. The chapter closes with an easy-to-understand explanation of gasoline and its properties, along with a sidebar on using alcohol as a race fuel.

The importance of Chapter 9, which is titled "Tuning for Street and Strip" needs to be established to those who have race entries, even though Chapter 10 is dedicated to race track preparation. Wanting to avoid lengthy repetition, the basics of spark advance, idle quality, jet sizes, squirter cam orifice, and secondary operation are covered. In contrast, Chapter 10 skips these fundamentals and reveals secrets for application-specific venues including drag and road racing. General competition carburetor tuning is discussed in length along with the unique requirements of alcohol and forced-induction applications. The chapter concludes by explaining the need for dyno tuning and how it is the most efficient and cost-effective method to obtain the best performance from not only the Demon carburetor, but the entire vehicle.

For the ultimate in performance and driveability, a Demon carburetor and a NitrousWorks nitrous oxide system are the ticket.

All of the cars at the Richard Petty Driving School are Demon-equipped for reliable performance and in total log more than 1.5 million high-speed miles per year.

The book closes with a glossary of approximately 460 terms that are relevant to the subject matter, either directly or indirectly. On its own the glossary makes for interesting reading, exposing the enthusiast to common engineering jargon while enriching the learning experience.

Happy reading.

Ray T. Bohacz
June 2001

A smoky burnout sounds powerful, but depending on the throttle angle, the engine may be running mostly on the idle and main-metering circuit.

How to Tune & Win with DEMON CARBURETORS
Back to Basics

For those of us who have a love affair with engines, the four-barrel carburetor holds a very special place in our hearts. During the heyday of the musclecar era, this style of induction was romanticized by both Detroit and the music industry. It became the focus of advertising campaigns, its presence was displayed with fender badges, and it was a dominant factor in determining the name of the Oldsmobile 442. It unequivocally represented the epitome of performance. Today the world is different, and the carburetor has been replaced by electronic fuel injection. Sadly, 35 years after its introduction in America, the last four-barrel-equipped engine rolled down an assembly line in 1987. It succumbed to the demands of emissions controls and corporate average fuel economy (CAFE) standards for production cars, but its dominance in street performance and racing has not wavered, and if anything, has increased.

Demon Carburetion founder and owner Barry Grant, a devoted drag racer, discovered early on that a prop-

The same fortitude and tenacity that made Barry Grant a successful racer drives Barry Grant, Inc.

erly tuned carburetor was the key to extracting the most performance from an engine. An inherent obstacle to that cause was the actual carburetors being used. In most instances, they were original equipment designs that were asked to supply needs beyond their ability. They suffered from inadequate fuel and airflow capacity, along with manufacturing and design issues, and so a subindustry that modified carburetors was born.

Though many tried their hands at this concept, Barry Grant was quickly recognized as being in the forefront of carburetor tuning. His goal progressed from modifying production carburetors to engineering and manufacturing a completely new design that would not require rework for use on a performance engine. This was the impetus for the extensive R&D program that gave birth to the Demon Carburetion line. Grant's company was restructured to include Demon Carburetion, BG Fuel Systems, and NitrousWorks under the corporate banner GPT (Grant Performance Technologies) 300, Inc. Effective May 1, 2001, the company changed its corporate name to Barry Grant, Inc.

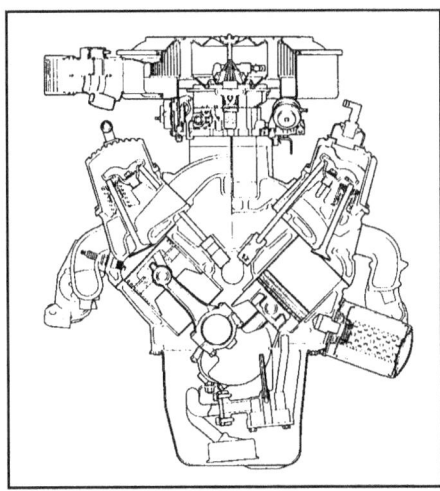

The popularity of V-8 engines such as this 1968 Ford 302 created the need for a more efficient fuel-metering device, which gave birth to the four-barrel carburetor.

The Demon brand offers a carburetor for nearly every application and is categorized by name. It begins with the Road Demon, an entry-level carburetor focused on the street-performance and replacement market. It not only offers increased power and driveability, but is attractively styled. Rated at 625 cfm, it is designed to serve the requirements of 289- to 355-cubic-inch engines.

The next step up is the Speed Demon, available in three different flow rates: 650, 750, and 850 cfm, with either vacuum or mechanical secondary. Aimed at the street/strip market, the Speed Demon series offers a higher level of tuneability and flow capacity than the Road Demon.

Serving the needs of the racer is the Race Demon, which is available with an RS suffix, identifying a removable sleeve. A unique feature of certain Demon models, it allows the flow rate of the carburetor to be changed by varying the venturi size with a sleeve kit. The Race Demon is also offered with a cast venturi and in flow rates of 650, 750, 825, and 1000 cfm. RS variants offer venturis to adjust the flow rate to 675, 775, 825, 950, 975, 1025, or 1050 cfm.

Rounding out the lineup is the King Demon, with either RS or fixed venturi. Designed as the ultimate race carburetor, it features cfm ratings of 795, 895, 995, 1090, 1095, 1190,

The Road Demon is designed for the street performance and replacement market. It can serve the needs of an engine up to 400 horsepower.

The Race Demon is a highly-refined competition carburetor that is offered with mechanical secondary operation.

1195, and 1295. All Demon carburetors offer design features that make them unique and will be covered in full as the text progresses.

HOW IT ALL STARTED

In 1673, Christian Huygens invented the first engine which was designed to pump water from the Seine River to King Louis XIV's Palace of Versailles. Built with an open combustion chamber, it con-

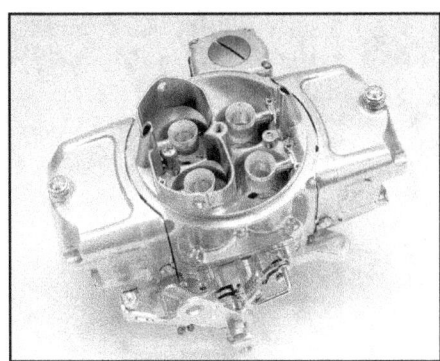

The Speed Demon is available in various flow sizes and with either a mechanical or a vacuum secondary. Designed to offer the fuel-metering accuracy of a race unit with the required manners of a street carburetor, it is a popular choice for a broad range of engines and applications.

A King Demon can be identified by the booster venturi support bridge. A true race-designed carburetor, three-circuit versions offer uncanny driveability around the pits or for Pro Street-style uses.

sumed gunpowder as a fuel. Though it was the first documented engine to be built, it had a striking resemblance to Leonardo da Vinci's drawing of 1509, which never came to fruition.

German Nicholaus Otto is general-

Every use requires a specific carburetor design and is the reason for the many different Demon part numbers, models, and calibrations.

How to Tune and Win with Demon Carburetors

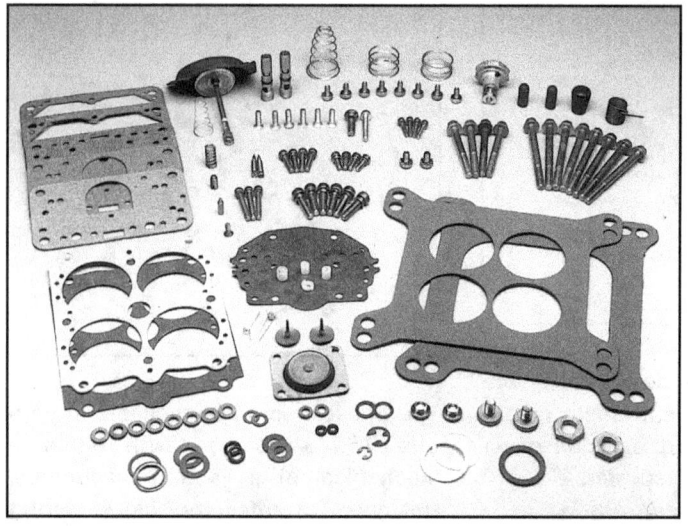
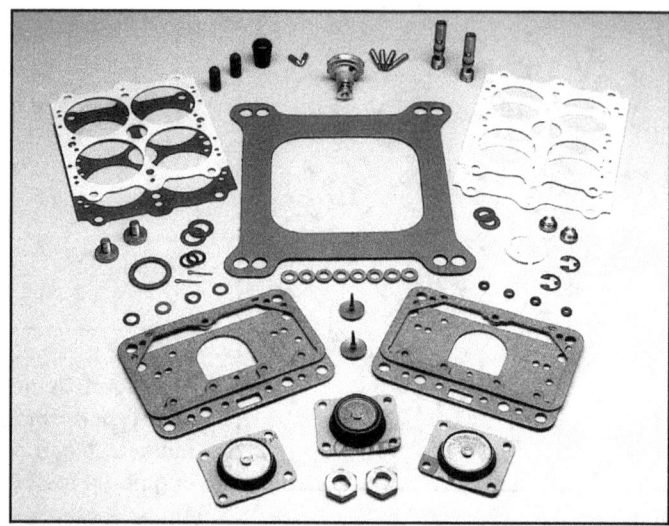

Major overhaul kits are available for all Demon carburetors through a nationwide dealer network.

Quick freshen-up kits keep your Demon carburetor at peak performance for many years.

ly credited with the creation of the first successful four-stroke powerplant that bears any resemblance to today's modern engine. Frenchman Alphonse Beau de Rochas fathered the original concept 14 years earlier in 1862, but he was not completely successful in getting it to work. Otto's original goal was to improve on the efficiency of the French Lenoir two-stroke, non-compression engine, and his inspiration came from watching steam rise from a smokestack. As a result, his surname is often used synonymously for the four-stroke cycle.

Common with any technological revolution, there must be parallel developments in other areas to spawn growth. For this reason, one individual is hardly ever credited with the development of a technology. As for the internal combustion engine, it needed to wait for the arrival of a suitable fuel.

Rudolf Diesel invented the compression ignition engine in 1897. Shortly thereafter, refining technology produced gasoline, albeit not in today's current form. Gasoline was basically a derivative of kerosene, a waste byproduct of early oil refining. It was considered a nuisance and was disposed of by being dumped onto the ground or into rivers.

The controlled release of the high energy content of gasoline was quickly recognized by inventors as a fuel that could advance engine development. The problem with gasoline was that it does not burn in liquid form. It needs to be atomized, emulsified, and vaporized to ignite. This means it must be broken down into small particles, be mixed with air, and undergo a phase change through heat, respectively. The carburetor's job is to accomplish the first two steps, while the law of physics known as the latent heat of vaporization takes credit for the last step. An additional function of the carburetor is to throttle the engine and supply the proper ratio of fuel to air to allow it to operate at varied speeds and loads. It accomplishes this by restricting airflow past the

Parent company Barry Grant, Inc. has a complete stock of service parts for all Demon carburetors housed in its glistening 50,000-square-foot facility, which is nestled in the mountains of Georgia.

RS model Race and King Demons offer replaceable inner sleeves to tailor the flow characteristics to your engine. Color-coded for identification, they offer the ultimate in tuning possibilities.

Through extensive engineering and testing, the booster design for each Demon was analyzed. Shown are a down-leg or drop booster alongside an annular design.

The task of reinventing the carburetor was a daunting one and included many hours of CAD/CAM and dyno time.

Acknowledging that a computer screen and dyno cell can only determine so much, actual on-vehicle testing was done during the development of each Demon model. Barry Grant's BG Fuel Systems Pro Stock Oldsmobile Cutlass was a test bed for both the Race and King Demon.

throttle plates and limiting the amount of charge that reaches the cylinders.

Carburetors are identified as wet-flow fuel systems, whereas a port EFI system is considered dry flow. In wet-flow systems, the fuel/air mixture courses the intake manifold runners, and as its name suggests, a dry system carries only air.

FOUR CYCLES OF AN ENGINE

The fundamental principles that affect carburetor performance and tuning are connected to how an engine works. An internal combustion engine is often compared to an air pump, and this is the basis of the old adage we have all heard: the more air pumped, the higher the output.

Early on, we all learned the four strokes of an engine: intake, compression, power, and exhaust. It seems simple at first, but it involves the elements of combustion that are under the influence of other factors. Air density, compression ratio, fuel octane, volumetric efficiency (VE), and air/fuel ratio are only some of the variables.

Let us expand upon this and consider the events of an engine in more depth. 1) How does the charge fill the bore during the intake stroke? From vacuum created by the piston or through atmospheric pressure? 2) Is the cylinder filled to capacity during every intake event? 3) How is compression ratio defined? How does it impact engine performance? 4) Why is expansion the proper name for the power stroke? 5) During the exhaust cycle, is the bulk of the end gas removed during blow-down or by the pumping action of the piston? Think about your answers and then read on.

Intake

Responsible for filling the cylinder with a combustible mixture, intake is also referred to as the induction stroke. During this event, the intake valve will be open and the exhaust valve closed, the piston will travel downward, and there will be no combustion present. The movement of the piston creates a low-pressure region in the bore and intake manifold and works in conjunction with atmospheric pressure to fill the cylinder. The intake stroke is initiated with the piston at top dead center (TDC) and ends at bottom dead center (BDC). To aid in filling the cylinder, the intake valve usually opens shortly before the stroke starts and closes after it ends, referenced in crankshaft angle degrees.

Airflow through an engine is a cumulative result of the low pressure created by the pumping action of the piston and the differential in pressure between atmosphere and the bore. In reality, the mixture is neither sucked nor pushed into the bore, but is a function of a delta pressure relationship. The quicker the piston moves, the greater the pressure differential becomes, and the more charge that is passed. If piston velocity is kept constant but the atmospheric pressure is varied, the amount of cylinder fill will change. This explains why your car

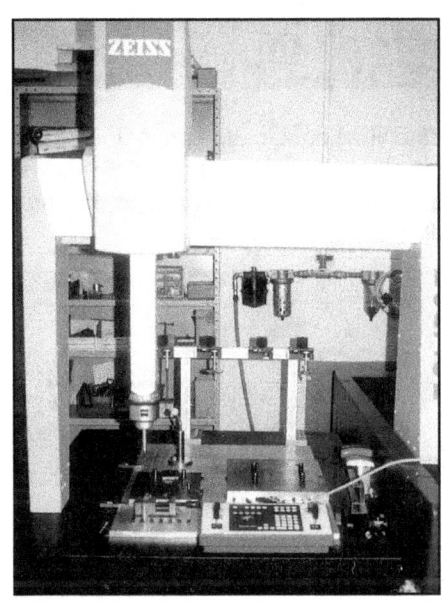

One of the aspects that make the Demon the best carburetor on the market is the manufacturing process. Sophisticated equipment such as this Zeiss coordinate measuring machine (CMM) at Industrial Castings in Macedonia, Ohio, became a key element.

A hand-built prototype of the main body is quality-control checked using the CMM before the design is released for final production.

How to Tune and Win with Demon Carburetors

Zinc/aluminum in the form of ingots will eventually become Demon float bowls, boosters, and main bodies through diecasting.

Twelve state-of-the-art CNC machines produce all of the billet-aluminum carburetor components at Barry Grant, Inc. in Dahlonega, Georgia.

Main bodies follow a mechanized high-pressure cleaning line to guarantee the highest in quality.

Demon engineer Mike Harris and Industrial Castings quality engineer John Quitter inspect a new industrial robot that will be used in a diecasting process.

A similar robot will remove castings from the mold before quenching.

will run better on a dry day with a high barometric reading. The higher atmospheric pressure will fill the bore more completely, while the lack of moisture will provide an oxygen-rich charge.

If you want to prove the theory of piston speed to airflow, connect a vacuum gauge to an engine, and with the ignition disabled, crank the engine over and record the reading. Then repeat the same test with the engine idling. Most V-8 engines with a mild cam profile will produce readings of one to four inches of mercury while cranking, and 11 to 17 inches of mercury running. The atmospheric pressure did not change, but the speed of the piston did.

Using a simple equation, the mean piston speed can be calculated in feet per minute: fpm = stroke X RPM/6. Determining the rate of acceleration of the piston would require advanced calculus and is too burdensome for our illustration. Plugging in some numbers, we would see that an engine with a 3.750-inch stroke cranking at 250 rpm would be experiencing a mean piston velocity of 156.25 fpm, but at 1200 rpm the speed will increase to 750 fpm.

If you leave the vacuum gauge connected and quickly snap the throttle to wide open from idle, the needle will swing to zero. How can this be when the piston is moving faster? With the throttle plate closed, a restriction is created, separating the low pressure in the bore from the atmosphere. At WOT this restriction is no longer there, and the engine is considered to have little or no vacuum, even with the increased piston velocity. The low-pressure region is still present, but the volume of the bore is not sufficient to create a differential that can be read in inches of mercury. For this reason, airflow testing done on a flow bench is measured with a manometer that registers in inches of water. Water has a lower specific gravity than mercury, which makes it more sensitive and adds accuracy to testing. Traditionally, a race engine at WOT would see six inches of water depression in the intake manifold, which would convert to .5 inch mercury.

Compression

As the piston sweeps toward TDC, it reduces the cylinder's effective volume and compresses the charge. During this time, both valves are closed, and at a defined point near the end of the stroke, the spark plug is

When the engineering specifications call for a quench, the robot can offer the precise timing required to achieve the desired results.

The Demon exclusive ConcentraCast method offers superior airflow and component stability with the minimization of core shift and the parting line.

arced. The difference in the combined cylinder and combustion chamber volumes measured with the piston at BDC and TDC defines the static compression ratio (CR). To apply numbers to this, a CR of 10.0:1 represents a cylinder volume that is 10 times greater at BDC than at TDC. The compacted charge when ignited creates a more powerful and efficient burn due to increased density and turbulence.

Contrary to popular belief, the CR of an engine has a more dominant effect on fuel efficiency than power production when working in a specified RPM range. The laws of thermodynamics are responsible for this. An increase in compression ratio from 8.00:1 to 11.00:1 will yield a power increase of only 5.2 percent, but a fuel economy gain of more than 20 percent if all other factors of the engine are kept constant. Increased compression ratio affects the engine in other ways though: improved throttle response and quicker acceleration of the crankshaft. Obviously, higher compression ratios impact the octane requirements and the engine's propensity to enter abnormal combustion.

The rate at which an engine converts fuel to power is measured as brake specific fuel consumption (BSFC) and is defined as the amount of fuel in pounds required to produce one horsepower. Often this is extrapolated further to include the pounds per horsepower per hour. A rule of thumb for a gasoline engine is .5 lbs./hp. To determine BSFC, the engine needs to be attached to a dyno with a fuel flow meter. The horsepower is measured along with the amount of fuel consumed. Many factors affect BSFC ratings beyond compression ratio; some are the design of the combustion chamber, the operating RPM, and the material of the cylinder head. For a modern engine with a high compression ratio and an efficient combustion chamber, a value of .45 BSFC is more

A float bowl mold is being loaded into a die casting machine.

Sophisticated machining processes go into every carburetor.

When all the high-tech machining and casting is complete, a skilled technician assembles each carburetor the old-fashioned way, by hand.

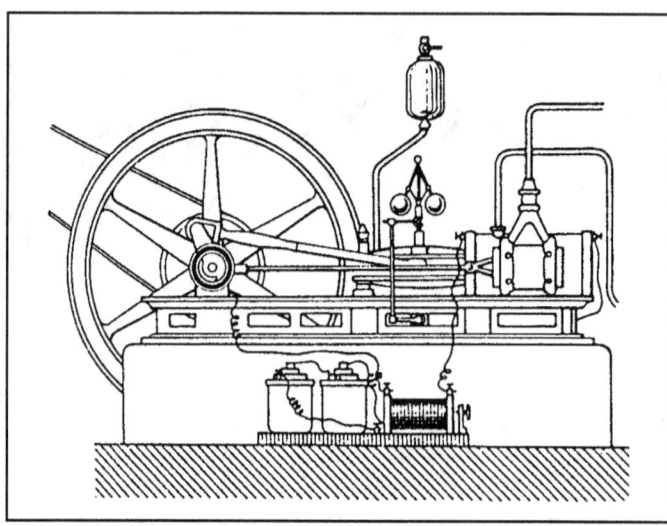

A conceptual drawing of what the first engine developed by Christian Huygens in 1673 may have looked like.

realistic. As an example, an NHRA Pro Stock-style engine with its nearly 17.0:1 compression ratio boasts a BSFC of approximately .32.

Cast iron is more thermodynamically efficient than aluminum and offers a better BSFC rating when the compression ratio is kept constant. With this in mind, the carburetor jetting requirements for identical engines with different-material cylinder heads would be dissimilar. A cast-iron head motor would use smaller jets than its aluminum-headed brother to produce the same power.

Power

When the arc across the spark plug ignites the mixture, a flame front is established and the temperature and pressure in the cylinder rise. As the flame front travels from burned to unburned regions, it expands and pushes the piston down in the bore. For this reason, the proper name for this stroke is expansion, and not power.

Approximately five times as much work is done by the piston during expansion than during compression. When this occurs, both valves are closed, the piston is traveling downward, and the combustion event ends. The rate at which the flame expands across the bore is measured in meters per second (m/s). Engineering studies have determined that the flame can have a velocity of anywhere between 10 and 25 m/s.

Many factors affect the flame speed, the dominant ones being the design of the combustion chamber and the location of the spark plug to the bore center. The speed of the flame affects the required spark advance curve and the exhaust gas temperatures in the port of the head, and when measured in the branch of the exhaust manifold or primary tube of a header.

Slower burn rates require the flame to have a head start so that it may keep pace with the piston. This is accomplished by lighting the spark plug while the piston is still on the compression stroke, or more commonly referred to as before top dead center (BTDC). To prove this concept, let us reference a mean flame speed of 15 m/s and a piston speed of 750 fpm. The mean piston speed when converted to m/s would be 41, substantially faster than the flame speed. Low compression ratios burn slower and require more spark lead, even if the combustion chamber design is kept constant. Slow burn rates tend to have the flame complete its burn in the exhaust port, which wastes energy and raises exhaust gas temperatures.

Exhaust

The true name for this event is the pumping loop, not the exhaust stroke. During this cycle, the remaining gases exit the bore, first because the cylinder pressure is substantially higher than the exhaust pressure, and then through the pumping action of the piston as it sweeps toward TDC. It is customary to open the exhaust valve 40-60 degrees before bottom dead center (BBDC); just as the valve opens

The engine in this race Nova has little visual resemblance to the first four-stroke cycle engine invented by Nicholas Otto, but it shares the same laws of combustion.

The Demon carburetor is a series of circuits that work together to create the most efficient wet-flow fuel-metering device on the market.

Crude oil requires many processing steps before it becomes gasoline to fill the float bowls of a Demon carburetor.

and the cylinder pressure is still high is known as blow-down.

Ideally, blow-down should occur while the piston is still stationary at BDC and should vacate the majority of exhaust. This is why the proper name for this event is the pumping loop, due to the work the piston does to expel the residual gases that did not evacuate during blow-down. Factors that impact the effectiveness of this cycle are independent of it and are traced to camshaft overlap, the time period when both the intake and exhaust valves are opened, and low-lift valve flow. During the pumping loop, the exhaust valve is open and the intake valve is closed, but the intake will start to open as the piston reaches TDC to create the overlap period. As the piston travels toward TDC on the pumping loop, there is no combustion present.

STATIC AND DYNAMIC COMPRESSION

With our review complete, let's look a little deeper into compression ratio and what can be derived from it. The mathematical computation of the change in volume at TDC vs. BDC will determine the static compression ratio. Though a mechanical compression test is an indicator of the dynamic compression ratio, the cranking compression test is used for diagnostic purposes and to determine the health of the engine, not as an indicator to choose parts such as a carburetor. There is no theoretical method to derive a static compression ratio from a cranking test result. This is due in part to the many factors that impact the reading. Camshaft design, cranking speed, and throttle position are some of the dominant concerns. Empirical data can be

More than 300 years later, tinkerers such as Leon Dick are still searching for the perfect combustion process. His Volcin Hot Fuel Injection system preheats the fuel by circulating it around the exhaust valve seat for advanced vaporization.

Not all racing is in a straight line. These varied requirements are represented by application-specific Demon carburetors for circle track, marine, and most other motorsports venues.

The design of the Demon carburetor produces lower BSFC ratings than competing brands. Not an important issue in drag racing, but a factor in other forms of motorsports.

How to Tune and Win with Demon Carburetors

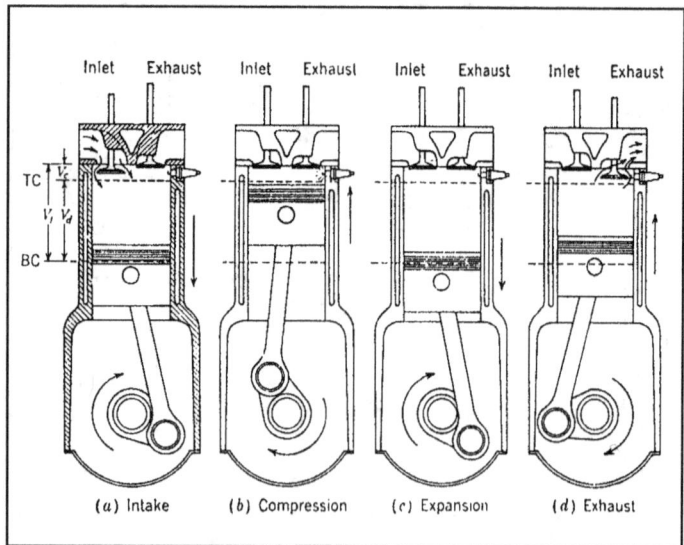

The four strokes of an engine are often called the Otto cycle, and they impact the carburetor function. Since the ignited flame expands as it travels and pushes against the piston, expansion rather than power is the technical name of the third event.

The difference between exhaust and intake pressure is what creates a reversion of inert exhaust gas back into the cylinder. For this reason, an engine requires a richer mixture at idle when the throttle plate is closed and the least fresh charge is introduced. During part-throttle operation, the required ratio becomes leaner.

obtained to estimate the static compression ratio from a dynamic test, but its accuracy will be vague.

Before considering any carburetor tuning or modifications, the mechanical health of both the engine and ignition system should be confirmed. As simple as a cranking compression test is, many still execute it incorrectly. It should be performed with the engine at operating temperature, the ignition system disabled, a fully charged battery, all of the spark plugs removed, and the throttle wide open. The engine should be cranked a minimum of four revolutions to achieve accurate results.

An old qualifier that many have forgotten is the first puff reading. When checking compression, the first pulsation of the gauge should yield a minimum of 40 percent of the final reading; if not, the rings or cylinder walls are in poor condition. A bore that reads significantly higher than the others could be a victim of carbon deposits or valve timing issues. On a mechanically sound engine, camshaft profiles and their impact on cylinder pressure rise can be compared with a dynamic compression test. Profiles that build cylinder pressure earlier will be seen during the first puff and are a good indicator of a cam that will build low-end grunt.

Another forgotten test is measuring the compression while the engine is running. With the ignition disabled on the test bore, start and idle the engine with the compression gauge installed. The piston will be moving faster now, but the throttle will be closed, so the value will be less than that of the cranking test. Typically, the reading will be 60-80 psi on a street engine. This is a good method to determine cylinder fill and will reveal

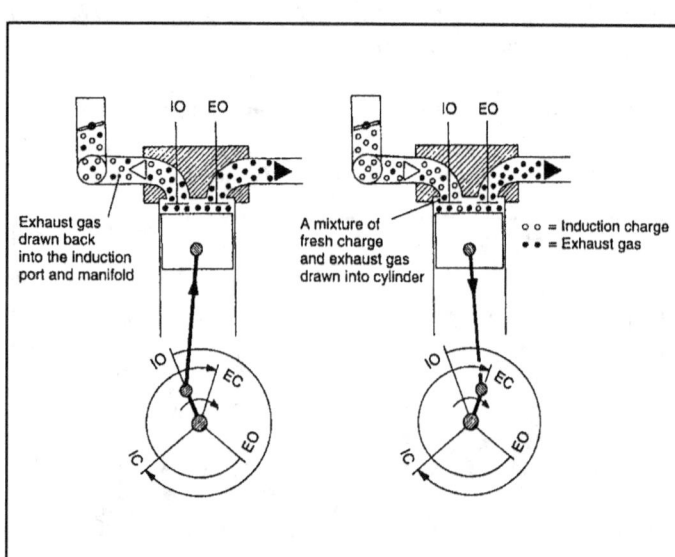

The reversion process occurs during valve overlap and is present in varying degrees in every engine.

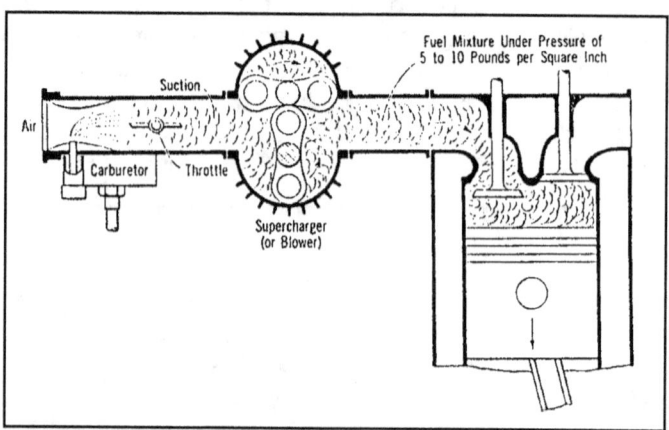

A normally aspirated engine uses the pressure differential between the atmosphere and the lower pressure region in the bore to fill the cylinders. A supercharger or turbocharger raises the pressure in the intake manifold and cylinder above atmospheric. Boost is always referenced to atmospheric pressure.

Land-speed racing puts extreme demands on the engine. The fuel-supply system needs to be able to keep the float bowls of the carburetor filled for proper performance.

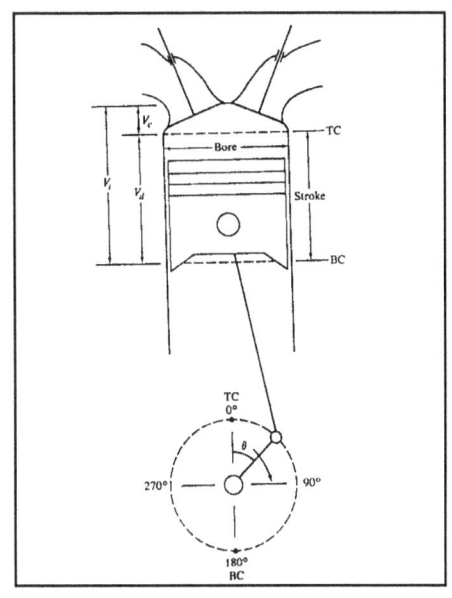

Compression ratio is calculated as the change in volume with the piston at BDC vs. TDC. VC represents the compression area that the charge is forced into.

flow deficiencies that may not be apparent during crank due to the slow piston speeds. After recording the results, snap the throttle quickly wide open. This will increase the airflow through higher piston velocity along with the elimination of the throttle restriction. The result will be a dramatic rise in cylinder pressure. Then again, volumetric differences will be exposed. A good rule is that the snap throttle test would indicate 80 percent of the crank reading. A very high reading may be indicative of a restriction in the exhaust, whereas a low value can be attributed to a restriction caused by carbon buildup on the intake valve.

THE EFFECT OF COMPRESSION RATIO ON OCTANE REQUIREMENTS

The term octane tolerance is used to identify an engine's antiknock requirements; lower octane tolerance equates to higher required fuel octane numbers. Compression ratio is a dominant factor in determining the fuel quality needed, but as represented previously, it is only one of many factors. Cylinder head material, cooling system design (including the water jackets in the cylinder head), intake charge temperature, piston crown design, and air/fuel ratio all contribute to or degrade octane tolerance.

Commonly overlooked are the weather conditions and the altitude at which the engine is operating. According to the Society of Automotive Engineers (SAE), for every one degree Fahrenheit rise in temperature, an engine will require a 0.054 increase in motor octane number (MON) of the fuel. Conversely, changes in weather that increase humidity decrease an engine's octane requirements. A drop of 0.035 MON is predicted for every grain of water per pound of dry air. A grain is 1/7000 of a pound. Altitude has the same effect on octane since the reduced atmospheric pressure creates less cylinder fill and causes the engine to run richer, hence octane requirements decrease as altitude increases. Even without a complete comprehension of meteorology, this information can be summarized to reveal that an engine will require higher-octane fuel as the air temperature increases or the humidity drops, and less octane as the humidity rises or the altitude increases.

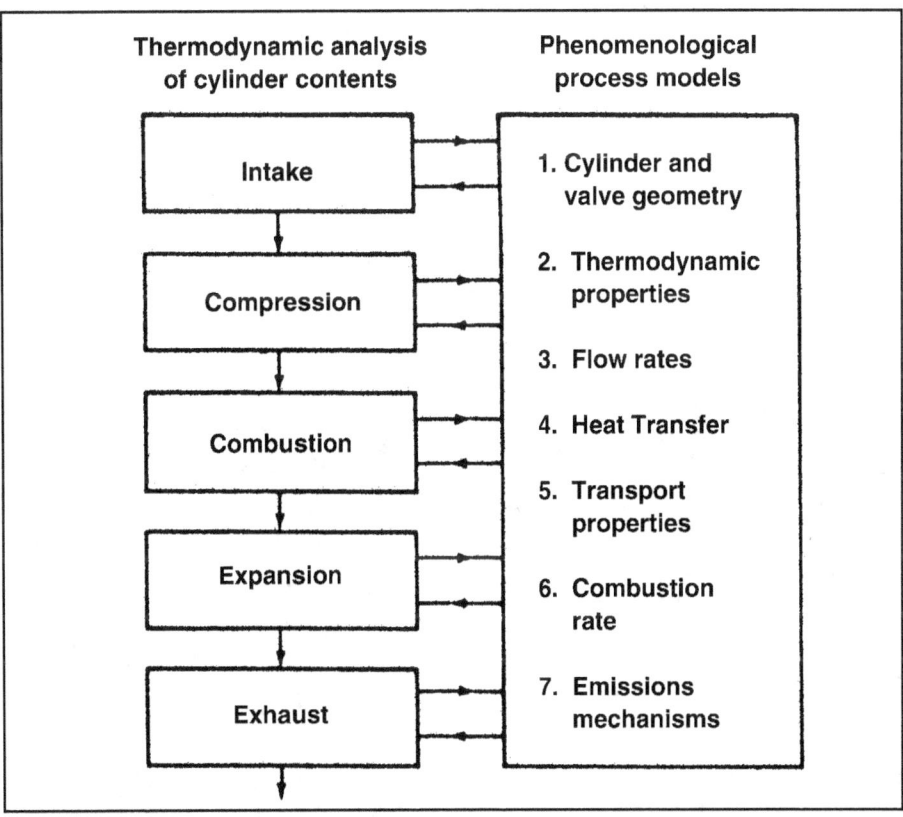

The elements of thermodynamics are impacted by the compression ratio of the engine. Higher ratios produce greater thermal efficiency and will decrease the required jet size in the carburetor with all other factors being equal.

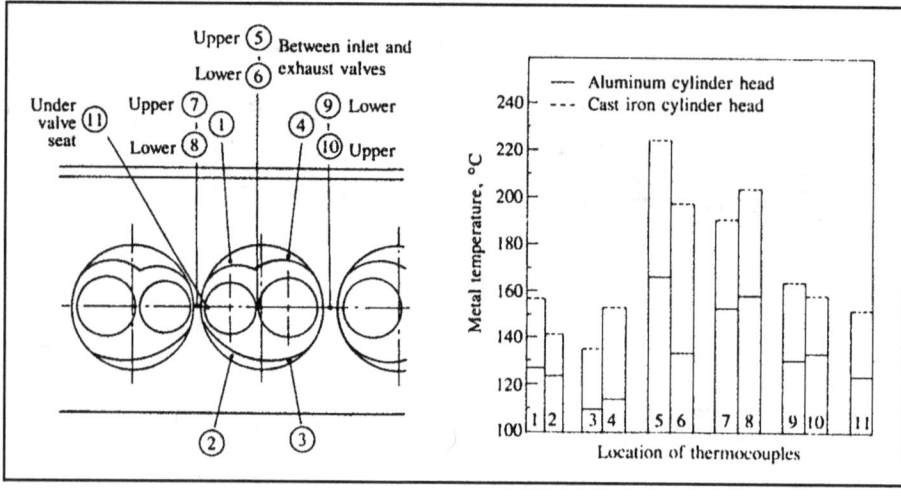

Aluminum dissipates more of the combustion heat, necessitating a higher compression ratio to maintain the same thermal efficiency as cast iron. Note the variation in temperatures at different locations in the combustion chamber for the two metals.

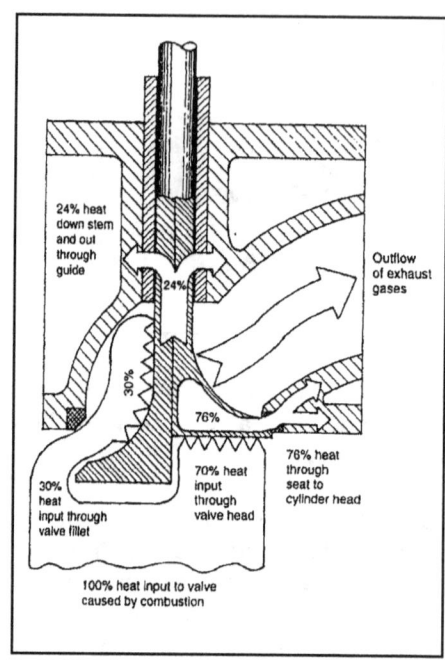

The heat input to the exhaust valve during combustion can be documented and will have an effect on the BSFC of the engine.

VOLUMETRIC EFFICIENCY

Contrary to what many believe, the cylinder is never completely filled with charge on a normally aspirated engine. The quantity is indicated as volumetric efficiency and is read in percent. At peak torque, the cylinder is the most full. Torque is defined as the amount of work an engine can accomplish, whereas horsepower indicates how quickly the work can be done. Therefore, RPM is required to produce horsepower.

It is important to acknowledge that horsepower is just a mathematical derivative of torque. It was the brainchild of James Watt, who in the early 1600s was searching for a standard to compare a steam engine's ability to do work against the then-common draft horse. Since no two horses have exactly the same strength, torque is a more accurate indicator of an engine's power. A dyno measures torque and then mathematically converts the amount of work to horsepower. The equation is: horsepower = torque X RPM/5252. This is why both horsepower and torque are equal at 5252 rpm. With the numerator and denominator of the equation being equal, it becomes one. Thus, horsepower and torque at that engine speed are the same.

Most production engines achieve a VE of only 85 percent at peak torque. A very defined race engine may see slightly more, but values of 100 percent and greater are possible only through forced induction. Factors that control VE beyond airflow are the intake manifold design and camshaft profile.

Some intakes are designed to tune at a specific RPM, and when the valve events are timed properly, it creates an effect known as inertia supercharging.

In simpler terms, the timing of the valve events, along with the length of the intake manifold runner, work to accelerate the charge and increase the amount of cylinder fill. A tuned induction tract works very well in a narrow RPM range, offering substantial gains in VE at the RPM point of tuning, but it is proportionally less efficient above and below that engine speed. As the length of the intake manifold runner increases, the low-RPM torque will be enhanced at the expense of high-RPM horsepower.

Short-intake manifold runners require more piston speed to effectively fill the cylinders, but they work efficiently at high engine speeds. When the acceleration of the charge occurs, the manifold is said to be resonating. It then becomes essential to have the valve event timed properly to utilize this energy. When the manifold resonates, it is advantageous to open the intake valve during the second pulse of the intake track. Identified as the second harmonic, it is accepted to be both the strongest and longest. The first pulse will collide with the closed intake valve

Race engines use high compression ratios to increase power and thermal efficiency. Higher compression ratio are required with camshafts that increase overlap.

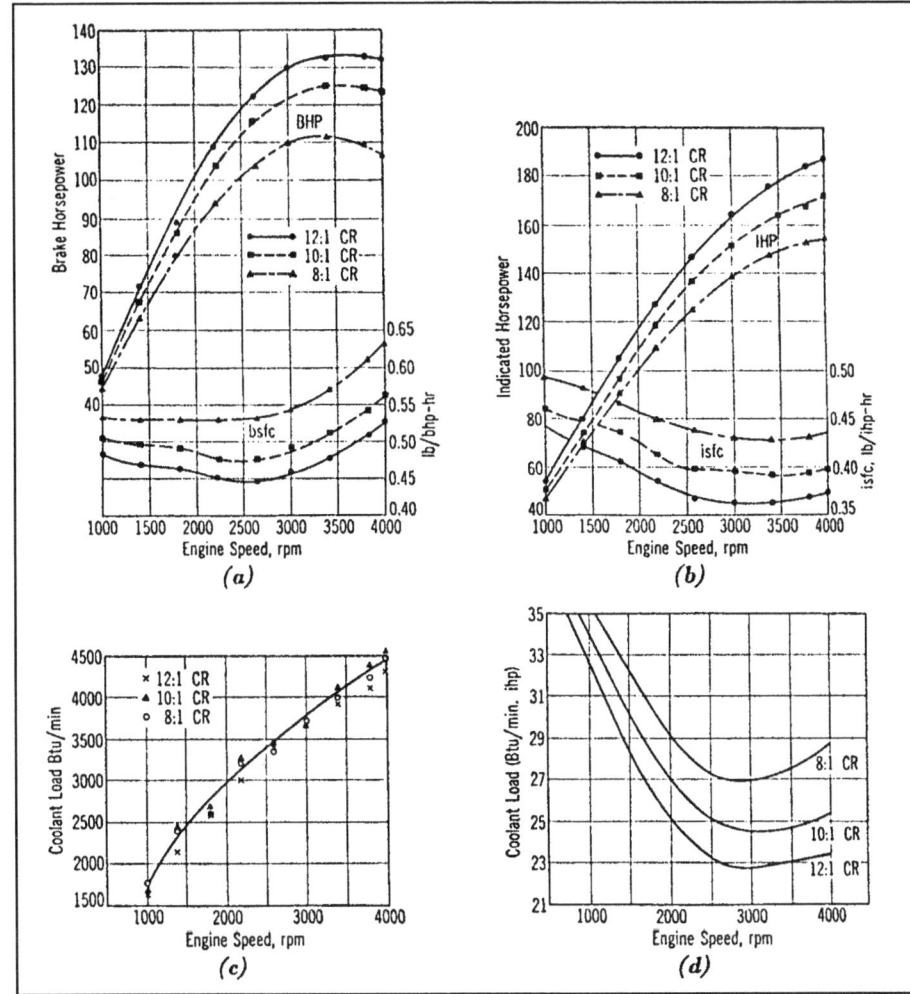

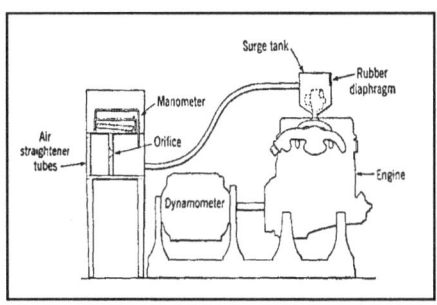

A modern dyno facility incorporates equipment that measures fuel flow, air induction, and torque. The horsepower rating is then mathematically converted from work over time.

A proper dyno cell will allow the engine to breathe ambient air, independent of the room's atmosphere. A high-output engine in an improperly vented dyno cell will actually suck all of the air from the room, lowering the barometric pressure.

These results are from a test done in the 1950s by Oldsmobile using its Rocket V-8 with varied compression ratios. The results show the dramatic affect higher thermal efficiency has on the amount of fuel required to support the power produced.

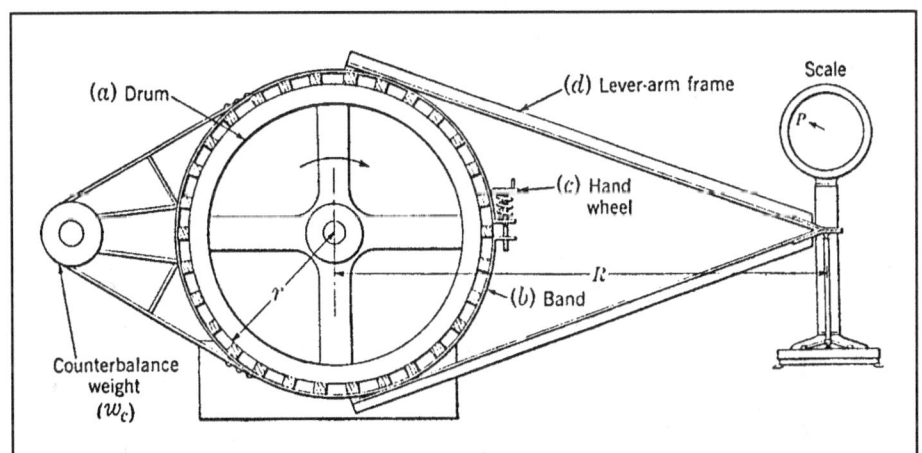

Though the aftermarket references horsepower, torque is a true indicator of an engine's ability to do work. This drawing illustrates a prony brake dyno.

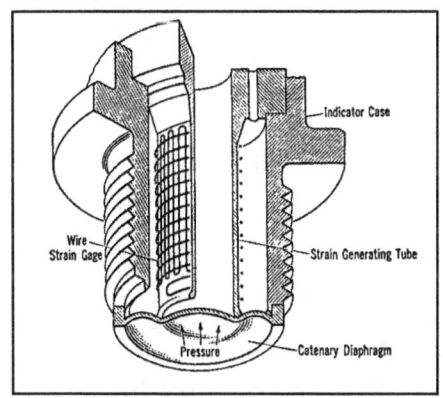

The true measure of an engine's power is cylinder pressure. To measure this, an engine cycle analyzer and quartz pressure transducers are required in each bore.

and bounce back up the runner and toward the plenum. If the valve event is timed properly, the valve will open just as the first pulse expends its energy and starts to fall back down the port. When this occurs, the second pulse carries the first reverted harmonic with it, increasing the volume of incoming charge, called a plug. Valve events that miss the second harmonic are less

How to Tune and Win with Demon Carburetors **17**

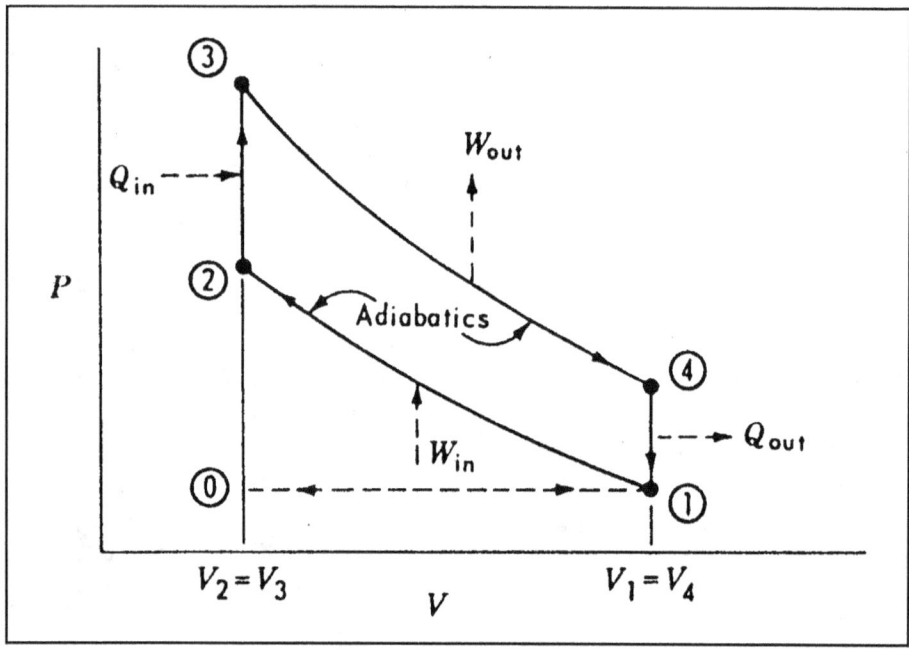

Engineers use a pressure-volume (P-V) log as an indicator of an engine's output. Position 1 is the piston at BDC after the intake stroke. The volume in the bore is high, the pressure at atmospheric. As the line sweeps toward 2, the volume of the bore decreases during the compression stroke, and the cylinder pressure rises. After ignition, the pressure spikes as the flame expands but has not induced enough rotational torque to turn the crankshaft. As the line travels from 3 to 4, the piston is traveling downward on the expansion or power stroke. The dotted line is the work the piston does on the exhaust stroke or pumping loop. Note how the volume decreases but the pressure stays low because the exhaust valve is open.

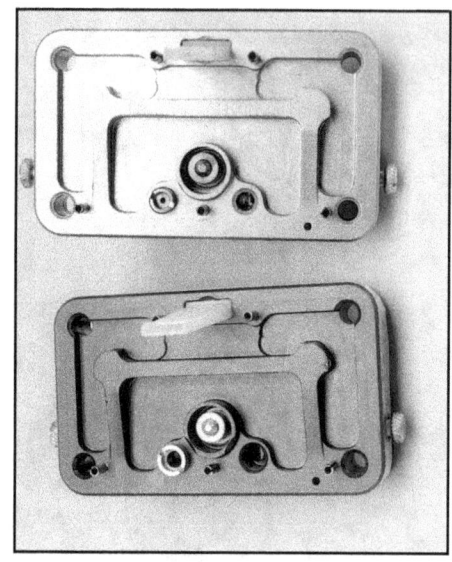

The stoichiometric rating of each fuel varies. For example, alcohol has one-half the energy content of gasoline. Note the size difference in the main jets on these two metering blocks. The bottom one is for alcohol.

CARBURETOR 101

One of the most visible parts of an engine, and often the most misunderstood, is the carburetor. Maligned and blamed for conditions and problems that it has no control over, it has been the victim of unjust persecution since its inception. When studying Demon carburetors, you need to bear in mind that as advanced and well-engineered as they are, the laws of physics still apply. Although every brand of carburetor has its own unique features, they basically all function under the same theory. If you can understand how one works, then you can understand them all. Though a carburetor plays an important role in determining how well an engine runs, it is only one part of a complex machine. Manifolding, valve events and timing, port and cylinder head considerations, compression ratio, and ignition timing all serve very important functions.

The most common device used to mix fuel with air, the carburetor comprises a series of different circuits and functions housed in one main body. For an engine to produce power, it needs to burn fuel, but that is in direct contradiction to the saying that "lean is mean." How can we make more power with less fuel? The job of the carburetor is not only to act as a mixing and throttling device, but to meet the air/fuel ratio requirements of the engine. This is an especially challenging task since an automobile engine is required to work at various loads, throttle angles, and RPM conditions.

The job of the carburetor designer for a steady-state engine or even a lawnmower is much easier due to the fixed engine speed and throttle position. The term air/fuel ratio needs to be

effective since the inertial effect has lost much of its energy, and the cylinder fill rate suffers accordingly.

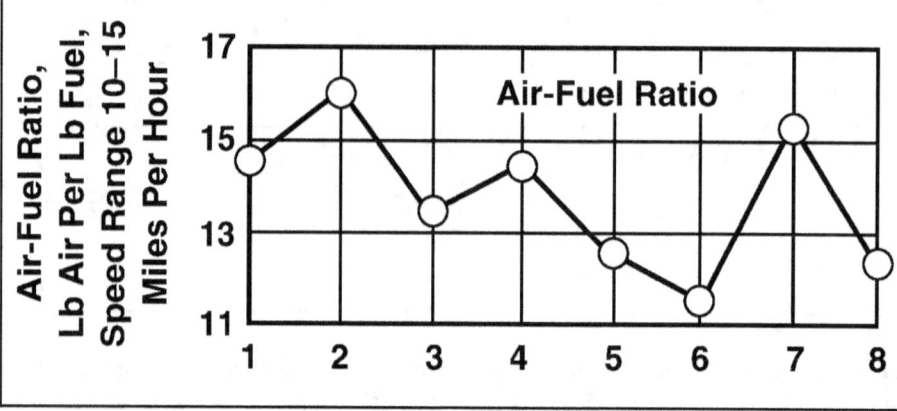

Most production carburetors only offer primary bore idle circuits, which then require the front of the intake manifold plenum to be flooded with fuel. Often this will create an uneven air/fuel ratio throughout the engine, especially at low speeds, as represented by this chart. All Demon carburetors use a four-corner idle to eliminate this condition.

18   *How to Tune and Win with Demon Carburetors*

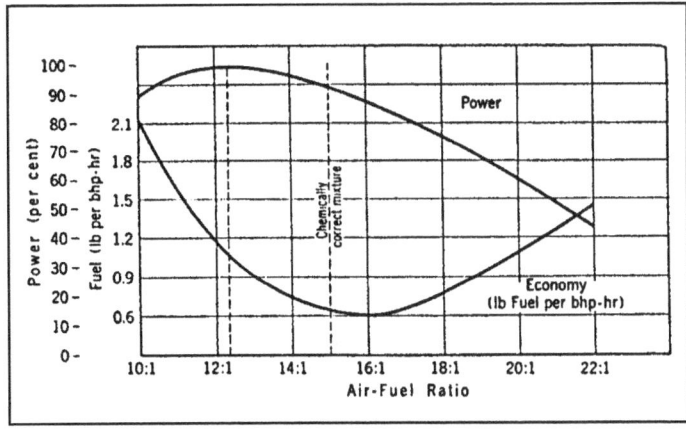

An engine produces the most power when there is a sufficient amount of fuel to burn all of the oxygen in the bore, not the other way around.

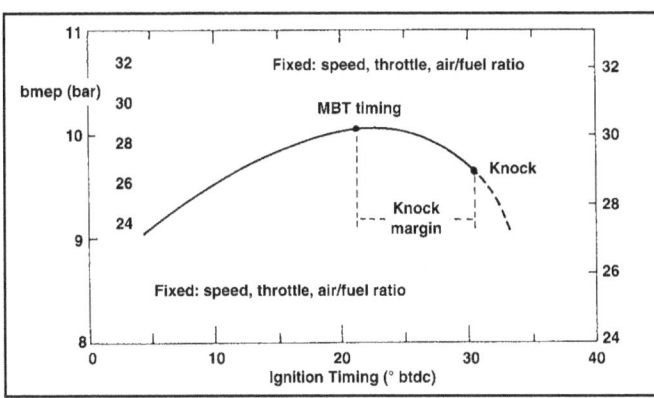

Spark timing is critical for proper carburetor performance. The rate at which the flame front expands is measured in meters per second and will determine the amount of spark lead the engine requires.

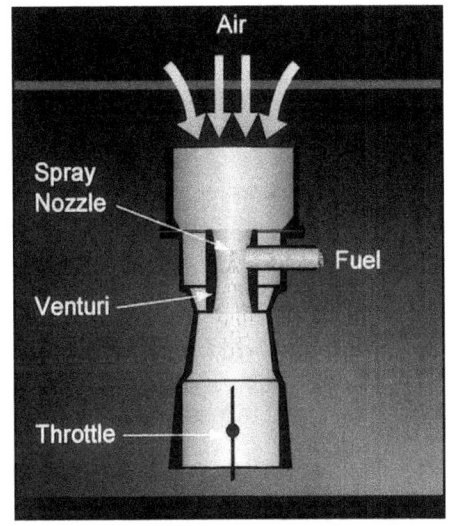

Every carburetor works on the venturi principle that creates a high-velocity, low-pressure region in the throat of the main body.

fully understood before exploring the workings of the Demon. It is the amount of air that is mixed with a constant part of fuel. Let's start with the ratio 14.7:1. If we were chefs we would say that 14.7 parts of air should be mixed with one part fuel. This shows that as the amount of air goes numerically lower, the recipe is biased toward fuel (richer), since the constant is being diluted less. Likewise, if the ratio goes numerically higher, the mixture is being excessively diluted (leaner).

What is interesting is that an engine requires a different air/fuel ratio for various load conditions. What is best for fuel economy is not the ratio for maximum performance. Let's first discuss the term *stoichiometric*. Abbreviated as stoich, it defines the ideal ratio for the optimum release of chemical energy from the fuel. Often this is simplified by stating that it is the ratio for the best burn, which in reality has removed a little too much from the definition. Unleaded gasoline has a stoichiometric value of 14.67:1 and is commonly rounded to 14.7:1. The ratio is different for other fuels: nitromethane 1.7:1, methanol 6.45:1, ethanol 9.0:1, and 100-octane race fuel 15.1:1.

In most engines at peak torque (remember this is also when the cylinder has the highest VE), the required ratio for gasoline is around 12.7-12.9:1, and at maximum horsepower, it's 12.9-13.2:1. That is just around 13 parts of air to one part of fuel. During full power, the engine will induct a constant amount of air, which is limited directly by the piston displacement.

If the fuel flow is increased by

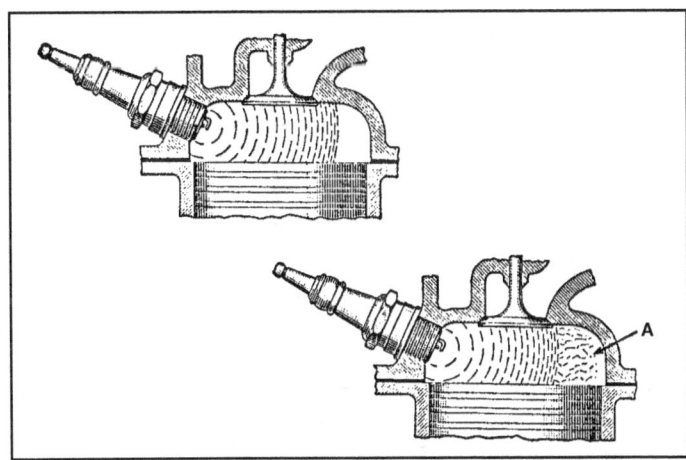

Excessive amounts of spark advance will create high cylinder temperatures and pressures, allowing an additional flame front to form. "A" represents the rogue flame front that occurs during abnormal combustion.

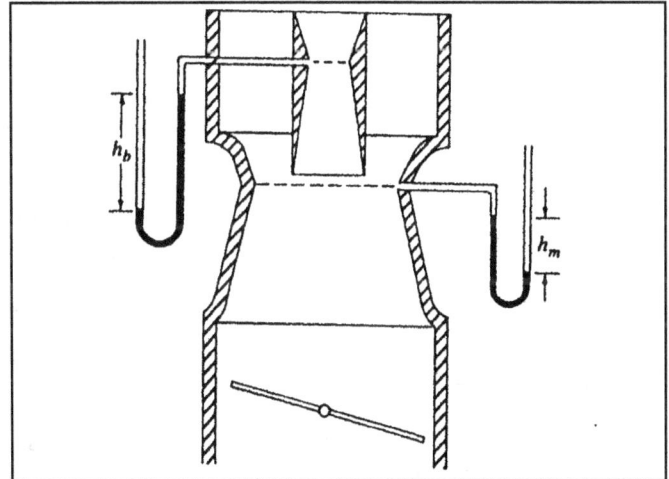

The pressure drop is much greater in the booster venturi section of the carburetor compared to a reading taken in the main body venturi.

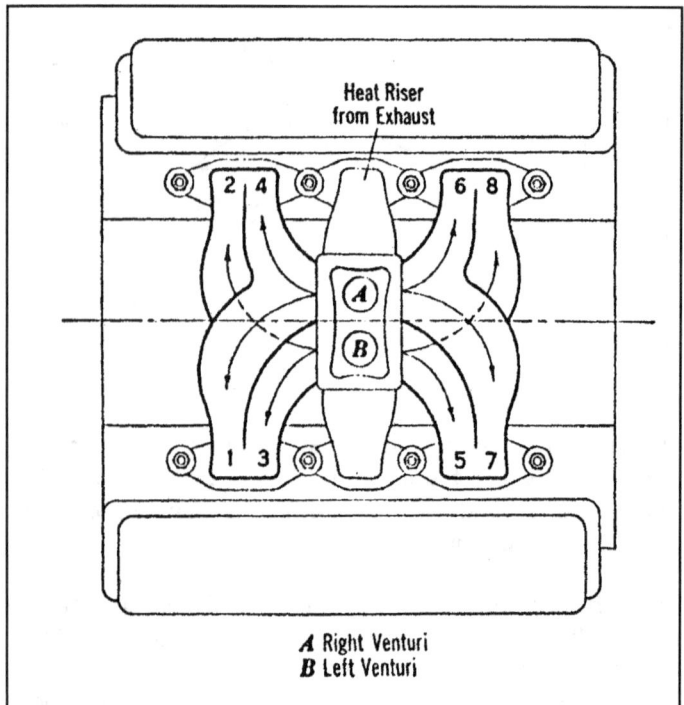

A Right Venturi
B Left Venturi

The heat-riser passage is used to help vaporize the cold fuel during engine warmup. The intake manifold design is an important element in cylinder-to-cylinder fuel distribution.

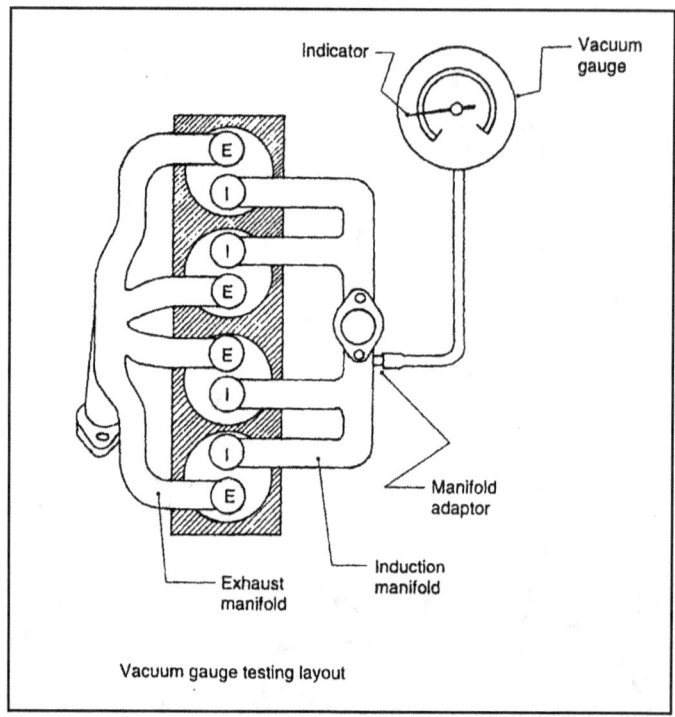

Vacuum gauge testing layout

A manifold or full-time vacuum reading is taken by accessing a port that is connected below the throttle plates of the carburetor.

changes in carburetor jetting, the power will rise due to the increased liberation of the chemical energy. The output of the engine will continue upward with an increase in fuel until a point is reached where all of the oxygen in the cylinder is effectively utilized for the combustion event. This will represent the optimum release in chemical energy when ignited. Since the fuel flow can be increased but the airflow of an engine is fixed by design and displacement, it is the air and not the fuel that imposes limits on power.

Maximum power is obtained when there is just enough fuel to consume all of the air in the cylinder. It must then be recognized that the fuel and air are never perfectly mixed with any carburetor or EFI system, that the fuel may not be completely vaporized, and that some of it is falling into crevice regions. Additionally, the cylinder almost always has a certain faction of exhaust gas present that effectively dilutes the concentration of fresh charge. Due to this, a mixture ratio substantially richer than stoichiometric is required to make power.

THE CARBURETOR NEEDS TO BE MATCHED TO THE ENGINE

Most of us in this hobby seem to suffer from the ailment identified as "drag racer syndrome," no matter what form of motorsports we are involved with. That disease clouds our judgment and causes us to feel that the bigger the component is, the better it is. It is especially prevalent when choosing a carburetor but also has revealed itself with camshaft selection and cylinder head port choices. If it is bigger it just has to go faster, right? Well, more often than not, if in doubt, err on the small side; it disappoints less.

When dealing with a carburetor, the trick is to provide bore and venturi sizes that do not limit the VE of the engine, but provide a strong pressure differential between the bore of the carburetor and the small inner bore called a venturi. This delta pressure relationship in carburetor language is called a signal and will be discussed in length as the text progresses. Too large a carburetor bore dimension and the pumping action of the piston will not create a strong enough signal to pull fuel from the discharge ports or tubes. If the carburetor is too small, it will offer excellent driveability, throttle response, and performance until it becomes a choke point and limits the VE of the engine and, thus, the power produced.

All Demon carburetors are considered modular-style designs. This name is attached to a carburetor that has a solid main body, a separate throttle body, isolated fuel bowls, and metering block. In direct contrast, a Rochester Quadra-Jet is considered a multi-piece carburetor.

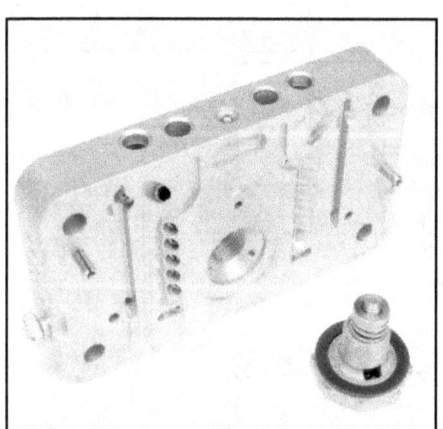

The metering block of a Demon carburetor is made from billet aluminum to avoid the porosity concerns of a casting. Here is a Race Demon version with five emulsion orifices and the power valve removed.

CAN VOLUMETRIC EFFICIENCY REALLY EXCEED 100 PERCENT?

In engineering terms, volumetric efficiency is a measure of the engine's ability to pump air. On the performance level, our only exposure to this ability is on a dynamometer. A simplified definition of VE would then become the amount of filling that the cylinder experiences.

Many engine builders brag about VE greater than 100 percent with a normally aspirated engine, which would mean that they are actually filling the cylinders beyond capacity and creating a pressure above atmospheric while the piston is still at or near BDC. This is usually accomplished through matching the camshaft profile with the design of the intake manifold and allowing the laws of physics and resonant tuning to come into play. However, most engineers agree that values of over 100 percent are not possible without forced induction. Since most engines experience only 80-85 percent VE at peak torque, a lot of resonant tuning would be needed to find the additional 15-20 percent of cylinder fill to reach that perfect goal, let alone surpass it. When scanning a dyno sheet for peak torque, it is easier to follow the VE column; when the cylinder is the most filled, the amount of work the engine can do is the greatest.

So is it possible to have VE greater than 100 percent? Most engine dynos in the performance industry determine VE through a data-acquisition system that calculates the total swept volume of the engine and then compare this to the incoming volume measured by a flow meter attached to the engine's inlet tract. If the cylinder volume is less than the incoming air volume, then it is considered that the VE exceeds 100 percent. The problem is that you must measure more than the incoming air; you must also measure the amount of exhaust volume and subtract that from the first value to calculate internal losses.

We must remember that when the engine is running, it is not completely sealed. There is leakage past the rings and valve seals, as well as what is scavenged during overlap of the cam.

These values are not taken into account when the amount of incoming air is all that is measured. However, don't be misled into thinking that VE values on a dyno sheet are useless. They are good indicators, and any increase will return higher output regardless of whether your engine is really seeing 100 percent or greater cylinder fill rates.

REVIEW QUESTIONS

(1) A more accurate name for the power stroke of a four-cycle internal combustion engine is:

a: torque
b: expansion
c: conversion
d: pumping

(2) How much depression will a typical race engine produce in the intake manifold at wide open throttle?

a: 6 inches of water
b: 6 inches of mercury
c: 14.7 psi
d: one-half the atmospheric pressure of the day

(3) As the static compression ratio of an engine is increased, the thermal efficiency will:

a: decrease
b: stay the same
c: it depends on the camshaft profile
d: increase

(4) The BSFC rating of an engine represents:

a: the rate at which fuel is converted to horsepower
b: the rate at which fuel is converted to RPM
c: the octane requirement of the engine
d: how large a venturi the carburetor will need

(5) The rate that the flame travels across the combustion chamber is measured in:

a: BSFC
b: torque
c: RPM
d: meters per second

(6) What is the mathematical equation to convert a cranking compression test result to a static compression ratio?

a: torque X RPM/5252
b: cranking RPM X 1/2 cranking compression
c: there is no equation to convert the results
d: atmospheric pressure X cranking compression PSI

(7) As the humidity in the air goes up, the octane requirement of the engine:

a: goes down
b: goes up
c: stays the same
d: humidity has no affect on octane requirement

(8) When does a normally aspirated engine experience the highest VE?

a: at idle
b: at peak torque
c: at peak horsepower
d: it is always the same

(9) Which of the following is not the responsibility of a carburetor:

a: vaporization
b: atomization
c: throttling of the engine
d: emulsification

(10) The venturi of a carburetor:

a: should always be as large as possible
b: should always be sized to find a balance between signal strength and airflow
c: has no affect
d: should always be as small as would fit the intake manifold

Answers: 1) B, 2) A, 3) D, 4) A, 5) D, 6) C, 7) A, 8) B, 9) A, 10) B

How to Tune and Win with Demon Carburetors

MEASURING HORSEPOWER AND TORQUE

How much power does it make? This question invariably surfaces in every conversation about an engine. Abiding by the laws of physics, power is required to change a body at rest into one in motion, and whatever has the most power goes the fastest. This now creates the need to determine an engine's output. Even though power can be calculated mathematically according to a vehicle's rate of acceleration or top speed, the ideal place to define the amount of grunt is at the flywheel or drivewheels during a dyno test. Most dyno sessions are used to sort out and tune combinations or parts, while others use the dyno to quantify and qualify the maximum output of the engine. Either way, valid documentation of engine output is the reason for investing in dyno time.

It is important to determine the proper dyno for the job: either engine or drivewheel. The benefit of engine dyno testing is the ease of swapping parts and attaching data acquisition and test equipment that might be difficult or impossible to use in the confines of the engine compartment. A chassis dyno, on the other hand, provides relative ease of testing, but limits changes and modifications. Until recently, most chassis systems were limited to wide-open throttle testing and were unable to sustain a given load for part-throttle tuning. Ancillary to this is the ability to record the air/fuel ratio and exhaust gas temperatures. Although working solely with power numbers is helpful, it lacks the depth needed to prescribe modification and tuning help. Ideally you should define your combination with the engine dyno, then put it in the car and run it on the chassis dyno to do the tune-up.

Power is found in the chemical-to-mechanical energy change that is created from the expansion of the flame front during ignition and through the power stroke. During this time, the cylinder pressure increases as the flame presses down on the piston. The real measure of an engine's ability to do work is the amount of cylinder pressure that is produced during the power stroke.

A dynamometer measures torque, which is defined as the amount of work that can be accomplished; horsepower is calculated as work over time. While torque is a valuable means of measuring the potential to do work, it is affected by the displacement of the engine. For this reason, OE engineers reference mean effective pressure (MEP), a parameter of force-per-unit area, rather than horsepower or torque. This can then be measured in terms of torque, which is referred to as brake mean effective pressure (BMEP). The maximum BMEP of an efficient engine is essentially constant over a wide range of engine displacements. Then the BMEP of an engine can be compared with those of other engines of varied size, and the engine's effectiveness to produce power can be compared to peers of different displacements. The aftermarket does not recognize BMEP but rather compares horsepower to cubic inches (hp/ci).

All dynamometers, except inertia-based chassis types, incorporate a device that applies resistance to the engine like a brake. It may build resistance via friction material or electrical current, but the most popular ones use hydraulics. Thus, the term "brake" was applied to the readings of both horsepower and torque because it was a measurement of the power consumed by the resistance mechanism. Today, brake has been replaced by flywheel power, delivered power, or drivewheel power. Power may also be registered as net, gross, peak, and continuous.

Before 1971, most OE manufacturers advertised gross power, or what the engine would produce on the dynamometer with intake and exhaust systems that were more efficient than the ones in the vehicle, and without any power-robbing accessories. The net rating, however, accounted for all of the components and accessories from the production car and reflected substantially lower output.

The aftermarket usually publishes gross peak readings because the exhaust and air intake systems from the vehicle are rarely included in the test procedure. Detroit publishes net continuous ratings, which is the power the engine can produce for extended periods without any anticipated failure while using the production ancillaries and drive loads.

Since an engine's ability to do work is affected by atmospheric conditions, correction factors are necessary to compare engine output. A test performed on a low-barometric-pressure day would yield different results than one done on a high-pressure day. Likewise, if the air temperature was to vary, the result would be affected also. Since we do not have the ability to control the atmosphere, the SAE has developed and identified test standards that include correction for temperature, barometer, and humidity. Since most correction factors are set at the dyno console, the phrase "spin the dial until the check will clear" has been applied by unscrupulous engine builders. They modify the correction factor to create a dyno sheet showing the power they promised you. If the multiplier on the dyno sheet is less than one, then the test occurred in weather conditions that surpassed the test standard. Conversely, if the multiplier is more than one, then the day was worse than the standard.

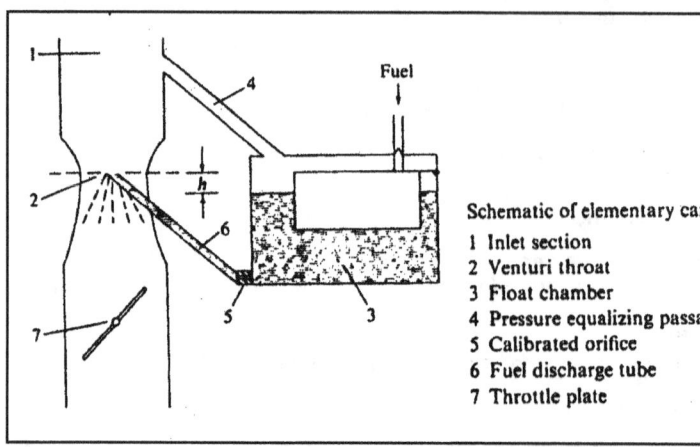

Schematic of elementary carburetor.
1 Inlet section
2 Venturi throat
3 Float chamber
4 Pressure equalizing passage
5 Calibrated orifice
6 Fuel discharge tube
7 Throttle plate

The elements of a simple carburetor.

How many parts of this simple carburetor can you identify?

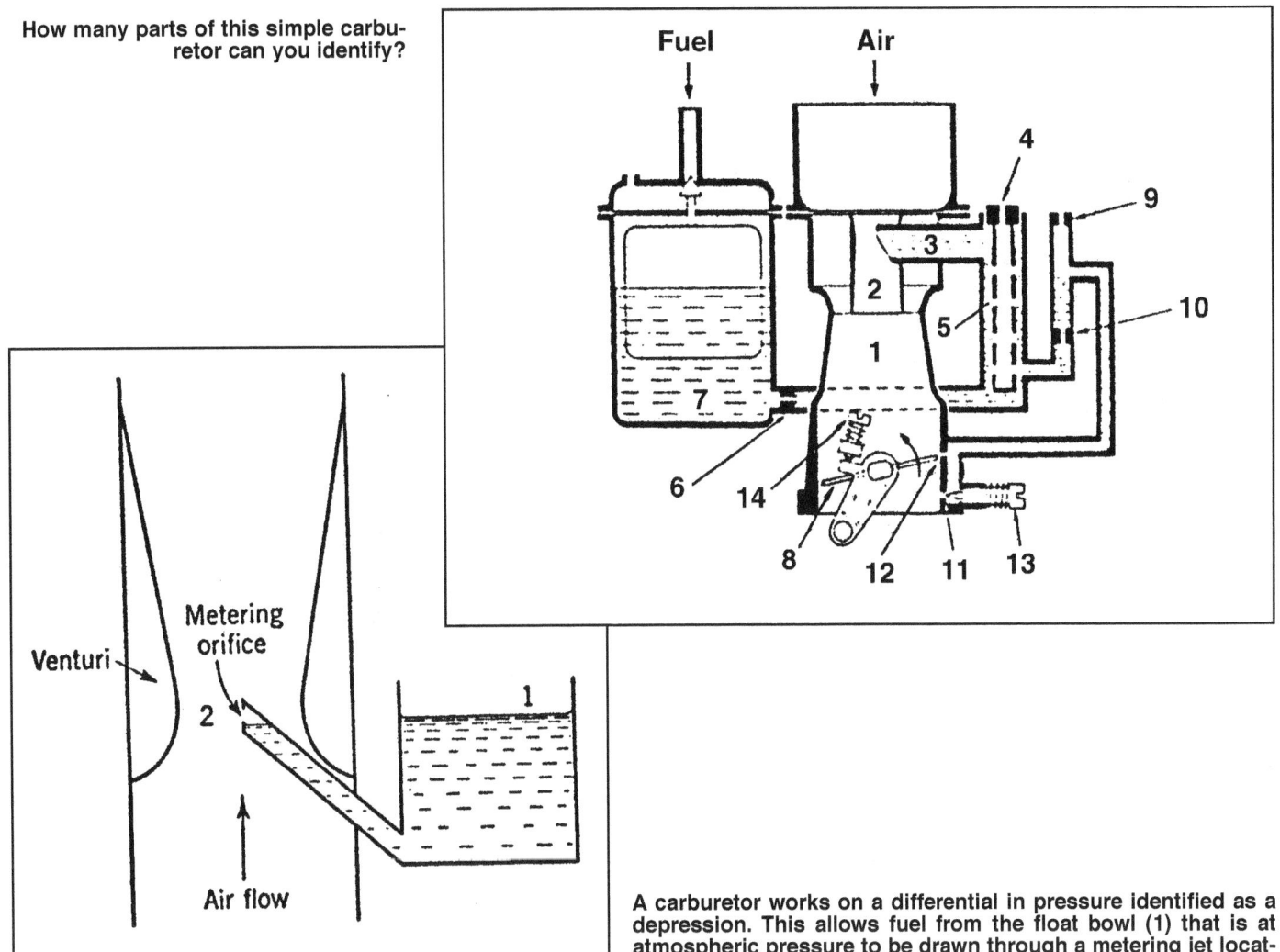

A carburetor works on a differential in pressure identified as a depression. This allows fuel from the float bowl (1) that is at atmospheric pressure to be drawn through a metering jet located in the low-pressure region created by the venturi (2).

WHAT IS AIR?

Any proper discussion of engines requires thought about the properties of air and the gas exchange process itself. It is commonly thought that air is a single element, and that misconception is further expanded when the word oxygen is used falsely as a synonym. By definition, it is accepted that air is 78 percent nitrogen, 21 percent oxygen, and one percent other gases. When we breathe, we take in air, use the oxygen, and exhale carbon dioxide, nitrogen, and the rest. An engine does exactly the same thing. It inputs the total air composition, uses the oxygen, and expels the rest. The oxygen content in air will vary as much as one percent in a normal day and is the result of changes in air density, which are caused by variations in temperature and humidity.

An engine needs to mix the air with fuel to produce power, hence the term air/fuel ratio. Using the stoichiometric figure of 14.7:1 as an example, we can draw conclusions with the introduction of some basic facts. One gallon of gasoline weighs approximately six pounds, whereas it would take 100 gallons of air to equal one pound. This makes fuel 600 times heavier than air. Therefore, to maintain a stoichiometric ratio, we would need to supply 8,820 gallons of air to burn one gallon of fuel.

Gasoline is a blend of light and heavy hydrocarbons obtained from crude oil. Chemically, it consists of hydrogen, carbon $C_6 H_{8-18}$, sulfur, and, in some race gas, lead. The energy content of fuel is measured by a caloric scale that is read in British thermal units (Btu). One pound of regular gasoline can deliver approximately 19,166 Btu of heat energy. Like air, gasoline density is affected by temperature. Other liquid fuels such as alcohol have only half the heat energy of gasoline and would require twice the amount to produce the same power. Consider that even the highest output engine to date is only marginally better in terms of thermal efficiency than the first engine ever produced, using 20-25 percent of the energy that is converted to heat. With this in mind, 75-80 percent of all fuel burned is turned into heat, but not used to produce power; it is transferred to the cooling system and out the exhaust.

During combustion, the hydrocarbons are broken down and take different forms. The proper name for this cycle is the gas exchange process. The laws of thermodynamics dictate that energy cannot be consumed or destroyed; only its state can change. When the spark plug initiates this event, the hydrocarbons break down into carbon and hydrogen. The hydrogen and carbon mix with the oxygen and results in heat, carbon dioxide, and water.

How to Tune and Win with Demon Carburetors

How to Tune & Win with DEMON CARBURETORS
The Circuits of a Carburetor

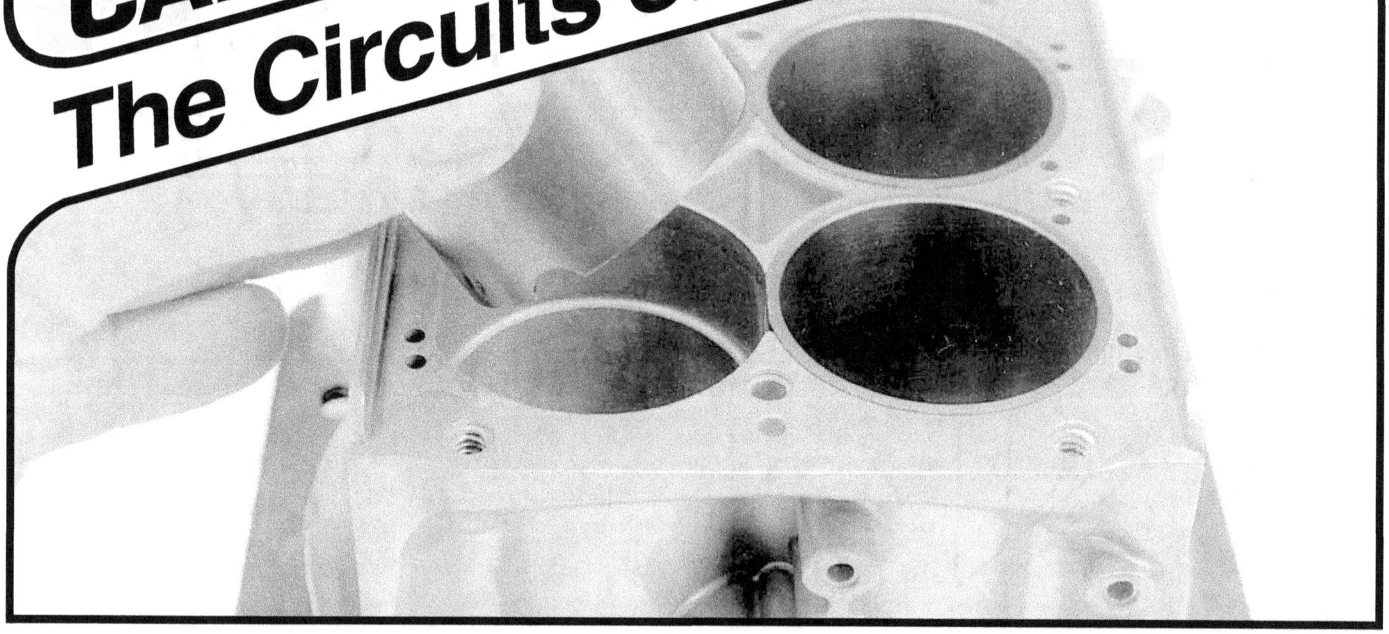

Just as an orchestra is composed of many different instruments, a carburetor is a series of interdependent circuits, each designed to serve a unique function. When an orchestra is properly conducted, a synergy occurs, and the result is beautiful music. However, listened to individually, the orchestral instruments may not sound so pleasing. The same theory can be applied to carburetion; when tuned to perfection, the result is a smooth, powerful engine with vibrant throttle response. Each interdependent circuit alone cannot run the engine, and if one is not functioning properly, poor performance is the result.

As established in Chapter 1, an engine will require distinct air/fuel ratios during different operating modes. The circuits that make up a carburetor are designed to accomplish this and are broken down into seven categories: float, choke, idle, main metering, power enrichment, squirter, and, if applicable, secondary barrels. Though each circuit provides a function, carburetor operation uses a building-block approach, retaining some circuits as others are added.

CARBURETOR HISTORY

As the gasoline engine (also referred to as a spark ignition (SI) engine) evolved, so did the carburetor. The Demon line of carburetors represents the most advanced theories in wet-flow fuel delivery and is designed with the latest computer-aided design/computer-aided manufacturing techniques based on years of practical experience. It was not always this way. The first carburetors were very crude devices.

One of the earliest carburetors was called the surface carburetor and functioned by having the intake charge drawn over a reservoir of gasoline. It generated an inconsistent mixture ratio and required the operator of the engine to constantly correct the air/fuel ratio with hand-operated air valves. An unforeseen problem when applied to an early automobile was the splashing of the gasoline due to vehicle motion and the negative impact that it had on vaporization.

The next evolutionary step was the wick carburetor; it had the inlet air

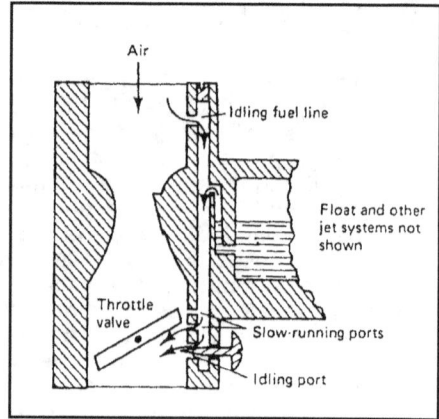

Since the throttle plates are almost fully closed at idle, the amount of depression created in the venturi of the main body is minimal. For this reason, the signal that initiates the fuel flow in the idle circuit is referenced below the throttle plates. That is why if you look down the carburetor throat when an engine is idling, no fuel can be seen.

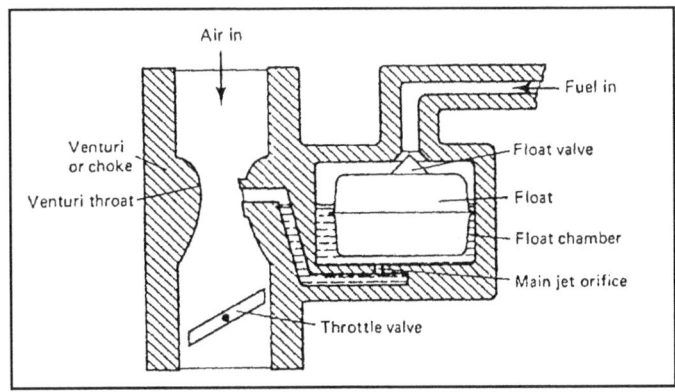

Every carburetor works on the fact that high pressure goes to low pressure. The venturi is used to create a low-pressure region that pulls fuel from the float bowl which is under the influence of atmospheric pressure.

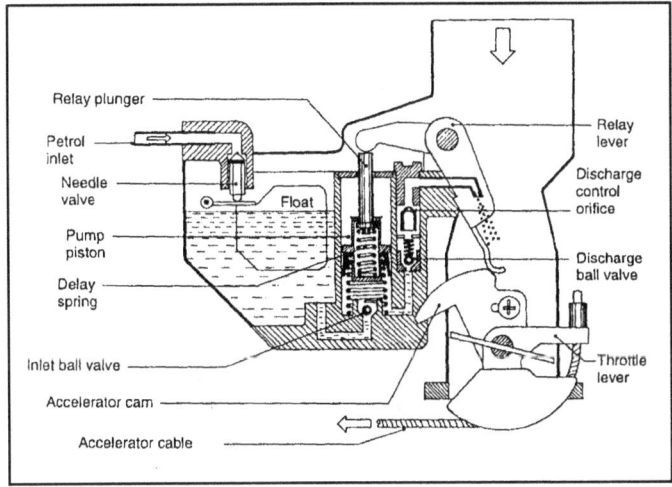

A Demon is considered a modular carburetor and uses a diaphragm-style accelerator pump. A multi-piece carburetor such as a Rochester uses a plunger-style accelerator pump, as shown in this generic drawing. Demon chose not to use the plunger design because it offers little or no tuneability, an important element of a performance carburetor.

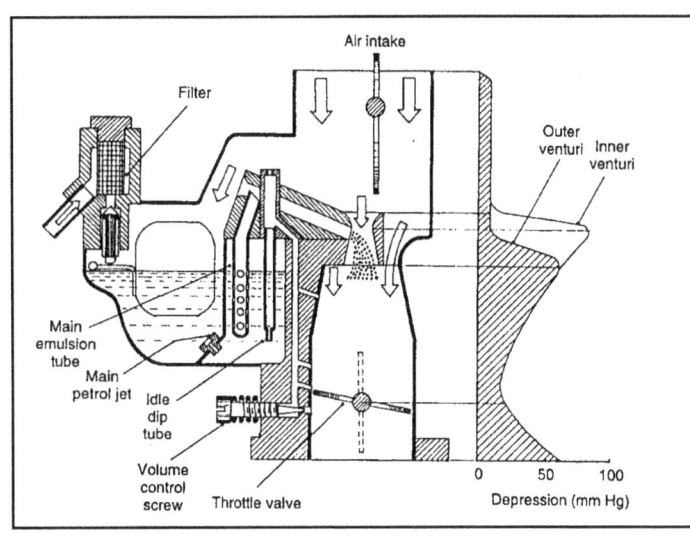

This cut-away drawing of a generic carburetor does not resemble a Demon in appearance but does a good job of showing how a carburetor works.

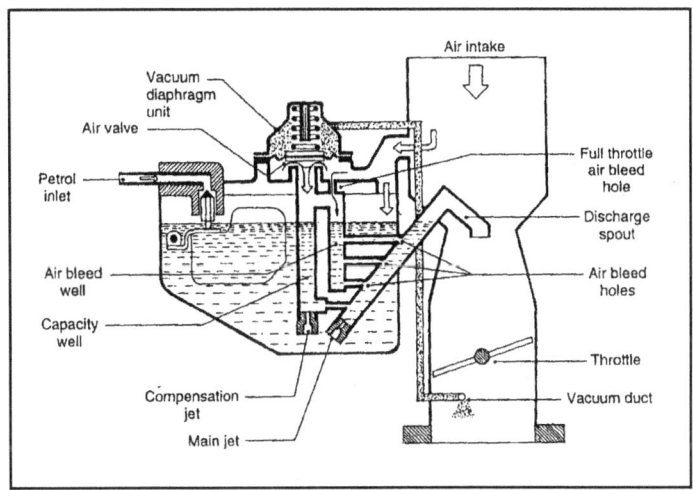

Though carburetor terms may vary by manufacturer, the theory of operation is the same.

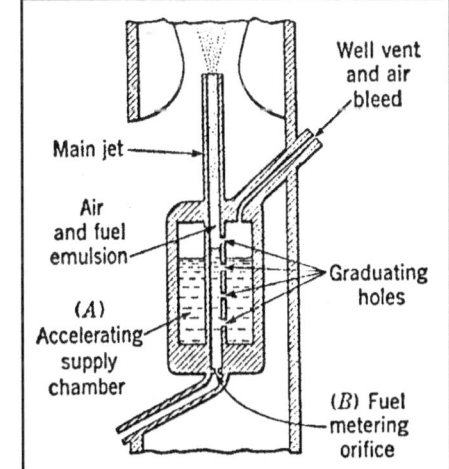

Fuel by itself will not burn and needs to be mixed with air. A carburetor uses air bleeds and emulsion holes to accomplish this.

pass around wicks that were placed in small bowls of gasoline. Capillary action maintained the part of the wick exposed to air in a state of saturation, so a sufficient amount of gasoline could be evaporated to provide a combustible mixture. A significant drawback was its considerable bulk and inaccurate mixture preparation.

Next in the time line was an adaptation of the surface carburetor by German Wilhelm Maybach in 1892; it was the forefather of today's modern carburetor. Identified as a spray carburetor, it measured the incoming airflow and metered in an appropriate amount of fuel. In its simplest form it was comprised of an air tube into which a fuel delivery jet was placed, so the engine's incoming air was forced to flow past the jet. It was discovered that a moving column of air exerts less sideways pressure than when it is stationary, hence the fuel entering the delivery jet from the float chamber is forced out into the air stream. This is a function of the atmospheric pressure on the fuel supply in the float chamber being greater than the pressure surrounding the jet. It is often thought that in a modern carburetor, the fuel is sucked through the jet; rather it is pushed from the jet due to a pressure differential between the pumping action of the piston and atmospheric pressure.

How to Tune and Win with Demon Carburetors

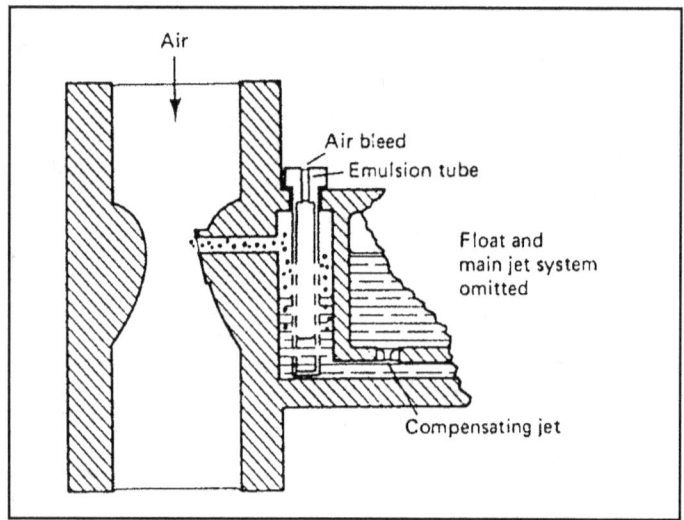

Air bleed and emulsion orifice size and placement control the timing of the fuel delivery of the carburetor in relationship to the amount of depression. Larger bleeds and orifices delay the operation of the main metering circuit.

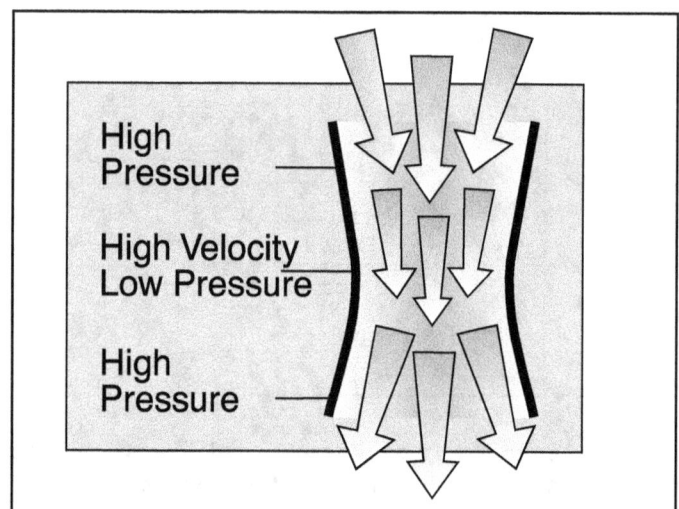

The venturi cast into the main body of a carburetor does not create enough depression for a multi-speed engine to control fuel properly. A constant-speed engine, such as that in a lawnmower, can get by with a single venturi and still run properly.

DEFINING VACUUM

When the basics of engine functions were reviewed in Chapter 1, it was stated that the movement of the piston created a vacuum in the bore and below the throttle plates in the intake manifold. Now the time is right to expand upon the definition of vacuum.

The standard to identify pressure is relative to the force of the atmosphere on the Earth, better known as atmospheric pressure. By definition, a vacuum is any pressure less than atmospheric. The many ways this is measured often lead to confusion: it can be represented in pounds per square inch, inches of mercury, or inches of water. According to McGraw-Hill's Dictionary of Engineering, atmospheric pressure is measured at sea level and is considered to be 14.70 psi, which is also called one atmosphere.

A typical vacuum test gauge reads in inches of mercury. If a vacuum gauge is attached to an engine and reads 15 inches of mercury, this can be interpreted that the low-pressure region created in the engine is sufficient for atmospheric pressure to push a test column of mercury 15 inches up into a tube. Expanding upon this, atmospheric pressure of 14.70 psi has the ability to push the same column of mercury 29.92 inches. In near terms, due to the difference in specific gravity, a manometer would read 406.78 inches of water at atmospheric pressure. So as you can see, what we accept as either pressure or vacuum is actually relative to the atmosphere.

The process of trying to draw fuel through the jet of a carburetor was met with difficulty; the frictional flow coefficient of the gasoline required a greater amount of depression than was available in the throat of the carburetor. Thus, a method was needed to increase the amount of depression, or in other terms, increase the pressure differential from atmosphere. Since the displacement of the engine is fixed, on its own it would not have this ability.

In the 18th century, Swiss scientist Daniel Bernoulli wrote extensively on the theory of hydraulics and quantified the Bernoulli principal. It stated

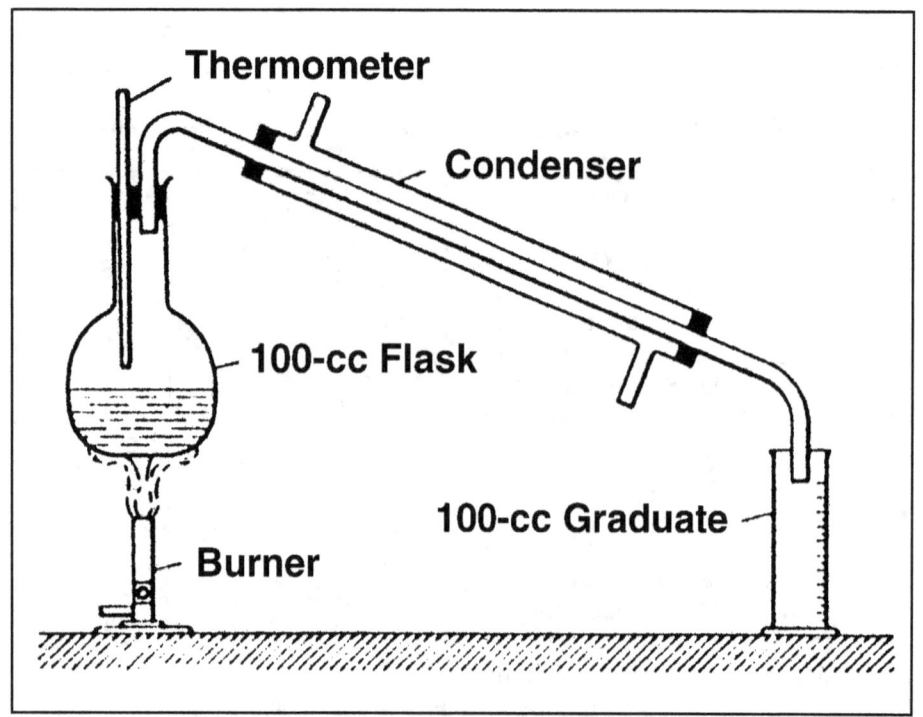

A distillation test is done on gasoline by the oil companies to determine the boiling point, vapor pressure, gum, and varnish production.

How to Tune and Win with Demon Carburetors

that the relationship between pressure and velocity in a flowing fluid is such that the total energy possessed by the flow is the same at every point along its path. The pressure of the fluid will therefore be reduced where velocity is increased, since the gain in kinetic energy must be offset by a loss in potential energy. This was further expanded upon by Giovanni Venturi, an Italian physicist who discovered that to increase the depression over a metering jet, the air inlet must be provided with a converging-diverging path, and it was so named after him. The Venturi principle works because the same volume of air must flow through all portions of the carburetor. It will be evident that the effect of introducing a constriction will increase the local air speed and cause a corresponding drop in pressure. With this in mind, every carburetor functions on the law of physics that states pressure moves from high to low.

When looking down the throat of an automotive carburetor, you will see a ring positioned in the bore and a converging-diverging casting in the main body. This is used to initiate the Venturi principle. The Demon uses an actual insert known as a booster venturi to create this high-velocity-low-pressure region and draw fuel from the float bowl. Demon carburetors offer three different styles of boosters to serve application specific needs, and will be discussed in length in Chapter 3.

These are two different straight boosters for Demon carburetors. Note how the internal diameter and shape of one is different from the other.

Automotive carburetors use a booster, or second, venturi within the main body venturi to amplify the signal. Demon uses many different styles and shapes of boosters to obtain the desired results for each application.

HOW A CARBURETOR WORKS

If asked to describe the function of a carburetor in elementary terms, it could be said that the air enters through the top, which is identified as the air horn, from an air cleaner assembly that is used to remove suspended dust particles. The air then flows into the venturi, where the air velocity increases and the pressure decreases. While this is happening, the float bowl acts as a fuel reservoir with the level maintained at a constant height. Connecting the float bowl to the venturi is a tube that contains a calibrated orifice better known

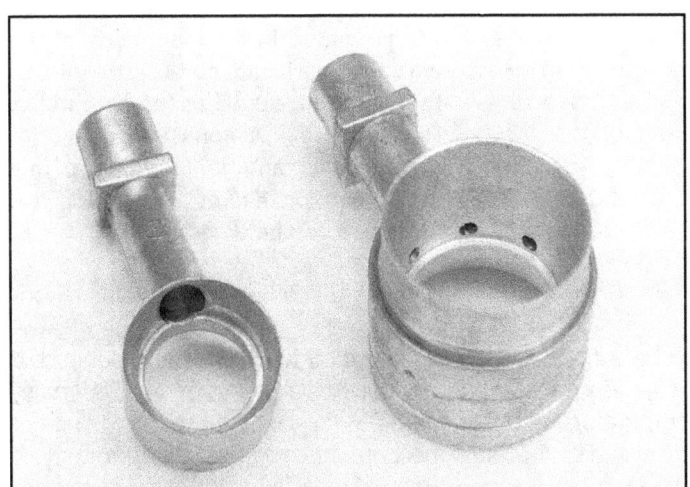

Most boosters discharge fuel from the main well through one hole in the booster circumference. In some applications, an annular booster is used and has multiple discharge holes around the internal ring.

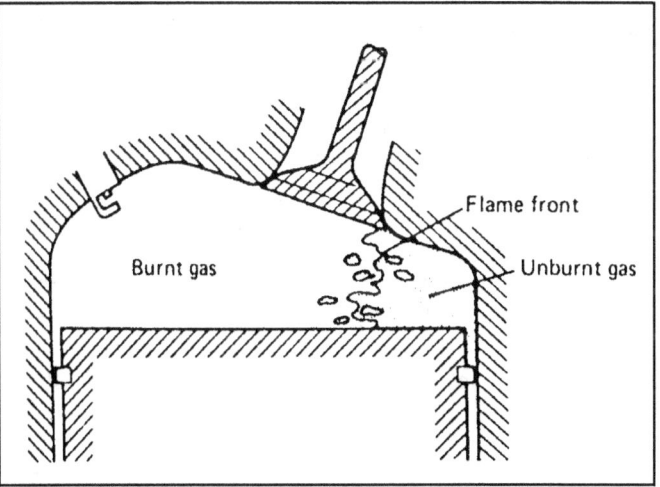

When the fuel and air mixture from the carburetor is ignited by the spark plug, the flame expands and travels from regions of burned to unburned gas. The expanding energy works against the piston and drives it down in the bore.

How to Tune and Win with Demon Carburetors

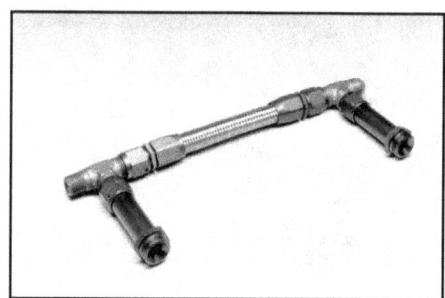

All Demon carburetors feature dual float bowls and require a dual inlet fuel line.

This is how the fuel is discharged by the booster when the engine is operating on the main metering circuit. The placement of the camera gives the false impression of uneven fuel discharge.

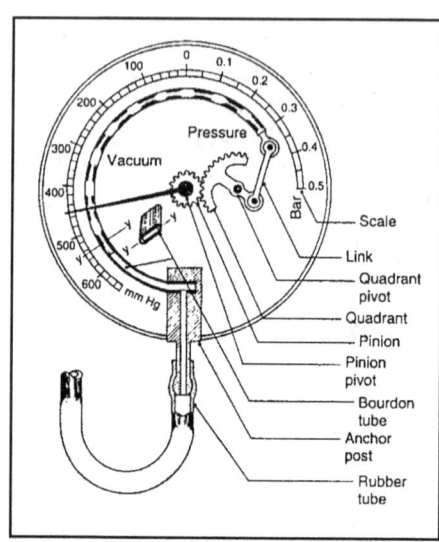

A vacuum/pressure gauge is an essential tool for tuning a carburetor properly. This drawing shows its internal workings. It must be remembered that all readings are referenced from atmospheric pressure.

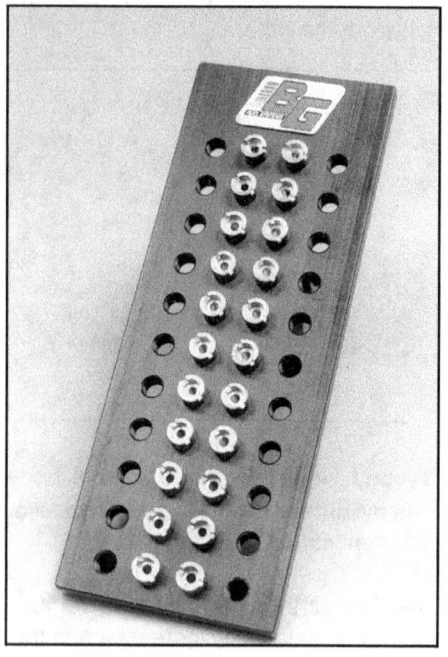

The size and design of the main jets affect the air/fuel ratio throughout the operating range. Air bleed and emulsion orifice dimensions affect the shape or timing of the fuel curve.

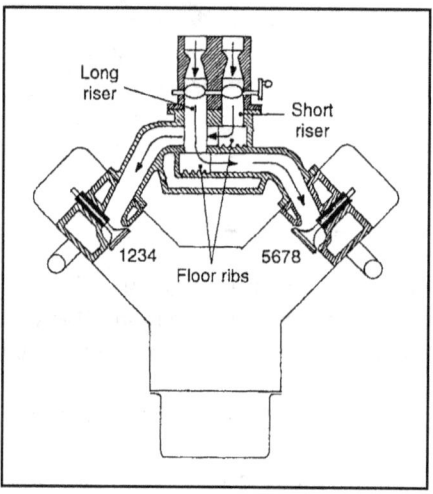

A dual-plane intake manifold will work better at low engine speeds, whereas a single-plane design favors high piston velocities.

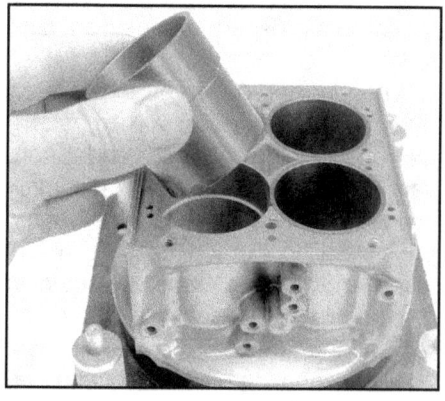

The action of the piston during the intake stroke creates the low-pressure region called the depression. The size of the venturi in the main body of the carburetor will affect the strength of the signal produced in the carburetor. Race and King Demon RS models offer replaceable venturis, so the optimal dimension for the best carburetor performance can be determined.

as a jet. As a result of the high velocity and low pressure at the tip of the jet, fuel is discharged into the air column, since the atmospheric pressure on the float bowl is greater than the pressure in the venturi. The fast-moving air stream carries away the fuel and further atomizes it by tearing. The newly created fuel/air mixture flows through the diverging section of the venturi, where it decelerates and recovers some pressure. The mixture then flows past the throttle plate and enters the intake manifold and is distributed to the cylinders.

The job of the carburetor is very demanding, serving the needs of the engine for both fuel and air delivery. Since no single design could accomplish this task satisfactorily for every possible engine combination and use, there are distinct models in the Demon line. The following overview provides generic descriptions. The exact design of the Demon circuits will be covered after these fundamentals are established.

Float System

Often considered to be a fuel reservoir, the float system supplies gasoline to all circuits of the carburetor. It consists of a float located at the end of a lever, which is attached by a pivot and rests against a needle valve. The action of the lever causes the needle valve to lift off its seat, allowing fuel to enter the bowl. The float, in conjunction with the needle valve, maintains a constant level of fuel in the bowl, but will also shut off fuel flow when required. If the correct amount of fuel is maintained in the bowl, the other circuits of the carburetor will function properly. If the float level is too high, a rich mixture will be induced; the signal created in the booster will pull fuel prematurely. Conversely, if the float level is low, a lean condition will occur because it will

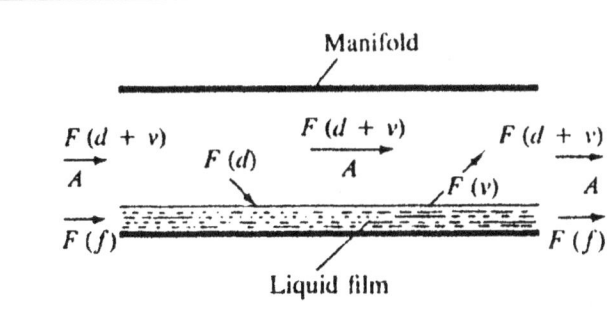

Schematic of fuel flow paths in the manifold when liquid film flows along the manifold runner floor.

- A Air
- F Fuel
- f Liquid fuel film
- d Liquid fuel droplets
- v Fuel vapor

Once the intake charge leaves the carburetor and enters the intake manifold, some of the fuel puddles and creates a boundary layer in the runners of the manifold. This creates a variation in the delivered vs. created air/fuel ratio. Engineers work to limit this puddling when they design an intake manifold.

be harder for the booster signal to lift the fuel the additional distance. When the booster signal is sufficient to initiate fuel flow, it is called "pull over."

Choke

A number of issues arise during crank due to the temperature of the air and the engine itself, along with the slow speed of the piston. Gasoline requires heat to vaporize, and as the ambient temperature drops, so does the rate of vaporization. At -45 F degrees, only 20 percent of the fuel will vaporize, and under these conditions a gasoline-powered engine will stop running. At 60 F degrees, the rate of vaporization is only up to 50 percent. Conversely, if the underhood temperature becomes excessive, the fuel vaporizes prior to entering the venturi area of the carburetor, not allowing the engine to start due to vapor lock or boiling. These concerns are addressed by the industry under the term hot fuel handling. Additionally, the speed at which the engine cranks becomes an issue, since the low piston velocity will not allow a significant amount of depression to occur, even with the benefit of a booster.

During crank, the mixture that would reach the cylinders is too lean to ignite, and until the intake components reach a certain temperature the fuel distribution would suffer. To overcome this and produce fast starts and acceptable engine operation during the transition period from a cold to a warm engine, the carburetor uses a choke to richen the air/fuel ratio. Once the manifold is hot enough to properly vaporize the fuel, the choke function must be extinguished. This circuit consists of a butterfly or plate located in the air horn and, in the case of most modern carburetors, a thermostatic spring and fast-idle cam. During crank, the choke closes by spring tension and exposes almost full manifold vacuum in the venturi, drawing a large amount of fuel through the main metering system. When the engine fires, the increased piston velocity partly blows the choke plate open against the spring tension to allow a sufficient amount of air to lean the mixture and reduces the signal in the venturi to avoid flooding.

Idle

Once the engine starts, the piston velocity increases and the signal provided by the booster is much stronger

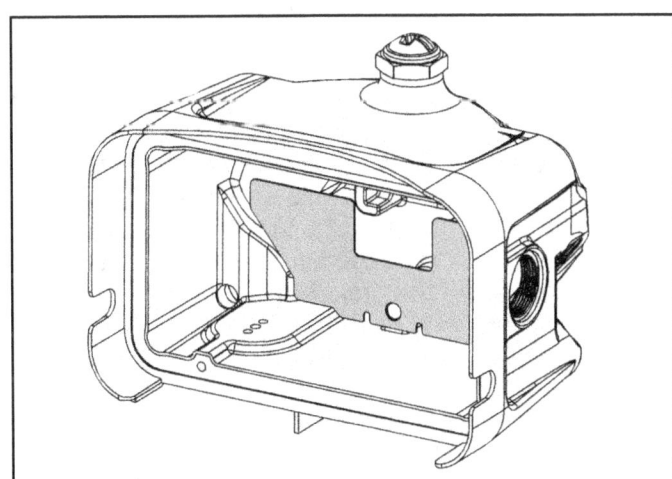

All Demons offer high-capacity float bowls for a good supply of fresh fuel to the carburetor. Some applications have a fuel dam to limit aeration while the bowl is filling, as shown in this drawing.

The first step for proper carburetor performance is to have the float level set properly. Kelly Ricketts of Barry Grant, Inc. was one of many highly-skilled people involved in the development process.

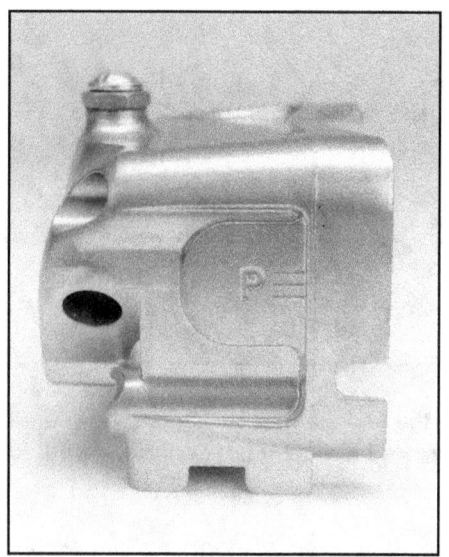

Primary and secondary float bowls are identified with either a P or an S.

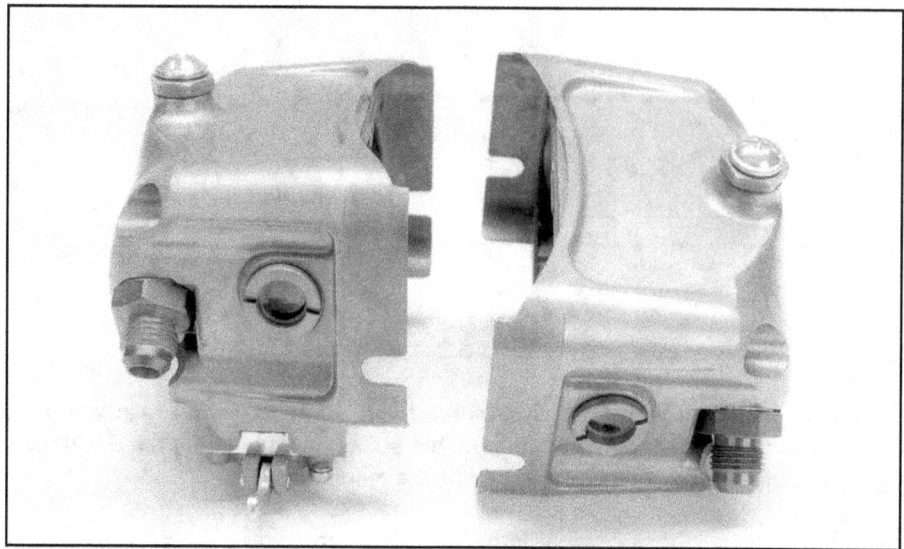

Single-accelerator pump models have the pump assembly mounted on the bottom of the primary float bowl.

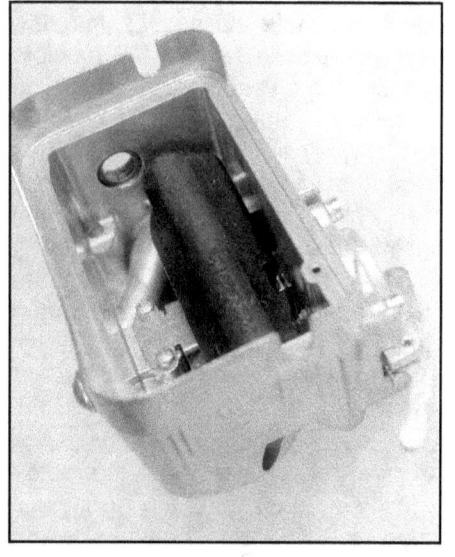

Demon float bowls use large, clear sight windows for safe and quick float level adjustment.

than during crank if no choke plate were present. An engine is considered to be at idle when no external load is placed upon it and the throttle plate is essentially closed. The idle circuit is required because in this state, the airflow through the carburetor is insufficient to create venturi depression to draw fuel through the main metering circuit. This is not to be confused with the fact that the engine vacuum is considered high below the throttle plates, but the lack of throttle opening impacts the signal in the venturi. The high-manifold vacuum signal is then used to control the idle circuit by connecting a fuel well to an orifice below the throttle plates (plenum side of the throttle plates).

The idle circuit is attached with an idle air bleed, idle mixture screw, and idle discharge port in the throttle body. The air bleeds are used to emulsify the charge and to reduce the pressure drop across the idle port and control the fuel circuit. As the throttle plates are opened further, the idle circuit still functions, but the idle fuel volume is controlled by the mixture screw.

An idling engine demands a mixture that in relative terms is richer than at part-throttle. As the throttle plates are opened, the mixture can be made leaner. An explanation for this is found by noting the pressures in the intake manifold and cylinder bore while idling. When the throttle plate is nearly closed, the pressure in the intake manifold is usually far below atmospheric (remember, though we call this a vacuum, it is relative to atmospheric pressure), while the pressure at the end of the exhaust stroke is close to atmospheric. Just as the intake valve opens, there is a higher pressure in the cylinder than in the intake manifold. This causes the relatively high-pressure exhaust gas to expand into the intake tract. As the piston starts to descend on the induction stroke, the reverted exhaust gas is drawn back into the cylinder along with the fresh charge. Thus, the overall mixture contains a high percentage of exhaust gas.

To offset the effects of the inert exhaust gas diluting and weakening the burnable mixture, the carburetor needs to supply a rich mixture. Though it has been well established that the pressure and temperature of the exhaust gas at the end of the exhaust stroke do not vary greatly with engine load, the clearance space in the cylinder remains constant, so the amount of trapped exhaust gas stays constant. The concern is the most prevalent at idle, since the throttle plates are almost closed and the engine requires a very small amount of fresh charge by weight to overcome internal friction. The VE of the engine is at its poorest, but the volume of reverted exhaust to fresh charge is high. This condition is present in all engines, even those with very mild cam profiles, but dilution is accentuated when cam overlap is increased. As a slower idle speed is demanded, a richer air/fuel ratio is required, or the idle speed must be raised to allow for an increase in fresh charge.

Main Metering

As the throttle plate is opened, the problem of exhaust gas dilution becomes less acute and the mixture can be leaned out. The concern now is to provide the proper amount of fuel to consume all of the oxygen in the bore, with the VE in a limited state. Identified as part-throttle or

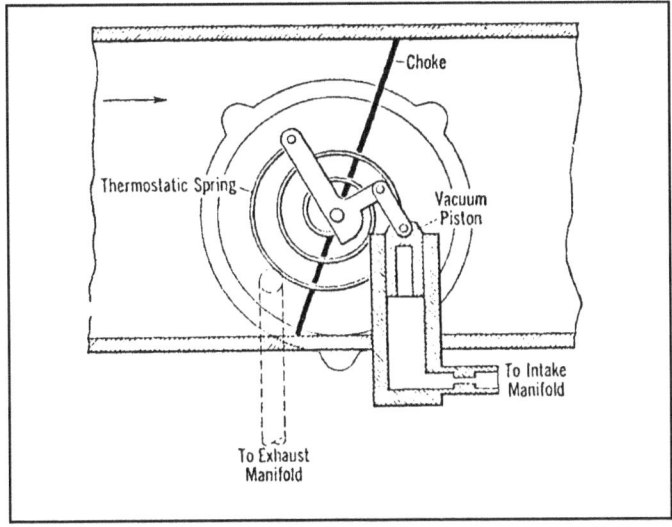

Many years ago, choke springs used heat from the exhaust manifold to expand the thermostatic spring and open the choke plate.

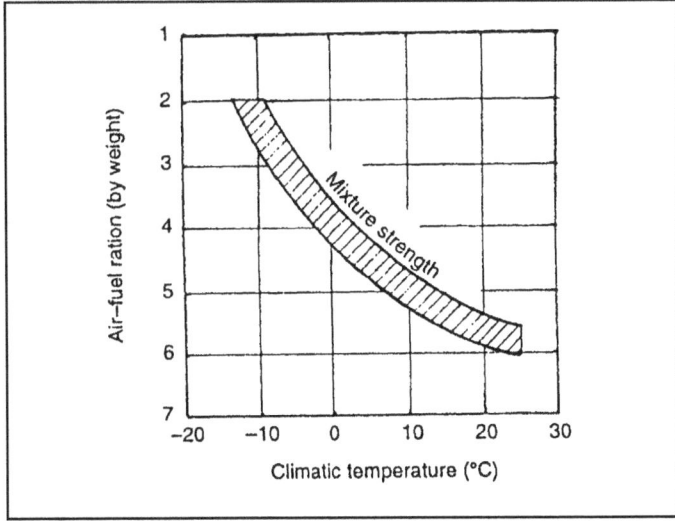

Gasoline needs heat to vaporize. The air/fuel ratio needs to be richer during starting and engine warm-up to make up for the poor rate of phase change.

Modern electric chokes require no exhaust heat source and are standard on Road Demons and optional on Speed Demons.

The period of time in crankshaft rotational degrees when both valves are open is defined as overlap. The reversion of inert exhaust gas into the intake manifold dilutes the fresh charge, requiring a richer mixture to be delivered by the carburetor.

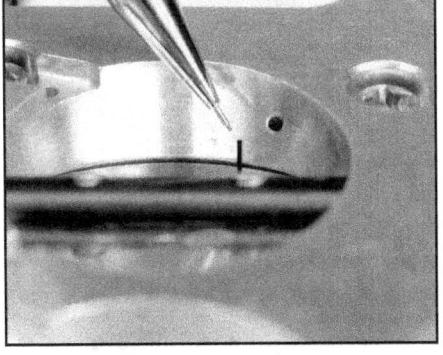

For proper tip-in driveability and throttle response, the transfer slot area in relation to the throttle plate is extremely critical on Demon carburetors.

light load, the engine is fueled by both the main metering system and with the idle circuit. To obtain the best driveability in this region, one must consider that the reduced volumetric efficiency will limit the dynamic compression ratio of the engine, and the best results will be obtained by tuning not only the air/fuel ratio, but also the spark advance curve.

As the signal at the venturi becomes stronger and more fuel is introduced, air is bled into the main fuel well by a series of bleeds. This reduces the pressure differential across the main fuel metering orifice, which is no longer experiencing full venturi vacuum. The air from the bleeds and the fuel become emulsified and atomize more uniformly to smaller droplet sizes when entering the venturi.

Accelerator Pump

The transition of the throttle plate from closed to open causes an elimination of some of the pumping restriction, and the result is a reduction in the pressure differential from atmosphere. Since the VE of the engine has increased, there is more combustible mixture in the bore, so the engine speed increases. Though this reaction may appear to happen instantaneously, there is a time period when the drop in vacuum is greater than the increase in flow through the carburetor. If this condition was not addressed by design, the engine would bog slightly because it would momentarily be starved for fuel.

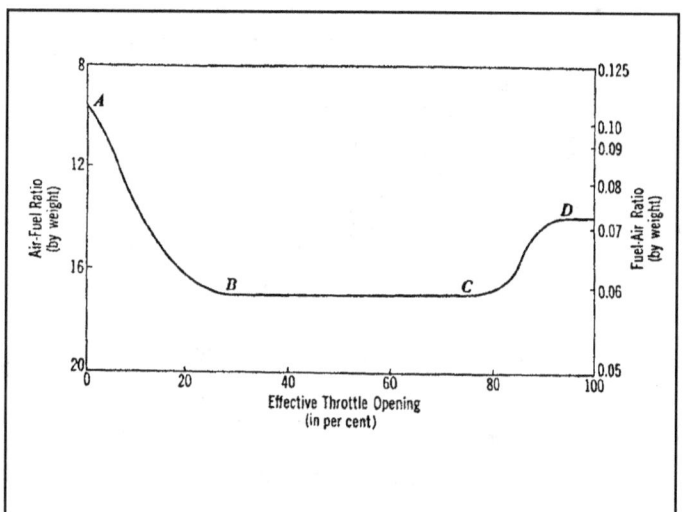

Plotting the mixture requirements of an engine reveals an inverse bell curve. The mixture needs to be the richest when the throttle plates are closed, and leans out as they are opened. As WOT is approached, the fuel requirement increases again.

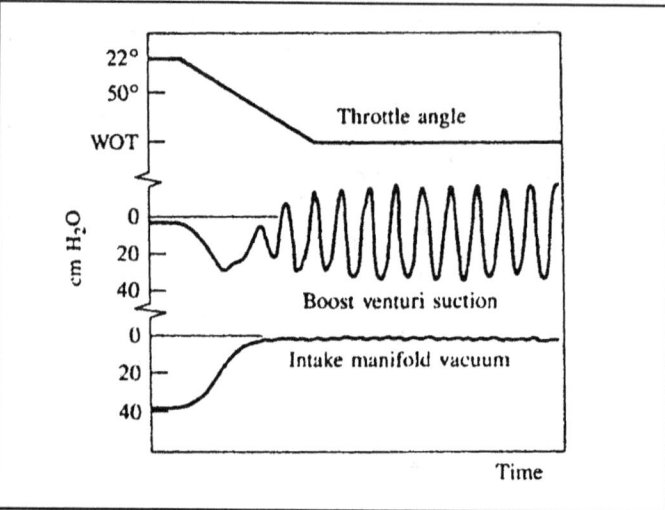

The relationship of the throttle angle vs. the booster signal and intake manifold vacuum. The sine wave effect of the booster signal is a result of the amplification of the pumping pulses of the piston. They are apparent in the intake manifold vacuum signal but are subdued.

If you were to study this condition in more detail, you'd see that fuel is approximately 600 times heavier than air. Though much of the fuel flow into the cylinder is in the form of vapor, there are small fuel droplets carried by the air stream, and a fraction of that fuel flows onto the manifold walls and forms a liquid film. This fuel then evaporates more slowly than the fuel carried by the air stream and produces a lag between the air/fuel ratio produced at the carburetor and the mixture delivered to the cylinders. In engineering terms this is called a puddling constant or coefficient.

When the throttle is opened quickly, the air will rush in, and even though the venturi principle will be present, the fuel, due to its weight, will lag behind the air. To combat this an accelerator pump, or squirter, is used. Mechanically linked to the throttle plates, it consists of a diaphragm (which acts like a reservoir), a spring, passages, a cam to control timing and volume, and a discharge nozzle. When the accelerator pump is triggered, the diaphragm overcomes the spring pressure behind it and forces fuel through a tube and calibrated restriction. It is positioned for the stream to hit on the top of the booster and break the fuel apart, atomizing it as it enters the incoming air flow. The output of the squirter is a function of throttle depression, spring pressure, squirter cam timing, and discharge orifice dimension. The fuel enrichment from the accelerator pump is over a time period and not delivered all at once.

Power Enrichment

Triggered from a manifold vacuum signal, the power valve supplies additional fuel through the main metering circuit and is designed to richen the air/fuel ratio the equivalent of eight steps larger in main jet size. Under wide-open or close to wide-open throt-

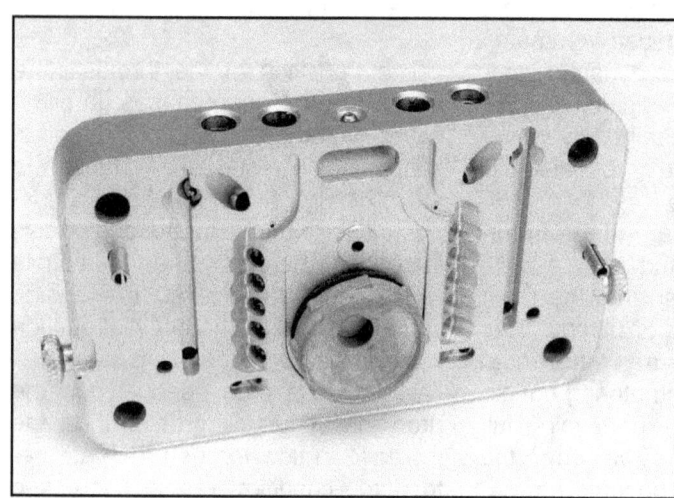

The main body side of the metering block reveals the power valve and emulsion orifices.

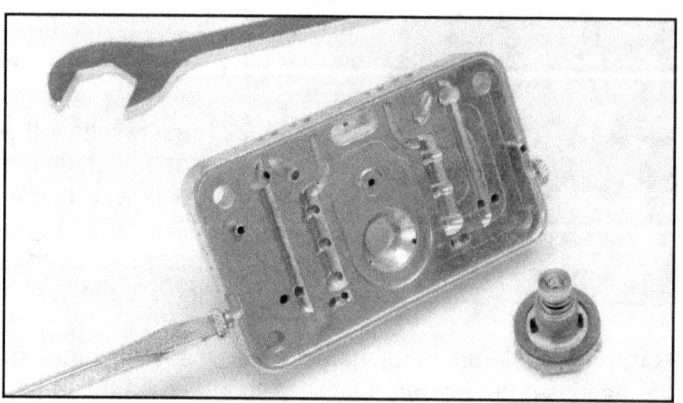

A thin-shank one-inch wrench is the proper tool for power valve removal. Remember, the power valve marking represents the opening vacuum of the valve and not the flow rate. The PVCR restrictor controls the amount of enrichment offered by the power valve. Most Demons are shipped with a PVCR that is eight steps larger than the main jets.

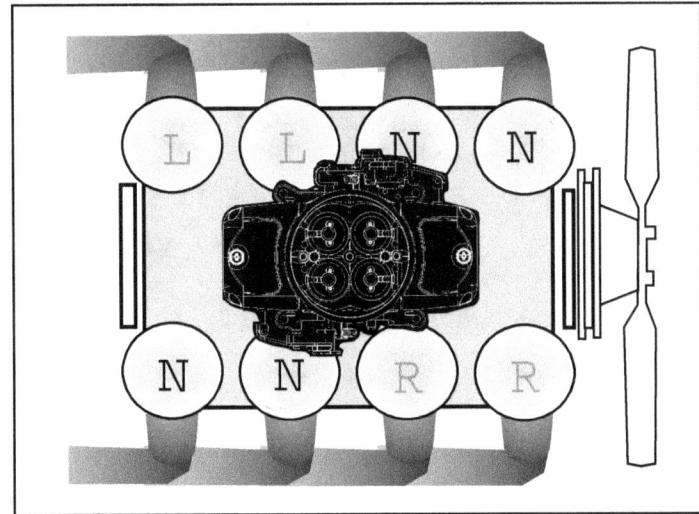

These are the mixture deficiencies with a primary side idle circuit only. L, N, R represent lean, neutral, and rich, respectively. All Demon models use a four-corner idle to eliminate this problem and achieve better idle quality.

The accelerator pump diaphragm is located on the bottom of the float bowl. Twin squirter models have accelerator pumps on both primary and secondary bowls.

tle conditions, the intake manifold pressure rises to a point where there is not enough of a variance between atmospheric pressure and manifold pressure to pull sufficient fuel through the normal main metering circuit. This condition can occur at wide-open throttle when the engine is loaded and the RPM is relatively low, such as when pulling a load or a trailer up a steep hill. The reduced piston velocity creates less velocity through the venturi, so the pressure drop and the amount of fuel pulled through the main metering circuits are less. Then the power valve supplies the additional fuel. Held closed by vacuum, as the manifold pressure rises (the amount of vacuum is less), the valve opens against a light spring and allows additional fuel to flow through the power valve channel restrictor (PVCR) circuit.

Secondary Barrels

Some may wonder why a four-barrel carburetor even exists. Why not use one large barrel? The use of carburetors with multiple venturis is an attempt to balance venturi signal for accurate metering of fuel, along with maintaining a high level of VE at wide-open throttle. If a single-barrel carburetor were used, as the venturi size is increased to provide higher airflow potential, the venturi length also increases and the metering signal generated at low flow rates suffers. A good rule is that maximum wide-open-throttle airflow can be as much as 70 times the idle airflow, which would make it very hard to design a single-

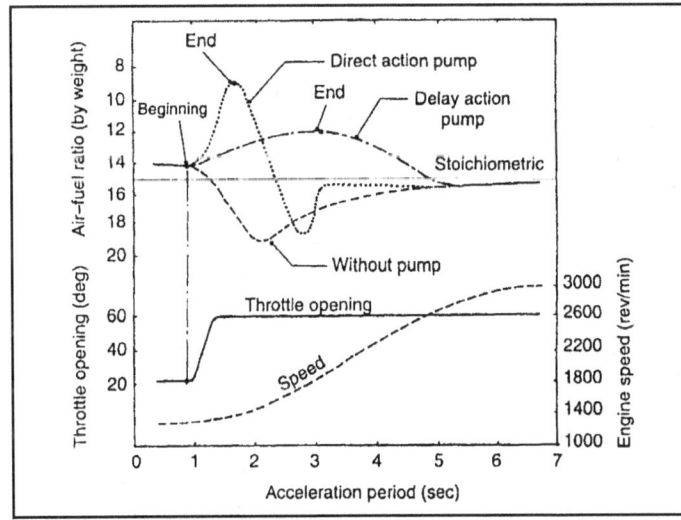

The accelerator pump delivers fuel over a time period in relation to the amount of throttle opening, as shown by this chart. The additional enrichment is required to eliminate the lean condition created by rapidly opening the throttle plates. Note the trace that represents the air/fuel ratio if no accelerator pump was used.

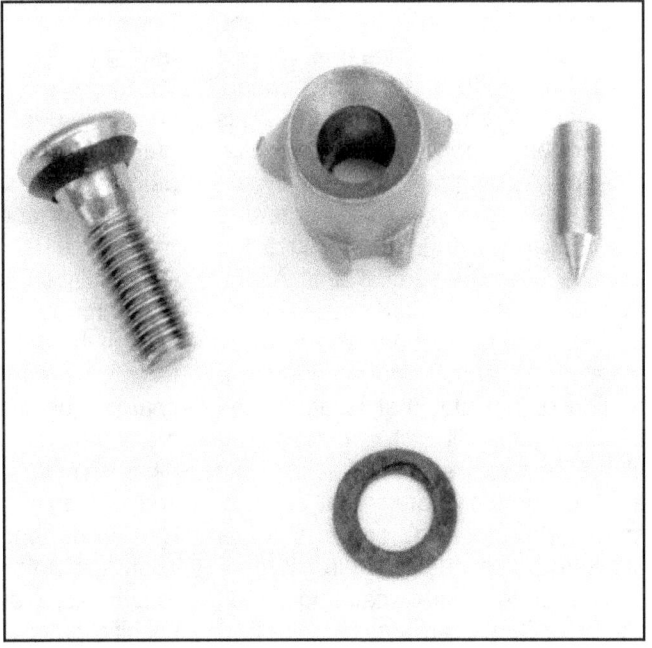

Most Demon models use standard-style squirters.

This 1980 Corvette is hiding a Road Demon under all of those vacuum hoses. This is an excellent choice as a replacement carburetor for the original Rochester Quadra-Jet.

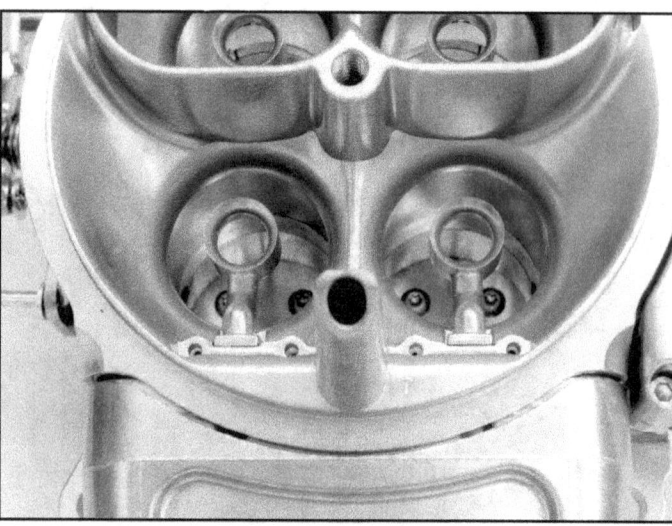

A four-barrel carburetor is more efficient because it allows the engine to run on small primary bores to generate a strong signal at part throttle. Under high load, the secondary barrels then limit the pumping losses.

bore carburetor that could work efficiently under these varied conditions.

All Demon carburetors are of the four-barrel design, with some models offering staged secondary butterflies. Race versions usually can be tailored to open all four barrels simultaneously.

Transfer Slots

Many carburetors also incorporate transfer ports that are timed or positioned to be exposed at predetermined throttle angles. Their function may be to supply either bleed air or a vacuum source to run an ancillary component, such as a spark advance unit.

As the throttle plates are opened, more air will enter the manifold. This will require more fuel to be discharged. As mentioned previously, the idle holes are a fixed size, whereas the idle air passages just above the throttle plates are vertical slots. As the throttle is opened, more of the slot will be exposed to vacuum and will use more of the area to deliver fuel. The portion of the slot that is above the throttle plate will still act as an air bleed. To avoid a lean condition just as the throttle plates are opened, most carburetors add one or two fuel discharge slots that are directly connected to the main metering circuit idle tube. Some carburetors use a port similar to this to supply a vacuum connection independent of the intake manifold and designed to be exposed at a specific throttle angle.

Air Bleeds, Emulsion Holes, and Jets

The internal part of a carburetor that most enthusiasts are familiar with is the jet. Used to control the amount of fuel in both the main and secondary circuits, it can be thought of as a calibrated orifice. Years ago it was common to correlate the jet size to a drill bit index. Though this practice is still used today, Barry Grant, Inc. offers tuning kits with incremental jet sizes, making drilling by the enthusiast obsolete. The theory behind jet changes will be discussed in depth in Chapters 9 and 10, but each jet number will alter the fuel delivery approximately four pounds per hour, or about three percent.

Gasoline is a liquid and therefore essentially incompressible, so the fuel flow through a jet is a function of the area of the orifice and the pressure differential across it. This is called the discharge coefficient. It is affected by many factors and is in no means one-dimensional. It includes, but is not limited to, the mass flow rate of the gasoline, orifice length, and diameter ratio, approach ratio, surface area, surface roughness, inlet and exit chamfers, the specific gravity, viscosity, and surface tension of the fuel. For these reasons, even though many modular carburetor jets may appear to be the same, only Demon-manufactured jets should be used to maintain the quality and performance of your carburetor. Additionally, the jet size and carburetor tuning need to be calculated using the specific gravity of the intended fuel.

A change in jet size impacts the air/fuel ratio throughout the engine operating range, while modifications to air bleeds and emulsion orifice size and placement control the RPM at which a given mixture ratio will be produced. The emulsion bleeds are located in the metering block, and their number and placement vary by Demon model. They function to control the density of the fuel by metering the amount of air that is introduced into the main well. They work in unison with the air bleeds in the main body to control the shape of the fuel curve relative to engine speed.

The air bleeds are located in the upper portion of the air horn between the wall and the venturi. There are at least eight in total on every Demon carburetor. The ones located closest to the air cleaner ring are for the idle circuit, the high-speed bleeds are found on either side of the vent tube, and the intermediates on three circuit models are located in between them. As the bleed orifice dimension is enlarged, it will slow down or delay the circuit activation, while smaller bleeds will quicken the response of the circuit. Opposite of jet changes, the essence of carbure-

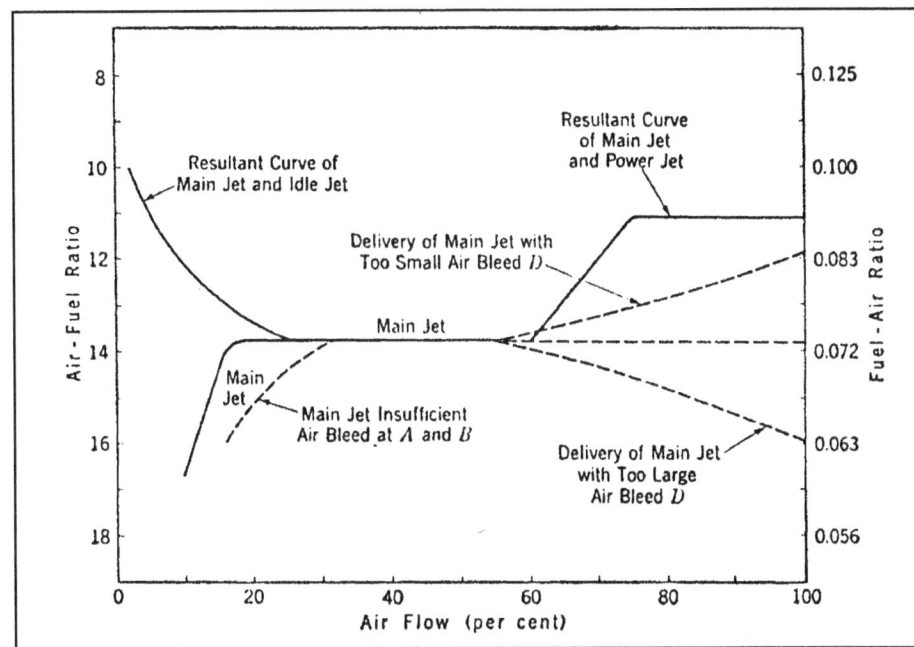

The air/fuel ratio created by the carburetor is determined by the size of the main jet. The horizontal axis of the graph represents airflow instead of RPM, since the piston velocity will impact the strength of the signal in the booster. Note how the air/fuel ratio timing is altered by varying the air bleed dimensions.

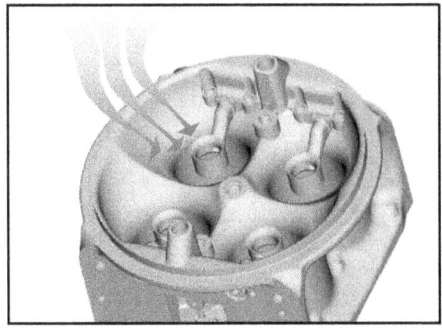

All Demon carburetors feature a patented sculptured air entry that increases horsepower, torque, and throttle response.

tor tuning is to find a balance of jet, air bleed, and emulsion hole dimensions.

PUTTING IT ALL TOGETHER

For a carburetor to be properly constructed, there are several design requirements.

(1) An idle circuit is required to meter the fuel and control the ratio of the charge during idle and light load conditions.
(2) The main metering circuit must provide the proper air/fuel ratio during engine operation for conditions when the engine is between 20 and 80 percent of its airflow potential.
(3) The squirter must inject additional fuel when the throttle is opened rapidly to maintain the proper delivered air/fuel ratio to the cylinders.
(4) A power-enrichment circuit is required to provide the additional fuel for high engine load conditions.
(5) It is necessary to increase the intensity of the pressure drop through the use of a booster to control fuel flow.
(6) A choke can be added on street-driven vehicles to enrich the mixture during engine starting and warm-up to provide fast starts and acceptable driveability until the intake manifold has sufficient heat to properly vaporize a majority of the fuel.

THE WORKINGS OF A DEMON

If all carburetors function on a pressure differential, then what makes the Demon brand better? Simply put, by design, it does a superior job of being a carburetor. Consisting of four distinct models, each has design and engineering features that are responsible for its superior performance. In subsequent chapters, the intricacies of each model will be explored in length. The following is an overview of similarities of all models.

Air Entry

In physics, air is considered a gas, which is defined as matter in its most rarefied state, opposed to a fluid or liquid. It has been well established that a gas does not like to make turns, succumbing to frictional flow losses when asked to travel in anything other than a straight path. Since this is not always possible, a good design minimizes these losses through understanding.

Demon recognized this basic law of physics and looked first to improve upon the air entry of the carburetor, known as the air horn. Traditional carburetor designs often neglected this, forcing the incoming air to turn abruptly against

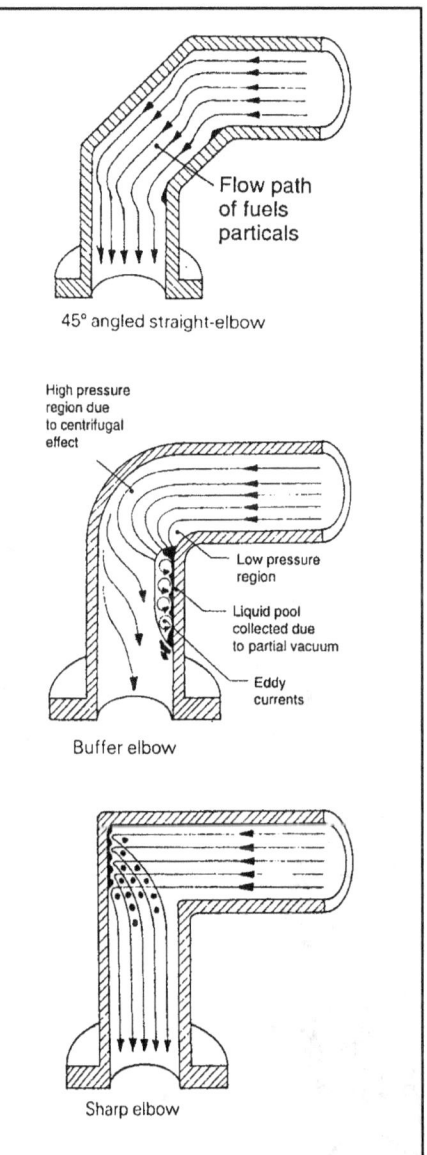

The ideal path for any gas is a straight line, but more often than not that is not possible. The Demon design team recognized that and spent much time studying the air entry of a carburetor before finalizing a design.

How to Tune and Win with Demon Carburetors

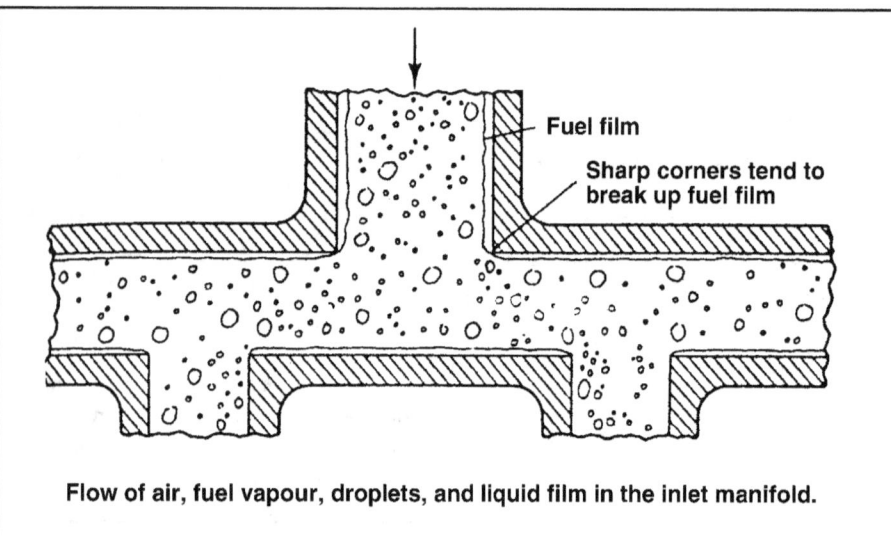

Flow of air, fuel vapour, droplets, and liquid film in the inlet manifold.

Sharp corners in the intake manifold tend to break up fuel film for a carburetor that does not do a good job of atomization. However, they also create a frictional flow loss.

sharp edges and multiple angles with a rough casting surface. Often overlooked is the effect that the surface of the casting has on the air. Anyone who has ever ported a cylinder head usually acknowledges this and polishes the surface after it is contoured by the abrasive cutting bit. When air is asked to flow over a rough surface, flow losses through friction occur that are different from those established by sharp turns, but nonetheless they are losses.

Demon took a very unique approach and was awarded Patent # 5863470 for its inlet-entry design, which is used in every model. The approach is multifaceted, incorporating a high-quality casting procedure that creates an extremely smooth surface, with a contoured radiused air inlet to better direct the air. This allows for a more efficient flow path, along with the ability to generate a superior signal in the booster and control fuel more accurately. This design pays dividends beyond the obvious and improves peak horsepower and torque and adds crispness to the throttle response of the engine.

Standard casting procedures usually leave a ridge where the two pieces of the mold are joined, known as a parting line. In a traditional carburetor, the parting line is usually located in the bore between the booster and the venturi. This seemingly small intrusion into the airflow path creates a substantial flow loss, which in turn affects the signal produced in the venturi, along with becoming a pumping loss for the engine. Recognizing there must be a better method, Demon joined forces with Empire Industrial Castings of Macedonia, Ohio, to be the first carburetor manufacturer to implement a new diecasting procedure called ConcentraCast. This procedure minimizes the parting line, misalignment, and core shift. Requiring a special mold making process, all Demon carburetors use this method and are void of any parting line in the venturi.

Float Circuit

Proper carburetor operation is founded on the requirements of keeping the float bowl filled to the correct level and offering enough capacity along with control of the fuel. These concerns were addressed by design and include a unique float circuit system. The Demon float bowls offer increased capacity from conventional modular carburetors and provide a more constant fuel reserve for consistent performance. Acknowledging the importance of proper float height, the traditional removable sight plug that was a potential fire hazard was replaced with a large, clear sight glass that is marked for the proper fuel level. No longer is the actual fuel level up to the interpretation of the tuner, adding inconsistency to the carburetor's ability to pull fuel properly. Additionally, some application-specific models have a unique anti-aeration dam installed in the float bowl that settles the fuel and reduces foaming. The float level is adjustable from the exterior of the carburetor and requires a wrench and properly-sized screwdriver.

Craig Mensching of Mensching Competition Engines uses a flow bench to test a cylinder head. Though the prescribed method, a flow bench cannot represent the true flow characteristics of a running engine.

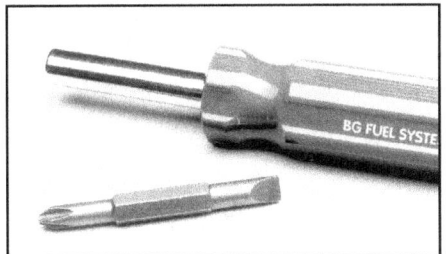

BG Fuel Systems is a full-line company offering all the tools you need to tune your Demon carburetor, fuel, or nitrous system.

Gathering the most facts about your engine will help the Demon staff choose the proper carburetor for your application.

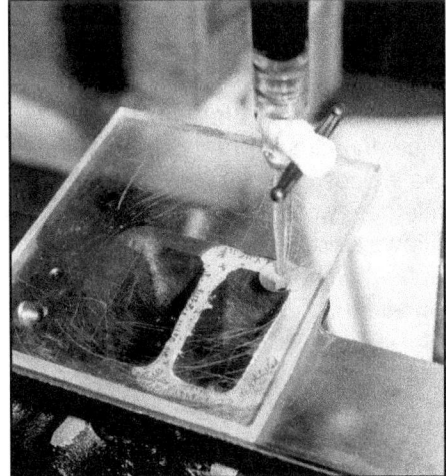

Calculating the compression ratio by using the cc method is the only accurate means of determining the difference in volumes.

Many racers believe that a 1:1 secondary link should always be used on a race engine, but in some instances a progressive link offers better performance.

There are applications that do require a mechanical secondary. Before any purchase is made, it is advisable to consult the Demon tech line.

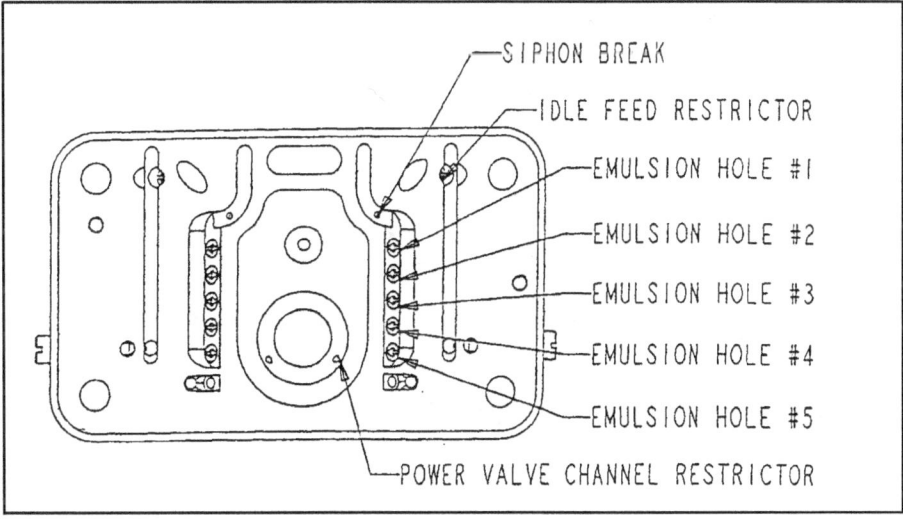

The billet-aluminum metering block used by Demon guarantees repeatable performance.

How to Tune and Win with Demon Carburetors

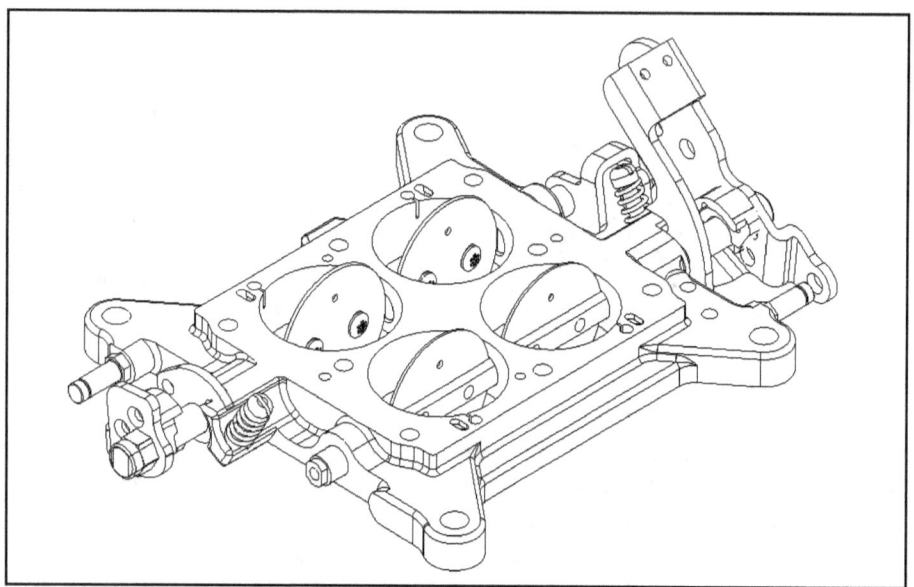

The Demon exclusive billet-aluminum base plate assembly is virtually unbreakable. Note the air bypass holes in each throttle plate in this engineering drawing. They are used on some race carburetors to help adjust the idle speed. Chapter 10 will cover this theory in detail.

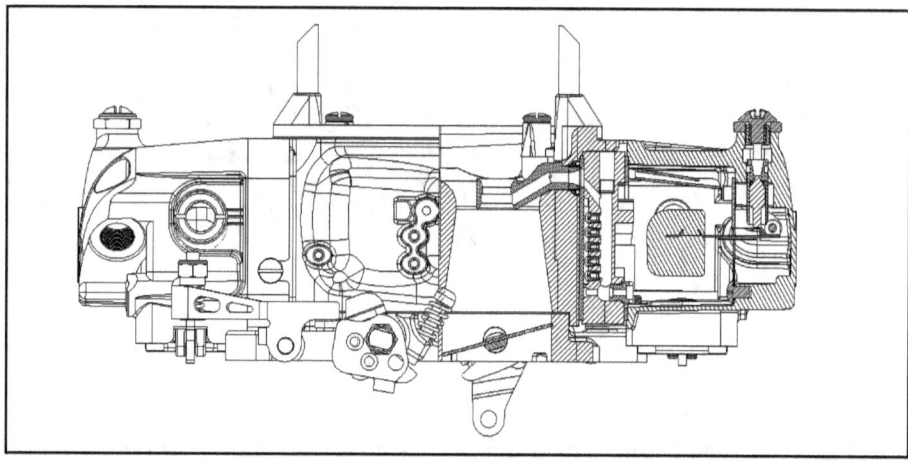

In this Demon cutaway drawing, you can see how the emulsion holes introduce air into the main well to be mixed with fuel before exiting the booster.

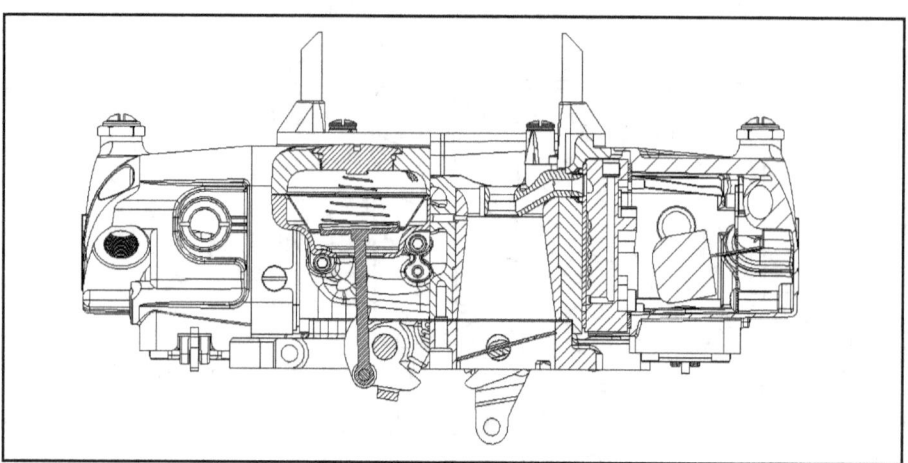

The vacuum secondary operates on venturi vacuum, not manifold vacuum. This is the signal produced in the venturi of the main body.

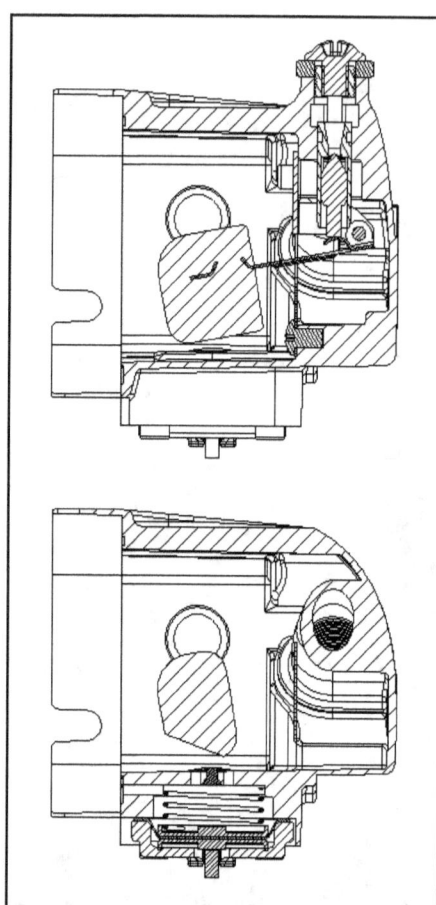

The float and accelerator pump circuit of a Demon carburetor is represented by these drawings.

Choke

Standard on the Road Demon and optional on Speed Demon is a choke kit. It is a very simple design consisting of an electric thermostatic spring with integral fast idle cam, linkage, choke butterfly, and shaft. Designed to increase the booster signal to pull additional fuel through the main metering circuit when cold, the choke plate does not fully block the air horn inlet as would an OE design. This allows for broad-based installation appeal without the complication of a pull-off mechanism.

Idle Circuit

Traditional carburetors offered only primary bore idle circuits and mixture screws. This creates an inherent distribution problem, forcing the front of the plenum to be flooded with fuel in the hope of being distributed to the rear cylinders. The end result was a poor

38 *How to Tune and Win with Demon Carburetors*

idle quality that was especially sensitive to cam overlap and the dilution of the charge created by reversion.

A simple cure was instituted by Demon with the integration of a four-corner idle mixture system. Offering an idle circuit and mixture screw at each bore guarantees fuel distribution and superior idle quality and throttle tip-in over applications with only primary bore circuitry. Located in the metering blocks, the idle mixture screws are knurled for easy adjustment without a screwdriver. It is important to recognize that the idle circuit is functioning throughout the carburetor operating range, and the more adjustability that is available, the easier it will be to perfect driveability and throttle response.

Demon carburetors also include an idle feed restrictor which is used to limit the fuel flow from the main jet well into the idle circuit. This is especially important as the jet size is increased to meet the air/fuel requirements of the engine under WOT. As jet orifice diameter is enlarged, the amount of fuel passed is greater, limiting the authority of the idle mixture screw. By integrating a fixed-orifice dimension, a smooth, clean idle is available to the user of a Demon carburetor, regardless of the jets needed to meet the engine's full-power fuel demand. The idle feed restrictor orifice size is listed in the specifications section for each series carburetor under the abbreviation I.F. Res.

Main Metering Circuit

The metering block of a Demon carburetor serves two functions: controlling the fuel flow into the venturi, and mixing the air and fuel prior to entering the carburetor bore. This is accomplished through a series of sized orifices that are drilled into the metering block assembly.

A unique aspect of the Demon metering block is its construction; it's made from billet aluminum instead of diecast zinc. Cast-zinc metering blocks have suffered from porosity that effectively bleeds the air and fuel circuits together, making tuning and consistent carburetor performance impossible. Being made of billet aluminum, the Demon metering block eliminates this condition, guaranteeing exacting performance over years of operation.

The number and position of emulsion bleeds varies with each Demon model and is identified numerically, with number one being at the top. By design, some models do not have every emulsion hole opened. This criteria allows the tuning of the fuel curve and will be investigated in depth for each model carburetor in the respective chapters of this book.

Squirter Circuit

The Demon line uses two different-style squirters: standard and tube-style. The tube type is easily identified by the short tubes extending from the exit orifice of the squirter. The exit orifice diameter of either design controls the duration of the pump shot. The standard volume as installed at the factory on most Demon models is 30cc, with a 50cc diaphragm and cover on the King Demon and available for some race models. The smaller the diameter of the exit orifice, the longer time it will take to empty the volume of the pump. A larger-diameter exit orifice will discharge the squirter's total fuel volume more quickly. Additional tuning of the squirter circuit is available by changing the squirter activation cam. Eight different cams are available and are color-coded for easy identification. As mentioned ear-

---

COOL SCHOOL

If you or someone you know ever wanted to find a place to learn about high-performance engines, your prayers have been answered by Loren Jarvis and the staff at the University of Northwestern Ohio, in Lima (419-227-3141). Working in concert with a standard automotive program, a course of study was added that includes suspension, steering, drivelines, engine machining, fuel systems/electronics/ignition, and custom engine building.

Situated on a beautiful 35-acre campus, the technological division encompasses more than 76,000 square feet of classroom and shop space. In addition to a fully-equipped machine shop, there is a complete cylinder head flow-testing room with multiple SuperFlow 600 benches, along with Audie Technologies swirl detection and camshaft inspection instrumentation. Airflow theories and machine shop skills are then put to the test in one of the school's two SuperFlow 901 dyno cells, each outfitted with a complete data-acquisition system.

Not limited to just engine building, the high-performance drivetrain and chassis programs teach the essentials of these theories. A partial list of subjects includes setting up rear end gears; adjusting and building a chassis for drag, dirt, and road racing; and tuning a four-link for better 60-foot times.

The university acknowledges that to be successful, skills beyond automotive performance are required. Addressing these needs, the associate's degree program covers mathematics, English, psychology, contract law, and introduction to business. The staff is comprised of hands-on instructors who collectively have more than 826 years of practical and theoretical experience. More important, they are hot-rodders at heart. This creates a common bond with the students that is not present in most institutions of higher learning.

Part of the curriculum is to gather practical experience around racing, so in an unprecedented move, Northwestern purchased nearby LimaLand Motorsports Park in 1997. At this location, student activities are at their best. Associate Dean Bill Sergent states, "Owning our own facility, where the students can work with our educators in an environment that includes a drag strip burnout pad for 60-foot shots and a complete quarter-mile dirt track and road race circuit, allows them to gain invaluable practical experience."

The school has an open admissions policy and accepts students who have earned a high school diploma or equivalent. There are no limits on age or past experience. Their mission statement is to offer quality diploma, associate, and baccalaureate programs to traditional and non-traditional students. Because the university is an accredited institute of higher education, tuition assistance is available with loans, grants, and work-study programs. Prospective employers acknowledge the prestige of being a Northwestern graduate, with students gaining employment at Mr. Gasket Company Inc., Summit Racing Equipment, and Skip Barber Racing School, along with major NHRA, NASCAR, and IRL racing teams.

CARBURETOR ICING

The problem of carburetor icing has been around as long as the carburetor itself. The vaporization of fuel removes heat from the intake manifold and carburetor venturi, which can cause ice deposits to occur when moist intake air condenses in the carburetor body or base plate assembly. This normally happens at ambient temperatures that are above freezing, and can occur even up into the middle 50 F degree range. Icing is most common, though, with air 25-45 F degrees that has a relative humidity of 80 percent or greater. At lower temperatures and humidity levels there is not enough water in the air to create the problem, and at higher ambient temperatures the evaporating gasoline cannot create the conditions to cause ice.

Ice deposits can be identified by the region of the carburetor on which they form and ultimately restrict the air or mixture flow. Where the formations occur varies with carburetor design and engine application and use. The location of the ice will determine how the driveability is impacted. If the ice forms on the throttle plates, it will have a significant effect on the air/fuel ratio only at very low throttle openings or when the throttle plate is closed completely, such as when the engine is required to idle. This type of icing is known as idle icing, most common in city driving during the engine warm-up period. During idle icing, the throttle plates become covered with ice and choke off the air causing the engine to stall.

Ice can also form in the venturi of the carburetor during cruise conditions which is known as cruise icing. These deposits tend to cause a power loss during cruise conditions, again because it restricts airflow or possibly the signal to the main metering circuit. The drop in power can be so great that the vehicle may come to a complete halt. Often this problem is hard to diagnose since it will take only a few minutes for the ice to melt and the power to return if the engine is shut off. This occurs because of the heat soak that warms the carburetor when the engine has stalled or has been turned off. The oil companies work hard to develop additives that will limit icing, but the laws of Mother Nature still prevail.

CLEAN COMBUSTION CHAMBERS

Every combustion process, even the most efficient one, creates carbon that becomes deposited on the combustion chambers of the cylinder head and on the crown of the piston. An additional area of concern about deposit formation is the back side of the intake valve and the intake track of the manifold during valve overlap and EGR operation, if the car is so equipped. These carbon-based deposits are detrimental to the engine, as they raise the octane requirements when found on the piston and combustion chambers, and absorb fuel when attached to the intake valve.

Many old-time mechanics used to carefully drip water down the carburetor with the engine running at high idle in the hopes of loosening and removing the combustion chamber formations. Others believe that using a drip of automatic transmission fluid applied with the same procedure as the water does the trick. Both methods have some intrinsic value for carbon removal, but their effectiveness is limited and, at times, costly. An uncontrolled drip of any liquid into the intake system of an engine affords the opportunity to hydrostatically lock the engine if too much is administered. Since a liquid is non-compressible, the connecting rod or piston gives instead. A concern with using water or transmission fluid to loosen deposits is rooted in the fact that the carbon is not loosened, but hammered from the parts.

Recognizing that there had to be a better way to remove deposits without dismantling the engine, C.A.T. Products (215 639-1839) developed the Run-Rite process to chemically dissolve both combustion chamber and intake valve deposits and let them burn off through normal combustion. A complete kit is offered for under $50, which includes a reusable applicator. A three-step process has one part added to the gas tank, another to the engine oil, and the third and final element safely dripped into a manifold vacuum source. The Run-Rite applicator is designed to limit the liquid throughput of the company's patented carbon-dissolving chemical. Simply connect the applicator bottle to the appropriate vacuum source, set the idle speed up, and in about 30 minutes the deposits will be removed, lowering the emissions and octane requirements and restoring full performance.

lier, a complete review of the theory and application of this modification will be covered in Chapters 9 and 10.

Power Valve Circuit

The power valve is located in the metering block between the two main jets. It offers an increase in available fuel to meet the requirements of the engine without creating an overly rich idle or part-throttle condition. All Demon power valves are marked clearly with a vacuum rating. This signifies the point at which the valve will open referenced against engine vacuum. The lower the rating, the more the vacuum has to drop in the engine before this circuit is evoked. The power valve is located only on the primary metering block of Road and Speed Demons. All others have a provision for power valves on both the primary and secondary blocks.

Secondary Circuit Control

Application-specific to the model carburetor is either mechanical or vacuum operated secondaries. All models that feature dual squirters (located on both primary and secondary barrels) are equipped with mechanical secondaries. Tuning kits are offered to modify the spring tension in the vacuum diaphragm and alter the secondary opening rate. For mechanical versions, there are two styles of secondary linkage available: 1:1 and progressive. The 1:1 link, which is the longer of the two, opens the secondaries at nearly the same rate as the primary bores. In contrast, the progressive linkage requires the primary side to be approximately one-third open before the secondaries begin to open.

Altering the link design has a huge impact on driveability. The non-progressive style increases both the fuel and airflow more rapidly, whereas the progressive version brings the additional barrels in over time.

Additional Features and Benefits

A long-standing problem of many carburetors were the brittleness of a diecast aluminum-based plate. For this reason, Demon offers the indus-

PCV vs. VALVE COVER BREATHERS

It's common practice to install a valve cover breather on a race or performance engine to allow any blow-by that migrates past the piston rings to escape the oil pan by traveling up past the lifter area and into the valve covers. If this path was not available, the oil pan would become pressurized and create resistance against the piston as it swept toward BDC. Additionally, the breather minimizes the possibility of oil leaks from a pressurized oil pan.

In contrast, a PCV system is a controlled vacuum leak that is used to siphon the blow-by and introduce it back into the induction track to be burned. The problem with a PCV system is that it works from manifold vacuum, better known as full-time vacuum. An engine will produce vacuum only at part throttle, thus the PCV valve does not evacuate the blow-by gases during WOT operation. This is not a problem for a street engine since the amount of time it spends at WOT is very minimal.

Often an enthusiast will install a valve cover breather and retain the PCV system. Unfortunately, this renders the PCV inoperative because the system is now open to the atmosphere and cannot create a vacuum in the valve cover. Real race engines often use a breather kit that is scavenged from the exhaust header collector to use the velocity of the exhaust gas and the expansion of the sound and pressure wave to pull a vacuum in the valve cover at high engine speeds. Under no circumstances should a valve cover breather be installed on an emissions-controlled vehicle. This would violate local and federal laws.

try's only billet-based plate, which is virtually unbreakable. Machined in-house, not only does the billet construction add strength, but dimensional tolerance and sealing are better than with cast designs.

Booster design concerns and installation procedures are mutually exclusive to Demon carburetors, offering three design styles: straight, drop leg, and annular. Each design offers distinct advantages and application specific theories. A full explanation of booster design will be covered in Chapter 3.

REVIEW QUESTIONS

(1) Fuel is discharged by the carburetor because of:

  a: the difference in pressure exerted on the fuel in the float bowl vs. the pressure in the venturi
  b: the pressure created by the fuel pump
  c: the overlap of the camshaft
  d: the compression in the cylinder

(2) The venturi in the carburetor creates a:

  a: low-pressure, high-velocity region
  b: high-pressure, low-velocity region
  c: high-pressure, high-velocity region
  d: atmospheric pressure

(3) At idle, the air/fuel ratio in relative terms needs to be:

  a: richer than part-throttle operation
  b: leaner than part-throttle operation
  c: the same as wide-open throttle
  d: constantly changed

(4) All Demon carburetors have a patented:

  a: choke plate design
  b: mounting bolt pattern
  c: contoured air inlet
  d: needle valve design

(5) The Demon exclusive ConcentraCast procedure produces:

  a: a rougher venturi surface to atomize the fuel
  b: a parting line that needs to be ground flush with the venturi bore
  c: a smooth venturi and bore surface free of a parting line
  d: none of the above

(6) The purpose of the Demon four-corner idle circuit is:

  a: to create even distribution of fuel in the plenum
  b: for more top-end power
  c: to allow the use of low-octane fuel
  d: to make the engine run richer

(7) The idle feed restrictor is used to:

  a: increase fuel flow to the idle circuit under high engine demand
  b: raise the idle speed
  c: make up for poor tuning
  d: limit fuel flow to the idle mixture screws

(8) All Demon metering block assemblies are made from:

  a: billet aluminum
  b: cast from ZA-3
  c: cast aluminum
  d: stamped from mild steel

(9) All Demon power valves are stamped with a number signifying the:

  a: amount of fuel in lbs. per hour
  b: size carburetor it is designed for
  c: amount of manifold vacuum when the valve will start to flow fuel
  d: amount of manifold vacuum when the valve will stop flowing fuel

(10) All Demon twin squirter carburetors feature:

  a: mechanical secondary operation
  b: either mechanical or vacuum secondary depending on model
  c: only vacuum secondary
  d: standard choke kits

Answers: 1) A, 2) A, 3) A, 4) C, 5) C, 6) A, 7) D, 8) A, 9) C, 10) A

How to Tune and Win with Demon Carburetors

How to Tune & Win with DEMON CARBURETORS
Choosing the Proper Carb

The decision to equip your engine with a Demon carburetor is an easy one; it is the best performing fuel-metering device you can buy. The difficult question is: Which Demon is right for you? With Road, Speed, Race, and King Demon variants, the proper carburetor for your application will need to be determined. Other features need to be considered as well; vacuum secondary, dual squirter, and size, all come into play after the model selection is made.

UNDERSTANDING AIRFLOW RATINGS

As mentioned previously, the thinking in this hobby is, the larger the part, the better it will perform. When applied to carburetors, choosing the proper flow rating is the key to obtaining the best performance. However, there has been much confusion over flow specification, test procedures, and their meanings. What's an enthusiast to do? The only logical approach is to establish a full understanding of airflow testing and an engine's requirements.

The industry standard for quantifying the amount of air passing through an induction system of an engine is a flow bench test. Carburetors are identified with flow ratings to quantify their size, but cylinder head flow testing is what has made airflow numbers a common topic during bench race sessions. The problem lies in how this information is derived, and that cylinder head airflow cannot be correlated to carburetor flow numbers.

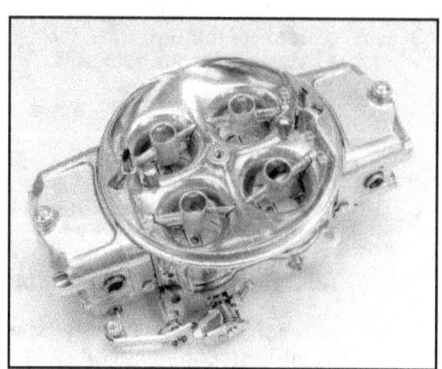

The King Demon is an impressive piece, but it does not belong on every engine.

The fact has been established that one of the keys to power in an engine is airflow; so measuring airflow, in theory, should enable one to establish potential output. The basis of the performance industry is founded on maximizing an engine on an individual component level. Then documented gains in airflow should produce predictable results in power production. The question could then be posed, why look at airflow and not power?

Whenever designing or modifying components in the induction track of an engine, the ideal procedure would be to install the part and then dyno check. This would be not only the most accurate, but also the least practical test method. Anyone who has ever ported a cylinder head while quantifying results on a flow bench can only imagine the arduous process of installing the head and running the engine after every port change. Early on it was recognized that a better method needed to be developed, and that became the flow test. A flow bench test allows a quick and easy means of quantifying gains or losses in airflow, but it does not simulate the actual flow process of the engine.

Most of the confusion in regard to carburetors is based on the fact that the industry as a whole has never really established a common guideline for a flow test. It is assumed that all carburetor manufacturers use the same amount of depression as a test value, but that is not always the case. A very basic law of physics is overlooked: two things cannot occupy the same place at the same time. Traditional flow benches are dry flow, moving air only, while a carburetor on an engine is moving both fuel and air simultaneously. So using a dry-flow test to determine the actual flow of a carburetor is a faulted procedure.

Recognizing this, Demon is the only carburetor manufacturer to use a wet-flow instead of dry-flow test bench. This was done to guarantee that as the Demon carburetor line was developed, all aspects of the design could be studied. It is one of the elements responsible for its stunning performance. This was a monumental undertaking, since a wet-flow bench of this capacity did not exist in production form. So Barry Grant, Inc. had to build its own.

Even though a specific test procedure and depression are not common in the industry, it would be safe to assign a depression of 1.5 inches of mercury (in./Hg) to a four-barrel, and

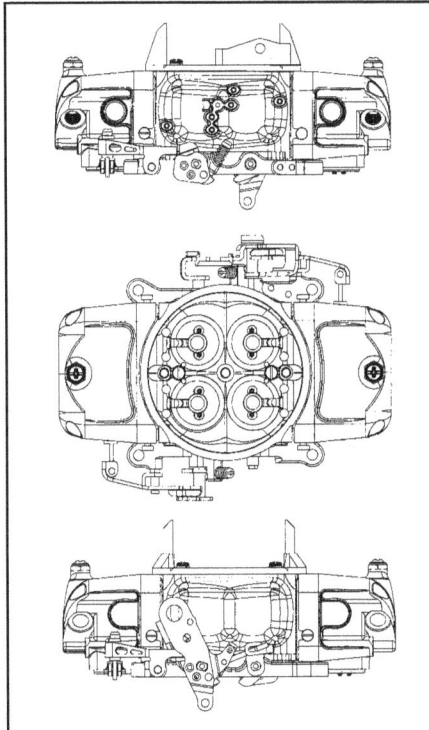

Although the four distinct models of Demon carburetors are different, they all share a family resemblance to this engineering drawing.

3.0 in./Hg for a two-barrel, for brands other than Demon. Since a flow bench is a series of vacuum motors, the higher the depression, the more powerful the bench needs to be. Manufacturers such as Holley, Edelbrock, and Carter, along with aftermarket carburetor tuning companies, use dry-flow testing on a flow bench that is calibrated to read

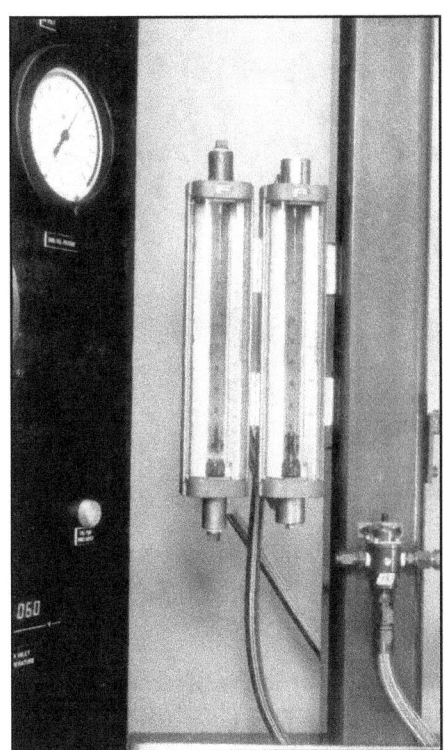

A nonflammable test fluid that has the same specific gravity of gasoline is used. The flow rate is controlled by the operator.

in inches of water, not mercury. A rule for conversion is: .5 in./Hg is equal to 6.79 inches of water. Thus, 1.5 in./Hg would be equivalent to 20.40 inches of water. As a side note, the aftermarket cylinder head industry uses 28 inches of water as a standard depression.

What is interesting about flow numbers is that they are meaningless

Cylinder head flow testing on a dry-flow bench, such as this SuperFlow SF-600, has become the industry standard but does not accurately determine carburetor flow characteristics.

Barry Grant and his engineers realized that to develop a new breed of carburetor, a wet-flow bench would be required. Since there was none commercially available, he spent over $250,000 designing and building the industry's first wet-flow carburetor test system.

How to Tune and Win with Demon Carburetors

To create a sufficient depression to start fuel flow during a static test, the Barry Grant, Inc. wet-flow bench uses two 60-horsepower electric motors.

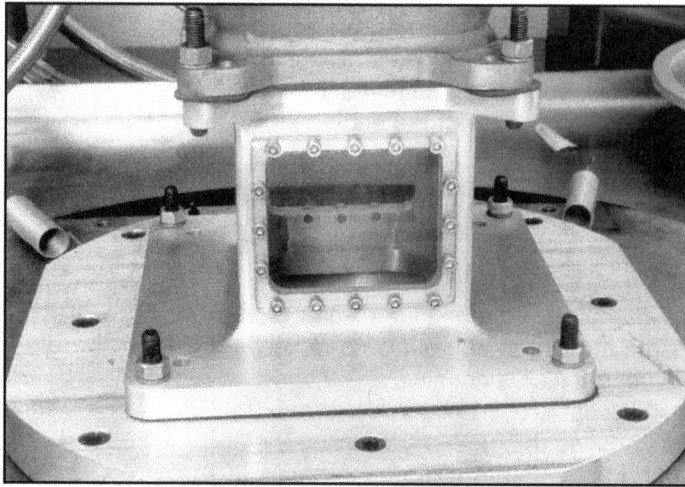
A glass chamber is located below the carburetor adapter on the Demon wet bench to check atomization.

unless you know the depression, much like a dyno sheet with corrected values to an unknown standard. With a flow bench, if you want to see higher cfm readings, just increase the depression. As an example, a test value of 250 cfm at 28 inches of water would equal 282.5 cfm at 36 inches of water. This created a dilemma for Demon because the industry was so deeply entrenched in bogus carburetor airflow numbers that revealing the true facts would confuse customers.

Referencing Chapter 1 and the discussion of vacuum in an engine, it was stated that a race engine will produce a depression of six inches of water at WOT. Testing at depressions higher than that become moot as reference numbers, but are required to try to simulate the conditions the carburetor will see on the engine. Because of its superior casting process and contoured air inlet, a smaller advertised Demon carburetor will outperform a higher-rated competitive brand.

Adding more confusion is whether all four barrels are open when testing, or flowed individually and added together. This procedure is used when a company has not made the investment in the proper flow equipment and its bench does not have the capacity to create sufficient depression for a meaningful test pressure. Demon ratings were derived with all barrels wide open and the carburetor flowing both air and a test fluid that has the same specific gravity as the appropriate fuel, at 1.5 in./Hg. So a Demon that is rated at 625 cfm wet will flow substantially more than that on a dry-flow test.

With this established, the next step is to determine the required flow capacity of the engine to choose the proper carburetor cfm rating. For years, a very fundamental equation has been used that makes many assumptions. It ignores compression ratio, bore and stroke ratio, combustion chamber design, etc., and historically yields a required carburetor size that is a good percentage higher than the engine needs to produce the best performance. Mathematically it only looks at maximum engine speed along with displacement. It is: cfm @ 100% VE = displacement X RPM/3456.

For example, let's take a 400-cubic-inch engine that will spin to a maximum

DEMON CARBURETION CARBURETOR FLOW CARD

IDLE FLOW: 75 % EMPLOYEE #: 41
WOT FLOW: 230 PPH LEAK CHECK: ✓
TIP-IN/FULL RANGE: ✓
SQUIRTER:
PRI: ✓   SEC: ✓
FLOAT LEVEL:
PRI: ✓   SEC:

ATTACHMENT OF THIS CARD CERTIFIES THAT THIS PRODUCT HAS BEEN FLOW TESTED BY THE MANUFACTURER.

GPT 300 INC
GRANT PERFORMANCE TECHNOLOGIES

Each Demon carburetor is flow-bench tested, calibrated, and adjusted before being shipped.

The quality of the booster discharge is important for proper carburetor and engine performance.

Extensive engineering goes into each calibration and is represented by the difference in boosters on these Speed Demons.

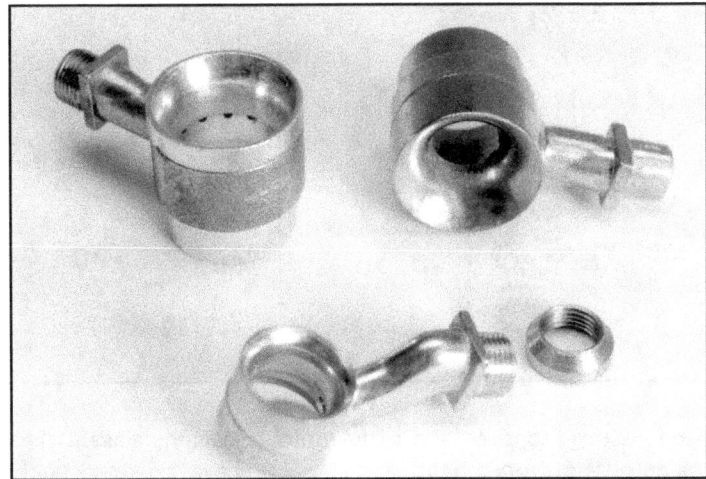

Booster design can be categorized into three classifications: straight, drop, or annular discharge.

of 6000 rpm. In theory, using the above equation, the engine would require a 694.44-cfm carburetor. Now let's explore other considerations. Assuming that at peak torque this engine would reach only 85% VE, the required airflow now becomes 590.27 cfm. If all aspects of the engine remained the same but the maximum engine speed was altered to 4000 and 7000 rpm, a carburetor of 462.96 cfm and 810.18 cfm at 100% VE would supposedly fit the bill, respectively.

Another way to examine the requirements is to consider the cfm required at 20.40 inches of water to support the horsepower of the engine: cfm = 1.68 X HP. Inserting numbers, a 400-horsepower engine would then require a 672-cfm carburetor. The problem with this equation is the lack of information required and not considering the RPM potential of the engine, and thus the pumping action of the piston. It may seem that there is no true mathematical method to determine carburetor size since the established equations all have an inherent error. Such is not the case.

As an industry, we measure the cubic feet of air per minute and not the mass or weight of the incoming air as we should. The work done by an engine depends on the amount of energy released when the mixture is burned. An important aspect is the air occupies a much greater volume than the fuel, and the induction of the air into the cylinder presents some difficulties. If the engine does not induct the largest possible amount of air, the power output will be limited, no matter how much fuel is added.

After Detroit designs an engine, the amount of air ingested in pounds per hour is measured to ensure that there are no restrictions that would prevent good breathing characteristics. Moreover, a knowledge of the quantities of air and fuel consumed by the engine enables the requirements for the proper air/fuel ratio to be mathematically computed. Measuring the airflow in cfm is a treacherous procedure; it does not take into consideration that air is a gas and expands and contracts with temperature, retains heat, or holds moisture, nor does it consider that the density of the oxygen molecules varies with atmospheric pressure. For this reason, cfm ratings are not accurate in determining carburetor size requirements and should be used as a guideline only.

Demon performs exhaustive testing on its dyno, along with inputting those results into the latest wave-dynamic engine-simulation software to determine the carburetors to offer.

The dimension of the main body venturi impacts the booster design. For this reason, all race-style Demons feature removable boosters.

The patented sculptured air inlet creates a more desirable flow path into the carburetor for superior performance. Note the screw-in idle and high-speed air bleeds on this model for easy tuning.

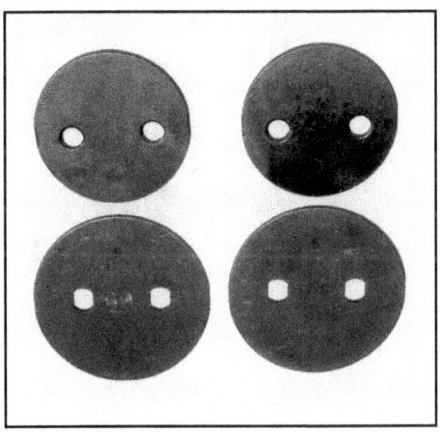

The dimension of the throttle plates affects the signal produced in the booster.

A bell is used to direct the airflow into the carburetor from a hood scoop.

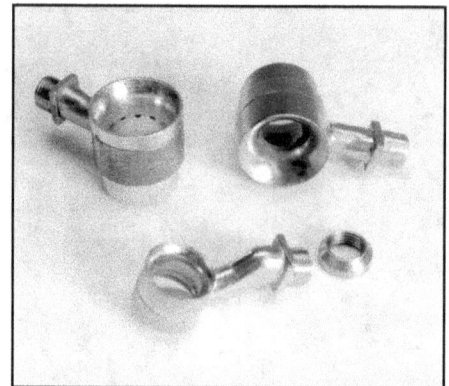

Demons classified as street carburetors have swedged boosters, whereas race versions have a replaceable style.

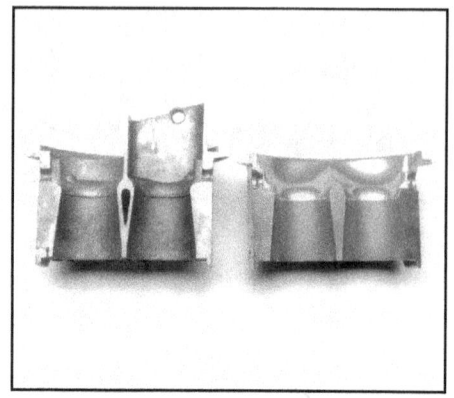

The Demon exclusive ConcentraCast method minimizes the parting line from the main body venturi.

Recognizing that this approach, though the proper one, would be met with resistance from the industry, it offers guidelines in its catalog and through a telephone hotline to assist the end user in choosing the proper Demon carburetor for each application.

VELOCITY vs. BOOSTER SIGNAL

Because the carburetor is an air/fuel-metering device, common logic would dictate that if it is sized too large for the engine, the result would be an over-fueling or extremely rich mixture.

Before reading on, think about this statement and decide why it might be true or false. If you chose false, you are correct. When a carburetor is sized too large, the net result will be a lean, not rich, condition. The reason is a reduction in the strength of the booster signal created and the resultant inability of the carburetor to pull fuel.

An aftermarket carburetor manufacturer such as Demon has an especially challenging task: its products are going to be installed on myriad engines with varied displacements, cylinder heads, and camshaft profiles. In contrast, an OE has the luxury of designing a carburetor to a fixed set of specifications. The design premise of all carburetors is to create as high a velocity in the booster as possible. This logic bows to the Bernoulli and Venturi principles by creating the most depression in the booster, allowing for the best atomization. All of the circuits will function best when the depression in the venturi is the highest: more depression equals more efficient circuit operation. This leads to better idle, fuel economy, BSFC, and throttle response.

When the booster signal is diminished, the job of the carburetor designer and tuner becomes more difficult. A parallel concern for a performance carburetor is limiting VE with a small venturi and butterfly area. The balancing act then becomes the ability to move a voluminous amount of air to feed the engine while maintaining a sufficiently small area to create a strong signal.

The maximum or ideal velocity of the air at the throat of the venturi can be

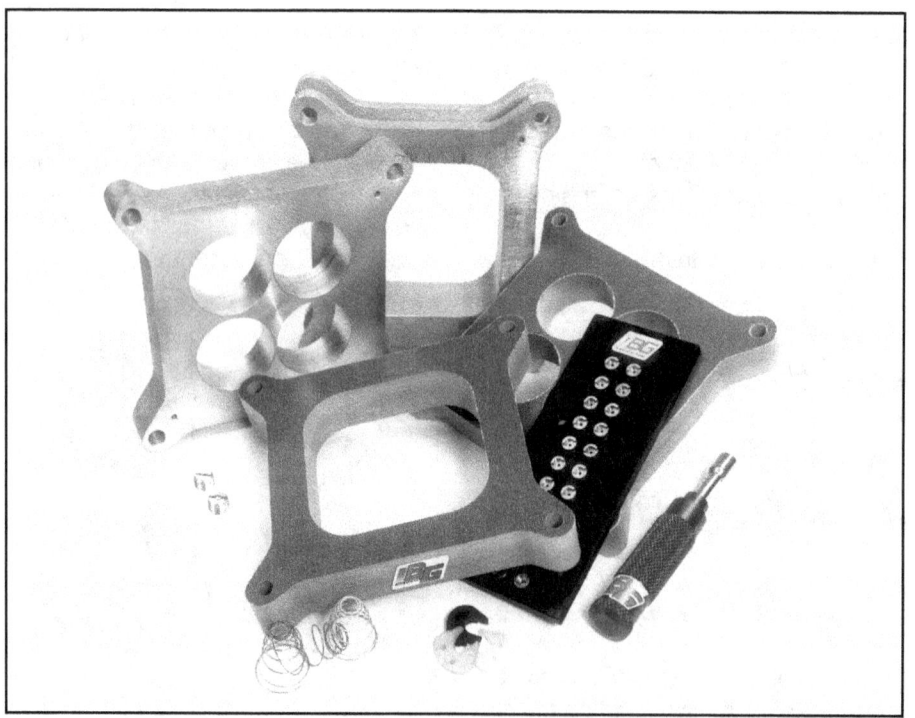

BG Fuel Systems manufactures all of the tuning equipment and parts to make your Demon perform like no other carburetor.

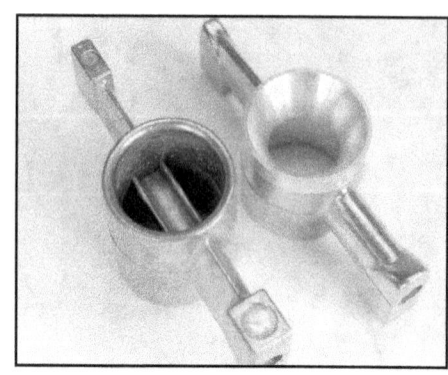

Not only are Demon boosters designed for improved performance, they are made from a material that is 40 percent stronger to eliminate fatigue.

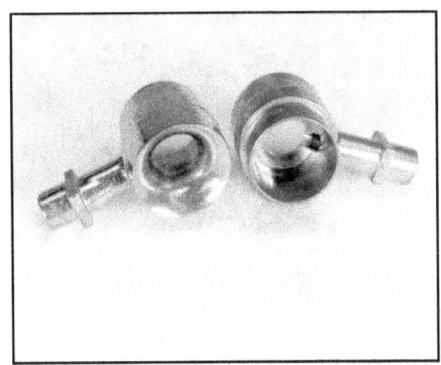

Swedge-installed boosters can be identified by the lack of thread on the leg.

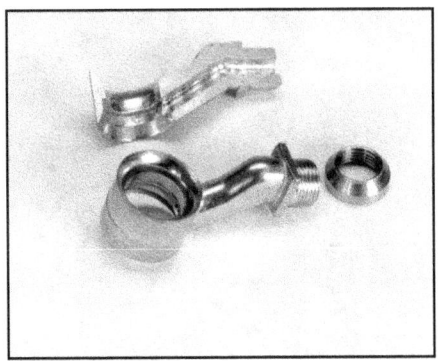

Removable boosters are threaded and are secured to the main body with a nut.

A special spanner-type wrench is required to remove the booster.

RS-model carburetors often require a booster change when the main body venturi dimension is altered.

Once secured, the booster is locked in place and cannot work loose.

determined mathematically using a steady-flow energy equation, if all factors of the engine are known. The carburetor design comes into play to determine the coefficient of discharge, which is a means of determining the flow loss from the carburetor itself due to casting flash, core shift, and obstructions in the flow path, such as the booster and choke plate.

In simpler terms, the coefficient of discharge is the difference from ideal frictionless flow to the real flow conditions. A perfectly smooth venturi with no restriction beyond a converging-diverging air path would realize a coefficient of 0.94 to 0.97, with 1.00 being no flow loss at all. Most production carburetors that do not share the design advantages of the Demon line usually have a coefficient of discharge around 0.80. The patented contoured entry and ConcentraCast smooth finish, along with other design intents, allow the Demon line collectively to boast a coefficient of discharge near 0.84 for street offerings, and approximately 0.90 for race versions.

A direct-port nitrous system from Nitrous Works is an excellent way of adding a substantial power gain while retaining driveability.

Demon engineers have a full understanding of carburetor workings and acknowledge that the airflow through the venturi is first accelerated in the converging section with a constant fall in pressure, and then decelerated in the diverging section with a constant rise in pressure. The rate of acceleration is easily accomplished, but the decelerating process is relatively inefficient since the air possesses inertia. Thus, the carburetor's ability to provide a strong signal while not becoming a pumping loss is not a one-dimensional design criterion attached strictly to venturi size. By carefully positioning the metering orifice in the venturi, and modifying the booster design and other components, the strength of the signal can be improved while allowing a large-capacity bore dimension to produce high-RPM horsepower. Additional engineering is done with position and placement of the air bleeds, emulsion orifice, and transfer slots.

It must be acknowledged that a carburetor intended to serve different driving scenarios is always a compromise, and for anything other than a dedicated drag-race application, the throttle spends more time partially closed than wide open. For this reason, the dominant concern is the fuel metering and booster signal during the conditions under which the engine will operate the majority of the time.

BOOSTER VENTURI DESIGN

All Demon carburetors use a booster that is positioned in the venturi of the main body casting. A booster venturi can be considered an amplifier to increase the depression over what can be accomplished from just the diverging/converging venturi cast into the main body. To obtain the optimal performance with every Demon model, three booster designs are used: straight, drop, and annular. The booster style installed in a specific Demon model is not a random process. The complete carburetor is engineered around this decision and represents many different design intents.

How to Tune and Win with Demon Carburetors

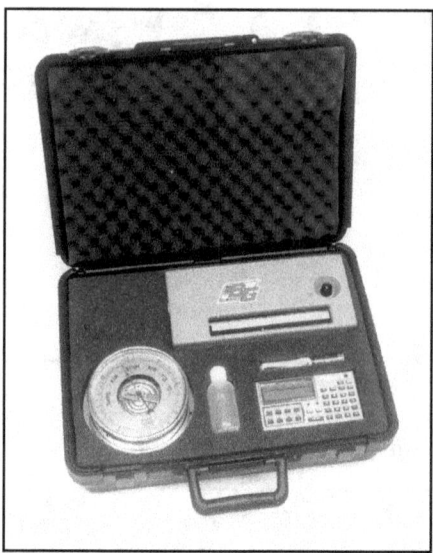

The BG Pro-Style weather station includes a Professor II computer, a premium-grade aneroid barometer, and electronic psychrometer for exact atmospheric readings to determine tuning.

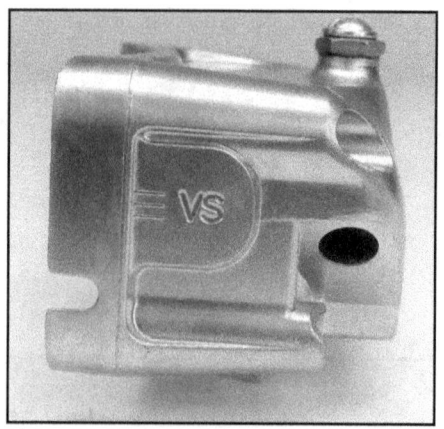

VS designates the secondary float bowl for a vacuum secondary carburetor.

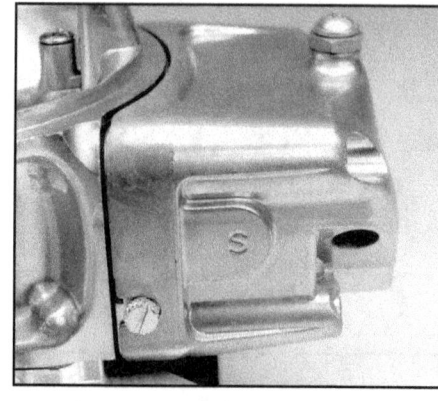

Mechanical secondary carburetors use dual accelerator pumps and have unique secondary float bowls.

Before working on the accelerator pump circuit on any Demon carburetor, the fuel should be drained from the bowl.

Test conditions	Research octane number	Motor octane number
Engine speed, rpm	600 ± 6	900 ± 9
Crankcase oil, SAE grade	30	30
Oil pressure at operating temperature, psi	25–30	25–30
Crankcase oil temperature	135 ± 15°F (57 ± 8.5°C)	135 ± 15°F (57 ± 8.5°C)
Coolant temperature		
Range	212 ± 3°F (100 ± 1.5°C)	212 ± 3°F (100 ± 1.5°C)
Constant within	± 1°F (0.5°C)	± 1°F (0.5°C)
Intake air humidity, grains of water per lb. of dry air	25–50	25–50
Intake air temperature	See *ASTM Standard Part 47*	100 ± 5°F (38 ± 2.8°C)
Mixture temperature		300 ± 2°F (149 ± 1.1°C)
Spark advance, deg. btdc	13	14–26 depending on compression ratio
Spark plug gap, in.	0.020 ± 0.005	0.020 ± 0.005
Breaker point, gap, in.	0.020	0.020
Valve clearances, in.		
Intake	0.008	0.008
Exhaust	0.008	0.008
Fuel/air ratio	Adjusted for maximum knock	

Gasoline is a commodity that we spend a lot of money on but do not see. The test procedure to determine both the motor and research octane is very specific.

The fuel from the main metering circuit enters the air stream through the booster, where it is quickly carried away and atomized while being mixed with air. Another design aspect is the size of the fuel passage in the booster and discharge orifice. Identified in the specifications for each carburetor as the booster leg, the dimension can vary from 0.140 to 0.189 inch. A four-barrel carburetor has the ability to create a stronger vacuum signal at the venturi throat along with higher velocities for improved atomization without increasing the overall pressure loss, compared with a two-barrel of the same flow capacity.

The booster venturi is usually positioned at the throat of the larger main venturi in the body casting, with its discharge at the location of maximum velocity in the main venturi. Only a fraction of the air the engine ingests flows through the booster, so the pressure at the booster exit is equal to the pressure at the main venturi throat. A pressure probe placed in the center of the booster venturi will reveal a much higher vacuum and is referred to as the signal. Velocity through the booster venturi can approach 200 m/s, which would convert to approximately 415.63 mph.

Another design advantage of the Demon line over other modular carburetors is the material used for the booster construction and method of

Every Demon carburetor is shipped with complete instructions and a video that will show you how to get the most from your purchase.

A Race Demon-equipped entry battles it out on the track.

The size of the intake valve in the cylinder head will impact the velocity of the charge, and ultimately affect the signal in the carburetor.

installation. Diecast from ZA-3, which is a zinc/aluminum mix, it offers much stronger construction and is resistant to fatigue. Most manufacturers other than Demon install the boosters with a swedging procedure, which works well for a street application but allows the booster to work loose from vibration in the extreme environment of motorsports. If this was to happen, the throttle could become jammed open. This is responsible for many crashes in NASCAR racing, as well as with other venues. Recognizing this, all Demon carburetors other than the Road and Speed Demons offer removable boosters that are bolted in, eliminating this concern.

The following is a design explanation of each style booster used by Demon. Application-specific booster styles for each model carburetor will be discussed in the appropriate chapters.

Straight

The main benefit of this design is its ability to position the booster higher in the main body venturi to act as an intentional airflow restrictor. This may at first seem counterproductive, but it is common practice in the industry to alter the booster design as an economical and effective means of decreasing the cast venturi area for better performance on small-displacement engines. It is easily identified by its thick leg and internal dimension, in reference to the external dimension of the booster. Fuel is discharged in the center of the booster venturi through a single hole. Known to produce a very strong signal, this design lends itself very well to street applications.

Down or Drop Leg

As its name implies, the shape of the booster leg resembles a dog leg and orients the booster lower in the main venturi area. This design is known for the best balance of airflow restriction

Intake and exhaust valve dimensions and placement are an exacting science, not a trial-and-error design method.

How to Tune and Win with Demon Carburetors

Valve head diameter in terms of cylinder bore B[11]			
Combustion chamber shape†	Inlet	Exhaust	Approximate mean piston speed, max power, m/s
Wedge or bathtub	$0.43-0.46B$	$0.35-0.37B$	15
Bowl-in-piston	$0.42-0.44B$	$0.34-0.37B$	14
Hemispherical	$0.48-0.5B$	$0.41-0.43B$	18
Four-valve pent-roof	$0.35-0.37B$	$0.28-0.32B$	20

Valve sizing takes the bore dimension and combustion chamber shape into consideration, along with the maximum piston speed.

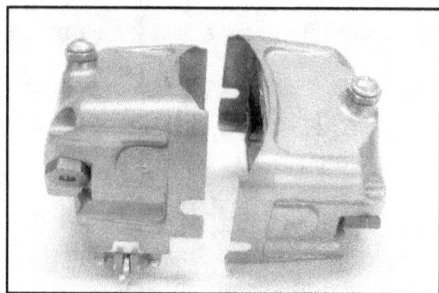

The King Demon float bowls are unique and are easily identified.

The shepherd's hook passageway on the main body metering block surface is the third or intermediate circuit on the King Demon.

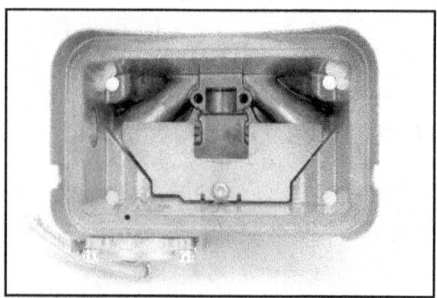

The float bowl and assembly may require special modifications, such as a fuel dam, for certain uses.

The King Demon is made from aluminum to reduce weight, since it is substantially larger than the rest of the line. Ease of tuning was a consideration with threaded air bleeds.

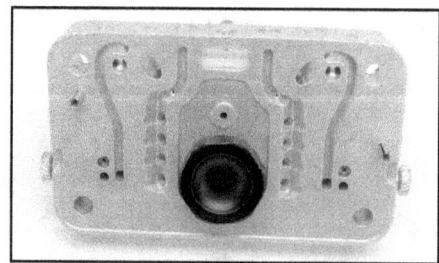

The same circuit can be seen on the metering block and allows this carburetor to offer extremely mild manners for the power it produces.

The squirter style is changeable on all Demons, but only a radical engine may require tuning of this circuit for maximum throttle response.

to booster signal. Placed lower in the bore, Demon offers designs that are application specific to the model carburetor by varying leg thickness and internal bore diameter. By design, the drop style does not produce a stronger signal than the straight leg, so a systems approach is used at the factory, modifying the carburetor design in regard to the air and emulsion bleeds. Most performance-style Demon carburetors incorporate a down leg booster. As with the straight booster, the fuel is distributed through a single hole.

Annular Discharge

A true race-style booster, the annular discharge offers improved atomization of the fuel for engines with large camshafts and poor velocity through the venturi at low RPM. It features eight fuel discharge holes around the internal ring of the booster on standard models, with an optional 14-hole discharge available by special order. The design has the ability to inflict a very minute flow penalty while creating a strong signal. It can be identified by the series of stepped rings inside the booster bore and is offered with either a single- or dual-leg mounting. Dual legs are used as a structural support member for larger carburetor bores, such as in the King Demon models. The additional support leg is solid and carries no fuel.

Often the difference in booster design creates confusion for the enthusiast. Though all boosters perform the same basic function, the complete engine and vehicle combination needs to be considered to produce the desired results. The best design is the one that the Demon technical department recommends for each application.

MECHANICAL vs. VACUUM SECONDARY

The method to open the secondary throttle butterflies of a Demon carburetor is determined by the engine's intended use and design. Vacuum secondary operation is the desirable choice for most applications that will see service on the street, and also in

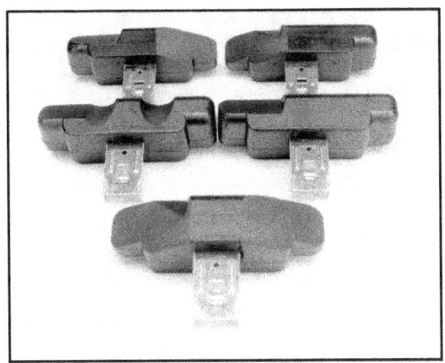

A float is not just a float. Demon offers specially designed floats for alcohol, road race, tunnel ram, oval track, and jet extensions.

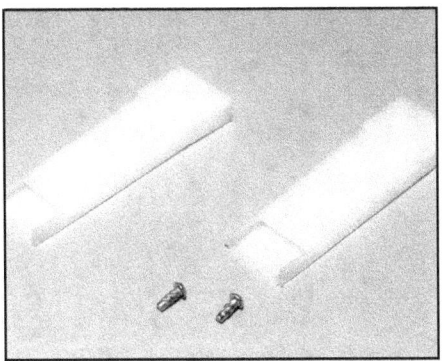

Vent baffles stop fuel from sloshing out of the bowl vent tubes and eliminate flooding.

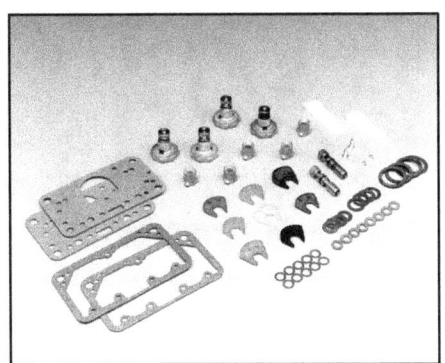

All Demons are factory equipped with reusable nonstick gaskets for the float bowls and metering block assembly, but a kit like this is good insurance if you plan on doing some trackside tuning. Note the different accelerator pump cams.

a majority of competition venues utilizing an automatic transmission. A mechanical secondary offers an increase in throttle response and performance, but only when fitted to the proper engine and use.

As mentioned previously, an engine is considered to be an air pump, and the ability to move air is scaled against piston velocity. The faster the piston moves, the greater the volume of air that will be pumped. This is a basic function that many ignore or don't consider when choosing secondary activation for a carburetor.

With a vacuum-controlled secondary, the butterfly opening rate is linked to the amount of airflow through the engine. This style automatically becomes a passive system, requiring piston velocity to create the pressure differential to open the additional throttle bores.

In contrast, a mechanical secondary is linked directly to the primary throttle bores, opening the secondary as a function of primary throttle angle, regardless of piston velocity. Some would like to think that a direct mechanical link to the primary throttle plate movement will provide quicker acceleration of the engine vs. a vacuum operation that will open over time, but this would be true only if the engine is designed to accept the additional airflow and accelerate the piston fast enough to put it to use. Historically, a mechanical secondary carburetor on an engine that is not equipped to produce the required rapid change in piston velocity suffers a performance penalty in the form of a severe bog or hesitation. This same application, when equipped with a vacuum secondary, offers linear performance with excellent driveability and will outperform the same engine when fitted with the wrong secondary actuation choice.

The Demon carburetor's secondary barrels work in conjunction with a vacuum diaphragm to open the butterflies. When the primary airflow reaches a specific point, the vacuum signal created in the primary venturi is referenced to the top portion of the diaphragm controlling the secondary. As the engine RPM climbs, the airflow throughput of the primary increases, along with a greater amount of depression in the venturi. This higher-velocity signal now allows the diaphragm to

A clean carburetor is a happy carburetor. Use a good spray carburetor cleaner to keep the venturi, bores, and air bleeds clean and functioning properly.

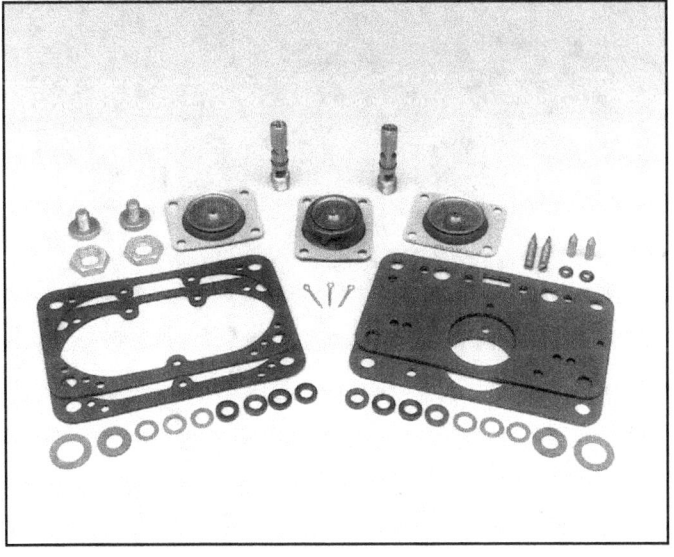

Always use BG brand parts to guarantee the performance of your Demon carburetor.

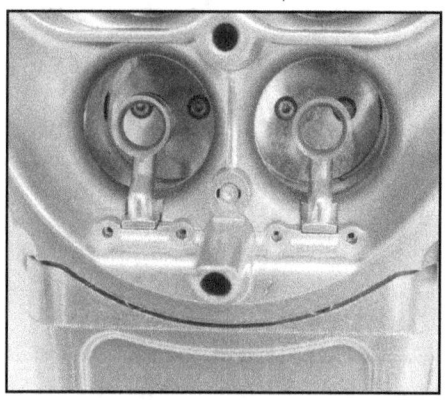

If the throttle plates are not oriented properly in relation to the transfer slot, the booster will start to pull fuel at idle.

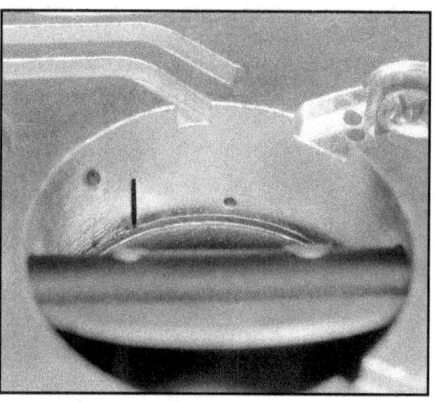

The passage that connects to the throttle bore is where the accessory manifold vacuum port receives its signal.

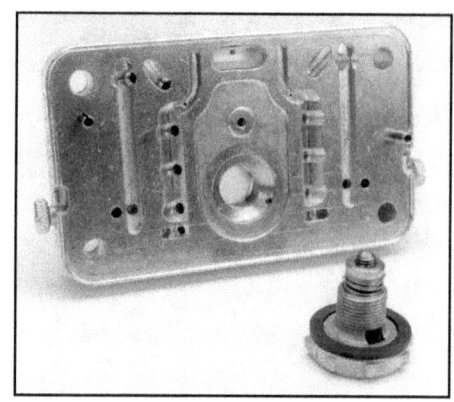

Road and Speed Demons use metering block assemblies with three emulsion holes. Race carburetors have five orifice blocks, but some applications have two of the five orifices plugged.

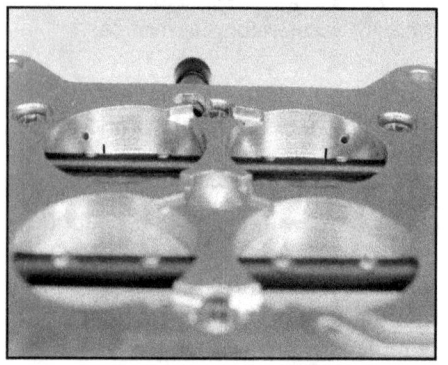

Follow the procedure in Chapter 9 to determine the proper transfer slot area.

release against the spring tension, further opening the butterfly and feeding the engine. For this reason, the secondary operation is sensitive to engine load and vacuum signal, so it will not open during free revving of the engine.

The secondary barrels are also equipped with booster venturi and function in a like manner as the primary side to pull fuel. Since all Demon carburetors are equipped with four-corner idle systems, fresh fuel is always available in the secondary float bowl even if the vehicle is driven in a very sedate manner, rarely evoking the secondary circuit. It must be considered that the function of the secondary diaphragm is to control the opening, not closing, rate of the secondary.

For tuning purposes, Demon offers seven different vacuum spring assortments to provide the proper opening rate for maximum performance, driveability and fuel economy. If the carburetor was too large for the engine, an insufficient amount of signal would be created, and thus the full potential for airflow would not be realized. The result would be an engine that would be self-throttled by limiting the secondary opening angle.

Demon mechanical secondary carburetors are designed to open the secondary bores as a function of primary throttle angle. On most models as shipped from the factory, this begins when the primary bores are approximately 45 degrees open, and then travel in lock step, reaching fully open simultaneously. This progressive function is controlled by the linkage design that attaches the primary and secondary halves of the carburetor together. A direct linkage, better known as a 1:1 linkage, is available and will open all four barrels simultaneously.

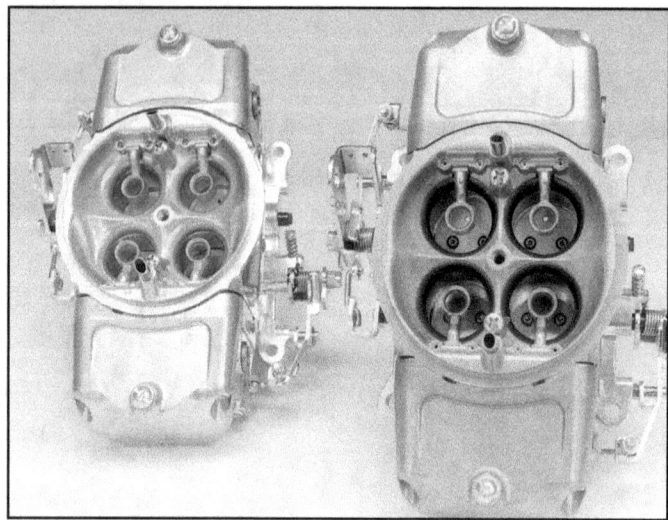

A carburetor that is sized too large for the engine will not generate enough signal and will not pull fuel, resulting in a lean condition.

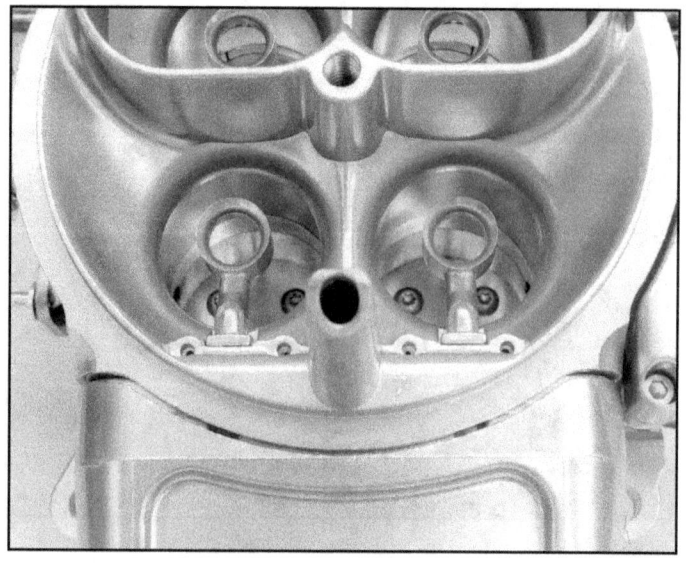

By varying the size and shape of the booster, Demon engineers can alter the flow characteristic of a carburetor.

A SYSTEMS APPROACH

To obtain the best performance from your engine, not only does it need a Demon carburetor, but the ignition system has to be able to arc the spark plug with a strong and long-firing event. The strength of an ignition system should be measured not only by its voltage output, but also by the length of time the arc of the spark plug can be maintained.

Anyone who has ever used an ignition oscilloscope is familiar with measuring burn time in milliseconds (1/1000 second), but a more accurate measure is crankshaft angle (CA) degrees. Most stock electronic ignition systems offer substantially more burn time than a breaker point system, but you must remember that horsepower is the result of cylinder pressure. Horsepower and cylinder pressure go up in lock step, so an ignition system that had sufficient power on a stock engine may become marginal when the power level is modified.

Most aftermarket ignition amplifiers, such as the ACCEL 300+, MSD, Mallory, Crane, and Jacobs, are identified as capacitor discharge (CD) ignitions, whereas an OE system charges the coil through inductance. As the RPM of an engine increases, there is less time in distributor rotational degrees, better known as dwell, to charge the coil. So in turn, the amount of CA the spark plug burns for is decreased with an inductive system. Since CD systems build the primary voltage in a capacitor, they charge the ignition coil with 300-600 volts depending on brand instead of the normal 14.6 volts of a modern alternator. An ignition system can be compared to a bank account: The more you deposit, the more you can withdraw. Your Demon carburetor can only deliver the proper mixture to the engine; the ignition system still needs to light it off.

WHAT A RUSH

The fact that a chain is only as strong as its weakest link holds true for most things in life, and a Demon carburetor is no exception. As good as these carburetors are, their performance to a great extent depends on the use of the proper air filter assembly and media. The aftermarket offers many high-flow filter elements but historically has neglected one critical aspect: the ability of the media to restrict the ingestion of airborne dirt particles.

Often sacrifices have been made to the filtering ability to increase the airflow in cfm. Recognizing that this one-dimensional approach was good for power but bad for engine life, Barry Grant, Inc. developed the Rush air filter line. Studying all of the currently available filtering media, Barry Grant discovered that American-grown cotton was world-renowned as one of the best materials for air filtration. Due to the climate, soil composition, and growing conditions, the cotton produced in the Southern U.S. is the finest worldwide.

Barry Grant, Inc. not only conducted its own testing, but enlisted the help of a major university's research lab to confirm the results. From this was born a complete line of high-flow air filters that are superior in filtration and airflow to any on the market. Independent tests using the same engine have proven a power gain when equipped with the Rush filter vs. all of the popular brand high-performance elements. Horsepower and long engine life are things we can all use.

This is primarily used in road racing and oval track racing for more precise throttle control. Many have tried this design on street engines and the result is a severe driveability problem.

SQUIRTERS

If one squirter is good, two must be better, right? Disappointingly, that is the logic of many enthusiasts and it cannot be more faulty when pertaining to the number of squirters. All Demon mechanical secondary carburetors are equipped with two 30cc squirters, while all vacuum secondary models use one 30cc squirter. The purpose of the additional squirter is to cover the hole in fuel delivery created by the secondary throttle plates opening quickly, before the main circuit can pull fuel.

The explanation for the existence of a squirter, found in Chapter 2, holds true for the secondary side when controlled mechanically instead of through vacuum. A dual-squirter carburetor will mask some of the inherent flaws in transition as the additional pair of butterflies open, but will have a serious negative impact on fuel economy and the amount of fuel that is left to puddle in the intake manifold runners and plenum. This creates an extreme variation in the created vs. delivered air/fuel ratio.

EASE OF TUNING

As you can see, many factors come into play when choosing the proper Demon carburetor for your application. An additional fact that needs to be considered is the amount of tuning that will be available. Throughout the complete carburetor line, tuning is a Demon forté, but due to the extreme care in design, manufacture, and wet-flow testing, the Demon carburetor will undoubtedly require the least amount of end-user tinkering for the ultimate

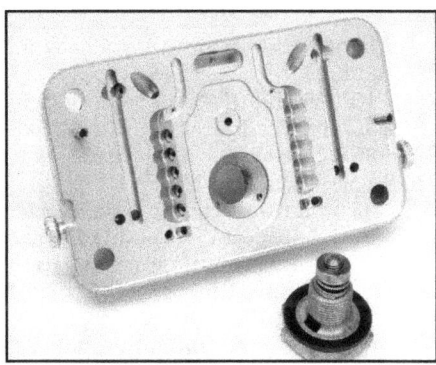

Race metering blocks feature threaded emulsion orifices for easy tuning. These are necessary since most race engines have very poor velocity through the booster at low speeds, along with high rates of dilution from camshaft overlap.

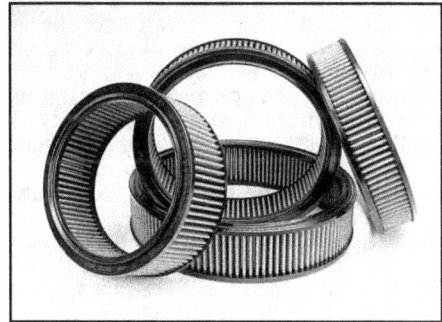

The Rush air filter line by Barry Grant, Inc. is the perfect complement to a Demon carburetor.

How to Tune and Win with Demon Carburetors

DEMON CARBURETOR RECOMMENDATIONS

Competition Light: Racecars and street bracket cars under 3000 lbs.
Competition Heavy: Racecars and street bracket cars over 3000 lbs.
Street Light: Lightened Camaros, Mustangs, Vegas, Monzas, and Dusters with fiberglass hoods and bumpers etc.
Street Heavy: Camaros, Mustangs, Roadrunners, Torinos, Chevelles, and Pick-ups.
Street Rod: Kit cars, pre-'50 coupes, sedans, and light vehicles exposed to hard driving. NO '50 Mercurys, '55 Chevys, '57 Caddies or '63 Impalas – see "Street Heavy."

HP/C.I.	Comp Light	Comp Heavy	Street Light	Street Heavy	Street Rod
GM					
300/350	675 Race	675 Race	625 Road	625 Road	625 Road
355/350(zz4)	675 Race	675 Race	650 Speed*3	650 SpeedV	650 Speed
375/350	675 Race	675 Race	650 Speed	650 SpeedV	650 Speed
502/502	1025 Race	975 Race	850 Speed*1*5	850 SpeedV*5	850 SpeedV
450/502	975 Race	825 Race	750 Speed	750 SpeedV	750 Speed
425/454	825 Race	775 Race	750 Speed	750 SpeedV	750 SpeedV*4
Ford					
320/302	675 Race	675 Race	625 Road	625 Road	625 Road
385/351	775 Race	675 Race	650 Speed*1*2	650 SpeedV	650 Speed*4
420/392	750 Race	750 Race	750 Speed*2	750 SpeedV	750 Speed*2
535/460	975 Race	825 Race	850 SpeedV*%	750 Speed*2	850 SpeedV*5
600/514	1095 King/1025 R	975 Race	975 Race	975 Race	975 Race
Mopar					
380/360	775 Race	675 Race	650 Speed*1*2	650 Speedv	650 Speed*4
610/528 Hemi	1095 King/1050 R	1025 Race	1025 Race	975 Race	1025 Race
545/500 Wedge	1095 King/1025 R	975 Race	975 Race	825 Race	975 Race
465/426 Hemi	975 Race	825 Race	850 Speed*2*5	750 Speed*2	850 SpeedV*5

*1 Manual transmission or automatic with 3000 + converter.
*2 Automatic transmission with stock or under 3000 converter may use a vacuum-secondary carb.
*3 On the dynamometer, the 650 Speed Demon has produced more torque and horsepower on this engine than any other carburetor – including both smaller and larger sizes from all other manufacturers.
*4 Use mechanically operated secondaries when car is driven hard. For best driveability during cruising use a carb with vacuum-secondaries.
*5 Annular discharge.

DO THE MATH

Engines are mathematical creations. The fact that most people do not like mathematics is another story, but when it comes to choosing parts for your engine combination, doing the math saves you big time in the dollars department. Today, thanks to the popularity of the home-based personal computer, you don't have to be a computer geek or a math wizard to run the numbers.

There are many inexpensive (usually under $60) software programs, such as Mr. Gasket's Desk Top Dyno, that allow the user to try different parts in the virtual world before paying for them in the real world, using a simple fill-in-the-blanks menu. Information on bore, stroke, valve size, compression ratio, valve events, and airflow are entered, and a graph of the calculated horsepower and torque is produced. Mr. Gasket Desk Top Dyno uses the theory of wave dynamics for cylinder filling and emptying, and the program is a good indicator of how the engine will respond.

Not meant to replace actual dyno tuning, the trends established by the computer simulation will factually determine if your combination will deliver approximately the performance you desire, or if your parts selection is a dud. As good as the Desk Top Dyno is, it can't replace the technical advice of the parts manufacturers.

in performance. If your engine combination requires additional tuning of the fuel system, then your Demon representative can recommend the proper changes and model carburetor that will offer the most adjustability to ensure that you are satisfied with your purchase.

As an example, the Race Demon models are available with screw-in air bleeds and removable venturi sleeves, whereas a comparable flow capacity Speed Demon has press-in air bleeds and fixed venturi dimensions. Due to the in-depth details that make each Demon model unique, a complete overview of each series will be required and begins in the next chapter with the Road Demon.

HOW TO IDENTIFY YOUR DEMON

EXAMPLE # 3282010BC

A) First digit <u>3</u>282010BC represents the series:

    1 = Speed Demons
    2 = Race Demons
    3 = Race Demon RS Series
        (Removable Sleeves)
    4 = Road Demons
    8 = King Demons
    9 = King Demon RS Series
        (Removable Sleeves)

B) Second & third digits 3<u>28</u>2010BC represent venturi diameter:

STANDARD & RACE R/S DEMONS:
    06 = 1.064" (orange)
    28 = 1.280" (green)
    37 = 1.375" (purple)
    40 = 1.400" (red)
         1.375" (purple)
    42 = 1.425" (blue)
    50 = 1.500" (gold)
    56 = 1.562" (black)
    59 = 1.590" (silver)

KING R/S DEMONS:
    50 = 1.064" (green)
    56 = 1.280" (red)
    62 = 1.375" (black)
    72 = 1.400" (blue)
    83 = 1.425" (gold)
    84 = 1.500" (silver)

C) Forth digit 328<u>2</u>010BC represents the b'fly size:

    0 = 1 7/16" (390 style)
    2 = 1 11/16"
    3 = 1 3/4"
    4 = 1 11/16" (830 style)
    8 = 2"
    9 = 2.100"

D) Fifth & sixth digit 3282<u>01</u>0BC shows booster type:

    01 = Down leg
    02 = Annular
    03 = Straight leg

E) Seventh digit 328201<u>0</u>BC shows fuel calibration:

    0 = Gasoline
        (silver metering blocks)
    5 = Methanol
        (black metering blocks)

F) Suffix 3282010<u>BC</u> shows preparation:

    BC = Blower Calibration
         (2x4 sideways)
    DR = Drag Race (single 4bl)
    GC = General competition
         (single 4bl)
    OT = Oval track (single 4bl)
    RR = Road race (single 4bl)
    TR = Tunnel ram (2x4 side)

REVIEW QUESTIONS

(1) Prior to shipping, all Demon carburetors are tested and calibrated on a:

   a: dry flow bench
   b: dyno
   c: wet flow bench
   d: simulator

(2) If the carburetor is sized too large for the engine, the effect would be:

   a: an insufficient booster signal to pull fuel
   b: an overly rich condition
   c: no effect since the throttle would regulate the airflow
   d: higher horsepower and torque

(3) Fuel from the main well enters the air stream through:

   a: the idle transfer slot
   b: the accelerator pump
   c: the booster
   d: the power valve

(4) When discussing accelerator pump diaphragms and covers, the volume is measured in:

   a: liters
   b: grams
   c: pounds
   d: cc

(5) On a mechanical secondary Demon carburetor, 1:1 links are best for:

   a: street use
   b: racing only
   c: trailer towing
   d: anytime you want the most power

(6) The additional leg on a King Demon booster is used:

   a: for carrying extra fuel
   b: for fuel storage
   c: for structural integrity
   d: to consume venturi area

(7) The Demon carburetor engineer may choose to use a straight booster as a design intent:

   a: to reduce cost
   b: to over fuel the engine
   c: as an airflow restrictor
   d: to create a lean mixture

(8) Before choosing a Demon carburetor model and size, it is best to:

   a: ask your friend which one will work better
   b: call the Demon tech line for the proper model and part number
   c: calculate the needed size using an equation for airflow in cfm
   d: take your best guess

(9) Dry-flow cfm is a poor indicator of carburetor size because:

   a: you may not own a dry-flow bench
   b: every engine is different
   c: they were developed without considering the mass of the fuel and at a depression that the engine will never be able to produce
   d: it ignores the camshaft profile of your engine

(10) The RS models were designed:

   a: to allow sleeve changes to compensate for the change in seasons
   b: to change a drag race carburetor to one for road racing
   c: to allow the end user to vary the venturi dimension and booster design as his engine combination changes
   d: for appearance at street rod shows

Answers: 1) C, 2) A, 3) C, 4) D, 5) B, 6) C, 7) C, 8) B, 9) C, 10) C

How to Tune and Win with Demon Carburetors

How to Tune & Win with DEMON CARBURETORS

Road Demon

Designed to meet the requirements of the entry-level street performance and replacement markets, the Road Demon is offered as a single model designated as 625. It includes all of the same manufacturing and design features of its companion Demon carburetors but is offered only with a vacuum secondary. It accepts most standard square-flange intake manifold mounting pads. Delivered with an electric choke, the Road Demon is ready for action in all climates and weather conditions. Designed to serve the needs of an engine between 289 and 355 cubic inches, with a camshaft specification of up to 220 degrees of duration at 0.050 inch lift at a maximum of 400 horsepower, it's the volume leader of all the Demon carburetors.

Part number 4282010VE sports a conventional linkage, and part number 4282010VFE is equipped with a Ford-style kick-down linkage. The Road Demon has design features that offer increased performance and easier tuning than any competing carburetor currently in the marketplace. In addition, two full-time (manifold) and one timed (ported) vacuum ports are included for easy accessory hook-up. Though considered an economy entry, the same quality manufacturing process and material that have earned the Demon line its blue ribbon credentials apply.

The main body is diecast from Zamak-3, using the Demon exclusive ConcentraCast procedure. The venturi

After the design and dyno work were complete, the final Road Demon calibration was done on this 350-equipped 1949 Chevy sedan delivery, which belongs to Barry Grant.

size is 1.280 inches to offer a good balance of flow capacity and booster signal for excellent fuel metering. Demon engineers decided that the best performance would be obtained by using a 0.059-inch primary bore idle air bleed; on the secondary side that dimension was enlarged to 0.063 inch. The high-speed air bleeds for both primary and secondary bores are alike, with the dimension being 0.039 inch. The booster design is also different on the primary and secondary barrels with a down-leg style in the front of the carburetor, whereas the rear venturi uses a straight design. The booster leg diameter on both bores is 0.140 inch in diameter, guaranteeing a sufficient supply of fuel for all driving needs.

The butterfly dimensions are also larger in the rear bores, featuring 1 9/16 inches and 1 11/16 inches front and rear, respectively. This is an especially interesting feature of the Road Demon. In conjunction with the down-leg booster, it provides a strong signal and excellent metering characteristics. This has earned the Road Demon

The Road Demon can be quickly identified by its choke, standard-style secondary pod, and down-leg boosters in the primary bores.

"Mr. Mopar," Len Valeo of Allamuchy, New Jersey, found the Road Demon to be the perfect carburetor for his 440-powered 1964 Dodge race car carrier.

my, throttle response, and fine tuning to help meet tailpipe emissions standards, when applicable. A 30cc accelerator pump diaphragm cover supplies fuel enrichment to a standard-style squirter with a 0.031-inch discharge dimension. The accelerator pump cam is pink in color and is a series #330 design.

The vacuum secondary is operated by a yellow spring in a standard-style pod in lieu of a quick-change version, as on the other Demons. This design was chosen as a way to keep costs down and was deemed superior for the intended market and the minimal tuning that this carburetor would see. The billet-aluminum metering blocks are silver in color and have a total of three emulsion holes for each main well. All three positions are sized at 0.031 inch. The emulsion orifices are used to help control the density of the fuel introduced into the main well by mixing it with air.

A siphon break is located above the top emulsion bleed to stop the fuel from flowing into the main well when the venturi signal is eliminated by a closed throttle. The dimension of the siphon break is 0.028 inch and is required since inertia would supply fuel even after the signal in the booster was diminished. Both the siphon break and the emulsion orifices are located on the main body side of the

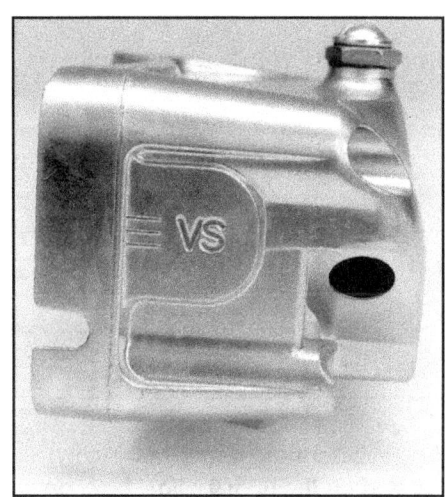

Secondary float bowls are clearly marked with the VS designation.

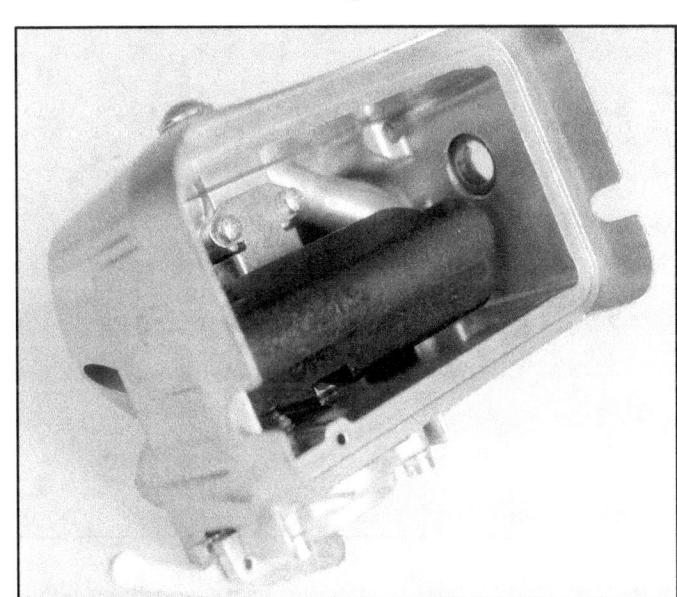

A standard-style float is used in both float bowls.

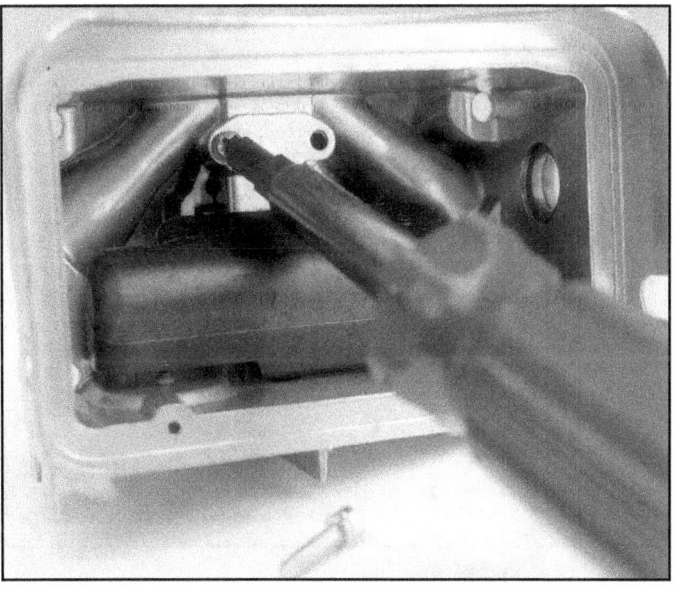

The float is easily removed for service.

How to Tune and Win with Demon Carburetors

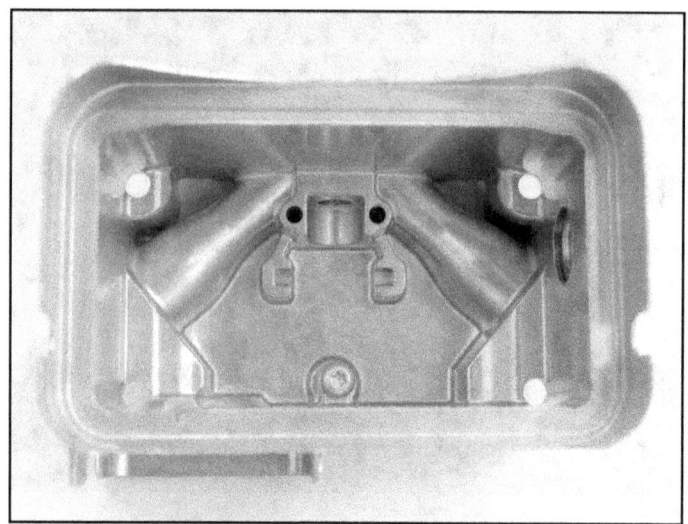

No fuel dam is used in the Road Demon.

Always use a stand when working on any Demon carburetor.

An accelerator pump assembly is located on the primary float bowl only.

metering block. The shape of the fuel curve is controlled by the placement and design of the emulsion holes and has been optimized by Demon engineers on a multitude of test engines and vehicles. The time spent in this area is responsible for this carburetor's stunning out-of-the-box performance on a wide array of engines.

The primary-side main jets are #70 and work well with the IFR dimension of 0.031 inch, a 6.5 power valve, and PVCR of 0.059 inch. The secondary side comes equipped with #78 main jets and an IFR dimension of 0.033 inch. Fuel is supplied by a 0.110-inch Viton needle and seat assembly, and dual inlets keep the float bowls full. All air bleeds and emulsion holes are of the press-in variety.

WARM BLOODED

Many people believe it is best to allow an engine to run on a cold winter day before driving. The assumption is that it is good for the engine to sit and idle, allowing the coolant temperature to build and warm air to start blowing from the heater ducts. The assumption is a good one, but it is not true.

The disk-shaped item under the spring is called a Renee valve and is used in all Demon carburetors.

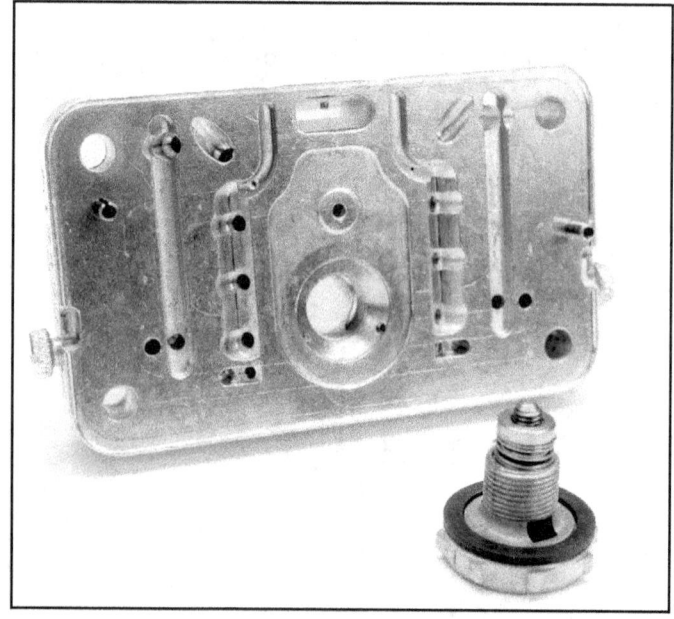

The Road Demon uses a metering block with three emulsion orifices for each main well. Here the power valve is removed exposing the two PVCR circuits, one for each well.

A standard-style squirter is used and is easily removed through the air horn.

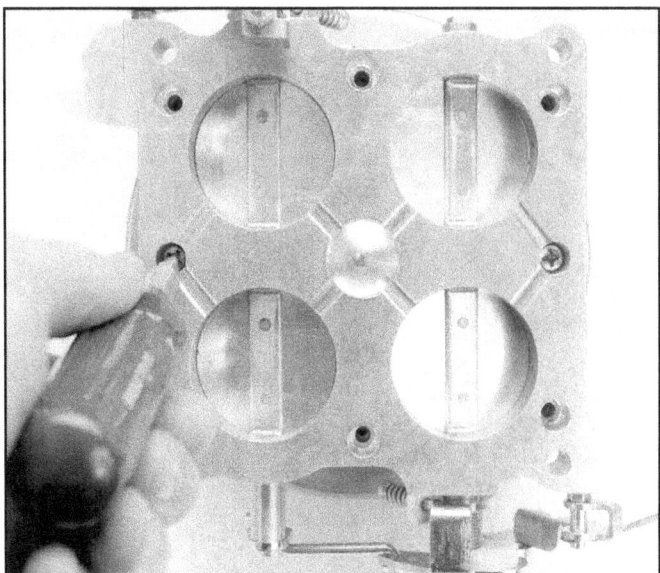
As with all Demon carburetors the base plate is separated from the main body by removing six screws.

When an engine is cold, many things happen that are detrimental to its longevity. The fuel mixture is extremely rich due to the reduced vaporization in the intake manifold from the lack of heat. That translates into liquid fuel entering the combustion chamber, where it washes the oil from the cylinder walls and enters the crankcase. During cold operation, test conducted by the Big 3 have proven that there is approximately 1000 percent more piston ring wear than when the coolant is at operating temperature.

With this in mind, the premise is to accelerate the warming process, or in other words, limit the amount of running time cold. This can be accomplished by driving the vehicle moderately as soon as the oil pressure has come up and stabilized. By placing a light load on the engine, it will build temperature sooner, decreasing the window of time that excessive wear takes place.

As an example, under light load it might take only two minutes of driving to reach a temperature where the wear is decreased. However, getting to the same point by idling may take 10 minutes. In addition, the complete drivetrain warms by driving, whereas during idle, only the engine and some of the transmission parts experience a rise in temperature. Often an excuse for warming an engine is the poor driveability it exhibits when cold. There is no excuse for this with a Demon carburetor that is equipped with a choke. Follow the instructions in Chapter 9 for perfect performance in any weather condition.

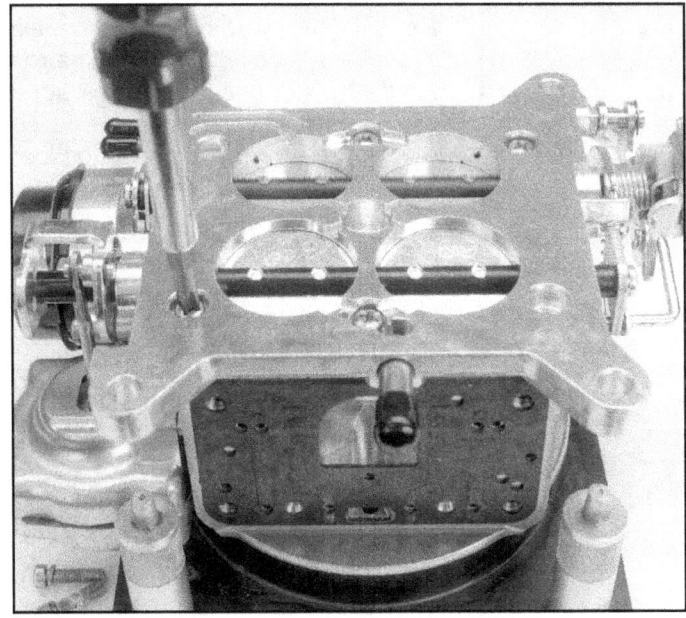
Seen here is the secondary-side metering block gasket. All Road Demons feature nonstick gaskets on the float bowl.

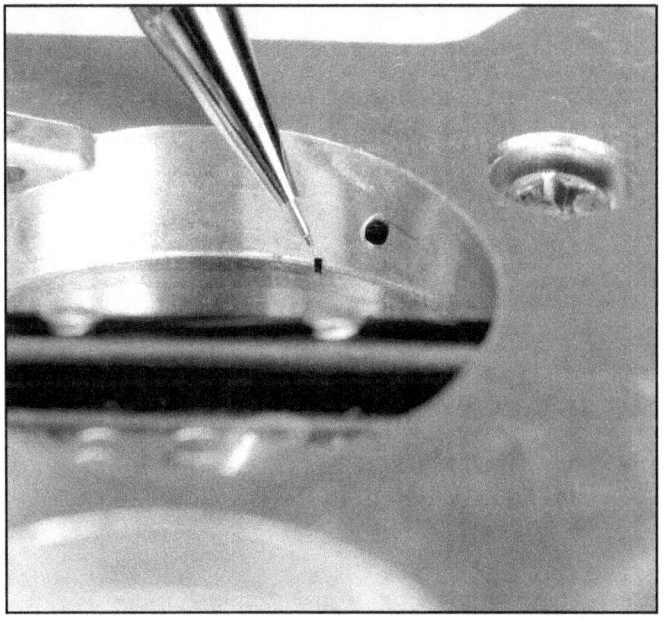
When the throttle plates are adjusted properly, there will be an approximate area of 0.020 inch of the transfer slot

How to Tune and Win with Demon Carburetors **59**

From street rod to car carrier, and many other applications in between, the Road Demon is a versatile carburetor.

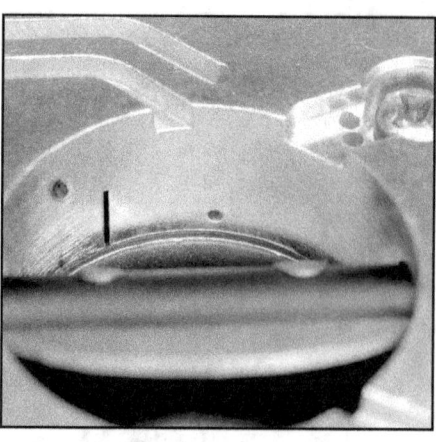

As the throttle plate sweeps open, more of the transfer slot is used to fuel the engine. Note the canal-like passages that supply vacuum to accessory ports.

ROAD DEMON SPECS

PART #:	4282010VE
VENTURI SIZE:	1.280"
IDLE AIR BLEEDS PRI:	.059"
IDLE AIR BLEEDS SEC:	.063"
H.S. AIR BLEEDS:	.039"
BOOSTER TYPE PRI:	DOWN LEG
BOOSTER TYPE SEC:	STRAIGHT
BOOSTER LEG:	.140"
SQUIRTER SIZE:	31
BUTTERFLY SIZE PRI:	1-9/16"
BUTTERFLY SIZE SEC:	1-11/16"
AIR HOLE SIZE:	NONE
PUMP CAM #:	# 330
PUMP CAM COLOR:	PINK
VACUUM SEC. SPRING:	YELLOW
METERING BLOCK # PRI:	A-12400
METERING BLOCK # SEC:	A-12402
SIPHON BREAK:	.028"
E-HOLE POS. #1:	.031"
E-HOLE POS. #2:	N/A
E-HOLE POS. #3:	.031"
E-HOLE POS. #4:	N/A
E-HOLE POS. #5:	.031"
P.V.C.R. SIZE:	.059"
I.F.R. PRIMARY:	.031"
I.F.R. SECONDARY:	.033"
MAIN JETS PRI:	# 70
MAIN JETS SEC:	# 78
POWER VALVE PRI:	6.5 STD
POWER VALVE SEC:	N/A
LINKAGE TYPE:	VACUUM
N&S SIZE/TYPE:	.110"-VITON
ACC. PUMP DIA. SIZE:	#30CC

A GOOD ALL-AROUND CARBURETOR

Everything in design and engineering is a compromise: horsepower for torque, fuel economy for performance, and simplicity for complexity. The street-performance market is not immune to these trade-offs. Often the logic is applied that if a component is considered a race part, it must be even better for street use. The problem is that this is a one-dimensional logic and does not recognize that the rigors of everyday driving in many instances are much more severe than those in racing. Motorsports usually stresses a component in a narrow band of conditions, whereas a street car is challenged in many different ways: long running times, varied load and weather conditions, extended idling in traffic, and usually less-than-ideal maintenance. All of this could potentially spell failure for a part that is designed only for racing.

Barry Grant, Inc. engineers recognized this and developed four distinct models of Demon carburetors. Often an enthusiast may overlook the attributes of using a Road Demon for the glamour of moving up to a Speed Demon. Though both excellent carburetors, the Road Demon fills the needs of a multitude of applications from street rods, pickup trucks, motorhomes, and restored musclecars, and deserves your consideration.

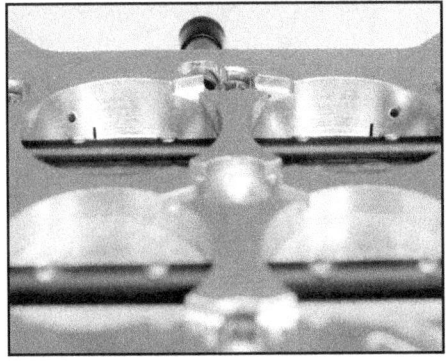

This shows the secondary butterflies and transfer slots. The Road Demon needs to have them adjusted so they are slightly more closed than the primary side.

Changing the secondary vacuum diaphragm spring requires removal of the pod.

This is how the fuel is discharged by the booster when the engine is operating on the main metering circuit. The placement of the camera gives the false impression of uneven fuel discharge.

REVIEW QUESTIONS

1) All Road Demon carburetors are factory equipped with:

   a: threaded air bleeds
   b: an electric choke
   c: annular boosters
   d: a yellow accelerator pump cam

2) The secondary butterfly dimensions on a Road Demon:

   a: are smaller than the primary butterfly
   b: are the same as the primary butterfly
   c: vary by model
   d: are larger than the primary butterfly

3) Road Demons come equipped with:

   a: down-leg boosters on the primary, straight on the secondary
   b: square jetting
   c: annular boosters
   d: 7.5 power valve

4) How many emulsion bleeds does each Road Demon main well have?

   a: 6
   b: 4
   c: 2
   d: 3

5) The Road Demon is available with:

   a: either mechanical or vacuum secondary
   b: vacuum secondary only
   c: dual squirters
   d: an alcohol calibration

6) The idle air bleeds on a Road Demon are:

   a: smaller on the primary side
   b: larger on the primary side
   c: the same on all four barrels
   d: threaded in

7) A unique feature of the Road Demon calibration is that:

   a: the metering block has extra emulsion holes
   b: the main jets are the same on each venturi
   c: a larger IFR is used on the secondary side
   d: it uses a yellow accelerator pump cam

8) The Road Demon metering block is:

   a: made of cast aluminum
   b: diecast from Zamak-3
   c: made of white metal
   d: made of billet aluminum

9) The Road Demon is offered only with:

   a: hand choke
   b: mechanical secondary
   c: optional choke
   d: four-corner idle

10) The Road Demon can support horsepower levels to:

    a: 400
    b: 300
    c: 450
    d: 500

Answers: 1) B, 2) D, 3) A, 4) D, 5) B, 6) A, 7) C, 8) D, 9) D, 10) A

How to Tune & Win with DEMON CARBURETORS

Speed Demon

The target market for the Speed Demon is the general performance segment, which is defined as both street and strip vehicles with a camshaft duration of less than 250 degrees and 0.050 inch of lift. The model line is offered in three different flow ratings, with either dual-squirter or vacuum secondary. The carburetor was designed to produce the airflow dynamics and fuel metering accuracy of a racing unit while integrating features required for a street application. An optional electric choke kit ensures rapid starts and excellent cold-engine performance regardless of the weather. The standard square-flange mounting pad (also known as 4150 style) and air cleaner ring make it a direct replacement for most engines with an aftermarket intake manifold. In addition, two full-time (manifold) and one timed (ported) vacuum junctions allow for easy accessory hook-ups.

Part number 1282010 is a twin squirter 650 intended for healthy 289- to 327-cubic-inch engines, or a mild 350- to 400-cubic-inch application. Part numbers 12802010VE and 12802010VFE boast the same specifications but designate vacuum secondary and Ford-style linkage with vacuum secondary, respectively. For larger engines of 350 to 427 cubic inches, or mild 427- to 455-cubic-inch displacements, part number 1402010

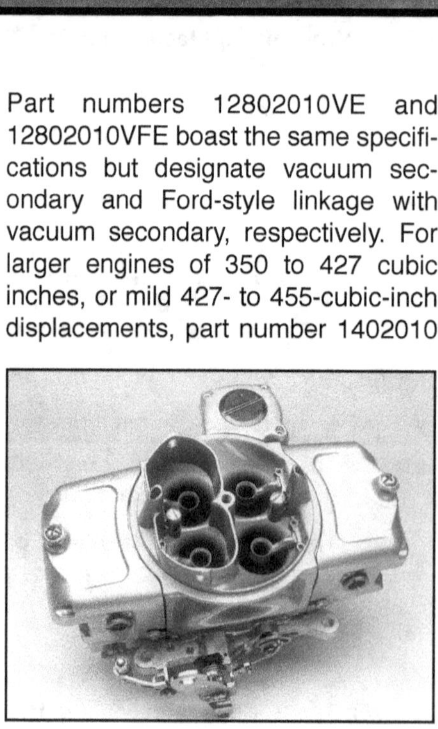

The vacuum-secondary Speed Demon features down-leg boosters on all barrels, along with a quick-change secondary pod. Starting in 2001, all Speed Demon vacuum-secondary carburetors are factory-equipped with an electric choke.

750 Speed Demon is recommended. As with its smaller brothers, the suffix identifying vacuum secondary and Ford linkage applies.

Rounding out the lineup is the 850 version cataloged under part number 1563010, with the same suffix added for secondary and linkage styles. This being the largest in the Speed Demon family, it is targeted to 460-cubic-inch and larger street engines. Within the 850 model designation, a unique Speed Demon is offered with an annular discharge booster. Intended for use with mild big-block applications, the annular booster allows for better atomization and has the ability to pull more fuel at wide-open throttle.

Common to all Speed Demon models are design features that offer increased performance, easier tuning, and quality manufacturing. The main body is diecast from Zamak-3, using the Demon exclusive ConcentraCast method. The following are the venturi dimensions: 650, 1.280-inch, 750, 1.400-inch, and 850, 1.562-inch. The billet base plate and

The Speed Demon is a good choice for street/strip action.

Vacuum and mechanical-secondary Speed Demons side by side.

metering blocks are considered important elements of this design. The butterfly size is 1 11/16 inch for the 650 and 750 versions, and the 850 boasts larger 1 3/4-inch throttle plates.

The billet-aluminum metering block is silver on all Speed Demon models and has a total of six emulsion bleeds, three for each main well along with a dedicated siphon break for each side. The emulsion holes are identified with bleed number one highest up on the metering block. The emulsion orifices are used to help control the density of the fuel introduced into the main well.

Emulsion holes one and three (the top and bottom) are fitted with a 0.031-inch orifice; the middle or number two position is not drilled and is solid. The shape of the fuel-delivery curve is controlled by the placement of these holes and has been decided by Demon engineers to obtain the best performance characteristics through a combination of hole size and placement. The emulsion orifice size and position are constant throughout the Speed Demon line.

Above the top emulsion bleed holes is a siphon break to stop the fuel from flowing into the main well when the venturi signal is eliminated by closing the throttle. This is required once the flow has been established because the fuel would continue to be pulled even after the throttle plates were closed and the booster signal intensity decreased. This can be likened to siphoning gas from a fuel tank with a rubber hose. The siphon break orifice is 0.028 inch, and along with the emulsion orifices, is located on the main-body side of the metering block.

Below the number three emulsion bleed is the idle feed restrictor, which is used to limit the amount of fuel introduced to the idle circuit. This increases the authority of the mixture

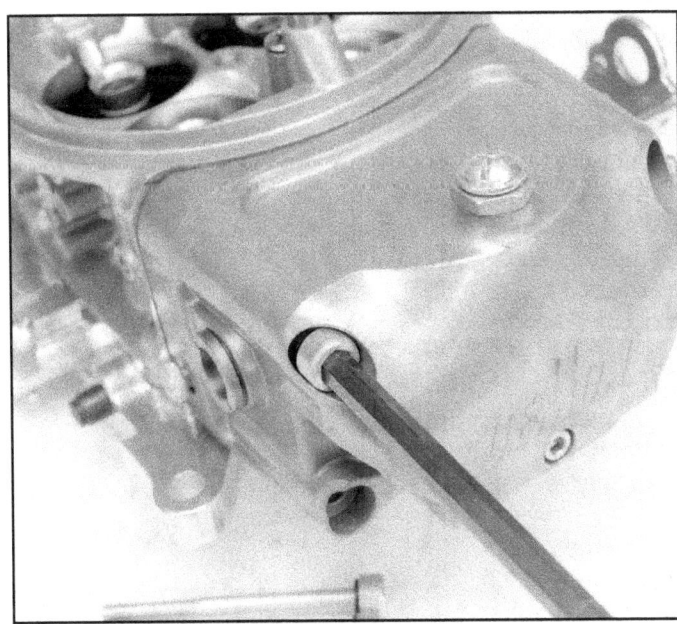
Float bowl removal is necessary for jet and power valve changes.

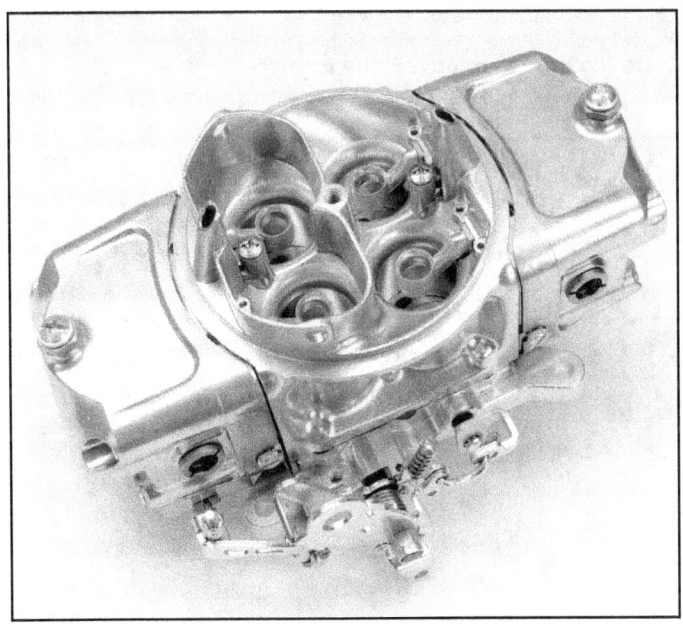
Mechanical secondary versions come with a progressive linkage.

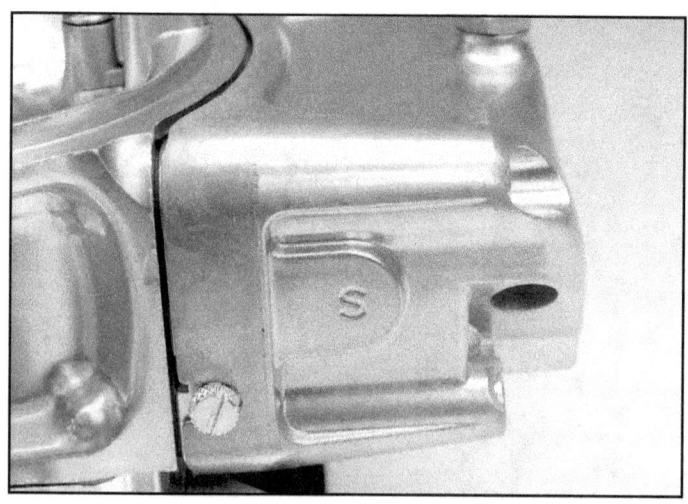

Mechanical-secondary carburetors have accelerator pumps on both the primary and secondary barrels. The float bowls are marked P or S.

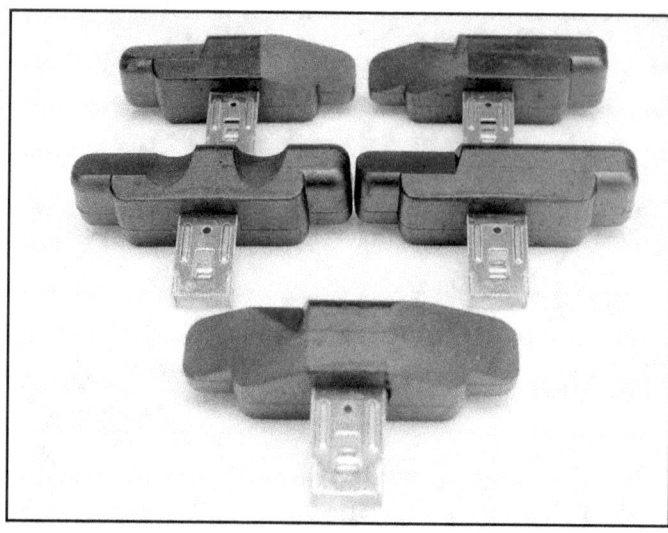

BG Fuel Systems offers floats for every use and Demon carburetor.

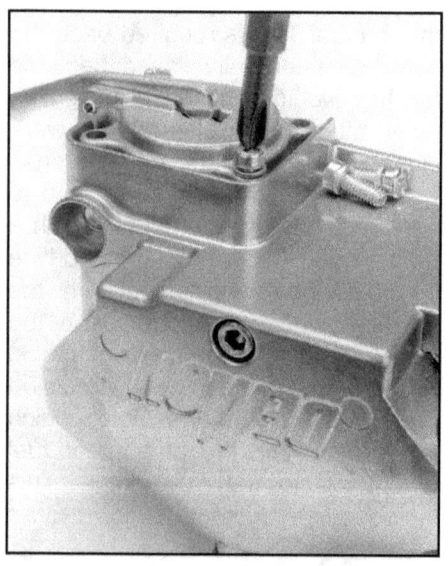

Once the bowl is removed, the accelerator pump is easily serviced.

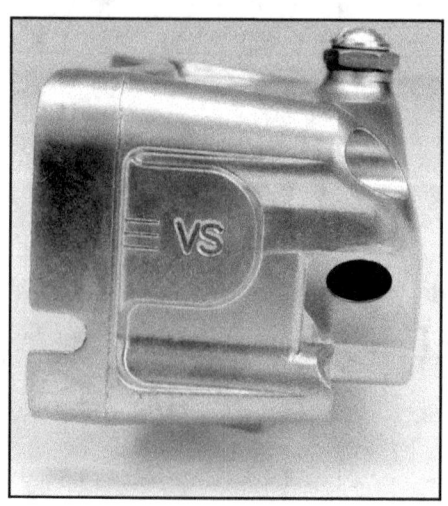

VS designates vacuum-secondary operation.

screw over the air/fuel ratio when excessively large main well jets are used. As the restrictor orifice goes larger, the amount of fuel introduced into the idle circuit increases. The 650, 750, and 850 models have restrictor orifices of 0.029, 0.033, and 0.035 inch, respectively.

There are two main well metering jets that supply fuel from the float bowl to the main metering circuit and are positioned on the fuel bowl side of the metering block. The jets control the amount of fuel to enter the metering block and, ultimately, the air/fuel ratio of the engine. If the mixture appears incorrect throughout the entire engine operating range, a jet change is in order. If the mixture is undesirable at only certain engine speeds, the air bleeds or emulsion orifice need to be altered. (Note: Always start with the air bleeds first.) Model 650 Speed Demons are shipped with #70 primary jets; the 750 and 850 are baselined with #76s and #85s, respectively. The secondary metering block is equipped with #78, #83, and #93 jets for 650, 750, and 850 models, respectively. By nature of design, Demon carburetors are extremely efficient and will produce very linear fuel curves as shipped from the factory.

Due to the improved atomization characteristics, tuners who reference BSFC values will notice readings that are lower than with other carburetors. Often this is misinterpreted and the carburetor calibration is jetted up to richen the mixture, resulting in sluggish performance. For this reason, if you attempt to match what would be considered normal BSFC values for other carburetors with a Demon, the result will be a carburetor and engine that function far below their potential.

Also located in the primary-side metering block are the power valve and power valve channel restrictor. All Speed Demon models are shipped from the factory with a .590-inch PVCR and a 6.5-inch mercury opening power valve. The PVCR is what controls the amount of fuel enrichment, and the vacuum rating of the power valve determines at what manifold vacuum the enrichment starts. All Demon power valves offer backfire protection.

Positioned in the air horn are the

The disk-shaped item under the spring is a Renee valve. It acts as a one-way check valve.

high- and low-speed air bleeds, with the idle bleeds closest to the air cleaner ring, and the four high-speed bleeds on either side of the squirter bosses. The air bleeds along with the emulsion orifices control the shape of the fuel curve, and the main jet size impacts the air/fuel ratio. Speed Demons use press-in air bleeds, so restrictors would be required to limit airflow. The air bleed orifice area can be enlarged by drilling. A larger bleed hole will slow down or delay the main metering circuit operation, and a smaller bleed will quicken the response. In other words, if the air bleed orifice dimension is made larger, a stronger booster signal will need to be produced before pulling fuel. All Speed Demons use a 0.067-inch idle air bleed restrictor; the 650, 750, and 850 have 0.041, 0.039, and 0.031-inch high-speed bleeds, respectively.

Vacuum secondary models are equipped with a quick-change spring cover, and mechanical secondary models feature progressive linkage. Standard squirters are of the flush, or straight, style and offer an orifice dimension of 0.028 for the 650, and 0.031 for 750 and 850 applications. The exit orifice dimension of the squirter controls the duration of fuel shot. A larger-diameter orifice discharges the pump's volume more quickly if the pump cam remains constant.

All Speed Demons use down-leg-style boosters made from diecast ZA-8, which are much stronger and fatigue-resistant than conventional designs. They feature fuel transfer passages of 0.140, 0.160, and 0.184 for the 650, 750, and 850 models, respectively. The same style booster is used on both primary and secondary bores. They are diecast from ZA-8 material and are attached by swedging.

Large-capacity float bowls offer a clear sight glass for float level adjustment and feature quick-release gaskets for easy jet changes. The needle and seat assembly are 0.110-inch high-flow units constructed from Viton. The standard Speed Demon float and assembly are designed for general street/performance use and shipped with no internal anti-foaming baffle.

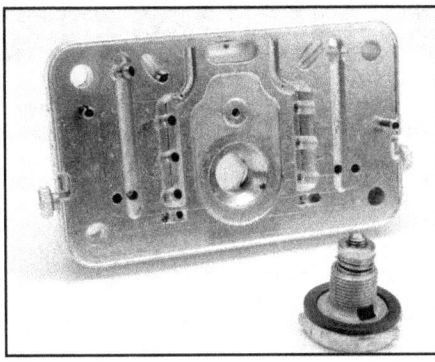

Speed Demons have three emulsion holes for each main well in the metering block. Note the two small holes where the power valve would attach. They are the PVCR, one for each well.

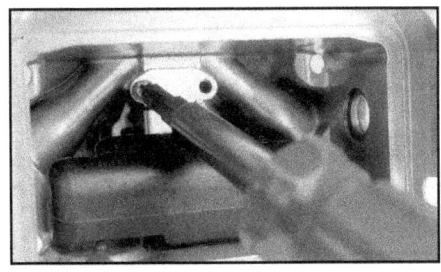

The float is easily removed once the bowl is detached from the main body.

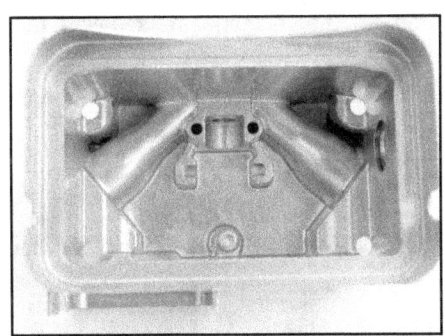

Speed Demons are not shipped with any fuel dams, but one can be user-installed if required.

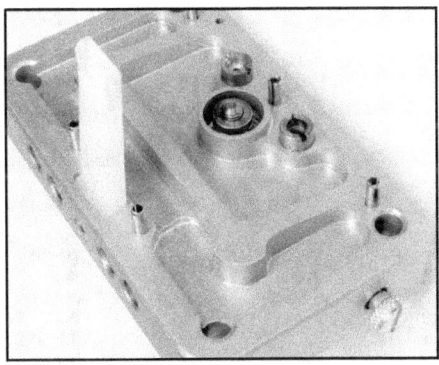

The plastic tube attached to the metering block is a bowl vent extension.

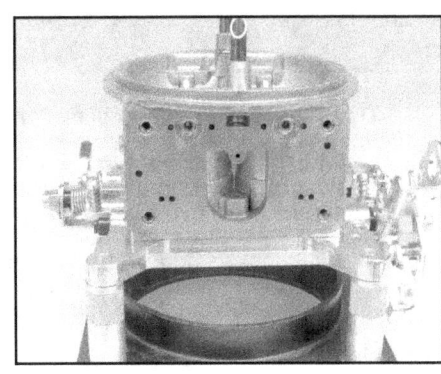

Whenever servicing a Demon carburetor, always use a stand.

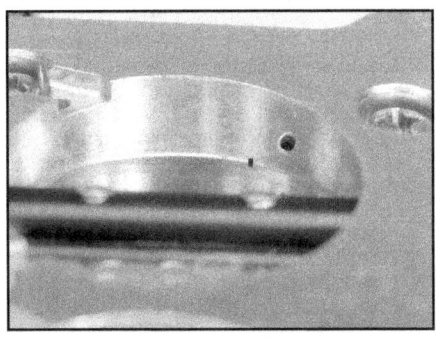

When the throttle plates are set properly, approximately 0.020 inch of the transfer slot area will be exposed.

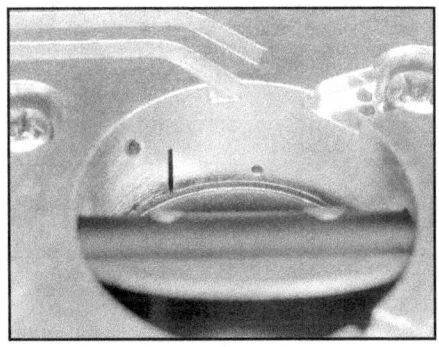

As the throttle is opened, it sweeps past the transfer slot allowing it to discharge fuel.

The secondary throttle plates need to be set the same as in the primary bore regarding transfer slot area.

How to Tune and Win with Demon Carburetors

THE CRATE MOTOR CARBURETOR

The old adage "the numbers don't lie" may apply to most aspects of life but cannot always be attached to engines, especially carburetors. Many in motorsports believe that the larger the component, the more power the engine will make. Chockfull of common sense, this logic often oversimplifies a complex subject. No better is this represented than when choosing a carburetor size and design.

A typical scenario would go like this. Scenario 1: You bring two different-size carburetors to dyno your street/strip big-block, a 750 and a 1000 model. The dyno sheet clearly proves the engine produced the most power with the 1000 monster installed. Scenario 2: Back at the track with a new level of confidence, your hopes for a personal best ET are shattered by lazy off-the-line performance and a disappointing rate of engine acceleration after gear changes. After weeks of frustration, you bolt the 750 back on and the engine performs like never before, running circles around the combination that proved killer on the dyno. What went wrong?

Carburetor size impacts the engine's ability to pump air, so the dimensions of the venturi and throttle plates are of paramount concern. In this fictitious example, the larger carburetor limited the pumping losses in the engine and was proven by the higher power levels on the dyno sheet. However, when the engine was bolted into a relatively heavy car, the airflow characteristics changed dramatically. If a strong signal cannot be produced in the carburetor venturi, the result would be a lack of fuel pulled through the main metering circuit, and poor atomization of the fuel that does arrive there. This plight is very common today, especially with the proliferation of large-cubic-inch crate engines. All of the Big 3 now offer street/strip big-block combinations that are designed to run on pump gas, utilizing a moderate compression ratio and a camshaft that is ground to produce low-speed torque with excellent driveability.

The GM 502/502, Ford 460, and new Mopar Hemi are all examples of this design intent. Historically, these engines find their way into a car that weighs more than 3,400 pounds, and for the sake of street manners, usually is equipped with a tight torque converter and a low numerical rear axle ratio. The natural assumption is to install a large carburetor, bowing to the engine's displacement. In reality, a combination such as this in a street/strip car requires a Dr. Jekyll-Mr. Hyde carburetor design. It would need to afford a sufficient amount of flow to achieve optimal volumetric efficiency while producing a very strong signal at low engine speeds. This is necessary to provide a well-atomized air/fuel ratio along with good mixture velocity. At first this would seem to be an impossible task, but through sound engineering and design, Demon Carburetion has found the solution to this dilemma. It is called the Speed Demon 850 Annular Discharge.

Identifying the need for a crate-motor-sized carburetor, Barry Grant, Inc. developed two 850 Annular Discharge models, a vacuum and a mechanical secondary. Cataloged under part numbers 1563020V and 1563020 respectively, they feature venturi dimensions of 1.562 inches and throttle plates of 1.750 inches, affording the ability to feed the engine with large volumes of air. What makes this 850 different is the use of annular boosters. The design offers improved atomization of the fuel for engines with relatively low velocities through the venturi at low engine RPM. Not a booster change alone, the 850 Annular Discharge is a complete design that includes alterations to the air bleed dimensions, jetting, booster fuel feed leg, and IFR.

The complexity of a carburetor's design and its impact on the engine's performance are often overlooked by the enthusiast and engine builder alike. Just because it may appear similar on the outside, what it does with the fuel and air on the inside is what counts. The Speed Demon 850 Annular Discharge is a welcome arrival to anyone who runs an engine of 430 cubic inches or larger that is tuned for street/strip action. This carburetor will improve throttle response, fuel economy, and emissions while producing more real-world horsepower and torque. All of this comes with a substantial decrease in drag-strip ET. In other words, it reacts like a smaller carburetor at low engine speeds, and a larger one at high RPM. In a world of compromise, Demon Carburetion has proven once again that technology and good design will always win.

SPEED DEMON SPECS

MODEL #:	650	750	850	850AD	650V	750V	850V	850ADV
PART #:	1282010	1402010	1563010	1563020	1282010V	1402010V	1563010V	1563020V
VENTURI SIZE:	1.280"	1.400"	1.562"	1.562"	1.280"	1.400"	1.562"	1.562"
IDLE AIR BLEEDS PRI:	.059"	.059"	.059"	.059"	.059"	.059"	.059"	.063"
IDLE AIR BLEEDS SEC:	.063"	.063"	.063"	.063"	.063"	.063"	.063"	.063"
H.S. AIR BLEEDS:	.041"	.039"	.028"	.028"	.041"	.039"	.028"	.028"
BOOSTER TYPE:	DOWN LEG	DOWN LEG	DOWN LEG	ANNULAR	DOWN LEG	DOWN LEG	DOWN LEG	ANNULAR
BOOSTER LEG:	.140"	.160"	.184"	STD.	.140"	.160"	.184"	STD.
SQUIRTER SIZE:	28 STD.	31 STD.	31 STD.	31 STD.	28 STD.	31 STD.	1 STD.	31 STD.
BUTTERFLY SIZE:	1-11/16"	1-11/16"	1-3/4"	1-3/4"	1-11/16"	1-11/16"	1-3/4"	1-3/4"
AIR HOLE SIZE:	NONE	NONE	NONE	NONE	NONE	NONE	NONE	NONE
PUMP CAM #:	# 330	# 330	# 330	# 330	# 330	# 330	# 330	# 330
PUMP CAM COLOR:	PINK	PINK	PINK	PINK	PINK	PINK	PINK	PINK
VACUUM SEC. SPRING:	N/A	N/A	N/A	N/A	YELLOW	PLAIN	PLAIN	PLAIN
METERING BLOCK # P:	A-12400	A-12400	A-12400	A-12400	A-12400	A-12400	A-12400	A-12400
METERING BLOCK # S:	A-12401	A-12401	A-12401	A-12401	A-12402	A-12402	A-12402	A-12402
SIPHON BREAK:	.028"	.028"	.028"	.028"	.028"	.028"	.028"	.028"
E-HOLE POS. #1:	.031"	.031"	.031"	.031"	.031"	.031"	.031"	.031"
E-HOLE POS. #2:	N/A	N/A	N/A	N/A	N/A	N/A	N/A	N/A
E-HOLE POS. #3:	.031"	.031"	.031"	.031"	.031"	.031"	.031"	.031"
E-HOLE POS. #4:	N/A	N/A	N/A	N/A	N/A	N/A	N/A	N/A
E-HOLE POS. #5:	.031"	.031"	.033"	.033"	.031"	.031"	.033"	.033"
P.V.C.R. SIZE:	.059"	.059"	.059"	.059"	.059"	.059"	.059"	.059"
TRANSFER SLOT RES:	OPEN	OPEN	.OPEN	.OPEN	OPEN	OPEN	.OPEN	.OPEN
IDLE FEED RESTRICTOR:	.033"	.033"	.035"	.035"	.033"	.033"	.035"	.035"
MAIN JETS PRI:	# 70	# 76	# 85	# 80	# 70	# 76	# 85	# 80
MAIN JETS SEC:	# 78	# 83	# 93	# 85	# 78	# 83	# 93	# 85
POWER VALVE PRI:	6.5 STD.	6.5 STD.	6.5 STD.	6.5 STD.	6.5 STD.	6.5 STD.	6.5 STD.	6.5 STD.
POWER VALVE SEC:	N/A	N/A	N/A	N/A	N/A	N/A	N/A	N/A
LINKAGE TYPE:	PROG.	PROG.	PROG.	PROG.	VACUUM	VACUUM	VACUUM	VACUUM
N&S SIZE/TYPE:	.110"-VITON	.110"-VITON	.110"-VITON	.110"-VITON	.110"-VITON	.110"-VITON	.110"-VITON	.110"-VITON
ACC. PUMP DIA. SIZE:	30CC	30CC	30CC	30CC	30CC	30CC	30CC	30CC

How to Tune and Win with Demon Carburetors

Bill Young, a student at the University of Northwestern Ohio in Lima, puts a Speed Demon to the test for *Corvette Fever*.

The base plate is easily removed from the main body. Always use a new gasket when reassembling.

Rich Smiecinski checks a spark plug on his 650V Speed Demon-equipped 355 Chevrolet. The engine made 398 hp and 456 lbs./ft. of torque on 92-octane fuel, and still passed smog testing.

REVIEW QUESTIONS

1) The target market for the Speed Demon line is:

   a: drag racing
   b: general performance
   c: alcohol applications
   d: marine

2) An annular discharge option is available on:

   a: all size Speed Demons
   b: no Speed Demons
   c: 850 models
   d: dual-squirter models only

3) The color of the Speed Demon primary and secondary metering blocks are:

   a: silver
   b: gold
   c: black
   d: any color you specify when ordering

4) On Speed Demons, how many emulsion bleeds are there in the metering block of each main well?

   a: 6
   b: 4
   c: 2
   d: 3

5) How many total air bleeds does a Speed Demon have?

   a: 8
   b: 6
   c: 4
   d: it varies by model

6) The IFR is used:

   a: to limit the amount of fuel that enters the idle circuit
   b: to richen the mixture off-idle
   c: so you can remove the power valve
   d: as a backup circuit in case the main well becomes plugged

7) All Speed Demons are shipped from the factory with:

   a: a choke kit
   b: dual squirters
   c: a 6.5 power valve
   d: jet extensions

8) The boosters on Speed Demons are attached by:

   a: swedging
   b: threads
   c: integral to the casting of the main body
   d: O-rings

9) Vacuum secondary Speed Demons feature:

   a: dual squirters
   b: quick-change secondary pod covers
   c: threaded air bleeds
   d: intermediate circuits

10) All Speed Demons except one model come with:

    a: straight boosters
    b: down-leg boosters
    c: annular boosters
    d: billet boosters

Answers: 1) B, 2) C, 3) A, 4) D, 5) A, 6) A, 7) C, 8) A, 9) B, 10) B

How to Tune & Win with DEMON CARBURETORS

Race Demon

As its name implies, the Race Demon is considered an off-road carburetor. Though the Road Demon is the sales leader, the Race Demon boasts the most individual part numbers, with 75 separate calibrations listed at the time of publication. If anyone was to ever doubt Barry Grant's commitment to making the Demon the best carburetor on the market, the fact that he has spent the time and money to develop so many calibrations of one model should be enough to convince you.

Due to these efforts, the Race Demon, when ordered properly, is undeniably the most closely tuned out-of-the-box fuel metering device in the world. You can now see why other brands of carburetors require so much rework to perform acceptably on a high-output engine; they offer only a few calibrations, if that. Featuring only mechanical secondary operation, the linkage is of the progressive style unless otherwise noted. The Race Demon shares all of the design features of the other models, with a few extras for its application-specific market. Also included are calibrations for alcohol and gasoline engines.

There are five distinct groups: drag race, general competition, road race, tunnel ram, and oval track. They expand further with the RS option, which offers a removable venturi sleeve.

All Race Demons will attach to an intake manifold with a 4150-style mounting pad and feature replaceable boosters and threaded air and emulsion bleeds. Depending on the calibration, the base plate will be either silver or black, representing 1 11/16-inch and 1 3/4-inch butterflies, respectively. Gasoline and most alcohol metering blocks have five emulsion holes with positions #2 and #4 generally plugged for gasoline, and #4 and #5 blocked for alcohol.

Due to the complex nature of the changes that define the distinct models of the Race Demon line, each category deserves to be explored individually. As mentioned previously, the main features common to all Demon carburetors will not be restated and should be referenced from previous chapters.

Drag Race Gas (DR)

Factory equipped to be used as a single four-barrel carburetor, it boasts jet extensions, clearanced floats, and specific fuel curve calibrations to promote clean idle, crisp throttle response, and consistent ETs. This is the perfect choice for a Bracket or Super class racer.

Meeting the demands of the drag racing market, the DR series comes equipped with jet extension and clearanced or notched floats on the rear bowl. It's offered in 650, 750, 825, 1000, and 820 AD versions. The 650 and 750 have silver base plates, and the rest use the larger black style. Down-leg boosters are used across the board except in the AD model.

Venturi sizing is 1.280, 1.400, 1.425, and 1.562 inch for the 650, 750, 825, 1000, respectively. The 820 AD uses the large 1.562 venturi also. Idle air bleeds are 0.070 inch for all except the 825, which uses a slightly smaller 0.067-inch diameter. The high-speed air bleeds vary from 0.031 to 0.041

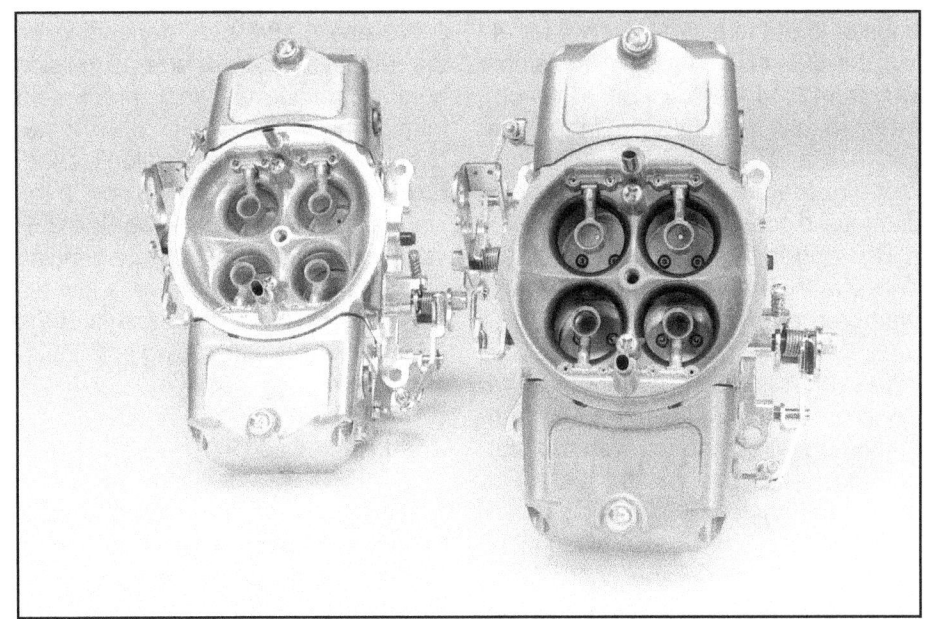

Race Demons can be easily identified by their lack of a choke horn. The carburetor on the right is an RS model.

The booster leg is the passage that carries the fuel as seen in the cutaway. All Race Demons have threaded boosters for a secure fit and easy tuning changes.

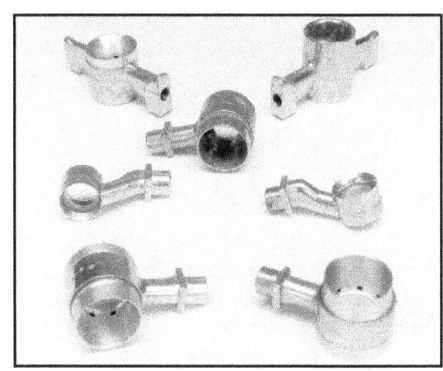

Barry Grant, Inc. went to a great effort to develop many different booster designs.

inch and should be referenced from the specifications chart. The squirter design is of the standard type, with a pink #330 cam allowing the fuel from a 30cc pump cover to discharge through a 0.028-inch-diameter orifice on the 650; the rest use a larger 0.031 hole.

All carbs in the DR series have air holes drilled into the four butterflies. They are precision drilled to a dimension of 0.093 inch and are used to allow the proper relationship of the throttle plate to the exposed transfer slot area. If this relationship is wrong, fuel will not be available in the transfer slot and will create a tip-in hesitation or bog as the throttle is opened. All DR carburetor production will switch to the Demon exclusive idle air bypass during spring 2001. This will alleviate the four throttle plate air holes, and instead there will be a tunable threaded bleed on the underside of the carburetor. The metering block is the standard silver A-12320 model with a 0.028-inch siphon break and five emulsion holes.

Drag Race Gas Removable Sleeve (DR RS)

The purpose of the removable sleeve design is to allow the end user to tune the flow and signal characteristic of the main body venturi by using a removable sleeve to change the dimension. The sleeves are color-coded and are offered in the following incremental sizes: green, 1.280 inch; red, 1.400 inch; blue, 1.425 inch; gold, 1.500 inch; black, 1.562 inch; silver, 1.590 inch. Demon offers the sleeves as a kit with the appropriate booster and instructions for changes to any air bleeds or emulsion orifices.

This tunable venturi version of the DR gasoline series is offered in eight sizes, six of them using down-leg boosters and two using annular discharge. Model designations are 675, 775, 825, 975, 1025, 1050, 820 AD, and 950 AD. The sleeve color coding is the same throughout the Race Demon series. The two smaller carburetors use the silver base plate and the others feature the large butterflies of the black base plate. Production before the first quarter of 2001 used one 0.093-inch air hole in each butterfly, which was phased out for the tunable air bypass. Idle air bleed dimensions measured in inches are 0.070 for all except the 825, which uses the smaller 0.067-diameter bleed. The high-speed bleeds are the following: 675, 0.041 inch; 775, 0.039 inch; 825, 0.039 inch; 975, 0.039 inch; 1025, 0.031 inch; 820 AD, 0.033 inch; 950 AD, 0.035 inch.

Siphon break, PVCR, and the use of five emulsion hole metering blocks stay constant with the other Race Demon models.

General Competition Gas (GC)

These calibrations are supplied with primary power valves that offer backfire protection for excellent idle and driveability. These are the only Race Demon models that feature vacuum ports, making them a perfect choice for a street/strip application.

Abbreviated GC, they are represented by five models, with the designations 650, 750, 825, 1000, and 820 AD, denoting annular discharge boosters. The venturi sizes vary according to model, from 1.280 to 1.562 inches. The 650 and 750 have a silver base plate, and the rest use the larger butterfly black base-plate assembly. Air bleed sizing for both idle and high-speed operation vary with calibration. The idle bleeds are 0.070 inch on all except the 825, which has a slightly smaller 0.067-inch orifice. The high-speed bleeds are as follows: 650, 0.041; 750, 0.039; 825, 0.039; 1000, 0.031; 820 AD, 0.033 inch. The

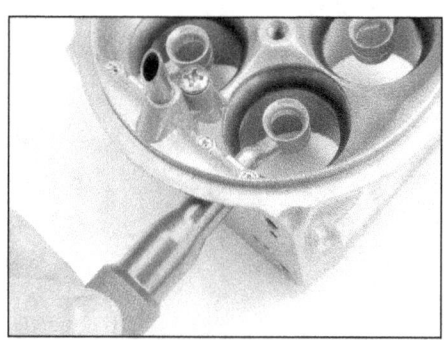

A special tool is required to remove the booster. It resembles a spanner wrench.

As easy as the boosters are to change on a Race Demon, remember, they are designed to work as a system with the emulsion bleeds.

RS models have the sleeves color-coded for easy recognition.

The venturi sleeves are stepped and are installed through the bottom of the main body after removing the boosters and base plate assembly.

booster is of the down-leg style for all but the 820 AD. The leg dimensions vary from 0.140 inch up to 0.184 inch. They all use standard squirters; the 650 has a 0.028 and the other four models feature larger 0.031-inch-diameter discharge orifices.

The butterflies have no air holes drilled in them, but carburetors manufactured after Spring 2001 will feature the Demon exclusive idle air bypass that is described at length in Chapter 9. This allows extra freedom in tuning by keeping the transfer slot relationship to the throttle plates at the proper angle.

All GC carburetors use #330 pink accelerator pump cams and 30cc pump covers. Common across the line is the 0.110-inch Viton needle-and-seat assembly. Standard Demon floats are used without jet extensions. Each carburetor uses the A-12320 metering block, which has five emulsion holes and is silver in color. Emulsion hole position #1, which is at the top of the block, is open and has a 0.031-inch dimension on each model. Likewise, position #2 is plugged across the board, with position #3 open and using the same dimension as the top hole. Bleed hole #4 is universally blocked, but #5 is open and uses a 0.031-inch orifice in all models except the 1000; that hole is enlarged to 0.033 inch.

The siphon break and PVCR dimension are the same for all models: 0.028 and 0.059 inch, respectively. The amount of fuel flow to the idle circuit is limited by an IFR of 0.029, 0.036, 0.037, 0.038 inch, for the 650, 750, 825, and 1000, respectively. The 820 AD IFR reverts to a 0.037-inch diameter. All models have the standard Demon 6.5-inch power valve on the primary side with the secondary metering block power valve cavity plugged. Refer to the specifications list at the end of this chapter for jet sizing.

General Competition Gas Removable Sleeve (GC RS)

The following models are offered in the GC RS line: 675, 775, 825, 1025, 1050, 820 AD, and 950 AD. Down-leg-booster venturis are used in all calibrations except the AD models. Booster leg dimensions vary between 0.140 and 0.184 inch, depending on the model and flow size. Emulsion hole dimensions and placement mimic the GC series, with minor changes in the specifications chart. Likewise, the PVCR dimension is the standard 0.059 inch, while the IFR varies from 0.029 to 0.039 depending on model. The power valve is located on the primary side only and is of the 6.5-inch variety with a plug in the secondary metering block.

Road Race Gas (RR)

Specifically engineered to handle the left-and-right turns of a road race circuit, they boast metering calibrations for the highest cornering and straightway speeds. The models 650, 750, and 825 comprise the offerings and are all down-leg-booster designs. Standard-style squirters are used with 0.028-inch discharge orifices for the 650; the two larger models use a 0.031-inch design. Most other aspects of this carburetor are similar to the RR RS version and can be compared in the specifications listing.

Road Race Gas Removable Sleeve (RR RS)

The requirements of the road racing market have been identified by Demon with exacting calibrations to fit this venue. Venturi dimensions create models 675, 775, and 825. They all use down-leg boosters but vary the booster-leg dimensions. Demon engineers found that the best performance would be obtained with a booster leg of 0.140 for the 675, and the two larger carburetors require the larger 0.160 sizing.

All three models use the silver base plate assembly and the traditional A-12320 five-hole metering block. An interesting feature on the RR RS series is the use of a 6.5-inch power valve in both the primary and secondary metering blocks. This dictates square jetting, meaning that the main jets are the same in all venturis. This series is offered only with a mechanical secondary 1:1 linkage, which means all four barrels will open simultaneously. Likewise, 0.093-inch air holes are used in early models, with later production switching to the idle air bypass orifice.

Road Race specific floats have modified corners to help control fuel movement under high cornering forces.

Tunnel Ram Gas (TR)

A unique calibration offered by Demon, these carburetors are designed to work in matched pairs on intake manifolds where the carburetors are mounted sideways.

The modular carburetor was originally designed to work while mounted parallel to the movement of the vehicle. The use of a tunnel ram intake manifold changes this orientation, making it perpendicular to the direction of motion. This creates issues with fuel movement in the float bowl that were addressed by Demon engineers in the TR series. An additional concern is the use of two carburetors on this style intake manifold, meaning that changes would be required to have the engine perform properly with eight throttle plates.

The TR series has four models: 650, 750, 825, and 1000 designations. The venturi dimensions are 1.280, 1.400, 1.425, and 1.562 inches for the 650, 750, 825, and 1000, respectively. They all use down-leg boosters. The 650 has a leg dimension of 0.140, the 750 and 825 share a 0.160, and the 1000 uses a 0.184-inch size. Base plate color is silver for the 650 and 750, and the larger models use the black 1 3/4-inch size.

Metering block choice, emulsion holes, and siphon break dimension follow suit with other Race Demons. The floats are a special design with one side modified and angle-cut. The modified floats are mounted in the bowls that would face the rear of the vehicle in a conventional installation, whereas the other bowl uses a standard float assembly. Due to the orientation of the carburetors, no jet extensions are used. Power valves are used on both primary and secondary metering blocks, so square jetting is employed in the design intent.

Due to the large area created by the eight throttle plates, no air holes are used in this design. A unique feature, though, is the implementation of a restrictor in the transfer slot circuit. This is used to limit the fuel flow and

Note the single air hole in each throttle plate, which will be replaced by a tunable air bypass passage in the center of the base plate during Spring 2001 production.

improve part-throttle engine performance and driveability. All other Race Demons use no restrictor, and this circuit is considered to be open. The restriction is varied with each model TR and is 0.076 in the 650 and 825 models. The 750 and 1000 use a smaller 0.063 orifice dimension.

**Tunnel Ram Gas
Removable Sleeve (TR RS)**

As with the other RS models, the sleeve sizing is color-coded and remains constant throughout the line. Down-leg boosters and the use of no power valves are common with the companion TR series.

Oval Track Gas (OT)

Designed for effortless driveability on dirt or asphalt, these carburetors have customized metering circuits developed to produce rapid throttle response and excellent midrange and top-end power.

As its name suggests, in this style racing, the vehicle constantly is traveling in a left turn. This needs to be considered in the design of the float so that both jets in each metering block stay immersed in gasoline. To accomplish this, Demon engineers use the same float as the TR-series carburetors but have installed them so the clearanced section is on the right side of the carburetor for left hand turns, and vice versa for tracks that run the opposite direction.

The five calibrations offered are: 650, 750, 825, 1000, and 820 AD. All models except the 820 AD use down-leg boosters. Both the 650 and 750 use the silver base plate, while the rest of the models employ the black assembly. As mentioned previously, each butterfly on OT series carburetors uses a 0.093-inch air bleed, but this will be phased out when the newer design goes into production. The metering block style is shared with the rest of the Race Demon line, and the specifications chart should be used as a reference. Power valves are employed on both metering blocks and are of the standard 6.5 variety.

**Oval Track Gas
Removable Sleeve (OT RS)**

Roundy-round racers can take advantage of the same unique RS feature as participants in other motorsports. Eight variations are included in this designation and are cataloged as the following models: 675, 775, 825, 975, 1050, 820 AD, 950 AD. Silver base plates are used on the 675 and 775 models, and the others use the black 1 3/4-inch style. Most other aspects of the design are similar to the OT series, but the 950 AD sports the larger 1.590-inch venturis.

**Blower Calibration
Removable Sleeve (BC RS)**

Designed for use on either draw-through or blow-through installation, there are five models available. A draw-through system places the carburetor before the blower and then compresses the mixed fuel and air charge. A Roots-style blower is a good example of this application. In contrast, a blow-through design places the carburetor after the supercharger, and thus the complete carburetor is exposed to boost pressure.

The BC RS is offered as a 675, 775, 825, 975, or 1025. All models feature down-leg boosters and standard-style squirters. The 675 and 775 use 0.028-inch-diameter discharge orifice squirters; the rest of the models use the larger 0.031-inch version. The Demon A-12320 metering block is specified for all BC RS carburetors,

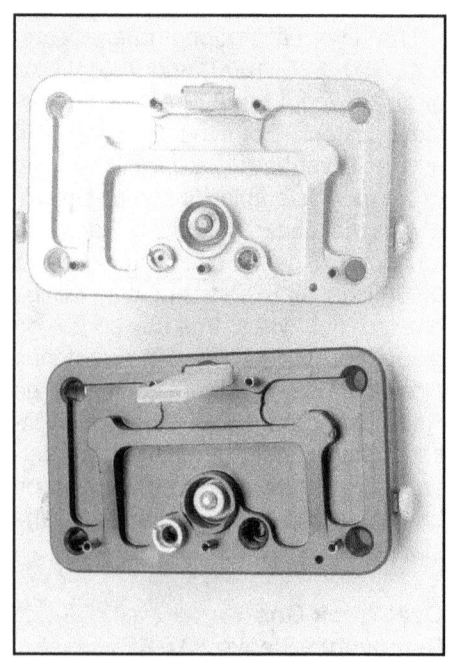

Alcohol requires much larger main jets and passages due to its lower energy content. All alcohol metering blocks are black for easy identification.

along with the standard 30cc accelerator pump and pink #330 cam.

Positions #2 and #4 in the metering block assembly remain plugged, and the PVCR is the standard-issue 0.059-inch calibration. The base plate assembly is blower-specific and features a port to boost reference the power valve that is used on the primary metering block alone. This is necessary since an application such as this can create a scenario that will place the engine under load while the blower is still pulling five to six inches of vacuum across the carburetor. By externally referencing the power valve from an intake manifold port, the circuit will be able to respond to the actual conditions in the manifold and not be tricked by the blower. In these applications the Demon factory installs a 4.5 power valve and uses transfer slot restrictors to help with driveability.

390 Removable Sleeve (390 RS) 750 Removable Sleeve Check Legal

Due to unique removable sleeve venturis, Demon has the ability to manufacture a "check legal" series of competition carburetors. Offered as both a 390 and a 750 model, they are designed to be checked with gauges by a racing association and can be used in these venues as long as no specific carburetor brand is required. Because of the unique calibration of the two carburetors and the ever-changing sanctioning body rules, please call the Demon technical line for current specifications.

ALCOHOL RACE DEMONS

When working with alcohol fuel, certain modifications have to be made over a standard gasoline unit. Stainless-steel high-flow needle valves and high-flow power valves are required. The metering block is alcohol-specific and is identified by its black color. In addition, all passages in the carburetor, booster leg, squirter, jets, and metering block need to be enlarged due to the fuel's lower Btu content than gasoline. It takes twice as much alcohol to support the same power level as gasoline.

Drag Race Alcohol (Alky DR)

The alcohol DR consists of three models: 650, 750, and 825. The venturi dimensions are 1.280, 1.400, and 1.425 inches for the 650, 750, and 825, respectively. The two smaller entries use the silver base plate, and the 825 is designed around the black.

It is interesting to look at the idle air bleed dimensions for carburetors using this fuel. Bleed sizing of 0.052 and 0.046 are used for the 650 and 750, respectively; the 825 shares the same idle air bleed with the 750. The high-speed air bleeds are 0.037 for the 650 and 0.033 for both the 750 and 825. Down-leg boosters are used in all models but have larger leg dimensions. Both the 750 and 825 use double stepped-down leg boosters, which increase the strength of the signal. The squirters are of the standard style but have been specially made with a 0.045- or 0.052-inch discharge orifice. The same #330 pink accelerator pump cam and 30cc cover is used as with gasoline models.

The metering block for alcohol Demons is identified by its black color. It has four emulsion holes and uses the first three with the #4 position plugged. In all three models, the emulsion orifice dimension for all positions is 0.028 inch. The siphon break size is 0.028 inch for the 650, but stepped down to 0.026 inch for the 750 and 825. Since no power valves are used in this application, the PVCR passage is nonexistent and the metering block is plugged. The needle and seat are stainless steel for corrosion resistance and are 0.150 inch in diameter. Early production versions use the throttle plate air hole, and later versions employ the Demon exclusive tunable idle air bypass.

Drag Race Alcohol Removable Sleeve (Alky DR RS)

The removable-sleeve version of this carburetor comes in four models with designations of 675, 775, 825, and 975. Double stepped-down leg boosters are featured in all but the 675, which has a conventional down-leg design. The squirter size is 0.045 inch for the 675, and 0.052 inch for the three larger models. The base plate assembly is silver for the 675 and 775, and black for the 825 and 975. The main jets are 0.144 inch all around, with jet extensions on the rear bowls. The metering block assembly is part number B-12325 and is color-coded black. Featuring four emulsion holes with positions #1, #2, and #3 all sized to 0.028 inch, the fourth position is plugged. Many other aspects of this calibration are shared with the Alky DR and can be referenced from the specifications.

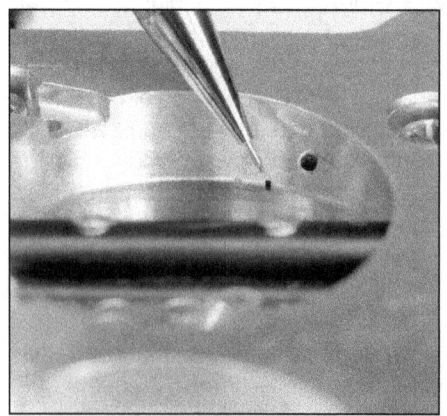

The idle air bypass will help keep the transfer slot relationship in check for an engine with a large camshaft.

Oval Track Alcohol (Alky OT)

To serve the unique requirements of this use, four models are currently offered in this classification: 650, 750, 825, and 1000. They feature 1.280-, 1.400-, 1.425-, and 1.562-inch venturi dimension for the 650, 750, 825, and 1000, respectively.

Some interesting aspects of these calibrations appear when comparing the idle and high-speed bleeds to the other alcohol Race Demons. The idle air bleed for the 650 through 825 is 0.067 inch, with the 1000 being 0.063 inch. The high-speed bleeds are 0.032 for the 650, and 0.033 for both the 750 and 825. The 1000 steps this dimension down to 0.028 inch.

All four models use standard down-leg boosters. High-flow 6.5 power valves are used on both primary and secondary metering blocks, with the 650 through 825 using the part number A-12325 with five emulsion positions, and the 1000 deviating from this by featuring the B-12325 version with four emulsion holes. Both metering blocks are color-coded black, and positions #1, #2, and #3 are used with the other positions plugged. The PVCR is 0.116 inch on all models and metering blocks regardless of position. As with the other Race Demon Alcohol calibrations, float and needle-valve assemblies are designed for submersion in alcohol. Squirters are of the tube type design for all models and only vary in the dimension of the discharge orifice.

Oval Track Alcohol Removable Sleeve (Alky OT RS)

This classification consists of five models starting with a 675 and progressing with 775, 825, 975, and ending with a 1025. Secondary operation is 1:1 style, and down-leg boosters are used exclusively. Tube-type squirters and black metering blocks are found in all models. Unique calibration features of these carburetors can be determined along with jetting from the specifications listing.

REVIEW QUESTIONS

(1) The letters RS when referring to a Race Demon carburetor denote:

   a: race series
   b: removable sleeve
   c: regular secondary
   d: race sleeve

(2) All GC series Race Demons have:

   a: vacuum secondary operation
   b: electric choke
   c: 30cc accelerator pumps
   d: black metering blocks

(3) Which Race Demon has threaded air bleeds?

   a: all
   b: GC
   c: TR
   d: alcohol calibrations

(4) What is the dimension of the butterfly air holes, if so-equipped?

   a: 0.005
   b: 0.93
   c: 0.03
   d: 0.093

(5) The AD suffix when used in the model designation refers to:

   a: automatic transmission drag race use
   b: booster design
   c: size of the venturi
   d: it has no meaning and is for inventory purposes

(6) Race Demons factory equipped without power valves have:

   a: square jetting
   b: staggered jets
   c: no PVCR in the metering block
   d: plugged emulsion holes in the metering block

(7) Road race versions have modified:

   a: accelerator pumps
   b: needle valves
   c: floats
   d: IFR circuits

(8) DR series carburetors that are fitted with jet extensions place them on:

   a: the primary side jets only
   b: all four main jets
   c: the secondary side only
   d: the right-hand side of the carburetor

(9) Blower-calibrated Race Demons have the power valve referenced from:

   a: boost
   b: external of the carburetor
   c: internal of the carburetor
   d: never use a power valve on a blower application

(10) Alcohol calibration uses:

   a: a stainless-steel needle-and-seat assembly
   b: smaller main jets
   c: 50cc accelerator pumps
   d: straight boosters

Answers: 1) B, 2) C, 3) A, 4) D, 5) B, 6) A, 7) C, 8) C, 9) A, 10) A

RACE DEMON GENERAL COMPETITION GAS (GC)

MODEL #:	650	750	825	1000	820 AD
PART #:	2282010GC	2402010GC	2423010GC	2563010GC	2563020GC
VENTURI SIZE:	1.280"	1.400"	1.425"	1.562"	1.562"
IDLE AIR BLEEDS:	.070"	.070"	.067"	.070"	.070"
H.S. AIR BLEEDS:	.041"	.039"	.039"	.031"	.033"
BOOSTER TYPE:	DOWN LEG	DOWN LEG	DOWN LEG	DOWN LEG	ANNULAR
BOOSTER LEG:	.140"	.160"	.160"	.184"	STD.
SQUIRTER SIZE:	28 STD.	31 STD.	31 STD.	31 STD.	31 STD.
BASEPLATE COLOR:	SILVER	SILVER	BLACK	BLACK	BLACK
BUTTERFLY SIZE:	1-11/16"	1-11/16"	1-3/4"	1-3/4"	1-3/4"
AIR HOLE SIZE:	NONE	NONE	NONE	NONE	NONE
PUMP CAM #:	# 330	# 330	# 330	# 330	# 330
PUMP CAM COLOR:	PINK	PINK	PINK	PINK	PINK
METERING BLOCK #:	A-12320	A-12320	A-12320	A-12320	A-12320
M-BLOCK COLOR:	SILVER	SILVER	SILVER	SILVER	SILVER
SIPHON BREAK:	.028"	.028"	.028"	.028"	.028"
E-HOLE POS. # 1:	.031"	.031"	.031"	.031"	.031"
E-HOLE POS. # 2:	PLUGGED	PLUGGED	PLUGGED	PLUGGED	PLUGGED
E-HOLE POS. # 3:	.031"	.031"	.031"	.031"	.031"
E-HOLE POS. # 4:	PLUGGED	PLUGGED	PLUGGED	PLUGGED	PLUGGED
E-HOLE POS. # 5:	.031"	.031"	.031"	.033"	.031"
P.V.C.R. SIZE:	.059"	.059"	.059"	.059"	.059"
TRANSFER SLOT RES:	OPEN	OPEN	OPEN	OPEN	OPEN
IDLE FEED RESTRICTOR:	.029"	.036"	.037"	.038"	.037"
MAIN JETS PRI:	# 71	# 75	# 76	# 85	# 80
MAIN JETS SEC:	# 79	# 83	# 84	# 93	# 88
POWER VALVE PRI:	6.5 STD.	6.5 STD.	6.5 STD.	6.5 STD.	6.5 STD.
POWER VALVE SEC:	PLUGGED	PLUGGED	PLUGGED	PLUGGED	PLUGGED
LINKAGE TYPE:	PROG.	PROG.	PROG.	PROG.	PROG.
N&S SIZE/TYPE:	.110"-VITON	.110"-VITON	.110"-VITON	.110"-VITON	.110"-VITON
ACC. PUMP DIA. SIZE:	30 CC	30 CC	30 CC	30 CC	30 CC

RACE DEMON DRAG RACE GAS (DR)

MODEL #:	650	750	825	1000	820 AD
PART #:	2282010DR	2402010DR	2423010DR	2563010DR	2563020DR
VENTURI SIZE:	1.280"	1.400"	1.425"	1.562"	1.562"
IDLE AIR BLEEDS:	.070"	.070"	.067"	.070"	.070"
H.S. AIR BLEEDS:	.041"	.039"	.039"	.031"	.033"
BOOSTER TYPE:	DOWN LEG	DOWN LEG	DOWN LEG	DOWN LEG	ANNULAR
BOOSTER LEG:	.140"	.160"	.160"	.184"	STD.
SQUIRTER SIZE:	28 STD.	31 STD.	31 STD.	31 STD.	31 STD.
BASEPLATE COLOR:	SILVER	SILVER	BLACK	BLACK	BLACK
BUTTERFLY SIZE:	1-11/16"	1-11/16"	1-3/4"	1-3/4"	1-3/4"
AIR HOLE SIZE:	(4) .093"	(4) .093"	(4) .093"	(4) .093"	(4) .093"
PUMP CAM #:	# 330	# 330	# 330	# 330	# 330
PUMP CAM COLOR:	PINK	PINK	PINK	PINK	PINK
METERING BLOCK #:	A-12320	A-12320	A-12320	A-12320	A-12320
M-BLOCK COLOR:	SILVER	SILVER	SILVER	SILVER	SILVER
SIPHON BREAK:	.028"	.028"	.028"	.028"	.028"
E-HOLE POS. #1:	.031"	.031"	.031"	.031"	.031"
E-HOLE POS. #2:	PLUGGED	PLUGGED	PLUGGED	PLUGGED	PLUGGED
E-HOLE POS. #3:	.031"	.031"	.031"	.031"	.031"
E-HOLE POS. #4:	PLUGGED	PLUGGED	PLUGGED	PLUGGED	PLUGGED
E-HOLE POS. #5:	.031"	.031"	.031"	.033"	.031"
P.V.C.R. SIZE:	.059"	.059"	.059"	.059"	.059"
TRANSFER SLOT RES:	OPEN	OPEN	OPEN	OPEN	OPEN
IDLE FEED RESTRICTOR:	.029"	.036"	.037"	.038"	.037"
MAIN JETS PRI:	# 71	# 75	# 76	# 85	# 80
MAIN JETS SEC:	# 79 W/EXT	# 83 W/EXT	# 84 W/EXT	# 93 W/EXT	# 88 W/EXT
POWER VALVE PRI:	6.5 STD.	6.5 STD.	6.5 STD.	6.5 STD.	6.5 STD.
POWER VALVE SEC:	PLUGGED	PLUGGED	PLUGGED	PLUGGED	PLUGGED
LINKAGE TYPE:	PROG.	PROG.	PROG.	PROG.	PROG.
N&S SIZE/TYPE:	.110"-VITON	.110"-VITON	.110"-VITON	.110"-VITON	.110"-VITON
ACC. PUMP DIA. SIZE:	30 CC	30 CC	30 CC	30 CC	30 CC

RACE DEMON REMOVABLE SLEEVE DRAG RACE GAS (DR RS)

MODEL #:	675	775	825	975	1025	1050	820 AD	950 AD
PART #:	3282010DR	3402010DR	3423010DR	3503010DR	3563010DR	3593010DR	3563020DR	3593020DR
VENTURI SIZE:	1.280"	1.400"	1.425"	1.500"	1.562"	1.590"	1.562"	1.590"
VENTURI COLOR:	GREEN	RED	BLUE	GOLD	BLACK	SILVER	BLACK	SILVER
IDLE AIR BLEEDS:	.070"	.070"	.067"	.070"	.070"	.070"	.070"	.070"
H.S. AIR BLEEDS:	.041"	.039"	.039"	.039"	.039"	.031"	.033"	.035"
BOOSTER TYPE:	DOWN LEG	DOWN LEG	DOWN LEG	DOWN LEG	DOWN LEG	DOWN LEG	ANNULAR	ANNULAR
BOOSTER LEG:	.140"	.160"	.160"	.184"	.184"	.184"	STD.	STD.
SQUIRTER SIZE:	28 STD.	31 STD.	31 STD.	31 STD.	31 STD.	31 STD.	31 STD.	31 STD.
BASEPLATE COLOR:	SILVER	SILVER	BLACK	BLACK	BLACK	BLACK	BLACK	BLACK
BUTTERFLY SIZE:	1-11/16"	1-11/16"	1-3/4"	1-3/4"	1-3/4"	1-3/4"	1-3/4"	1-3/4"
AIR HOLE SIZE:	(4) .093"	(4) .093"	(4) .093"	(4) .093"	(4) .093"	(4) .093"	(4) .093"	(4) .093"
PUMP CAM #:	# 330	# 330	# 330	# 330	# 330	# 330	# 330	# 330
PUMP CAM COLOR:	PINK	PINK	PINK	PINK	PINK	PINK	PINK	PINK
METERING BLOCK #:	A-12320	A-12320	A-12320	A-12320	A-12320	A-12320	A-12320	A-12320
M-BLOCK COLOR:	SILVER	SILVER	SILVER	SILVER	SILVER	SILVER	SILVER	SILVER
SIPHON BREAK:	.028"	.028"	.028"	.028"	.028"	.028"	.028"	.028"
E-HOLE POS. # 1:	.031"	.031"	.031"	.031"	.031"	.031"	.031"	.031"
E-HOLE POS. # 2:	PLUGGED	PLUGGED	PLUGGED	PLUGGED	PLUGGED	PLUGGED	PLUGGED	PLUGGED
E-HOLE POS. # 3:	.031"	.031"	.031"	.031"	.031"	.031"	.031"	.031"
E-HOLE POS. # 4:	PLUGGED	PLUGGED	PLUGGED	PLUGGED	PLUGGED	PLUGGED	PLUGGED	PLUGGED
E-HOLE POS. # 5:	.031"	.031"	.031"	.031"	.033"	.033"	.031"	.031"
P.V.C.R. SIZE:	.059"	.059"	.059"	.059"	.059"	.059"	.059"	.059"
T.S. RES:	OPEN	OPEN	OPEN	OPEN	OPEN	OPEN	OPEN	OPEN
I.F. RES:	.029"	.036"	.037"	.037"	.038"	.038"	.037"	.037"
MAIN JETS PRI:	# 72	# 76	# 78	# 84	# 84	# 84	# 88	# 84
MAIN JETS SEC:	# 80 W/EXT	# 84 W/EXT	# 86 W/EXT	# 92 W/EXT	# 93 W/EXT	# 96 W/EXT	# 90 W/EXT	# 92 W/EXT
POWER VALVE PRI:	6.5 STD.	6.5 STD.	6.5 STD.	6.5 STD.	6.5 STD.	6.5 STD.	6.5 STD.	6.5 STD.
POWER VALVE SEC:	PLUGGED	PLUGGED	PLUGGED	PLUGGED	PLUGGED	PLUGGED	PLUGGED	PLUGGED
LINKAGE TYPE:	PROG.	PROG.	PROG.	PROG.	PROG.	PROG.	PROG.	PROG.
N&S SIZE/TYPE:	.110"-VITON	.110"-VITON	.110"-VITON	.110"-VITON	.110"-VITON	.110"-VITON	.110"-VITON	.110"-VITON
ACC. PUMP DIA. SIZE:	30 CC	30 CC	30 CC	30 CC	30 CC	30 CC	30 CC	30 CC

RACE DEMON REMOVEABLE SLEEVE ROAD RACE GAS (RR RS)

MODEL #:	675	775	825
PART #:	3282010RR	3402010RR	3423010RR
VENTURI SIZE:	1.280"	1.400"	1.425"
VENTURI COLOR:	GREEN	RED	BLUE
IDLE AIR BLEEDS:	.070"	.067"	.067"
H.S. AIR BLEEDS:	.041"	.039"	.039"
BOOSTER TYPE:	DOWN LEG	DOWN LEG	DOWN LEG
BOOSTER LEG:	.140"	.160"	.160"
SQUIRTER SIZE:	28 STD.	28 STD.	31 STD.
BASEPLATE COLOR:	SILVER	SILVER	BLACK
BUTTERFLY SIZE:	1-11/16"	1-11/16"	1-3/4"
AIR HOLE SIZE:	(4) .093"	(4) .093"	(4) .093"
PUMP CAM #:	# 330	# 330	# 330
PUMP CAM COLOR:	PINK	PINK	PINK
METERING BLOCK #:	A-12320	A-12320	A-12320
M-BLOCK COLOR:	SILVER	SILVER	SILVER
SIPHON BREAK:	.028"	.028"	.028"
E-HOLE POS. # 1:	.031"	.031"	.031"
E-HOLE POS. # 2:	PLUGGED	PLUGGED	PLUGGED
E-HOLE POS. # 3:	.031"	.031"	.031"
E-HOLE POS. # 4:	PLUGGED	PLUGGED	PLUGGED
E-HOLE POS. # 5:	.031"	.031"	.031"
P.V.C.R. SIZE:	.059"	.059"	.059"
T.S. RES:	OPEN	OPEN	OPEN
I.F. RES:	.029"	.037"	.037"
MAIN JETS PRI:	# 72	# 76	# 78
MAIN JETS SEC:	# 72	# 76	# 78
POWER VALVE PRI:	6.5 STD.	6.5 STD.	6.5 STD.
POWER VALVE SEC:	6.5 STD.	6.5 STD.	6.5 STD.
LINKAGE TYPE:	1-1	1-1	1-1
N&S SIZE/TYPE:	.110"-VITON	.110"-VITON	.110"-VITON
ACC. PUMP DIA. SIZE:	30 CC	30 CC	30 CC

How to Tune and Win with Demon Carburetors

RACE DEMON ROAD RACE GAS SPECIFICATIONS (RR)

MODEL #:	650	750	825
PART #:	2282010RR	2402010RR	2423010RR
VENTURI SIZE:	1.280"	1.400"	1.425"
IDLE AIR BLEEDS:	.070"	.067"	.067"
H.S. AIR BLEEDS:	.041"	.039"	.039"
BOOSTER TYPE:	DOWN LEG	DOWN LEG	DOWN LEG
BOOSTER LEG:	.140"	.160"	.160"
SQUIRTER SIZE:	28 STD.	31 STD.	31 STD.
BASEPLATE COLOR:	SILVER	SILVER	BLACK
BUTTERFLY SIZE:	1-11/16"	1-11/16"	1-3/4"
AIR HOLE SIZE:	(4) .093"	(4) .093"	(4) .093"
PUMP CAM #:	# 330	# 330	# 330
PUMP CAM COLOR:	PINK	PINK	PINK
METERING BLOCK #:	A-12320	A-12320	A-12320
M-BLOCK COLOR:	SILVER	SILVER	SILVER
SIPHON BREAK:	.028"	.028"	.028"
E-HOLE POS. # 1:	.031"	.031"	.031"
E-HOLE POS. # 2:	PLUGGED	PLUGGED	PLUGGED
E-HOLE POS. # 3:	.031"	.031"	.031"
E-HOLE POS. # 4:	PLUGGED	PLUGGED	PLUGGED
E-HOLE POS. # 5:	.031"	.031"	.031"
P.V.C.R. SIZE:	.059"	.059"	.059"
TRANSFER SLOT RES:	OPEN	OPEN	OPEN
IDLE FEED RESTRICTOR:	.029"	.037"	.037"
MAIN JETS PRI:	# 71	# 75	# 76
MAIN JETS SEC:	# 71	# 75	# 76
POWER VALVE PRI:	6.5 STD.	6.5 STD.	6.5 STD.
POWER VALVE SEC:	6.5 STD.	6.5 STD.	6.5 STD.
LINKAGE TYPE:	1-1	1-1	1-1
N&S SIZE/TYPE:	.110"-VITON	.110"-VITON	.110"-VITON
ACC. PUMP DIA. SIZE:	30 CC	30 CC	30 CC

RACE DEMON RS TUNNEL RAM GAS (TR)

MODEL #:	675	775	825	975	1025
PART #:	3282010TR	3402010TR	3423010TR	3503010TR	3563010TR
VENTURI SIZE:	1.280"	1.400"	1.425"	1.500"	1.562"
VENTURI COLOR:	GREEN	RED	BLUE	GOLD	BLACK
IDLE AIR BLEEDS:	.067"	.070"	.070"	.067"	.070"
H.S. AIR BLEEDS:	.033"	.031"	.035"	.035"	.031"
BOOSTER TYPE:	DOWN LEG	DOWN LEG	DOWN LEG	DOWN LEG	DOWN LEG
BOOSTER LEG:	.140"	.160"	.160"	.184"	.184"
SQUIRTER SIZE:	28 STD.	28 STD.	31 STD.	31 STD.	31 STD.
BASEPLATE COLOR:	SILVER	SILVER	BLACK	BLACK	BLACK
BUTTERFLY SIZE:	1-11/16"	1-11/16"	1-3/4"	1-3/4"	1-3/4"
AIR HOLE SIZE:	NONE	NONE	NONE	NONE	NONE
PUMP CAM #:	# 330	# 330	# 330	# 330	# 330
PUMP CAM COLOR:	PINK	PINK	PINK	PINK	PINK
METERING BLOCK #:	A-12320	A-12320	A-12320	A-12320	A-12320
M-BLOCK COLOR:	SILVER	SILVER	SILVER	SILVER	SILVER
SIPHON BREAK:	.028"	.028"	.028"	.028"	.028"
E-HOLE POS. # 1:	.031"	.031"	.031"	.031"	.031"
E-HOLE POS. # 2:	PLUGGED	PLUGGED	PLUGGED	PLUGGED	PLUGGED
E-HOLE POS. # 3:	.031"	.031"	.031"	.031"	.031"
E-HOLE POS. # 4:	PLUGGED	PLUGGED	PLUGGED	PLUGGED	PLUGGED
E-HOLE POS. # 5:	.031"	.031"	.031"	.031"	.033"
P.V.C.R. SIZE:	N/A	N/A	N/A	N/A	N/A
T.S. RES:	.076"	.063"	.076"	.076"	.063"
I.F. RES:	.029"	.035"	.035"	.035"	.033"
MAIN JETS PRI:	# 76	# 78	# 80	# 88	# 86
MAIN JETS SEC:	# 76	# 78	# 80	# 88	# 86
POWER VALVE PRI:	PLUGGED	PLUGGED	PLUGGED	PLUGGED	PLUGGED
POWER VALVE SEC:	PLUGGED	PLUGGED	PLUGGED	PLUGGED	PLUGGED
LINKAGE TYPE:	PROG.	PROG.	PROG.	PROG.	PROG.
N&S SIZE/TYPE:	.110"-VITON	.110"-VITON	.110"-VITON	.110"-VITON	.110"-VITON
ACC. PUMP DIA. SIZE:	30 CC	30 CC	30 CC	30 CC	30 CC

RACE DEMON TUNNEL RAM GAS (TR)

MODEL #:	650	750	825	1000
PART #:	2282010TR	2402010TR	2423010TR	2563010TR
VENTURI SIZE:	1.280"	1.400"	1.425"	1.562"
IDLE AIR BLEEDS:	.067"	.070"	.070"	.070"
H.S. AIR BLEEDS:	.033"	.031"	.035"	.031"
BOOSTER TYPE:	DOWN LEG	DOWN LEG	DOWN LEG	DOWN LEG
BOOSTER LEG:	.140"	.160"	.160"	.184"
SQUIRTER SIZE:	28 STD.	28 STD.	31 STD.	31 STD.
BASEPLATE COLOR:	SILVER	SILVER	BLACK	BLACK
BUTTERFLY SIZE:	1-11/16"	1-11/16"	1-3/4"	1-3/4"
AIR HOLE SIZE:	NONE	NONE	NONE	NONE
PUMP CAM #	# 330	# 330	# 330	# 330
PUMP CAM COLOR:	PINK	PINK	PINK	PINK
METERING BLOCK #:	A-12320	A-12320	A-12320	A-12320
M-BLOCK COLOR:	SILVER	SILVER	SILVER	SILVER
SIPHON BREAK:	.028"	.028"	.028"	.028"
E-HOLE POS. # 1:	.031"	.031"	.031"	.031"
E-HOLE POS. # 2:	PLUGGED	PLUGGED	PLUGGED	PLUGGED
E-HOLE POS. # 3:	.031"	.031"	.031"	.031"
E-HOLE POS. # 4:	PLUGGED	PLUGGED	PLUGGED	PLUGGED
E-HOLE POS. # 5:	.031"	.031"	.031"	.033"
P.V.C.R. SIZE:	N/A	N/A	N/A	N/A
TRANSFER SLOT RES:	.076"	.063"	.076"	.063"
IDLE FEED RESTRICTOR:	.029"	.035"	.035"	.033"
MAIN JETS PRI:	# 74	# 77	# 78	# 84
MAIN JETS SEC:	# 74	# 77	# 78	# 84
POWER VALVE PRI:	PLUGGED	PLUGGED	PLUGGED	PLUGGED
POWER VALVE SEC:	PLUGGED	PLUGGED	PLUGGED	PLUGGED
LINKAGE TYPE:	PROG.	PROG.	PROG.	PROG.
N&S SIZE/TYPE:	.110"-VITON	.110"-VITON	.110"-VITON	.110"-VITON
ACC. PUMP DIA. SIZE:	30 CC	30 CC	30 CC	30 CC

RACE DEMON OVAL TRACK GAS (OT)

MODEL #:	650	750	825	1000	820 AD
PART #:	2282010OT	2402010OT	2423010OT	2563010OT	2563020OT
VENTURI SIZE:	1.280"	1.400"	1.425"	1.562"	1.562"
IDLE AIR BLEEDS:	.070"	.070"	.067"	.070"	.070"
H.S. AIR BLEEDS:	.041"	.039"	.039"	.031"	.033"
BOOSTER TYPE:	DOWN LEG	DOWN LEG	DOWN LEG	DOWN LEG	ANNULAR
BOOSTER LEG:	.140"	.160"	.160"	.184"	STD.
SQUIRTER SIZE:	28 STD.	31 STD.	31 STD.	31 STD.	31 STD.
BASEPLATE COLOR:	SILVER	SILVER	BLACK	BLACK	BLACK
BUTTERFLY SIZE:	1-11/16"	1-11/16"	1-3/4"	1-3/4"	1-3/4"
AIR HOLE SIZE:	(4) .093"	(4) .093"	(4) .093"	(4) .093"	(4) .093"
PUMP CAM #:	# 330	# 330	# 330	# 330	# 330
PUMP CAM COLOR:	PINK	PINK	PINK	PINK	PINK
METERING BLOCK #:	A-12320	A-12320	A-12320	A-12320	A-12320
M-BLOCK COLOR:	SILVER	SILVER	SILVER	SILVER	SILVER
SIPHON BREAK:	.028"	.028"	.028"	.028"	.028"
E-HOLE POS. # 1:	.031"	.031"	.031"	.031"	.031"
E-HOLE POS. # 2:	PLUGGED	PLUGGED	PLUGGED	PLUGGED	PLUGGED
E-HOLE POS. # 3:	.031"	.031"	.031"	.031"	.031"
E-HOLE POS. # 4:	PLUGGED	PLUGGED	PLUGGED	PLUGGED	PLUGGED
E-HOLE POS. # 5:	.031"	.031"	.031"	.033"	.031"
P.V.C.R. SIZE:	.059"	.059"	.059"	.059"	.059"
TRANSFER SLOT RES:	OPEN	OPEN	OPEN	OPEN	OPEN
IDLE FEED RESTRICTOR:	.029"	.036"	.039"	.039"	.037"
MAIN JETS PRI:	# 71	# 75	# 76	# 85	# 80
MAIN JETS SEC:	# 71	# 75	# 76	# 85	# 80
POWER VALVE PRI:	6.5 STD.	6.5 STD.	6.5 STD.	6.5 STD.	6.5 STD.
POWER VALVE SEC:	6.5 STD.	6.5 STD.	6.5 STD.	6.5 STD.	6.5 STD.
LINKAGE TYPE:	1-1	1-1	1-1	1-1	1-1
N&S SIZE/TYPE:	.110"-VITON	.110"-VITON	.110"-VITON	.110"-VITON	.110"-VITON
ACC. PUMP DIA. SIZE:	30 CC	30 CC	30 CC	30 CC	30 CC

RACE DEMON REMOVEABLE SLEEVE TUNNEL RAM GAS (TR RS)

MODEL #:	675	775	825	975	1025
PART #:	3282010TR	3402010TR	3423010TR	3503010TR	3563010TR
VENTURI SIZE:	1.280"	1.400"	1.425"	1.500"	1.562"
VENTURI COLOR:	GREEN	RED	BLUE	GOLD	BLACK
IDLE AIR BLEEDS:	.067"	.070"	.070"	.067"	.070"
H.S. AIR BLEEDS:	.033"	.031"	.035"	.035"	.031"
BOOSTER TYPE:	DOWN LEG	DOWN LEG	DOWN LEG	DOWN LEG	DOWN LEG
BOOSTER LEG:	.140"	.160"	.160"	.184"	.184"
SQUIRTER SIZE:	28 STD.	28 STD.	31 STD.	31 STD.	31 STD.
BASEPLATE COLOR:	SILVER	SILVER	BLACK	BLACK	BLACK
BUTTERFLY SIZE:	1-11/16"	1-11/16"	1-3/4"	1-3/4"	1-3/4"
AIR HOLE SIZE:	NONE	NONE	NONE	NONE	NONE
PUMP CAM #	# 330	# 330	# 330	# 330	# 330
PUMP CAM COLOR:	PINK	PINK	PINK	PINK	PINK
METERING BLOCK #:	A-12320	A-12320	A-12320	A-12320	A-12320
M-BLOCK COLOR:	SILVER	SILVER	SILVER	SILVER	SILVER
SIPHON BREAK:	.028"	.028"	.028"	.028"	.028"
E-HOLE POS. # 1:	.031"	.031"	.031"	.031"	.031"
E-HOLE POS. # 2:	PLUGGED	PLUGGED	PLUGGED	PLUGGED	PLUGGED
E-HOLE POS. # 3:	.031"	.031"	.031"	.031"	.031"
E-HOLE POS. # 4:	PLUGGED	PLUGGED	PLUGGED	PLUGGED	PLUGGED
E-HOLE POS. # 5:	.031"	.031"	.031"	.031"	.033"
P.V.C.R. SIZE:	N/A	N/A	N/A	N/A	N/A
T.S. RES:	.076"	.063"	.076"	.076"	.063"
I.F. RES:	.029"	.035"	.035"	.035"	.033"
MAIN JETS PRI:	# 76	# 78	# 80	# 88	# 86
MAIN JETS SEC:	# 76	# 78	# 80	# 88	# 86
POWER VALVE PRI:	PLUGGED	PLUGGED	PLUGGED	PLUGGED	PLUGGED
POWER VALVE SEC:	PLUGGED	PLUGGED	PLUGGED	PLUGGED	PLUGGED
LINKAGE TYPE:	PROG.	PROG.	PROG.	PROG.	PROG.
N&S SIZE/TYPE:	.110"-VITON	.110"-VITON	.110"-VITON	.110"-VITON	.110"-VITON
ACC. PUMP DIA. SIZE:	30 CC	30 CC	30 CC	30 CC	30 CC

RACE DEMON REMOVEABLE SLEEVE OVAL TRACK GAS (OT RS)

MODEL #:	675	775	825	975	1025	1050	820 AD	950 AD
PART #:	3282010OT	3402010OT	3423010OT	3503010OT	3563010OT	3593010OT	3563020OT	3593020OT
VENTURI SIZE:	1.280"	1.400"	1.425"	1.500"	1.562"	1.590"	1.562"	1.590"
VENTURI COLOR:	GREEN	RED	BLUE	GOLD	BLACK	SILVER	BLACK	SILVER
IDLE AIR BLEEDS:	.070"	.070"	.067"	.070"	.070"	.070"	.070"	.070"
H.S. AIR BLEEDS:	.041"	.039"	.039"	.039"	.031"	.031"	.033"	.035"
BOOSTER TYPE:	DOWN LEG	DOWN LEG	DOWN LEG	DOWN LEG	DOWN LEG	DOWN LEG	ANNULAR	ANNULAR
BOOSTER LEG:	.140"	.160"	.160"	.184"	.184"	.184"	STD.	STD.
SQUIRTER SIZE:	28 STD.	31 STD.	31 STD.	31 STD.	31 STD.	31 STD.	31 STD.	31 STD.
BASEPLATE COLOR:	SILVER	SILVER	BLACK	BLACK	BLACK	BLACK	BLACK	BLACK
BUTTERFLY SIZE:	1-11/16"	1-11/16"	1-3/4"	1-3/4"	1-3/4"	1-3/4"	1-3/4"	1-3/4"
AIR HOLE SIZE:	(4) .093"	(4) .093"	(4) .093"	(4) .093"	(4) .093"	(4) .093"	(4) .093"	(4) .093"
PUMP CAM #	# 330	# 330	# 330	# 330	# 330	# 330	# 330	# 330
PUMP CAM COLOR:	PINK	PINK	PINK	PINK	PINK	PINK	PINK	PINK
METERING BLOCK #	A-12320	A-12320	A-12320	A-12320	A-12320	A-12320	A-12320	A-12320
M-BLOCK COLOR:	SILVER	SILVER	SILVER	SILVER	SILVER	SILVER	SILVER	SILVER
SIPHON BREAK:	.028"	.028"	.028"	.028"	.028"	.028"	.028"	.028"
E-HOLE POS. # 1:	.031"	.031"	.031"	.031"	.031"	.031"	.031"	.031"
E-HOLE POS. # 2:	PLUGGED	PLUGGED	PLUGGED	PLUGGED	PLUGGED	PLUGGED	PLUGGED	PLUGGED
E-HOLE POS. # 3:	.031"	.031"	.031"	.031"	.031"	.031"	.031"	.031"
E-HOLE POS. # 4:	PLUGGED	PLUGGED	PLUGGED	PLUGGED	PLUGGED	PLUGGED	PLUGGED	PLUGGED
E-HOLE POS. # 5:	.031"	.031"	.031"	.031"	.033"	.031"	.031"	.031"
P.V.C.R. SIZE:	.059"	.059"	.059"	.059"	.059"	.059"	.059"	.059"
T.S. RES:	OPEN	OPEN	OPEN	OPEN	OPEN	OPEN	OPEN	OPEN
I.F. RES:	.029"	.036"	.039"	.039"	.039"	.039"	.037"	.037"
MAIN JETS PRI:	# 72	# 76	# 78	# 84	# 85	# 88	# 82	# 84
MAIN JETS SEC:	# 72	# 76	# 78	# 84	# 85	# 88	# 82	# 84
POWER VALVE PRI:	6.5 STD.	6.5 STD.	6.5 STD.	6.5 STD.	6.5 STD.	6.5 STD.	6.5 STD.	6.5 STD.
POWER VALVE SEC:	6.5 STD.	6.5 STD.	6.5 STD.	6.5 STD.	6.5 STD.	6.5 STD.	6.5 STD.	6.5 STD.
LINKAGE TYPE:	1-1	1-1	1-1	1-1	1-1	1-1	1-1	1-1
N&S SIZE/TYPE:	.110"-VITON	.110"-VITON	.110"-VITON	.110"-VITON	.110"-VITON	.110"-VITON	.110"-VITON	.110"-VITON
ACC. PUMP DIA. SIZE:	30 CC	30 CC	30 CC	30 CC	30 CC	30 CC	30 CC	30 CC

RACE DEMON DRAG RACE ALKY (DR)

MODEL #:	650	750	825
PART #:	2282015DR	2402015DR	2423015DR
VENTURI SIZE:	1.280"	1.400"	1.425"
IDLE AIR BLEEDS:	.052"	.046"	.046"
H.S. AIR BLEEDS:	.037"	.033"	.033"
BOOSTER TYPE:	DOWN LEG	DOWN LEG	DOWN LEG
BOOSTER LEG:	.184"	.189" DBL	.189" DBL
SQUIRTER SIZE:	45 STD.	52 STD.	52 STD.
BASEPLATE COLOR:	SILVER	SILVER	BLACK
BUTTERFLY SIZE:	1-11/16"	1-11/16"	1-3/4"
AIR HOLE SIZE:	(4) .093"	(4) .093"	(4) .093"
PUMP CAM #	# 330	# 330	# 330
PUMP CAM COLOR:	PINK	PINK	PINK
METERING BLOCK #:	B-12325	B-12325	B-12325
M-BLOCK COLOR:	BLACK	BLACK	BLACK
SIPHON BREAK:	.028"	.026"	.026"
E-HOLE POS. #1:	.028"	.028"	.028"
E-HOLE POS. #2:	.028"	.028"	.028"
E-HOLE POS. #3:	.028"	.028"	.028"
E-HOLE POS. #4:	PLUGGED	PLUGGED	PLUGGED
P.V.C.R. SIZE:	N/A	N/A	N/A
TRANSFER SLOT RES:	OPEN	OPEN	OPEN
IDLE FEED RESTRICTOR:	.063"	.063"	.063"
MAIN JETS PRI:	.140"	.185"	.185"
MAIN JETS SEC:	.140" W/EXT	.185" W/EXT	.185" W/EXT
POWER VALVE PRI:	PLUGGED	PLUGGED	PLUGGED
POWER VALVE SEC:	PLUGGED	PLUGGED	PLUGGED
LINKAGE TYPE:	1-1	1-1	1-1
N&S SIZE/TYPE:	.150"-S/S	.150"-S/S	.150"-S/S
ACC. PUMP DIA. SIZE:	30 CC	30 CC	30 CC

RACE DEMON REMOVEABLE SLEEVE DRAG RACE ALKY (DR RS)

MODEL #:	675	775	825	975
PART #:	3282015DR	3402015DR	3423015DR	3503015DR
VENTURI SIZE:	1.280"	1.400"	1.425"	1.500"
VENTURI COLOR:	GREEN	RED	BLUE	GOLD
IDLE AIR BLEEDS:	.052"	.046"	.046"	.046"
H.S. AIR BLEEDS:	.037"	.033"	.033"	.028"
BOOSTER TYPE:	DOWN LEG	DOWN LEG	DOWN LEG	DOWN LEG
BOOSTER LEG:	.184"	.189" DBL	.189" DBL	.193" DBL
SQUIRTER SIZE:	45 STD.	52 STD.	52 STD.	45 STD.
BASEPLATE COLOR:	SILVER	SILVER	BLACK	BLACK
BUTTERFLY SIZE:	1-11/16"	1-11/16"	1-3/4"	1-3/4"
AIR HOLE SIZE:	(4) .093"	(4) .093"	(4) .093"	(4) .093"
PUMP CAM #:	# 330	# 330	# 330	# 330
PUMP CAM COLOR:	PINK	PINK	PINK	PINK
METERING BLOCK #:	B-12325	B-12325	B-12325	B-12325
M-BLOCK COLOR:	BLACK	BLACK	BLACK	BLACK
SIPHON BREAK:	.028"	.026"	.026"	.026"
E-HOLE POS. # 1:	.028"	.028"	.028"	.028"
E-HOLE POS. # 2:	.028"	.028"	.028"	.028"
E-HOLE POS. # 3:	.028"	.028"	.028"	.028"
E-HOLE POS. # 4:	PLUGGED	PLUGGED	PLUGGED	PLUGGED
E-HOLE POS. # 5:	N/A	N/A	N/A	N/A
P.V.C.R. SIZE:	N/A	N/A	N/A	N/A
T.S. RES:	OPEN	OPEN	OPEN	OPEN
I.F. RES:	.063"	.063"	.063"	.063"
MAIN JETS PRI:	.144"	.189"	.189"	.213"
MAIN JETS SEC:	.144" W/EXT	.189" W/EXT	.189" W/EXT	.213" W/EXT
POWER VALVE PRI:	PLUGGED	PLUGGED	PLUGGED	PLUGGED
POWER VALVE SEC:	PLUGGED	PLUGGED	PLUGGED	PLUGGED
LINKAGE TYPE:	1-1	1-1	1-1	1-1
N&S SIZE/TYPE:	.150"-S/S	.150"-S/S	.150"-S/S	.150"-S/S
ACC. PUMP DIA. SIZE:	30 CC	30 CC	30 CC	30 CC

RACE DEMON OVAL TRACK ALKY (OT)

MODEL #:	650	750	825	1000
PART #:	2282015OT	2402015OT	2423015OT	2563015OT
VENTURI SIZE:	1.280"	1.400"	1.425"	1.562"
IDLE AIR BLEEDS:	.067"	.067"	.067"	.063"
H.S. AIR BLEEDS:	.032"	.033"	.033"	.028"
BOOSTER TYPE:	DOWN LEG	DOWN LEG	DOWN LEG	DOWN LEG
BOOSTER LEG:	.184"	.189"	.189"	.193" DBL
SQUIRTER SIZE:	40 T.T.	40 T.T.	42 T.T.	45 T.T.
BASEPLATE COLOR:	SILVER	SILVER	BLACK	BLACK
BUTTERFLY SIZE:	1-11/16"	1-11/16"	1-3/4"	1-3/4"
AIR HOLE SIZE	(4) .093"	(4) .093"	(4) .093"	(4) .093"
PUMP CAM #:	# 330	# 330	# 330	# 330
PUMP CAM COLOR:	PINK	PINK	PINK	PINK
METERING BLOCK #:	A-12325	A-12325	A-12325	B-12325
M-BLOCK COLOR:	BLACK	BLACK	BLACK	BLACK
SIPHON BREAK:	NONE	NONE	NONE	NONE
E-HOLE POS. # 1:	.025"	.028"	.028"	.028"
E-HOLE POS. # 2:	.028"	.028"	.028"	.028"
E-HOLE POS. # 3:	.028"	.028"	.028"	.028"
E-HOLE POS. # 4:	PLUGGED	PLUGGED	PLUGGED	PLUGGED
E-HOLE POS. # 5:	PLUGGED	PLUGGED	PLUGGED	N/A
P.V.C.R. SIZE:	.116"	.116"	.116"	.116"
TRANSFER SLOT RES:	OPEN	OPEN	OPEN	OPEN
IDLE FEED RESTRICTIOR:	.067"	.067"	.067"	.067"
MAIN JETS PRI:	.136"	.161"	.161"	.201"
MAIN JETS SEC:	.136"	.161"	.161"	.201"
POWER VALVE PRI:	6.5 HI FLO	6.5 HI FLO	6.5 HI FLO	6.5 HI FLO
POWER VALVE SEC:	6.5 HI FLO	6.5 HI FLO	6.5 HI FLO	6.5 HI FLO
LINKAGE TYPE:	1-1	1-1	1-1	1-1
N&S SIZE/TYPE:	.150"-S/S	.150"-S/S	.150"-S/S	.150"-S/S
ACC. PUMP DIA. SIZE:	30 CC	30 CC	30 CC	30 CC

RACE DEMON REMOVEABLE SLEEVE OVAL TRACK ALKY (OT RS)

MODEL #:	675	775	825	975	1025
PART #:	3282015OT	3402015OT	3423015OT	3503015OT	3563015OT
VENTURI SIZE:	1.280"	1.400"	1.425"	1.500"	1.562"
VENTURI COLOR:	GREEN	RED	BLUE	GOLD	BLACK
IDLE AIR BLEEDS:	.067"	.067"	.067"	.063"	.063"
H.S. AIR BLEEDS:	.032"	.033"	.033"	.028"	.028"
BOOSTER TYPE:	DOWN LEG	DOWN LEG	DOWN LEG	DOWN LEG	DOWN LEG
BOOSTER LEG:	.184"	.189"	.189"	.193" DBL	.193" DBL
SQUIRTER SIZE:	40 T.T.	40 T.T.	42 T.T.	45 T.T.	45 T.T.
BASEPLATE COLOR:	SILVER	SILVER	BLACK	BLACK	BLACK
BUTTERFLY SIZE:	1-11/16"	1-11/16"	1-3/4"	1-3/4"	1-3/4"
AIR HOLE SIZE:	(4) .093"	(4) .093"	(4) .093"	(4) .093"	.093"
PUMP CAM #:	# 330	# 330	# 330	# 330	# 330
PUMP CAM COLOR:	PINK	PINK	PINK	PINK	PINK
METERING BLOCK #:	A-12325	A-12325	A-12325	B-12325	B-12325
M-BLOCK COLOR:	BLACK	BLACK	BLACK	BLACK	BLACK
SIPHON BREAK:	NONE	NONE	NONE	.026"	NONE
E-HOLE POS. # 1:	.028"	.028"	.028"	.028"	.028"
E-HOLE POS. # 2:	.028"	.028"	.028"	.028"	.028"
E-HOLE POS. # 3:	.028"	.028"	.028"	.028"	.028"
E-HOLE POS. # 4:	PLUGGED	PLUGGED	PLUGGED	PLUGGED	PLUGGED
E-HOLE POS. # 5:	PLUGGED	PLUGGED	PLUGGED	N/A	N/A
P.V.C.R. SIZE:	.116"	.116"	.116"	.116"	.116"
T.S. RES:	OPEN	OPEN	OPEN	OPEN	OPEN
I.F. RES:	.067"	.067"	.067"	.070"	.067"
MAIN JETS PRI:	.144"	.169"	.169"	.201"	.209"
MAIN JETS SEC:	.144"	.169"	.169"	.201"	.209"
POWER VALVE PRI:	6.5 HI FLO	6.5 HI FLO	6.5 HI FLO	6.5 HI FLO	6.5 HI FLO
POWER VALVE SEC:	6.5 HI FLO	6.5 HI FLO	6.5 HI FLO	6.5 HI FLO	6.5 HI FLO
LINKAGE TYPE:	1-1	1-1	1-1	1-1	1-1
N&S SIZE/TYPE:	.150"-S/S	.150"-S/S	.150"-S/S	.150"-S/S	.150"-S/S
ACC. PUMP DIA. SIZE:	30 CC	30 CC	30 CC	30 CC	30 CC

RACE DEMON REMOVEABLE SLEEVE BLOWER CARB (BC RS)

MODEL #:	675	775	825	975	1025
PART #:	3282010BC	3402010BC	3423010BC	3503010BC	3563010BC
VENTURI SIZE:	1.280"	1.400"	1.425"	1.500"	1.425"
VENTURI COLOR:	GREEN	RED	BLUE	GOLD	BLUE
IDLE AIR BLEEDS:	.067"	.070"	.070"	.067"	.070"
H.S. AIR BLEEDS:	.033"	.031"	.035"	.035"	.028"
BOOSTER TYPE:	DOWN LEG	DOWN LEG	DOWN LEG	DOWN LEG	DOWN LEG
BOOSTER LEG:	.140"	.160"	.160"	.184"	.184"
SQUIRTER SIZE:	28 STD.	28 STD.	31 STD.	31 STD.	31 STD.
BASEPLATE COLOR:	SILVER	SILVER	BLACK	BLACK	BLACK
BUTTERFLY SIZE:	1-11/16"	1-11/16"	1-3/4"	1-3/4"	1-3/4"
AIR HOLE SIZE:	NONE	NONE	NONE	NONE	NONE
PUMP CAM #:	# 330	# 330	# 330	# 330	# 330
PUMP CAM COLOR:	PINK	PINK	PINK	PINK	PINK
METERING BLOCK #:	A-12320	A-12320	A-12320	A-12320	A-12320
M-BLOCK COLOR:	SILVER	SILVER	SILVER	SILVER	SILVER
SIPHON BREAK:	.028"	.028"	.028"	.028"	.028"
E-HOLE POS. # 1:	.031"	.031"	.031"	.031"	.031"
E-HOLE POS. # 2:	PLUGGED	PLUGGED	PLUGGED	PLUGGED	PLUGGED
E-HOLE POS. # 3:	.031"	.031"	.031"	.031"	.031"
E-HOLE POS. # 4:	PLUGGED	PLUGGED	PLUGGED	PLUGGED	PLUGGED
E-HOLE POS. # 5:	.031"	.031"	.031"	.031"	.033"
P.V.C.R. SIZE:	.059"	.059"	.059"	.059"	.059"
TRANSFER SLOT RES:	.076"	.063"	.076"	.063"	.076"
IDLE FEED RESTRICTOR:	.029"	.035"	.035"	.038"	.038"
MAIN JETS PRI:	# 70	# 74	# 76	# 82	# 82
MAIN JETS SEC:	# 78	# 82	# 84	# 90	# 90
POWER VALVE PRI:	4.5 STD.	4.5 STD.	4.5 STD.	4.5 STD.	4.5 STD.
POWER VALVE SEC:	PLUGGED	PLUGGED	PLUGGED	PLUGGED	PLUGGED
LINKAGE TYPE:	1-1	1-1	1-1	1-1	1-1
N&S SIZE/TYPE:	.110"-VITON	.110" VITON	.110"-VITON	.110" VITON	.110"-VITON
ACC. PUMP DIA. SIZE:	30 CC	30 CC	30 CC	30 CC	30 CC

RACE DEMON REMOVEABLE SLEEVE GENERAL COMPETITION GAS (GC RS)

MODEL #:	675	775	825	975	1025	1050	820 AD	950 AD
PART #:	3282010GC	3402010GC	3423010GC	3503010GC	3563010GC	3593010GC	3563020GC	3593020GC
VENTURI SIZE:	1.280"	1.400"	1.425"	1.500"	1.562"	1.590"	1.562"	1.590"
VENTURI COLOR:	GREEN	RED	BLUE	GOLD	BLACK	SILVER	BLACK	SILVER
IDLE AIR BLEEDS:	.070"	.070"	.067"	.070"	.070"	.070"	.070"	.070"
H.S. AIR BLEEDS:	.041"	.039"	.039"	.039"	.031"	.031"	.033"	.035"
BOOSTER TYPE:	DOWN LEG	DOWN LEG	DOWN LEG	DOWN LEG	DOWN LEG	DOWN LEG	ANNULAR	ANNULAR
BOOSTER LEG:	.140"	.160"	.160"	.184"	.184"	.184"	STD.	STD.
SQUIRTER SIZE:	28 STD.	31 STD.	31 STD.	31 STD.	31 STD.	31 STD.	31 STD.	31 STD.
BASEPLATE COLOR:	SILVER	SILVER	BLACK	BLACK	BLACK	BLACK	BLACK	BLACK
BUTTERFLY SIZE:	1-11/16"	1-11/16"	1-3/4"	1-3/4"	1-3/4"	1-3/4"	1-3/4"	1-3/4"
AIR HOLE SIZE:	NONE	NONE	NONE	NONE	NONE	NONE	NONE	NONE
PUMP CAM #:	# 330	# 330	# 330	# 330	# 330	# 330	# 330	# 330
PUMP CAM COLOR:	PINK	PINK	PINK	PINK	PINK	PINK	PINK	PINK
METERING BLOCK #:	A-12320	A-12320	A-12320	A-12320	A-12320	A-12320	A-12320	A-12320
M-BLOCK COLOR:	SILVER	SILVER	SILVER	SILVER	SILVER	SILVER	SILVER	SILVER
SIPHON BREAK:	.028"	.028"	.028"	.028"	..028"	.028"	.028"	.028"
E-HOLE POS. # 1:	.031"	.031"	.031"	.031"	.031"	.031"	.031"	.031"
E-HOLE POS. # 2:	PLUGGED	PLUGGED	PLUGGED	PLUGGED	PLUGGED	PLUGGED	PLUGGED	PLUGGED
E-HOLE POS. # 3:	.031"	.031"	.031"	.031"	.031"	.031"	.031"	.031"
E-HOLE POS. # 4:	PLUGGED	PLUGGED	PLUGGED	PLUGGED	PLUGGED	PLUGGED	PLUGGED	PLUGGED
E-HOLE POS. # 5:	.031"	.031"	.031"	.031"	.033"	.033"	.031"	.031"
P.V.C.R. SIZE:	.059"	.059"	.059"	.059"	.059"	.059"	.059"	.059"
T.S. RES:	OPEN	OPEN	OPEN	OPEN	OPEN	OPEN	OPEN	OPEN
I.F. RES:	.029"	.036"	.037"	.037"	.038"	.038"	.037"	.037"
MAIN JETS PRI:	# 72	# 76	# 78	# 84	# 84	# 88	# 82	# 84
MAIN JETS SEC:	# 80	# 84	# 86	# 92	# 93	# 96	# 90	# 92
POWER VALVE PRI:	6.5 STD.	6.5 STD.	6.5 STD.	6.5 STD.	6.5 STD.	6.5 STD.	6.5 STD.	6.5 STD.
POWER VALVE SEC:	PLUGGED	PLUGGED	PLUGGED	PLUGGED	PLUGGED	PLUGGED	PLUGGED	PLUGGED
LINKAGE TYPE:	PROG.	PROG.	PROG.	PROG.	PROG.	PROG.	PROG.	PROG.
N&S SIZE/TYPE:	.110"-VITON	.110"-VITON	.110"-VITON	.110"-VITON	.110"-VITON	.110"-VITON	.110"-VITON	.110"-VITON
ACC. PUMP DIA. SIZE:	30 CC	30 CC	30 CC	30 CC	30 CC	30 CC	30 CC	30 CC

How to Tune and Win with Demon Carburetors

How to Tune & Win with DEMON CARBURETORS

King Demon

Designed for the most powerful race engines, the King Demon stands alone as the most advanced carburetor of its kind. Designed as a direct replacement for a Holley® Dominator®, it uses the 4500-series intake manifold bolt pattern and boasts removable boosters and deep streamlined air intakes, along with other traditional Demon features. All King Demons are manufactured from aluminum instead of ZA-3 due to their size as a weight-saving measure, but they still employ the Demon exclusive ConcentraCast method that eliminates all parting lines and core shift.

The King Demon is available in three different classifications: general competition, tunnel ram, and drag race. None of the classifications offer vacuum port access.

General Competition Gasoline (GC)

These carburetors are designed for good idle quality and driveability while providing outstanding performance on a large-cubic-inch engine. The model designations for this classification are listed as a 1090 AD, 1090 STD, and 1190 AD. The AD and STD suffixes denotes the use of annular and straight boosters, respectively.

The venturi size is considerably larger than those of the other Demons, with both 1090 models using a 1.720-inch diameter, and the 1190 AD a huge 1.812-inch dimension. The idle air bleeds are 0.046 inch for the 1090 entries and 0.040 inch for the 1190 AD. Intermediate circuit air bleeds are 0.043 inch for the 1190 AD and are enlarged to 0.070 inch for the other two models. High-speed air bleeds are 0.029 inch for the 1090s and are enlarged only 0.001 from that specification for the 1190 AD. The booster-leg dimension for all three models is fixed at 0.169 inch. All King Demon boosters feature an additional leg as a structural support due to the size of the venturi.

The squirter is fed by a 50cc pump cover and has a discharge orifice dimension of 0.035 inch for the two 1090 models; this steps up to 0.042 inch on the 1190 AD. No air holes are offered in the throttle plates, but as with the companion Demons, Spring 2001 production will feature the Demon exclusive idle air bypass passage with tunable orifice dimension.

A King Demon exclusive is the use of a yellow part number 643 accelerator pump cam on the A-12330 metering block assembly. This block is silver and has four emulsion orifices, all of which are used. The emulsion hole dimension is 0.029 inch in all positions and for all three models of GC King Demons. The standard 0.028-inch siphon break is sufficient for these calibrations and is used across the range of models. The IFR was calculated to be 0.029 inch for all GC models, and no transfer slot restrictor is employed. The intermediate circuit uses a 0.040-inch pickup for all three calibrations, but the intermediate feed restrictor is dimensioned at 0.046 inch for the 1090 series, 0.063 inch on the 1190 AD. All use square jetting and no power valves, along with a progressive linkage. The needle-and-seat assembly is

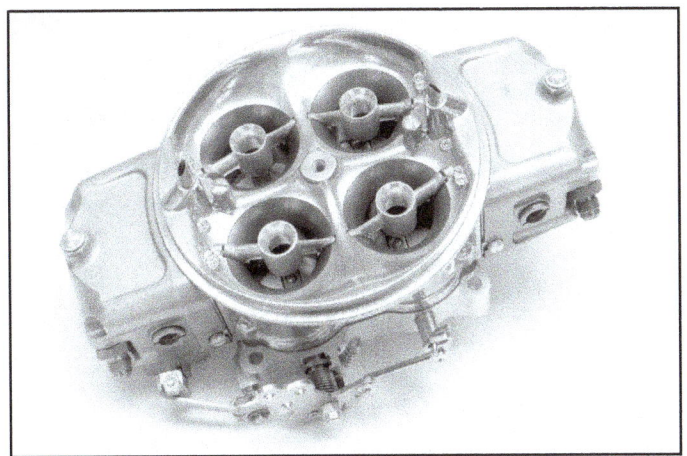

The King Demon can be identified by its size and additional support leg on the boosters.

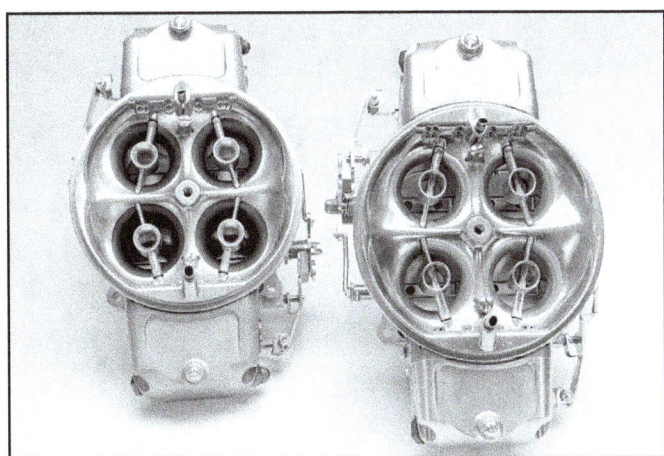

The King Demon is offered with either fixed or removable venturis.

of the Viton variety and is a large-capacity 0.130-inch dimension.

Drag Race
Removable Sleeve (DR RS)

Single four-barrel carburetors are provided with jet extensions, clearanced floats, and specific fuel-curve calibrations to promote a clean idle, crisp throttle response, and consistent ETs. The perfect choice for a bracket or super-class drag car.

The unique needs of the drag race market are met with eight DR RS offerings: model designations 795 AD, 895 AD, 995 AD, 995 ST, 1095 AD, 1095 ST, 1195 AD, and 1295 AD. The venturi dimensions are as follows: 795 AD, 1.500 inches; 895 AD, 1.562 inches; 995 AD, 1.625 inches; 995 ST, 1.625 inches; 1095 AD, 1.720 inches; 1095 ST, 1.720 inches; 1195 AD, 1.812 inches; 1295 AD, 1.838 inches.

Idle air bleed dimensions are 0.046 inch for all calibrations except the 1195 AD. The intermediate circuit air bleed is 0.070 inch for all except the 1195 AD and 1295 AD, which use 0.043 and 0.035 inch, respectively. High-speed air bleeds vary from 0.028 inch up to 0.035 inch depending on the model and should be referenced from the specifications chart. Both annular discharge and straight boosters use a 0.169-inch leg dimension. The butterfly size is 1.800 inch for the 795 and 895, and the rest use the large 2.00-inch version. Likewise, the two smaller models are equipped for power valves in the primary metering block with a 6.5-inch mercury opening calibration. All linkages are of the progressive style, and the obligatory King Demon 50cc accelerator pump cover is used.

The King Demon removable sleeve dimension are color coded as follows: 1.500 inches, green; 1.562 inches, red; 1.625 inches, black; 1.720 inches, blue; 1.812 inches, gold; 1.838 inches, silver.

The King Demon float bowls are unique and are marked for identification.

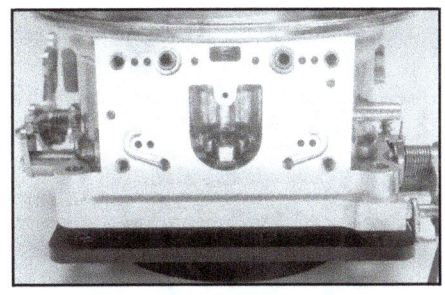

The King Demon main body is constructed from aluminum for weight savings. The fish-hook passage connects the intermediate circuit to the metering block.

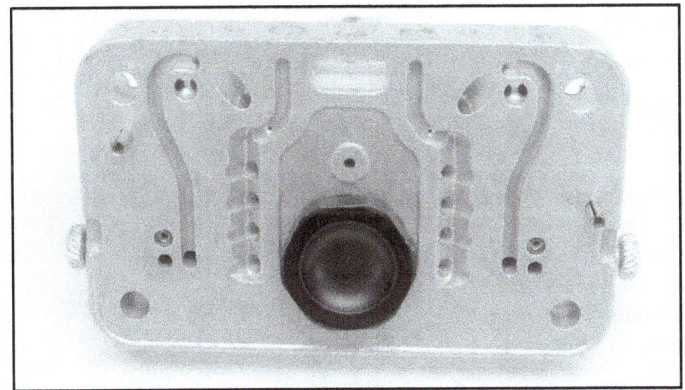

The King Demon uses unique metering block assemblies. The shepherd's hook passage is for the intermediate circuit.

All air bleeds are threaded for easy tuning. The bleed closest to the bowl vent is for the intermediate circuit.

How to Tune and Win with Demon Carburetors

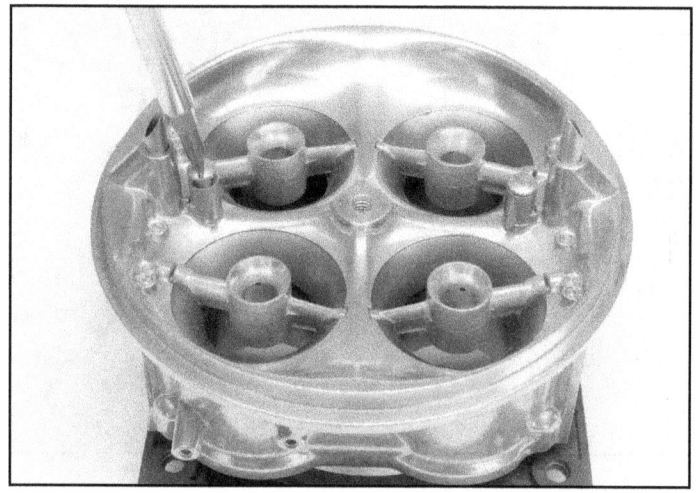

Squirters are easily tuned on both the primary and secondary barrels.

RS models have color-coded venturis for easy identification.

The venturis are replaced through the bottom of the main body.

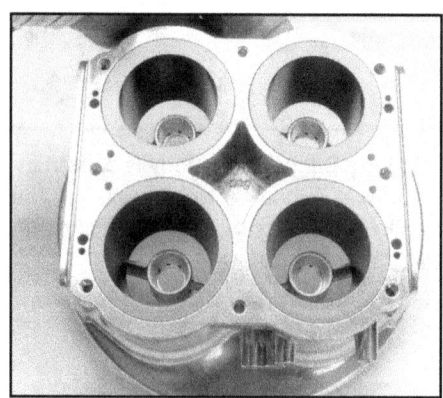

The venturis are stepped and lock in place. Note the discharge holes in annular boosters.

Tunnel Ram Removable Sleeve (TR RS)

These models are calibrated to function in matched pairs on 2 x 4 intake manifolds where the carburetors are mounted sideways. Sharing the unique design attention to the float assemblies as other Demon tunnel ram applications, three different calibrations are offered. A 1095 AD and ST offer annular discharge and straight boosters, respectively. A 1195 AD is the largest of the TR RS models. The venturi size is 1.720 inch for the two 1095 models, and the 1195 AD has 1.812-inch venturis. The venturi insert color is blue for the 1.720-inch size; the 1195 uses a gold color. The butterfly size is shared by all three and measures 2.00 inches. The A-12330 metering block assembly uses 0.029-inch emulsion holes in all positions and for all models. Square jetting is engineered into the design, and the specifications chart should be referenced for the actual jet sizes.

INTERMEDIATE CIRCUIT

As engines grow larger, so do the dimensions of the venturi and butterflies to provide a sufficient amount of area so as not to limit the VE. At some point this presents a problem in providing the proper amount of fuel during throttle tip-in or transition, as the signal produced at low piston speeds is usually very weak. In most instances, the accelerator pump squirter cannot cover the lean spot created during the transition between the idle and main metering circuits when the throttle is opened.

To alleviate this and produce smooth driveability during low-engine-speed operation, Demon engineers included an additional method of providing enrichment, identified as an intermediate circuit. It functions to provide the needed fuel that the squirter can't supply. To accomplish this, an additional pickup path is employed for the fuel and includes an intermediate tube that is installed in the center section. It can be considered an additional main metering circuit that is designed to pull fuel as the butterfly sweeps past the intermediate transfer slot that is located between the idle and main metering positions.

Fuel is supplied to the intermediate well from the float bowl through an additional pickup orifice located next to the main jet. It functions under the same theory as a main metering circuit jet but is smaller in physical dimensions. The orifice is threaded for easy tuning and is listed in the specifications as Int. pickup.

As with the idle circuit, a restrictor is in place and is identified as the Int.

The additional leg on the King Demon booster is for support and carries no fuel.

84 *How to Tune and Win with Demon Carburetors*

The Blasi family uses the tuneability of a three-circuit King Demon for winning performance with its Van Iderstine Speed Shop-sponsored 1968 Chevelle.

All service procedures are shared with the other Demon models.

feed restrictor. It's located on the main body side of the metering block assembly. An air bleed for the intermediate circuit is situated on the top of the main body casting nearest the bowl vent.

Since the intermediate circuit discharges fuel at the base of the main body venturi, the circuit is functional at all engine RPMs that expose the intermediate transfer slot. As with the main metering circuit, the diameter of the air bleed and the pickup orifice controls the timing and amount of fuel delivered. This feature is standard on all King Demons, allowing the third or intermediate circuit to provide another area of fine tuning and ability to increase the performance of the engine.

The majority of the King Demon development was done with Barry Grant's Pro Stock Oldsmobile.

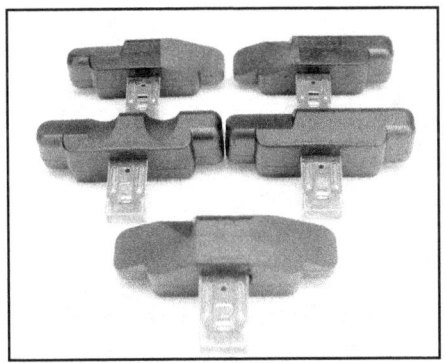

Demon installs specific floats for each application.

The King Demon is the ultimate in racing carburetors.

Demon technical representative Travis Abernathy races with the parts he sells. His Super Gas GTO is Pontiac- and King Demon-powered.

How to Tune and Win with Demon Carburetors

KING DEMON GENERAL COMPETITION GAS SPECIFICATIONS (GC)

MODEL#:	1090 AD	1090 STD	1190 AD
PART #:	8728020GC	8728030GC	8838020GC
VENTURI SIZE:	1.720"	1.720"	1.812"
IDLE AIR BLEEDS:	.046"	.046"	.040"
INT. AIR BLEEDS:	.070"	.070"	.043"
H.S. AIR BLEEDS:	.029"	.029"	.028"
BOOSTER TYPE:	ANNULAR	STRAIGHT	ANNULAR
BOOSTER LEG:	.169"	.169"	.169"
SQUIRTER SIZE:	35	35	42
BUTTERFLY SIZE:	2.00"	2.00"	2.00"
AIR HOLE SIZE:	NONE	NONE	NONE
PUMP CAM #:	YELLOW	YELLOW	YELLOW
PUMP CAM COLOR:	643	643	643
METERING BLOCK #:	A-12330	A-12330	A-12330
M-BLOCK COLOR:	SILVER	SILVER	SILVER
SIPHON BREAK:	.028"	.028"	.028"
E-HOLE POS. #1:	.029"	.029"	.029"
E-HOLE POS. #2:	.029"	.029"	.029"
E-HOLE POS. #3:	.029"	.029"	.029"
E-HOLE POS. #4:	.029"	.029"	.029"
P.V.C.R. SIZE:	.059"	.059"	.059"
I.F. RES:	.029"	.029"	.029"
T.S. RES:	OPEN	OPEN	OPEN
INT. PICK UP:	.040"	.040"	.040"
INT. FEED RES:	.046"	.046"	.063"
MAIN JETS PRI:	# 93	# 94	#96
MAIN JETS SEC:	# 93	# 94	# 96
POWER VALVE PRI:	PLUGGED	PLUGGED	PLUGGED
POWER VALVE SEC:	PLUGGED	PLUGGED	PLUGGED
LINKAGE TYPE:	PROG.	PROG.	PROG.
N&S SIZE/TYPE:	.130"-VITON	.130"-VITON	.130"-VITON
ACC. PUMP DIA. SIZE:	50CC	50CC	50CC

KING DEMON TUNNEL RAM REMOVABLE SLEEVE SPECIFICATIONS

MODEL#:	1095 AD	1095 ST	1195 AD
PART #:	9728020TR	9728030TR	9838020TR
VENTURI SIZE:	1.720"	1.720"	1.812"
VENTURI COLOR:	BLUE	BLUE	GOLD
IDLE AIR BLEEDS:	.046"	.046"	.040"
INT. AIR BLEEDS:	.070"	.070"	.043"
H.S. AIR BLEEDS:	.029"	.029"	.028"
BOOSTER TYPE:	ANNULAR	STRAIGHT	ANNULAR
BOOSTER LEG:	.169"	.169"	.169"
SQUIRTER SIZE:	35	35	42
BUTTERFLY SIZE:	2.00"	2.00"	2.00"
AIR HOLE SIZE:	NONE	NONE	NONE
PUMP CAM #:	YELLOW	YELLOW	YELLOW
PUMP CAM COLOR:	643	643	643
METERING BLOCK #:	A-12330	A-12330	A-12330
M-BLOCK COLOR:	SILVER	SILVER	SILVER
SIPHON BREAK:	.028"	.028"	.028"
E-HOLE POS. #1:	.029"	.029"	.029"
E-HOLE POS. #2:	.029"	.029"	.029"
E-HOLE POS. #3:	.029"	.029"	.029"
E-HOLE POS. #4:	.029"	.029"	.029"
P.V.C.R. SIZE:	.059"	.059"	.059"
I.F. RES:	.029"	.029"	.029"
T.S. RES:	OPEN	OPEN	OPEN
INT. PICK UP:	.040"	.040"	.040"
INT. FEED RES:	.046"	.046"	.063"
MAIN JETS PRI:	# 88	# 89	# 94
MAIN JETS SEC:	# 88	# 89	# 94
POWER VALVE PRI:	PLUGGED	PLUGGED	PLUGGED
POWER VALVE SEC:	PLUGGED	PLUGGED	PLUGGED
LINKAGE TYPE:	PROG.	PROG.	PROG.
N&S SIZE/TYPE:	.130"-VITON	.130"-VITON	.130"-VITON
ACC. PUMP DIA. SIZE	50 CC	50 CC	50 CC

KING DEMON REMOVEABLE SLEEVE DRAG RACE GAS SPECIFICATIONS (DR RS)

MODEL#:	795 AD	895 AD	995 AD	995 ST	1095 AD	1095 ST	1195 AD	1295 AD
PART #:	9406020DR	9567020DR	9627020DR	9627030DR	9728020DR	9728030DR	9838020DR	9849020DR
VENTURI SIZE:	1.500"	1.562"	1.625"	1.625"	1.720"	1.720"	1.812"	1.838"
VENTURI COLOR:	GREEN	RED	BLACK	BLACK	BLUE	BLUE	GOLD	SILVER
IDLE AIR BLEEDS:	.046"	.046"	.046"	.046"	.046"	.046"	.040"	.046"
INT. AIR BLEEDS:	.070"	.070"	.070"	.070"	.070"	.070"	.043"	.035"
H.S. AIR BLEEDS:	.032"	.032"	.035"	.035"	.029"	.029"	.028"	.032"
BOOSTER TYPE:	ANNULAR	ANNULAR	ANNULAR	STRAIGHT	ANNULAR	STRAIGHT	ANNULAR	ANNULAR
BOOSTER LEG:	.169"	.169"	.169"	.169"	.169"	.169"	.169"	.169"
SQUIRTER SIZE:	35	35	35	35	35	35	42	42
BUTTERFLY SIZE:	1.800"	1.800"	2.00"	2.00"	2.00"	2.00"	2.00"	2.10"
AIR HOLE SIZE:	NONE	NONE	NONE	NONE	NONE	NONE	NONE	NONE
PUMP CAM #:	YELLOW	YELLOW	YELLOW	YELLOW	YELLOW	YELLOW	YELLOW	YELLOW
PUMP CAM COLOR:	643	643	643	643	643	643	643	643
METERING BLOCK #:	A-12330	A-12330	A-12330	A-12330	A-12330	A-12330	A-12330	A-12330
M-BLOCK COLOR:	SILVER	SILVER	SILVER	SILVER	SILVER	SILVER	SILVER	SILVER
SIPHON BREAK:	.028"	.028"	.028"	.028"	.028"	.028"	.028"	.028"
E-HOLE POS. #1:	.029"	.029"	.029"	.029"	.029"	.029"	.029"	.029"
E-HOLE POS. #2:	.029"	.029"	.029"	.029"	.029"	.029"	.029"	.029"
E-HOLE POS. #3:	.029"	.029"	.029"	.029"	.029"	.029"	.029"	.029"
E-HOLE POS. #4:	.029"	.029"	.029"	.029"	.029"	.029"	.029"	.029"
P.V.C.R. SIZE:	.059"	.059"	.059"	.059"	.059"	.059"	.059"	.059"
I.F. RES:	.029"	.029"	.029"	.029"	.029"	.029"	.029"	.029"
T.S. RES:	OPEN	OPEN	OPEN	OPEN	OPEN	OPEN	OPEN	OPEN
INT. PICK UP:	.040"	.040"	.040"	.040"	.040"	.040"	.040"	.046"
INT. FEED RES:	.046"	.046"	.046"	.046"	.046"	.046"	.063"	.067"
MAIN JETS PRI:	# 72	# 76	# 85	# 85	# 93	# 94	#96	# 96
MAIN JETS SEC:	# 82	# 86	# 85	# 85	# 93W/EXT	# 94W/EXT	# 94 W/EXT	# 96 W/EXT
POWER VALVE PRI:	6.5 STD.	6.5 STD.	PLUGGED	PLUGGED	PLUGGED	PLUGGED	PLUGGED	PLUGGED
POWER VALVE SEC:	PLUGGED	PLUGGED	PLUGGED	PLUGGED	PLUGGED	PLUGGED	PLUGGED	PLUGGED
LINKAGE TYPE:	PROG.	PROG.	PROG.	PROG.	PROG.	PROG.	PROG.	PROG.
N&S SIZE/TYPE:	.130"-VITON	.130"-VITON	.130"-VITON	.130"-VITON	.130"-VITON	.130"-VITON	.130"-VITON	.130"-VITON
ACC. PUMP DIA. SIZE:	50 CC	50 CC	50 CC	50 CC	50 CC	50 CC	50 CC	50 CC

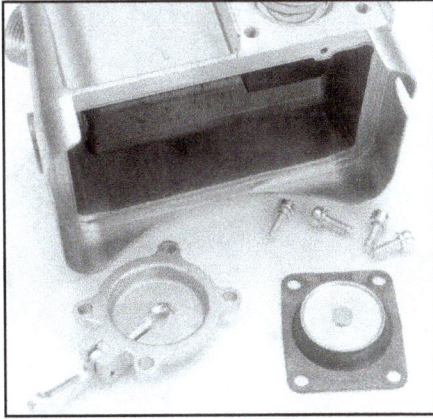

All King Demons use 50cc accelerator pumps.

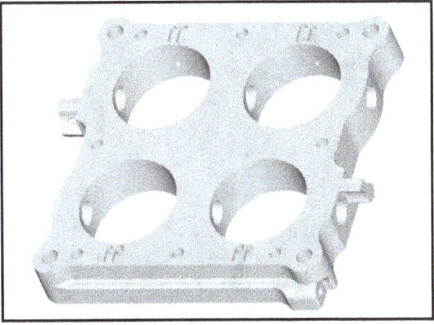

The King Demon has a unique base plate.

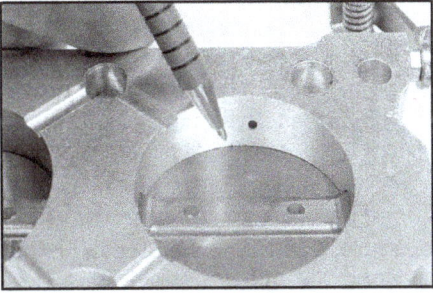

The amount of transfer slot area exposed at idle is critical on the King Demon also.

The accelerator pump arm adjustment affects performance. See Chapter 10 for the proper procedure.

REVIEW QUESTIONS

1) All King Demons use:

   a: a 0.130-inch Viton needle-and-seat assembly
   b: ZA-3 main body construction
   c: straight boosters
   d: pink accelerator pump cams

2) The King Demon series uses:

   a: a 30cc accelerator pump
   b: no accelerator pumps due to the intermediate circuit
   c: a 50cc accelerator pump
   d: a vacuum secondary

3) The intermediate circuit is used to:

   a: help fuel the engine during throttle transition
   b: improve idle quality
   c: increase top-end power
   d: compensates for the lack of an accelerator pump on certain models

4) The King Demon uses how many throttle plate air holes?

   a: 4
   b: 2
   c: 8
   d: 0

5) What feature is standard on all King Demons?

   a: choke assembly
   b: secondary power valves
   c: 1:1 secondary linkages
   d: progressive secondary operation

6) All King Demons uses metering blocks with how many emulsion holes per main well?

   a: 4
   b: 5
   c: 3
   d: 0

7) Which King Demon offers manifold vacuum ports for accessory hookup?

   a: none
   b: TR applications
   c: GC applications
   d: all

8) How is the intermediate circuit jet installed?

   a: swedged
   b: pressed
   c: drilled
   d: threaded

9) A clearanced float is used:

   a: when fueled by alcohol
   b: when jet extensions are installed
   c: with power valves
   d: for blowers

10) King Demons shipped with square jetting have:

    a: no intermediate circuit
    b: no power valves
    c: removable venturis
    d: intermediate circuits

Answers: 1) A, 2) C, 3) A, 4) D, 5) D, 6) A, 7) A, 8) D, 9) B, 10) B

How to Tune and Win with Demon Carburetors

How to Tune & Win with DEMON CARBURETORS
The Fuel System

Until now, our discussion has worked under the assumption that the fuel will be delivered in the required quantity and pressure to the carburetor in order for the engine to perform properly. Often the enthusiast and professional consider only the carburetor, neglecting the importance of the fuel-delivery process. Strange or inconsistent behavior by the engine in any street, towing, or race application can usually be traced to a poor-performing fuel-delivery system. It is common to think that the problem can only be a lack of fuel, but often, and especially at light engine loads, the exact opposite can be true. Diagnosing a fuel-delivery issue can be tricky at times because the same engine performance symptoms can be caused by non-fuel-related components. Even though your engine may not miss, pop, bang, skip, tug, or do anything else peculiar, the fuel system may still not be meeting its requirements.

PRESSURE AND FLOW

Referencing basic hydraulics, the relationship of pressure and flow can be likened to the sides of a seesaw: As one goes up, the other goes down. When there is flow, the pressure is reduced; when there is pressure, the flow decreases. This concept needs to be fully grasped since it is often confused with fuel volume. The amount of fuel pumped is generally measured as a volume per unit time standard. In the domestic performance industry, we rate fuel-delivery capacity in gallons per hour (GPH). To build pressure, the fluid needs to be forced through an orifice, and since a liquid is considered non-compressible, the pressure rises.

If you were to think in depth about the fuel-delivery process some questions would come up. Give thought to the following and see if you can explain their function before we proceed:

1) Why does an engine need to have a fuel pump?

2) What fuel pressure is used with a Demon carburetor and why is the pressure necessary?

3) **When the needle valve is closed, what happens to the fuel that is delivered by a standard block-mounted diaphragm pump?**

An automobile engine uses a fuel pump, but not all engines do. As an example, a lawn mower has fuel fed to it by gravity, as did early automobile and farm tractors. This method of delivery proved undesirable for a motor vehicle since it could not always provide a sufficient volume of fuel for every driving scenario. As the engine evolved and operating speeds increased, gravity alone was not sufficient to keep the float bowl full. Also, this feed method required that the fuel tank would always have to be higher than the carburetor, posing severe packaging problems as styling and aerodynamics started coming into play.

Back in the days of the Model T Ford, if the fuel tank was low, the driver would be forced to back up a hill to keep the pickup tube submerged and the engine running. This would obviously be unacceptable in today's soci-

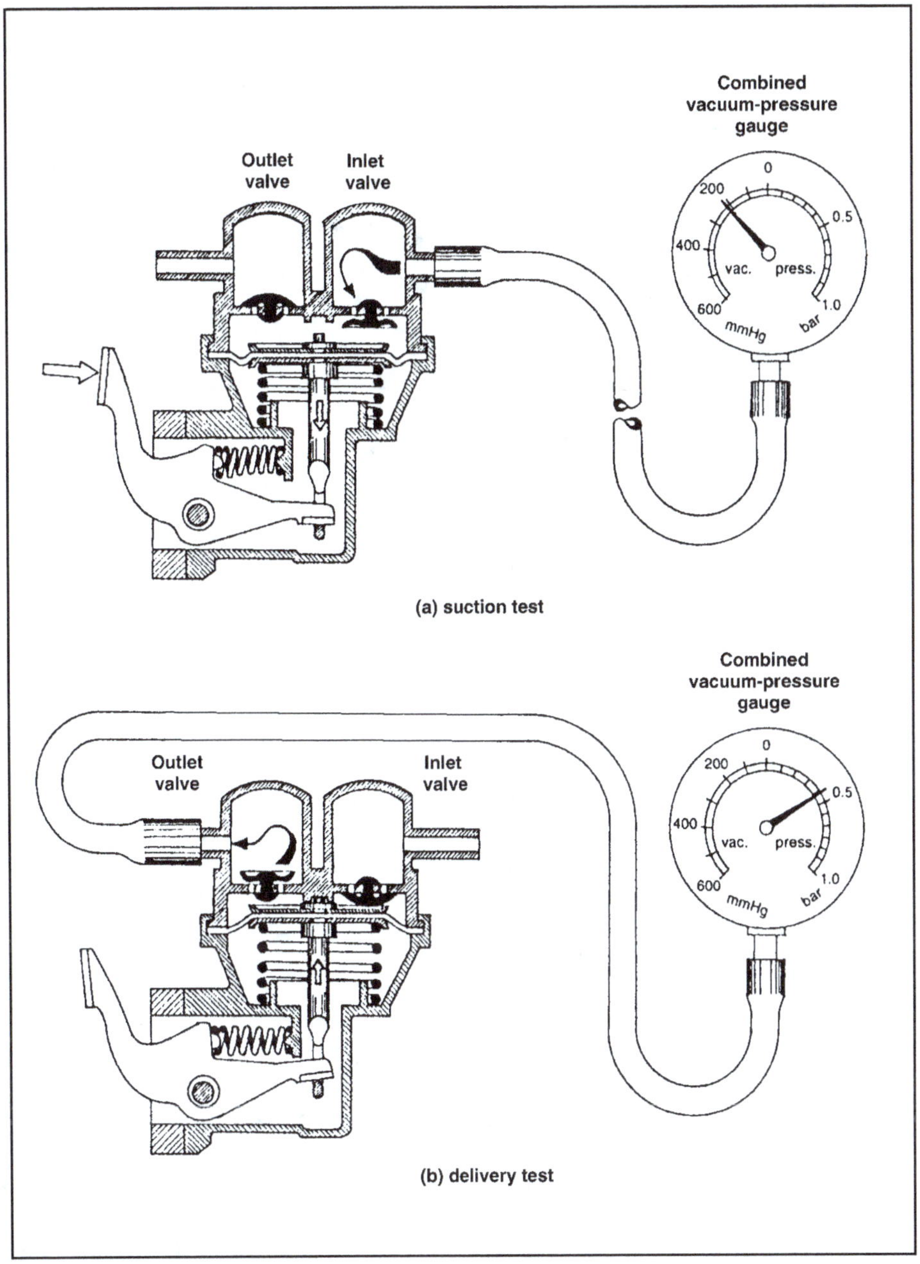

(a) suction test

(b) delivery test

Diaphragm pumps produce both pressure and suction.

The BG Super Speedway fuel pump is the most reliable high-volume pump available. It is a diaphragm style and is offered for popular Ford and Chevrolet engines.

The electric BG 220RR is an extended-duty pump designed for road racing and other continuous uses. It features an external adjustable bypass and requires a conventional fuel pressure regulator to control the inlet pressure at the carburetor.

All BG fuel pumps are hand assembled and tested on a dedicated assembly line at the Barry Grant, Inc. facility in Georgia.

Barry Grant used his extensive background in hydraulics, along with dyno testing, to design each model fuel pump in the BG line.

How to Tune and Win with Demon Carburetors

A dampened fuel pressure gauge allows for accurate readings and tuning.

All of the products produced by Barry Grant, Inc. are race-track-proven on the company's Oldsmobile Cutlass NHRA Pro Stock test vehicle.

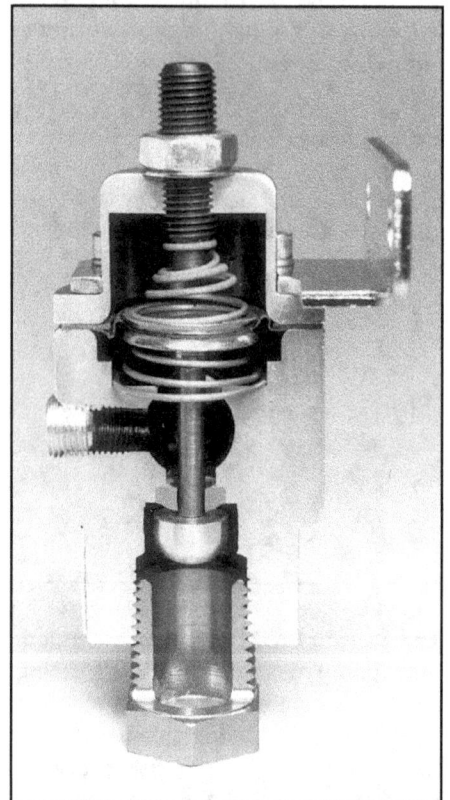

A fuel pressure regulator is a mechanical device; it is either open or closed.

A proper fuel system installation includes a secure mounting for the electric pump. BG Fuel Systems offers these heavy-duty clamps that make the job fast and easy.

ety, let alone dangerous. Another downfall of gravity feed was the inability to sufficiently filter the gasoline; it would not have the force to be pushed through a filtering media. Instead, these early fuel-delivery attempts used a sediment bowl in hopes of driving any contaminates out of the solution. Along with other concerns, this became the impetus for the integration of a pressurized fuel-delivery system on modern engines.

The Demon carburetor was designed to operate when being fueled with gasoline at a delivery pressure of 6-8 psi. An alcohol application requires 4-5 psi at idle, and 9-12 psi at wide-open throttle. The pressure in the fuel line is created by the force of the fuel pump working against the restriction of the needle valve. Beyond having a constant supply of fuel ready to keep the float bowl filled, the pressure raises the boiling point of the gasoline and helps to avoid vapor-lock. This condition can occur when high underhood temperatures allow the gasoline to boil and turn to vapor. During normal engine running, the cycling of the needle valve creates a rise and fall in pressure. This is normally dampened in the mechanism of the fuel pressure gauge so that an accurate reading can be taken.

FUEL PUMP TYPES

There are two different methods of supplying the carburetor with fuel: a mechanical system or an electric pump. The mechanical system is further defined as either a block-mounted diaphragm or belt-driven gear type. Electric pumps are designated by their flow ratings in gallons of fuel per hour. Barry Grant, Inc. manufactures fuel pumps, regulators, bypass, and filters through the BG Fuel Systems Division. All BG Fuel Systems components are designed to work with Demons, as well as other brands of carburetors.

BG Fuel Systems offers three models of block-mounted fuel delivery pumps: Six Valve, Super Speedway, and marine. The basic operation is shared by all three and can be described as being activated through an arm that rides on an eccentric ground into the camshaft. As the camshaft turns, the diaphragm lever is forced downward against the resistance of the diaphragm spring. This spring controls the upward movement of the diaphragm because the lever is hinged to the operating lever. During this pumping action, a low pressure is created in the fuel pump chamber and fuel is drawn from the fuel tank. On the return stroke, the diaphragm is forced up by the internal spring, thus closing the inlet valve and opening the outlet valve, and allowing fuel to be pumped to the carburetor. A pump of this design delivers fuel to the carburetor only when the fuel pressure is less then the pressure maintained by the diaphragm spring; in other words, only when the needle valve is open in the carburetor.

Answering the third question that was posed in the beginning of this chapter, there is no fuel delivered by a diaphragm-style pump when the float bowl is full and the needle valve is closed. As soon as the float level drops in the bowl of the carburetor, the pressure changes and the fuel pump will

A high-horsepower engine needs the fuel volume that only a belt-driven pump can supply.

The demand of an engine is elastic, and the fuel system needs to deliver under all conditions.

again resume its duties. Due to this design feature, a pump of this style will generally produce the highest pressure at idle when the flow is least, and the lowest pressure at maximum speed when the fuel flow is greatest.

In contrast to the diaphragm-style mechanical design, a belt-driven remote pump supplies fuel constantly. As the speed of the pump is varied, the output will also change. Commonly referred to as a belt-driven fuel pump, BG Fuel Systems also offers the same pump that is hex-driven, eliminating the belt. Since either drive configuration has no impact on the function or theory of pump operation, the term belt drive or belt style will be used in our discussion. Being indifferent to the position of the needle valve in the carburetor, a belt-driven fuel system needs to incorporate a diaphragm bypass.

An electric fuel pump operates as an integral electric motor and pump assembly. Though there are many styles of electric fuel pumps used in the OE market, BG Fuel Systems has found favor with the vane-and-rotor positive-displacement design. It works by using variable-sized circulating chambers to expose a supply orifice and draw in fuel as the volume of the pump expands. Once the maximum volume is reached, the supply orifice closes and the discharge orifice opens. The fuel is now forced out as the effective volume in the chamber decreases.

The chambers of this style of fuel pump are formed as the rollers circulate in a rotor plate assembly. A combination of centrifugal force and fuel pressure forces them outward against the eccentric roller path. The eccentricity between the roller plate and roller path provides the constant increase and decrease in chamber volume. An electric fuel pump offers constant fuel flow regardless of engine load and carburetor float bowl level, so a regulator or diaphragm bypass needs to be installed.

HOW MUCH FLOW?

The process of producing horsepower revolves around the conversion of fuel into energy. In Chapter 2, it was established that the amount of fuel required to produce 1 horsepower is measured as BSFC. It needs to be recognized that if an engine produces more power, then a greater volume of fuel needs to be supplied, even if the rate of conversion efficiency is high. With horsepower data you can then easily estimate the fuel requirements.

For example: The fuel needs of an engine that makes 500 horsepower and has a BSFC of 0.45 can be calculated by multiplying the power by the BSFC. This would yield the consumption of the engine in one hour at maximum output, measured in pounds. For demonstration purposes, let's round the weight of the gasoline to 6 lbs. per gallon. Then the equation would become: 500 hp x 0.45 = 225 lbs. per hour required. Now we need

A fuel check bleed is used to provide a fuel sample for a sanctioning body test without disconnecting the fuel line.

Stackable modular regulator assemblies can be attached to a common manifold to feed multiple carburetors and nitrous systems.

to convert the fuel from pounds to gallons: gallons = 225/6, or 37.5 gallons per hour.

The problem now becomes the method the performance industry uses to rate fuel pump volume. Similar to what happened to carburetor flow ratings over the years, fuel pump ratings also need to be interpreted. Referencing the BG Fuel Systems catalog, we see that the smallest electric pump offered is rated at 220 gph, which would equate to 1320 lbs. of fuel per hour, substantially more than the 225 lbs. our subject engine needs. The key here is that the rating is for open port flow, which means that there is no pressure being built. It can be compared to the rating of a sump pump for the basement of your home. A pump that is rated at 225 gph will move that volume of fuel when no restriction is present.

Thinking back to the basics of hydraulics in the beginning of this chapter, we know that as the pressure rises, flow decreases. This rating standard is not necessarily problematic if you realize that the pump is only required to keep the float bowls of the carburetor filled, and cycles from flow to no flow continuously. The performance industry usually does not measure part-throttle and light-load BSFC values, but it needs to be recognized that during most driving scenarios, a street car produces a very small percentage of its maximum power output. On average, even the least aerodynamic vehicle will still only require approximately 25-30 hp to cruise at 65 mph.

Although the efficiency of the engine decreases due to the pumping losses of a predominantly closed throttle, the amount of fuel required is still much less than at full power. Consequently, the fuel system needs to adapt to the elastic demand of a street engine. A race engine, on the other hand, has a complete other set of concerns, and needs large amounts of fuel. However, all race applications cannot be grouped together. A drag race car would require a different fuel system design than a road-race or dirt-track entry. The pump is considered the heart of the fuel system, but it needs to have the proper ancillary components to function.

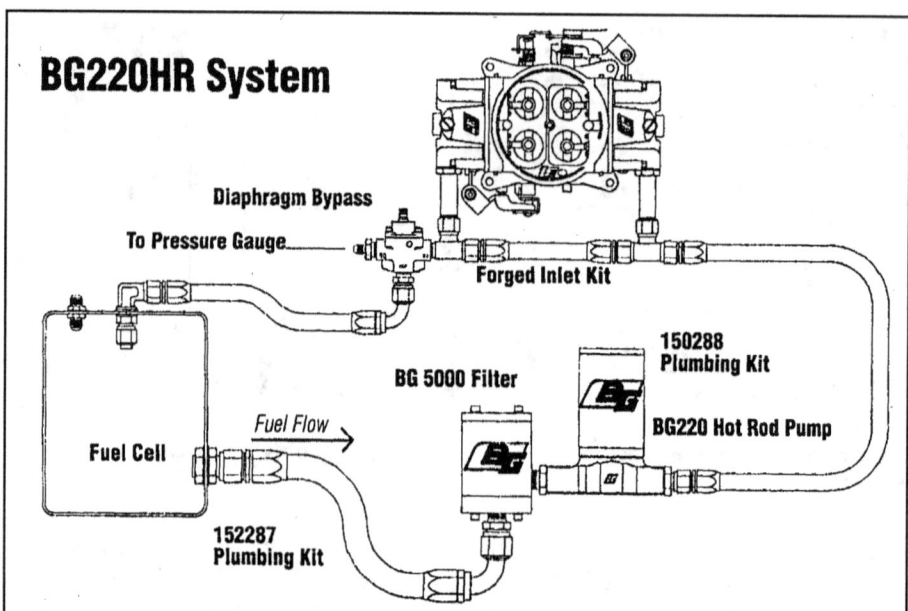

The BG 220HR is a great choice for a street/strip car.

CHOOSING THE PROPER FUEL PUMP

In engineering, less is more, and this logic is responsible for the KISS acronym: keep it simple, stupid. The fact remains that though a trick fuel system is impressive, most engines do not require the expense and complication that it brings. When designing the fuel system for your application, ask yourself the following questions:

1) Are you using gasoline or alcohol?

2) Is a dyno sheet available to quantify horsepower and BSFC?

3) What will the use be (street/strip, drag race, oval track, etc.)?

4) Where will the fuel tank or cell be mounted?

5) Does the engine run an alternator?

6) Does a sanctioning body dictate the fuel system?

Now let's apply logic to these considerations. The type of fuel is important since the stoichiometric value of alcohol is double that of gasoline. An engine that runs on alcohol will require twice as much fuel to produce the same power. An additional concern is the corrosiveness of the alcohol, so the fuel pump and components need to survive in this environment.

A dyno sheet with valid BSFC and power results will allow the fuel system to be targeted exactly to the needs of the engine with no guess work. If this is not available, then an educated guess will have to be applied.

The intended use of the engine determines the fuel pump model in regard to cycle or run time. As an example, a drag-race-only pump is designed to produce high volumes of fuel but is not intended to operate for hours at a time, the way a street car would.

The location of the fuel tank is critical since some fuel pumps are not designed to suck fuel for more than a few feet. Additionally, if it is a drag car and the fuel cell is mounted in the front, the force of acceleration will help carry the fuel to the engine, so a smaller pump can be used.

If the engine is not using an alternator, then the battery voltage becomes critical with an electric fuel pump. As the voltage input to the electric motor drops, so does the throughput of the pump.

If the car is going to be raced, the rules of a sanctioning organization will dictate the fuel system. Certain motorsports sanctioning bodies allow only certain fuel system designs and, thus, need to be acknowledged.

With all these facts quantified, you can now make an intelligent decision about the necessary fuel system components.

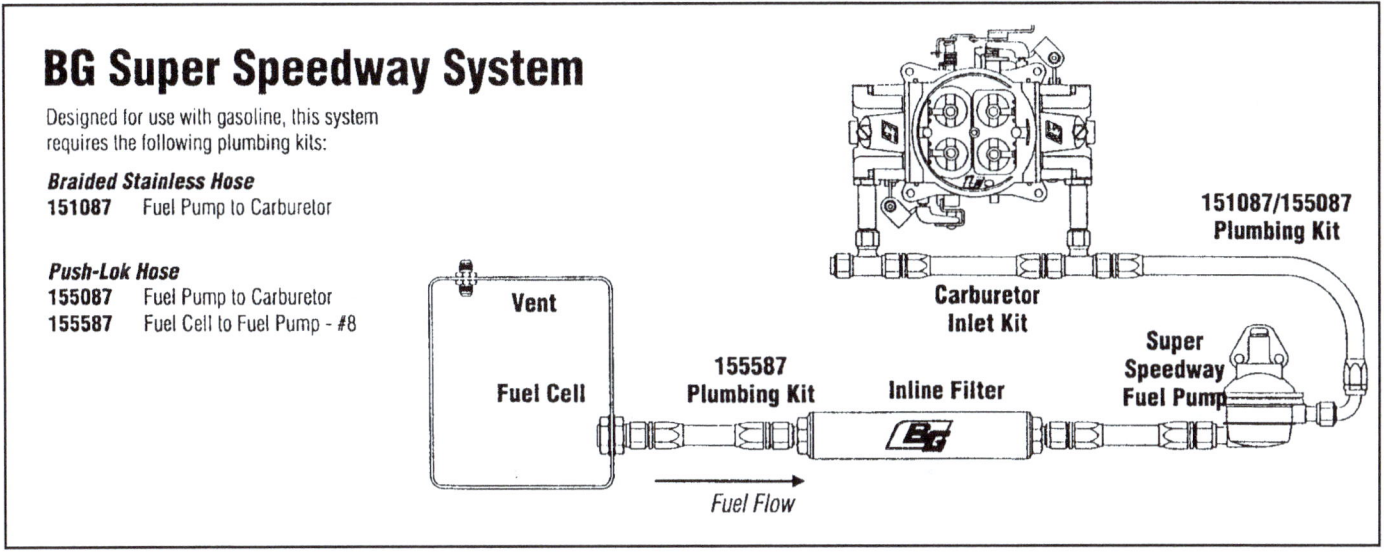

Since the Super Speedway pump is self-regulating by design, no bypass or regulator is required.

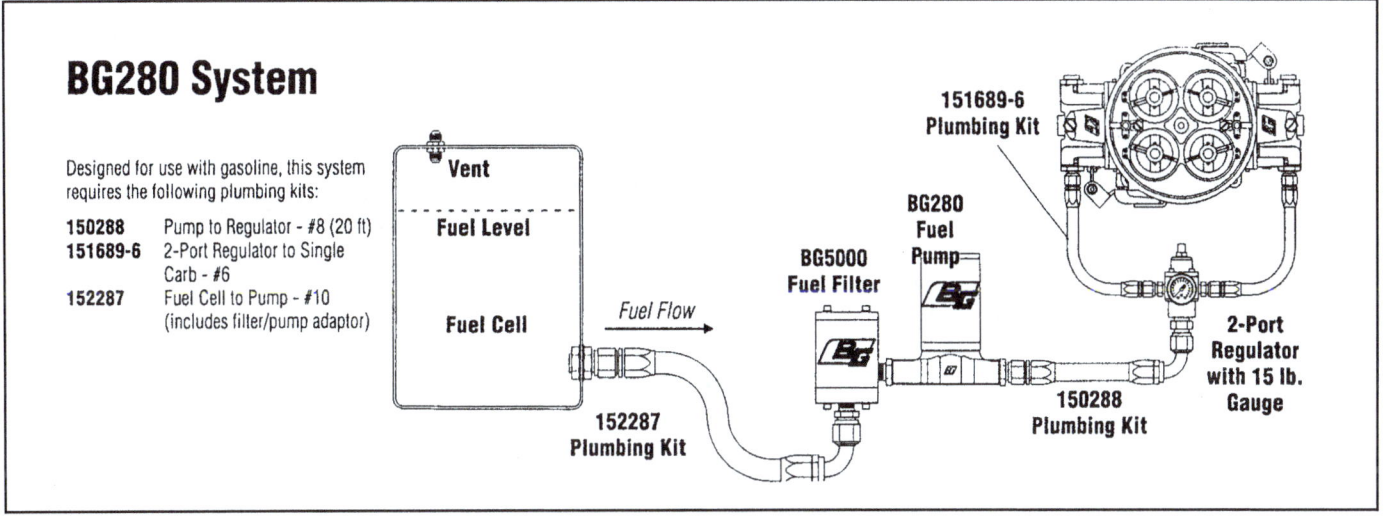

The BG280 includes an integral bypass so no return line is required.

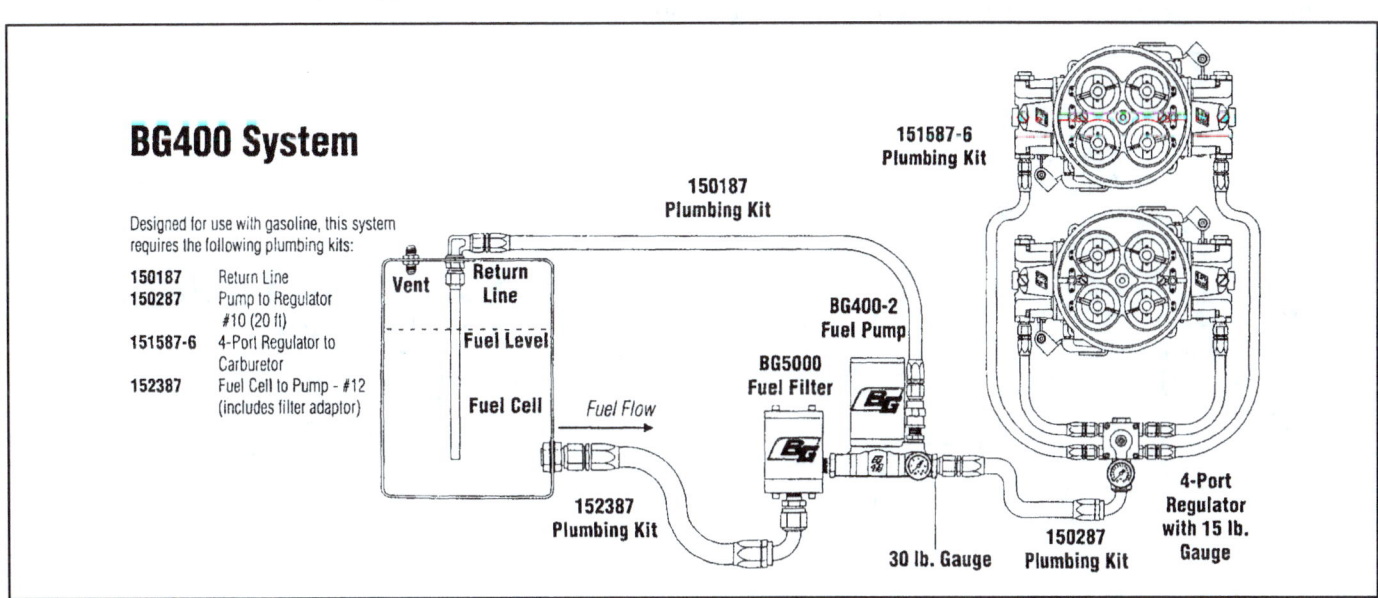

One four-port BG regulator can handle the requirements of twin King Demons.

How to Tune and Win with Demon Carburetors

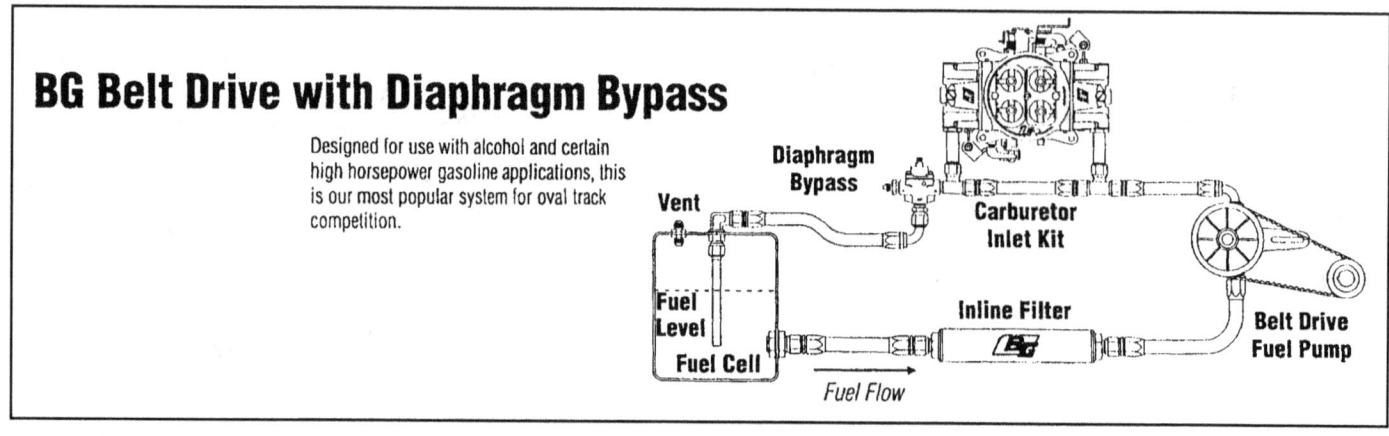

A belt-style pump varies its output with engine RPM and requires a diaphragm bypass and return line to the fuel source.

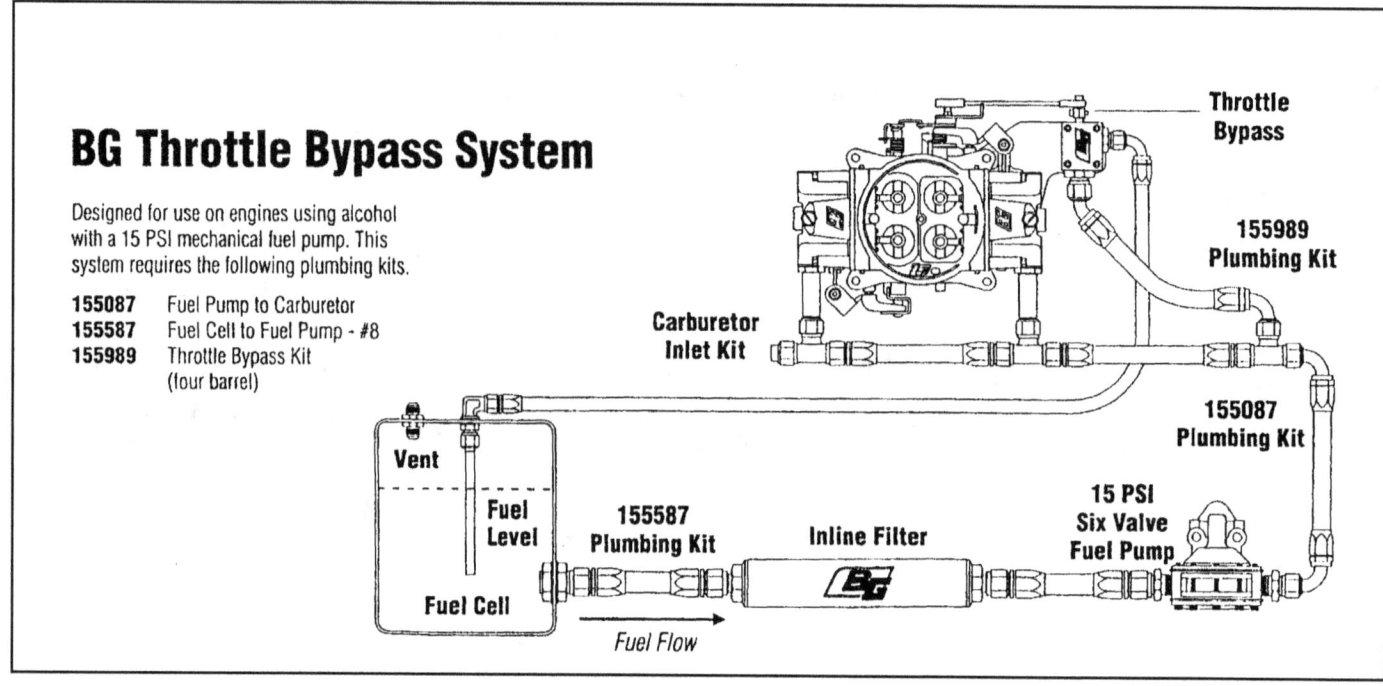

A throttle bypass is necessary when a Six Valve diaphragm pump is used with alcohol.

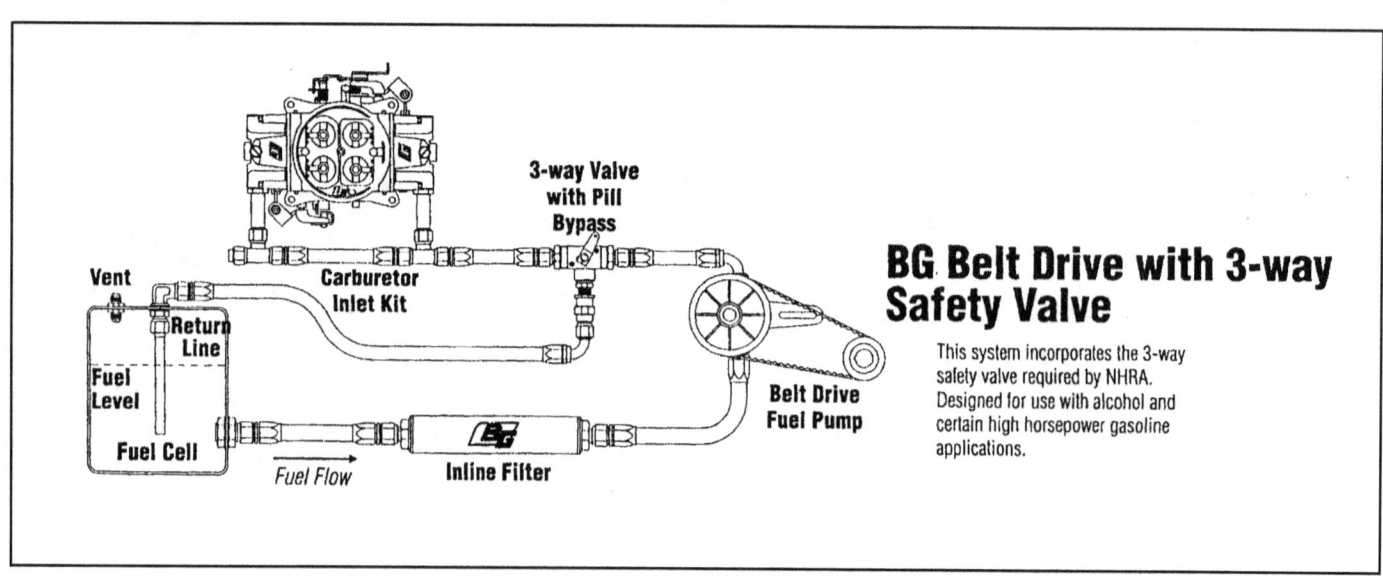

When a belt- or hex-drive fuel pump is used, the NHRA mandates the fuel system includes a shutoff valve.

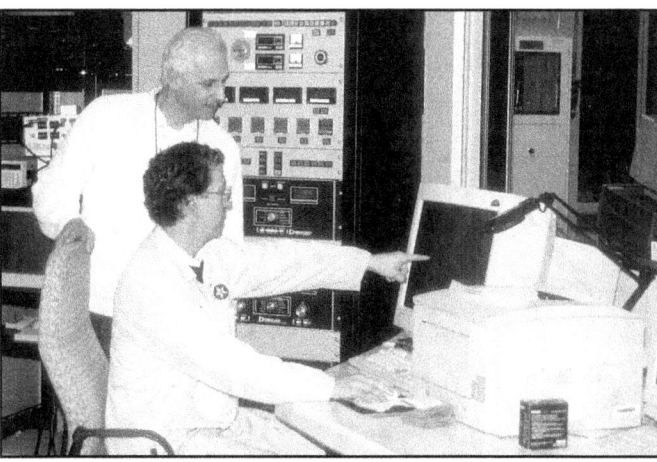

A wheels-in-the-air launch with a rear-mounted fuel cell means the fuel pump needs to fight the forces of gravity.

TAI engineer Joe Valentine and senior chemist Michael Rawdon analyze data from a combustion test.

In oval-track applications, a BG Belt Drive pump is preferred where the use of a mechanical pump is specified. This style offers the highest fuel-delivery volume of any mechanical pump yet maintains a lower fuel pressure at slow engine speeds. This alleviates a loading up of the engine from a rich mixture that is created when the fuel pressure is too high and unseats the needle valve in the carburetor. The BG Six Valve and Super Speedway models are excellent for street and high-performance applications that require no more than 130 gph. For drag-race cars, a BG400-2 Electric Fuel Pump is the best way to guard against fuel starvation.

If a drag car seems lazy at mid-track or lays down then pulls well in a higher gear, it may be experiencing intermittent fuel starvation. This is typically created by an emptying of the float bowls. The car will leave hard since the float bowls are full, but the delivery system cannot meet the demand as the vehicle accelerates. In the lower gears, the rapid acceleration will drain the bowls, creating a lean condition. When this happens the car will nose over from fuel starvation. The decreased rate of acceleration will now allow the fuel pump to recharge the bowls, and since the engine speed increases more slowly in a higher gear, the performance returns.

A test for adequate fuel volume is the system's ability to fill a 1-gallon metal gas can at the carburetor inlet in less than 25 seconds. A certified 1-gallon metal can should be used since a Super Jug or anti-freeze container is not an accurate volume. Large-displacement, high-horsepower engines should have a fuel pump that can accomplish this task in 20 seconds. For the engine to perform, the jets in the carburetor need to be covered with fuel. If there is no apparent reason for a lack of performance, the fuel delivery rate is the first thing to check. Contrary to what may be assumed, single four-barrel applications are more prone to fuel starvation issues than multiple carburetors. This stems from the four barrel possessing only two float bowls, inlet valves, and seat assemblies. With dual four barrels, there are now four float bowls and assemblies to act as reservoirs. This effectively doubles the fuel storage and handling capabilities.

For the same reason, the filter should be designed to match the flow rate and requirements of the fuel pump. Even the most powerful race engine should use a filter and, if designed properly, will not impart any flow restriction. Ideally, the filter should be placed on the suction side of the pump, removing any foreign material before entering the tight clearances of the fuel pump.

For alcohol applications, a belt-drive pump is desirable even though the BG Six Valve is compatible with this fuel. Inherently a diaphragm pump will not offer the required pressure differential keyed to engine speed, so a throttle bypass would be required. The alcohol version is designed to produce 15 psi, which is excessive at idle and very light load. The integration of a throttle bypass is required. It is a linkage-controlled device that mounts under the carburetor and returns the excess fuel to keep the fuel pressure at the proper setting.

PLUMBING AND INSTALLING YOUR FUEL SYSTEM

The best fuel system components in the world are useless if they are installed incorrectly. The amount of attention paid to detail will either make or break your fuel system long after the parts are paid for. The good thing is that a proper installation is not difficult to perform once the theory is understood. There are three distinct areas of concern: component choice, plumbing, and, if applicable, electrical.

Often a fuel system is sized too large, working under the theory that the fuel will be there if your engine program steps up a few notches. This is not necessarily a faulty logic if kept within reason, but as with most aspects of this sport, excess seems to be the norm. The problem with using an excessively large fuel pump, especially on a street engine, revolves around the need to control not only the fuel pressure at the carburetor, but also the delivery rate. At light loads, an excessive amount will need to be bypassed and will result in heating the fuel excessively, along with the possibility of cavitation and destroying an electric fuel pump.

Line size and material are other areas of confusion. A good rule to follow for sizing is to maintain the same

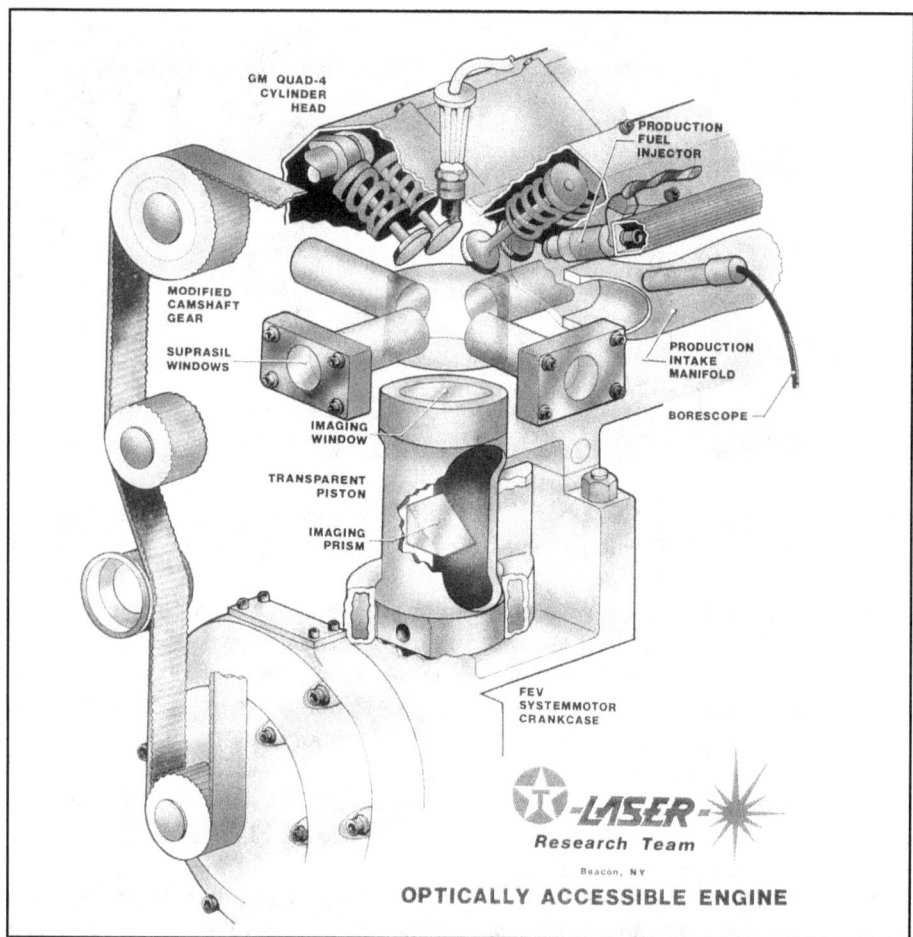

Texaco Additives International (TAI) R&D of Beacon, New York, has developed an optical one-cylinder engine that uses a laser beam to measure the effect additives have on combustion. (Illustration by Joe Valentine)

The one-cylinder optical engine features four windows into the combustion chamber.

This is the octane test engine used by the petroleum industry worldwide. Note the three cylindrical containers. They are the carburetor bowls for the test and reference fuels.

outlet dimension of the fuel pump. Anything larger will add storage capacity to the system but will not necessarily have any impact on delivery pressure and volume. However, the feed line from the fuel cell or gas tank to the fuel pump should be at least one complete size larger than the outlet dimension of the pump. Braided steel line may look tricky but is usually very expensive overkill for most installations. A good compromise is the use of aluminum tubing; it is strong, light, and easier to form than plain steel tubing, though it is more expensive. The use of rubber line should be limited to the flex area, where the fuel line leaves the frame of the vehicle and is moving to the engine. Many sanctioning bodies limit the amount of rubber line that can be used. For example, the NHRA will not allow more than one foot total of rubber fuel line in the entire vehicle. Systems that require a return line need to keep this dimension one size smaller than the line from the outlet of the pump to the carburetor or regulator.

Whenever a fluid is asked to make a turn, frictional flow losses occur, limiting flow in GPH while raising the pressure the pump must work against. Although it would be impossible to create a fuel system that makes no turns, some time spent studying and planing your installation can often eliminate many unnecessary maneuvers.

The ideal path would be as straight as possible from the fuel cell or tank to the inlet of the carburetor. When the direction of the fuel line must change, the gentler the bend, the happier the fuel will be. This means that a 45-degree turn is always better than a 90-degree. If the installation demands a 180-degree turn, it is best to go up one tubing size for that fitting and break it into multiple gentler bends.

Just remember: As the area of the radius increases, the frictional flow loss decreases. Often it looks as if the installer thought he was making a moonshine still instead of a fuel system. The style of fitting and connections will also impact flow losses. AN connections are the least restrictive and should be favored over the less expensive NPT style.

When installing an electric fuel pump, the use of a relay in the circuit with a fusible connection will be the safest and best performing. An electric motor follows Ohm's Law and works on watts, which are derived from volts multiplied by amps. Since an OE charging system is designed to put out approximately 14.6 volts DC, most fuel pumps are intended to work on at least 13.6 volts. Ohm's Law dictates that if the voltage supply is lowered, the current draw will increase.

By incorporating a relay from a switched ignition source, the fuel pump can be powered directly from the alternator or battery with the proper-size wire. All electrical connections should be soldered and shrink-wrapped for protection against moisture and corrosion. The ground wire of the pump should run back to the engine block at the same point where the battery ground strap attaches. This will ensure that the circuit will operate on the same ground plane with the least resistance.

USING A FUEL PRESSURE REGULATOR OR A DIAPHRAGM BYPASS

Deciding when to use a fuel pressure regulator or a diaphragm bypass is often the most confusing aspect of the fuel system installation. Before you can choose the proper equipment, you must understand the function of each. A regulator can be considered a digital device; it is either open or closed. When the port is open the fuel flows to the carburetor, and when it is closed no flow is present.

In contrast, a bypass of either a poppet- or diaphragm-style is analog in operation, controlling the fuel pressure to the carburetor by varying the flow and returning the excess. For the bypass to function, a return line needs to be installed to the fuel source.

Deciding which to use depends on the style pump employed. If the fuel pump design includes an internal bypass, then a regulator can be used; if it does not, then a diaphragm bypass is a necessity.

Traditionally, most block-mounted pumps are self-regulating by design, as previously explained. An exception to this rule is the BG Six Valve 15-psi model, which would require a bypass to step down the pressure. A belt-driven pump will require the use of a bypass since there is no practical method of incorporating this into the design.

UNDERSTANDING GASOLINE

With approximately 130 billion gallons of gasoline sold yearly in America, the phrase "fill 'er up" is very common. To most of the motoring public, gasoline is just a necessary part of life, but enthusiasts usually take their fuel purchases a lot more seriously. Many of us can be considered aficionados of this petroleum concoction, seeking out a special brand and octane, whiffing its aroma at every opportunity. The fact remains that very little is known about this petroleum distillate, and usually what we take as gospel is rife with error and misunderstanding. The following can be considered a crash course on gasoline, debunking the common myths about fuel.

Where Oil Comes From

Almost all of the automotive fuel consumed in the United States is derived from petroleum, which is a complex mixture of hydrocarbon compounds, identified before refining as crude oil. In some parts of the country, petroleum-based gasoline is mixed with fuels created from farm products, and the result is a gasoline/grain alcohol mix marketed under the name Gasohol.

The origin and evolution of petroleum in both liquid and gaseous states is not truly known, but it is accepted that it is found most abundantly in certain rock formations. It is believed that marine organic material on the bottom of the ocean was covered by rock layers and was subjected to very high pressures, eventually decomposing into what we know as petroleum. It is also thought that the original organic matter contained oxygen, although petroleum consists mainly of carbon and hydrogen compounds. It is postulated that bacterial action may have been responsible for the elimination of the oxygen. Another theory assumes that continuous exposure over time to slight radioactive charges from rock formations destroyed the oxygen. Despite all the theories, its disappearance remains a mystery.

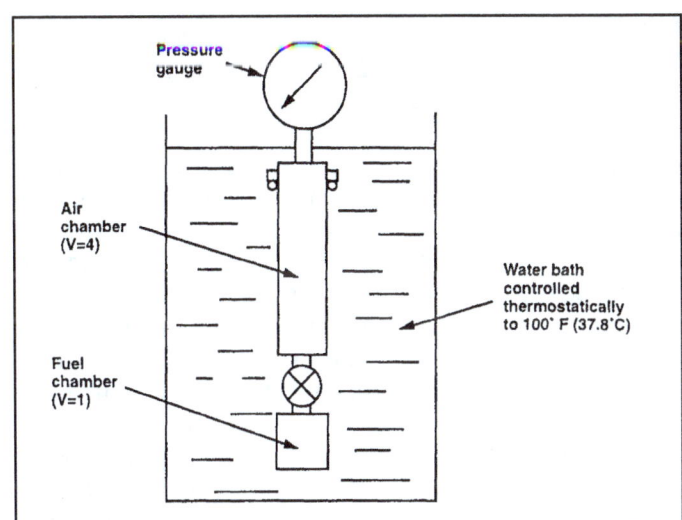

The test for RVP is performed in a device called a bomb.

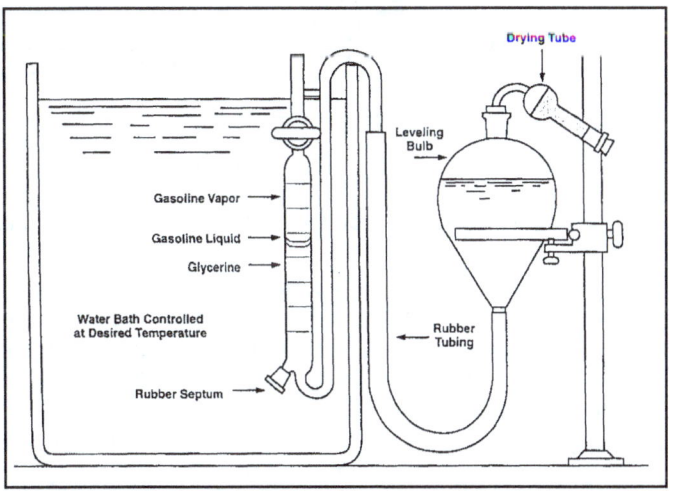

A liquid/vapor test is the best indicator to determine a fuel's propensity toward vapor-lock.

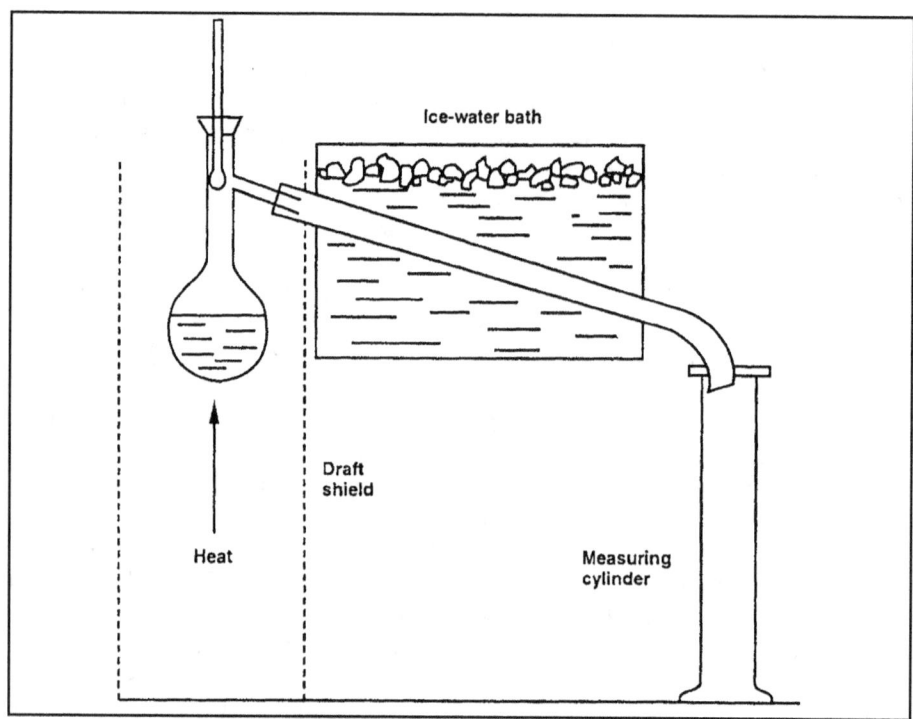

A distillation test determines the boiling point of the components that make up the fuel.

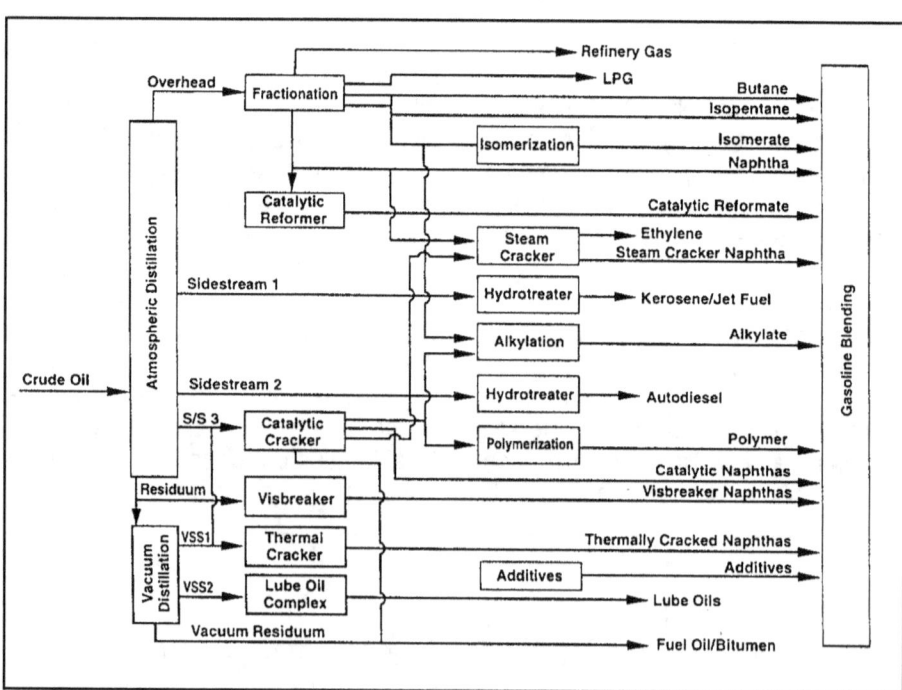

Considering the complexity of a refinery, gasoline is a very inexpensive commodity.

Regardless of how it was produced, petroleum is the fuel that has driven the world. Today, crude oil is found in porous rock formations, sand, and limestone. These underground traps are called pools and contain not only the petroleum, but gases and salt water. The salt water is believed to have been retained in the pores of the rock from when the organic material was deposited. Tar sand sediments are another form of petroleum and consist of common sand that is bonded with a viscous tar of petroleum origin. Oil shale is still another source and is found in hard rock formations that contain veins of petroleum-based material. The oil can be freed from the shale by crushing and heating the rock, but the cost of producing fuel from regions such as these is considerably more than that of oil pumped from an underground pool.

Through experience and test drilling, geologists can determine with great accuracy the amount of crude oil a pool contains. This is called the proven reserves. However, that does not necessarily represent the total of the pool, defined by the term resources, which is a combination of the discovered and estimated undiscovered petroleum. Often a pool contains more crude oil than can be documented during geological testing.

Crude petroleum is a mixture of an almost infinite number of hydrocarbon compounds ranging from light gases of simple chemical structure to heavy tar-like liquids and waxes of complex chemical composition. The oil as it comes from the well also contains varied amounts of sulfur, nitrogen, sand, and water. It has been established that the amount of carbon varies from 83 to 87 percent, and the hydrogen from 13 to 14 percent. The many compounds that comprise crude oil belong to the paraffin, naphthene, and aromatic families, along with a considerable amount of asphalic materials of unknown chemical structure. However, a finished petroleum product cannot be so easily divided into these molecular structures since they are made up of molecules from several families. Thus, a ring nucleus may be joined to a chain compound, or several rings of either the same or different families may be joined together to form a single molecule. Because of this, gasoline is a complex chemical composition, with each element affecting the performance of an engine.

Refining is the process that alters the composition of crude oil into a multitude of petroleum products. The making of gasoline for today's modern engine is no simple task. Crude oil contains only a limited amount of the hydrocarbons suitable for direct use in an engine. Therefore, other components need to be added to meet the requirements of a motor fuel.

By definition, a refinery is a system of processing units used to convert crude petroleum into fuels, lubricants, and other petroleum-based products. A very large investment is required to build a refinery, along with a multitude of environmental concerns. Because of this, no two refineries are exactly alike, even if they are owned by the same company. There are many different types of refineries, and they are usually identified by the processes performed there.

It must be realized that gasoline can differ quite widely in components from each refinery, even if the fuel is considered the same grade. In addition to the processing differences at each facility, the crude oil that is refined can be very different, and can even vary daily. In addition, the operating conditions at the plants themselves need to be modified according to the seasons, and influence the quality of the product produced.

Much of the work done at a refinery is through heating and separating the components of the crude oil. Therefore, the maximum use from the heating process is designed into the refinery layout. As an example, a process that heats the oil may then have the preheated crude boil another component before being cooled.

Following are some of the steps taken during the refining process of gasoline and are condensed descriptions.

Distillation. This is the initial process used at all refineries with the goal of separating the crude oil into different boiling range factions, each of which may eventually be a product on its own. Crude oil consists of thousands of different hydrocarbons, each with its own boiling point. The term ends is applied, and thus each component is identified as either a light or heavy end. The lightest are usually the gases at normal ambient temperature that will remain dissolved in the heavier hydrocarbons unless heated. The heaviest components are solids at ambient temperatures but are able to stay in solution except at extremely low temperatures. Distillation does not chemically change the crude oil in any way, but instead separates it into groups, each with its own boiling point.

Cracking process. There are two generally accepted methods of cracking: thermal and catalytic. Regardless of the procedure, cracking is defined as the process used to reduce the molecular weight of hydrocarbons by breaking the molecular bonds. Thermal cracking is now obsolete for

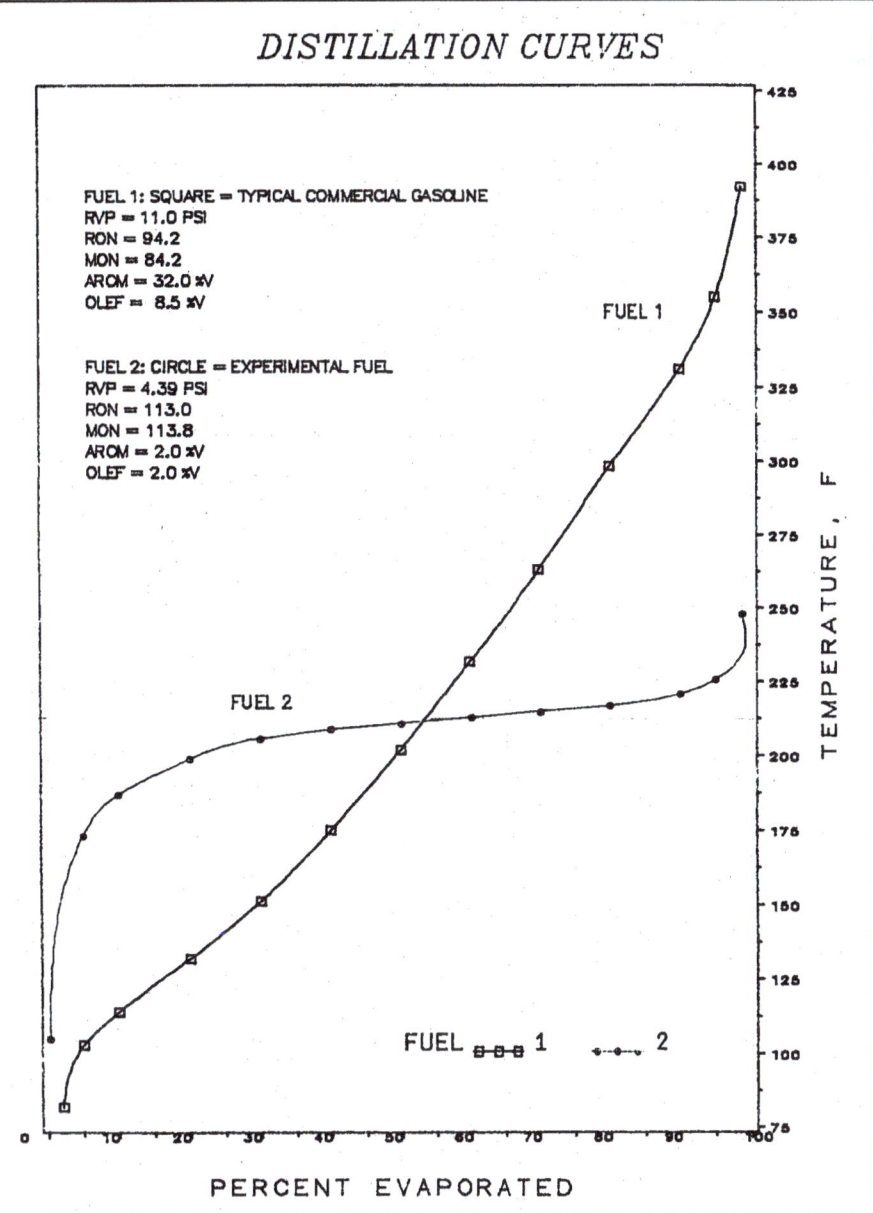

A distillation plot for conventional fuel (1) and race fuel (2).

the production of gasoline since many superior processes have been discovered. Thermal cracking required the petroleum to be exposed to a temperature of approximately 868 F degrees at 1015 psi. Visbreaking is a low-severity form of thermal cracking originally developed to reduce the viscosity of the residual fuel. Similar to conventional thermal cracking, the crude would be heated to the same temperature, but at a lower pressure of 290 psi.

Catalytic cracking is the most widely used form for the production of gasoline today. It allows the creation of more usable product from the crude oil consumed. It functions by exposing the petroleum to a catalytic material in the form of a bed that is made of an aluminum silicate known as zeolite, which suppresses the formation of light olefins.

Reforming. This process converts low-octane gasoline into higher-octane stocks suitable for blending into a finished product. It can be accomplished through either a thermal or a catalytic process. This is not to be confused with reformulated gasoline, which has an oxygenate added and will be discussed later.

Alkylation. The opposite of cracking, alkylation makes larger hydrocarbon units from smaller ones. It produces gasoline-range liquids from

SPECIFIC GRAVITY TO API GRAVITY CONVERSION CHART

API Gravity 60°F	Specific Gravity 60/60°F	Density 15°C	API Gravity 60°F	Specific Gravity 60/60°F	Density 15°C	API Gravity 60°F	Specific Gravity 60/60°F	Density 15°C
0.0	1.0760	1.0754	5.0	1.0366	1.0360	10.0	1.0000	0.9994
0.1	1.0752	1.0745	5.1	1.0359	1.0352	10.1	0.9993	0.9987
0.2	1.0744	1.0737	5.2	1.0351	1.0345	10.2	0.9986	0.9980
0.3	1.0736	1.0729	5.3	1.0344	1.0337	10.3	0.9979	0.9973
0.4	1.0728	1.0721	5.4	1.0336	1.0330	10.4	0.9972	0.9966
0.5	1.0720	1.0713	5.5	1.0328	1.0322	10.5	0.9965	0.9959
0.6	1.0712	1.0705	5.6	1.0321	1.0315	10.6	0.9958	0.9952
0.7	1.0703	1.0697	5.7	1.0313	1.0307	10.7	0.9951	0.9945
0.8	1.0695	1.0689	5.8	1.0306	1.0300	10.8	0.9944	0.9938
0.9	1.0687	1.0681	5.9	1.0298	1.0292	10.9	0.9937	0.9931
1.0	1.0679	1.0673	6.0	1.0291	1.0285	11.0	0.9930	0.9924
1.1	1.0671	1.0664	6.1	1.0283	1.0277	11.1	0.9923	0.9917
1.2	1.0663	1.0656	6.2	1.0276	1.0270	11.2	0.9916	0.9910
1.3	1.0655	1.0648	6.3	1.0269	1.0262	11.3	0.9909	0.9903
1.4	1.0647	1.0640	6.4	1.0261	1.0255	11.4	0.9902	0.9896
1.5	1.0639	1.0632	6.5	1.0254	1.0247	11.5	0.9895	0.9889
1.6	1.0631	1.0624	6.6	1.0246	1.0240	11.6	0.9888	0.9882
1.7	1.0623	1.0616	6.7	1.0239	1.0233	11.7	0.9881	0.9875
1.8	1.0615	1.0609	6.8	1.0231	1.0225	11.8	0.9874	0.9869
1.9	1.0607	1.0601	6.9	1.0224	1.0218	11.9	0.9868	0.9862
2.0	1.0599	1.0593	7.0	1.0217	1.0210	12.0	0.9861	0.9855
2.1	1.0591	1.0585	7.1	1.0209	1.0203	12.1	0.9854	0.9848
2.2	1.0583	1.0577	7.2	1.0202	1.0196	12.2	0.9847	0.9841
2.3	1.0575	1.0569	7.3	1.0195	1.0188	12.3	0.9840	0.9834
2.4	1.0568	1.0561	7.4	1.0187	1.0181	12.4	0.9833	0.9827
2.5	1.0560	1.0553	7.5	1.0180	1.0174	12.5	0.9826	0.9821
2.6	1.0552	1.0545	7.6	1.0173	1.0166	12.6	0.9820	0.9814
2.7	1.0544	1.0537	7.7	1.0165	1.0159	12.7	0.9813	0.9807
2.8	1.0536	1.0530	7.8	1.0158	1.0152	12.8	0.9806	0.9800
2.9	1.0528	1.0522	7.9	1.0151	1.0145	12.9	0.9799	0.9793
3.0	1.0520	1.0514	8.0	1.0143	1.0137	13.0	0.9792	0.9787
3.1	1.0513	1.0506	8.1	1.0136	1.0130	13.1	0.9786	0.9780
3.2	1.0505	1.0498	8.2	1.0129	1.0123	13.2	0.9779	0.9773
3.3	1.0497	1.0491	8.3	1.0122	1.0116	13.3	0.9772	0.9766
3.4	1.0489	1.0483	8.4	1.0114	1.0108	13.4	0.9765	0.9760
3.5	1.0481	1.0475	8.5	1.0107	1.0101	13.5	0.9759	0.9753
3.6	1.0474	1.0467	8.6	1.0100	1.0094	13.6	0.9752	0.9746
3.7	1.0466	1.0460	8.7	1.0093	1.0087	13.7	0.9745	0.9739
3.8	1.0458	1.0452	8.8	1.0086	1.0080	13.8	0.9738	0.9733
3.9	1.0451	1.0444	8.9	1.0078	1.0072	13.9	0.9732	0.9726
4.0	1.0443	1.0436	9.0	1.0071	1.0065	14.0	0.9725	0.9719
4.1	1.0435	1.0429	9.1	1.0064	1.0058	14.1	0.9718	0.9713
4.2	1.0427	1.0421	9.2	1.0057	1.0051	14.2	0.9712	0.9706
4.3	1.0420	1.0413	9.3	1.0050	1.0044	14.3	0.9705	0.9699
4.4	1.0412	1.0406	9.4	1.0043	1.0037	14.4	0.9698	0.9693
4.5	1.0404	1.0398	9.5	1.0035	1.0029	14.5	0.9692	0.9686
4.6	1.0397	1.0390	9.6	1.0028	1.0022	14.6	0.9685	0.9680
4.7	1.0389	1.0383	9.7	1.0021	1.0015	14.7	0.9679	0.9673
4.8	1.0382	1.0375	9.8	1.0014	1.0008	14.8	0.9672	0.9666
4.9	1.0374	1.0308	9.9	1.0007	1.0001	14.9	0.9665	0.9660
5.0	1.0366	1.0360	10.0	1.0000	0.9994	15.0	0.9659	0.9653

refinery gases. It was extensively used during World War II for its ability to raise octane for military aircraft.

Polymerization. Similar to alkylation, this process is a method of making gasoline from refinery olefinic gases, linking them together to form olefinic liquids. Any paraffin-based gases that enter the process are left unaltered.

Isomerization. As its name implies, it is a method of converting chemical compounds into their isomers, rearranging the way they are put together without changing their size or chemical composition. Straight molecular-chained heptane was chosen to represent zero on the octane scale, and could then be isomerized to a mixture of isoheptanes that were rated at more than 100 octane to blend a fuel.

What is octane?

By definition, octane is fuel's ability to resist auto-ignition from pressure and heat. In other words, it is the fuel's resistance to combustion until ignited with a spark. The number value assigned to the octane of gasoline is a measure of its antiknock performance; the higher the value, the greater the fuel's resistance to knock. There are two main tests to determine the octane of a fuel. They are the motor octane number (MON) and the research octane number (RON). Recently, another rating has been developed, the AKI, or antiknock index. It is the average of the RON and MON and is displayed with the formula RON + MON/2.

Gasoline RON and MON ratings are derived in a laboratory using a single-cylinder variable-compression-ratio test engine designed specifically for this task. During the RON testing, the engine is run at 600 rpm with an air intake temperature of 125 F degrees at standard barometric pressure. The MON schedule uses the same engine but runs at 900 rpm with an intake charge temperature of 300 F degrees. What is important is that the temperature referenced for the MON rating is at the entry of the intake port of the cylinder head, after the vaporization of the fuel has removed heat from the charge air.

In contrast, the RON procedure allows the engine to ingest air at

PERFORMANCE COMPARISON

PROPERTY	NITROFUEL®	METHANOL	ISO-OCTANE
Brake Mean Effective Pressure[1] (psi)	450	290	170
Horsepower/ cubic inch[1]	5.2	3.3	2.0
Fuel Metering	Fuel Injection	Fuel Injection	Carburetion
Manifold Pressure (HG)	90	90	Naturally aspirated
Static Comp. Ratio	7:1	10:1	13:1
Motor Octane #	-1000[2]	92	100

1 Approximate for selected representative applications in drag racing
2 Extrapolated estimate

HANDLING COMPARISON WITH OTHER RACING FUELS

PROPERTY	NITROFUEL®	METHANOL	GASOLINE
Corrosiveness	Low	High	Low
Lubricity	Low	Low	Medium
Storage Stability	High	Medium	Low
Solubility in Methanol in Gasoline	High Very Low	— Low	Very Low —

THERMODYNAMIC PROPERTIES COMPARISON

PROPERTY	NITROFUEL®	METHANOL	ISO-OCTANE
Chemical Formula	CH_3NO_2	CH_3OH	C_8H_{18}
Oxygen Content (weight) %	52.5	49.9	0
Lower Heating Value (BTU/pound)	4,993	8,644	19,065
Air/Fuel Ratio	1.7:1	6.45:1	15.1:1
Specific Energy (BTU/ pound air)	2,937	1.340	1.263
Specific Energy Ratio	2.33	1.06	1.0
Mole Ratio of Products and Reactants[1]	1.30	1.06	1.06
Theoretical Flame Temperature, °F	5,149	3,732	3,867

1 Computer equilibrium products at 0 = 1

Not all race cars require the same fuel. The needs of each engine are considered by the chemist.

125 F degrees. During the MON test the inlet air is substantially hotter than 300 F degrees, since this value represents the temperature after the latent heat of vaporization. The test engine is manufactured by the Waukesha Company of Wisconsin. The variable compression ratio is obtained by making the head and cylinder one unit. Then the cylinder can be raised or lowered by a hand crank, varying the compression volume and, therefore, the compression ratio of the engine, since the piston stroke is constant. The RPM of the engine is held steady by a synchronous generator that is driven by the engine and connected to an AC powerline. The generator then acts like a brake, limiting the engine speed to a multiple of the line frequency. The carburetor for the engine has three bowls, and the fuel fed from each bowl can be varied, thus altering the air/fuel ratio. The test fuel is placed in one bowl while blends of the reference fuels are in the other two bowls.

During the MON and RON testing, the amount of knock is registered by a vibration meter. For these tests, the engine is run under the specified conditions but with a defined compression ratio and blend of reference fuel. The knock obtained under these standard conditions is called the standard knock and is used to adjust the sensitivity of the knock meter to 55 units. This standardizes the intensity of knock, which now can be reproduced at different compression ratios. The unknown octane rating of the test fuel is determined by operation and adjusting the mixture ratio for maximum knock. The compression ratio is then varied until the knock intensity is at the standard 55 units. With the compression ratio locked at this setting, known blends of reference fuels are placed in the two other carburetor bowls.

Each fuel is then tested in turn, and the knock meter readings are recorded. Eventually, the original knock meter reading of 55 units will be bracketed by readings from the two known fuels. One blend will have a higher octane number than the unknown sample, and the second blend will have a lower number. The two known blends should differ by not more than two octane numbers from each other before interpolation of the readings to find the equivalent octane rating of the unknown fuel. In contrast, the aviation procedure uses the same engine but measures the temperature of a mixture of 87 percent iso-octane and 13 percent heptane as its reference.

The chemical iso-octane, which is a hydrocarbon trimethylpentane, has eight carbon atoms and is used as the primary reference fuel; it has been assigned values of 100 for both RON and MON. The octane rating of the fuel is then determined by the amount of iso-octane that is blended with heptane (zero octane) that will yield the same knock intensity as the fuel being tested in the engine.

Most consumers think that a higher-octane fuel is more powerful than a lower-rated one. This is not true. The energy content of fuel is measured in British thermal units and is not a function of octane, but density. The procedures used to raise the octane may actually lower the energy content. The proper way to measure Btu content of a fuel is in units of energy per pound of fuel, since that is the method used to measure the induction process of an engine. All calculations for air/fuel ratio are made in pounds of air to pounds of fuel. Since we purchase gasoline in gallons, then a good value to assign for energy content is 115,000 Btu per gallon. If your engine makes more power or travels farther on a tank of higher-octane fuel, it most likely is due to the increased cylinder pressure from the absence of abnormal combustion, not a higher energy content.

Early on, it was discovered that the introduction of tetraethyl lead, or TEL (what we call lead), was a very effective, inexpensive way to substantially raise the octane of fuel. In the United States, unleaded fuel had to be available since July 1, 1974, and from the late 1970s, all automobiles sold had to use unleaded fuel. The removal of lead from gasoline was nothing new, though. During WWII, a large-scale effort was going on in the U.S. and created many patented procedures. The concern was to remove large amounts of lead from small amounts of gasoline so it could be used by troops in the field as a cooking fuel and for lighting. Lead introduced into fuel was generally TEL, tetramethyl lead (TML), or a mix of these two compounds, identified as TMEL. With the required removal of all lead from motor fuels, other methods needed to be employed to raise the octane and have added substantially to production costs.

What am I buying?

The fact remains that little is known about the fuel we purchase at the pump or race track. Companies such as Union 76, Sunoco, and VP, which produce and market race gas, usually provide a list of specifications for their products. If you are not a chemist, these specifications are usually meaningless beyond the octane. During the refining process, the final product is considered to be base fuel. The industry defines that as a fuel that has not yet been additized, meaning no additives have been introduced. Since there are not refineries on every corner, the oil companies purchase base fuel from one another. The amount and composition of the additives each company includes in the final product makes it brand specific.

In parts of the country that don't have refineries, the fuel is made into the specifications of the brand at the distribution center or terminal. The necessary additives are fed into the tanker truck, and then the base fuel is added. Gasoline is considered fungible, meaning its characteristics are so similar that it can be mixed with other brands with no adverse affect, other than possibly diluting the additives. To represent this, think of a bank savings account. If you deposit $10 today and then withdraw $10 tomorrow, you don't care if you receive the same exact bill back, as long as the withdrawn amount is equal to $10. Money in this term can then be considered fungible, just like gasoline.

The purpose of additives is usually to decrease deposit formation on the intake valves, known as IVD, and in the combustion chamber, which is abbreviated CCD. The components that are added to the base fuel then comprise its composition and, due to the different approaches taken, can alter the octane, burn rate, and boiling point.

The density of the fuel is the only true indicator of the Btu content but is not readily available. Most specifications for gasoline list the specific gravity of the fuel, but the indicator for density is the American Petroleum Institute's (API) gravity test at 60 F degrees. Many motorsports organizations use a specific gravity test as a fuel check, and that value is published for high-octane race gas. The specific gravity can be converted to the API gravity results using the chart elsewhere in this chapter. When reading the API scale, the lower the value, the more dense the fuel. The density is where the energy content of the fuel lies and is a function of the base fuel and the refining process.

What does the engine want?

The main concern when purchasing a motor fuel is to provide sufficient octane so that a normal combustion event occurs at all times. Since an engine operates under different loads and conditions, normal combustion becomes a moving target. That is the

---

FUEL TEST POINTS

The following is a description of test points and their impact on fuel. The letter "T" designates a test temperature and the hyphenated numeral is the percent of the fuel evaporated.

T-10
In general, a lower reading defines a fuel that will cold start easier. However, if it is too low, it may contribute to carburetor icing and stalling during warmup. This plot in the curve is usually altered to create what is known as summer or winter gas.

T-50
While the T-10 identifies ease of starting, this point on the curve indicates the ability of the gasoline to supply a proper mixture during most of the warmup or intermediate period of engine operation. The lower this plot, the faster the engine will warm up. Carburetor icing can be reduced when the 50-percent point is increased.

T-90
This defines the amount of high-boiling-point components in the gasoline. At the proper engine temperature, these ingredients contribute to good fuel mileage. Offsetting this is their tendency to cause poor mixture distribution in a cold intake manifold. The T-90 point for most street gasoline is 300-350 F degrees.

Final Boiling Point (FBP)
This is the end point of the gasoline that indicates the extent to which heavy ends are present. When the difference between the T-90 and the FBP exceeds 70 F degrees, there is the possibility that the quantity of heavy ends may create excessive engine deposits.

Aromatics
The term was originally applied to benzene and its derivatives because of their unique odor. The aromatics are a family of ring-type hydrocarbons that contain three double bonds in the ring. The basic structure of aromatics is typified by benzene itself but embraces many related compounds such as toluene, xylene, and cumene. They are all components that can be used to blend a fuel.

As a consumer, you want the highest-density fuel without over-purchasing the amount of octane to support maximum power in your engine. Most major metropolitan areas sell reformulated gasoline (RFG) that contains the oxygenate MTBE. The purpose of this fuel is to reduce cold-start carbon monoxide emissions before the catalytic converter becomes functional. Gasoline that is categorized as RFG is less dense and consequently produces less power and fuel economy.

---

purpose of the RON and MON procedures, with the former addressing the fuel's antiknock ability under part-throttle light load, and the latter concerned more with higher loads and throttle openings.

Compression ratio is a major factor in determining the octane tolerance of an engine, but not the only one. Octane tolerance defines the minimal amount of octane required to support normal combustion. As the octane tolerance of an engine is increased, it is able to withstand lower-grade fuel with no adverse affect on power. However, the compression ratio is not the only factor. An engine is a systems approach, and the required octane is determined by the combustion chamber design and material, air/fuel ratio, charge air temperature, cam profile, and effectiveness of the cooling system, among other things. Octane allows the design and the tuning of the engine to be brought closer to optimal.

Cylinder pressure is what drives the crankshaft, and the higher the Btu content of the fuel, the greater the force against the piston.

As an example, nitromethane used in dragsters and funny cars has a negative octane rating. How does an estimated MON of -1000[2] hit you? A drop of nitromethane placed on a table and hit with a rubber mallet will explode from the induced pressure. That is why an engine that runs on this fuel sounds like it does; it can be likened to placing a stick of dynamite in the cylinder for every firing event. It builds about three times the cylinder pressure of pure iso-octane.

Empirically, many racers believe that higher-octane fuels burn slower, requiring more spark advance. The burn speed is not a function of octane, though components in the base fuel and the composition of the final blend will affect the burn rate and, in turn, the amount of required spark advance.

How to Tune and Win with Demon Carburetors

RACE GASOLINE

The objective in motorsports is to maximize an engine's power output while working within any imposed restrictions on fuel quality and requiring the engine to survive the duration of the race. The factors that become important in a racing gasoline are as follows:

Heating value. The greater the heat content of the fuel, the higher the potential energy output.

Stoichiometry. The lower the stoichiometric air/fuel ratio, the more fuel can be introduced into the combustion chamber.

Ratio of products to reactants. The higher this ratio, the higher the combustion pressure in the cylinder, and potentially the higher the power produced by the engine.

Resistance to detonation and pre-ignition. The severe duty experienced during racing may mean that the MON rating is more important than the RON as a guide to the fuel's anti-knock performance when the engine is normally aspirated. For forced-induction engines, the reverse would be true. However, under the extreme conditions of a race, the RON and MON of the fuel may not have very much meaning in terms of predicting whether knock or pre-ignition from knock will occur.

Flammability limits. This should be such that the rich air/fuel ratios can be used that maximize power.

Flame speeds. A fast burn rate is important in a racing engine since it helps to maintain good combustion under varying conditions of speed, load, air/fuel ratio, and also because combustion needs to be virtually complete before the expansion stroke is over in order to maximize thermal efficiency. Engines that operate over 10,000 rpm have a very limited combustion event time for this to happen.

Heat of vaporization. A high heat of vaporization will increase the volumetric efficiency of an engine by cooling the intake charge as the fuel evaporates, and increases its energy density.

Volatility. A fuel must have a boiling range that allows it to be transported readily in liquid form and yet volatilize satisfactorily in the intake system.

Safety. Fuel must be stable enough to ensure that it does not cause an explosion hazard during use or when being transported and handled under normal conditions.

Since it is not possible to produce a fuel that has optimum levels of all of these characteristics, race gas, like most things, is a compromise. One important method of comparing the heat release of different brands of fuel in an engine is the specific energy (SE). The theoretical SE is calculated by dividing the lower-rated heating value by the air/fuel ratio so that it represents the fuel energy delivered to the combustion chamber per unit mass of air inducted. It is often calculated for the stoichiometric air/fuel ratio. The actual SE is calculated from the actual heat of combustion and the actual air/fuel ratio. SE changes with air/fuel ratio and is only valid within the flammability limits of the fuel.

That is why, for maximum performance at the track, your tune-up should be done with the fuel being a constant.

Everyday motor fuels represent other concerns beyond octane, including the way the fuel responds to being heated, or the lack of heat. A street car endures a completely different set of circumstances than a race car, and so what is a concern for your everyday car is not an issue for a race car. Alcohol is an easy way to raise octane, but the problem is that it absorbs moisture and has only half the energy content of gasoline. This means that it is very corrosive and requires double the amount to produce the same power levels. Many companies add alcohol to raise the octane, but these fuels deliver less power and economy since they are less dense.

Since a street fuel needs to be vaporized at low temperature while remaining liquid to avoid vapor-lock at higher temperatures, these become the main concerns of the chemist. Following are terms used to describe gasoline's response when heated.

Reid vapor pressure (RVP). This is the vapor pressure obtained when the fuel is heated to 100 F degrees in a vessel called a bomb. It is determined by filling a metal chamber with chilled samples of gasoline and connecting it to an air chamber, which is then connected to a pressure gauge. The complete assembly is then immersed in a water bath at 100 F degrees and shaken periodically until a constant pressure is obtained, which is then identified as the RVP.

The significance of this test is to partially determine the fuel's resistance to vapor-lock and heat-soak. For automotive fuels, an RVP of 9 psi in the summer and 12 psi in the winter is considered normal. The true indicator of the fuel's ability to withstand vapor-lock is the vapor/liquid test procedure.

The distillation test. Gasoline is made up of many different components, and they do not all boil at the same time. The distillation test creates a plot or curve that is used to determine the amount of fuel boiled, read in percent at varied temperatures. Consider a pot of water placed on a kitchen stove at atmospheric pressure. When the water reaches 212 F degrees it will boil. If you were to add another component to the water that does not boil until 250 F degrees, then eventually the water would dissipate by way of steam, and the heavier, higher boiling point element would be left. That is what a distillation test determines; it identifies the boiling point for each component of the gasoline.

Initial boiling point (IBP). This usually occurs between 85 and 95 F degrees. The terms front-end volatility,

---

WHAT DO CARBURETORS HAVE TO DO WITH SHOCK ABSORBERS?

Since carburetors work primarily on a pressure differential that creates a liquid flow, they became a course of study in fluid dynamics for a designer of shock absorbers. Even though each fluid possesses its own properties, the carburetor shares many design elements and theories with a shock absorber. Frictional flow losses, surface tension, and flow through an orifice are shared elements of both a carburetor and a shock absorber. So the next time you are under your vehicle and see the shocks, know that they are a distant cousin to the Demon carburetor.

ALCOHOL AS RACE FUEL

Straight methanol commonly used as a racing fuel has many advantages over hydrocarbon-based fuels. It is somewhat better than gasoline in terms of specific energy since its low heating value is more than offset by a low stoichiometric air/fuel ratio. In addition, maximum power is obtained at very rich mixtures of 4:1 so that under these conditions, the SE is considerably higher than that of gasoline, where maximum power is obtained at a ratio of approximately 20 percent richer than stoichiometric. Methanol has excellent antiknock properties that allow high compression ratios to be used. It also has a high heat of vaporization, providing good volumetric efficiency, and it's readily available and relatively inexpensive.

The main problem is the high fuel consumption rate, particularly when operating at the air/fuel ratio for maximum power. At the required air/fuel ratio of 4:1 the engine will run cool, and as the mixture is leaned from there, economy will increase but power production will drop. Cold starting can be an issue with straight methanol because it has a very low vapor pressure and small amounts of hydrocarbons are added to combat this concern. Because methanol boils at a single temperature, carburetion calibration can be difficult.

Ethanol, which is commonly used as a race fuel, is intermediate in properties between methanol and gasoline. The air/fuel ratio for maximum power is approximately 7:1, and the relatively high heat of vaporization makes it a good choice for a race engine. The term aliphatic is used to describe the composition of alcohol and denotes a hydrocarbon compound with open carbon chains rather than ring structures. As the aliphatic scale goes higher, the combustion characteristics approach those of gasoline. Though the performance industry uses the term alcohol, it is actually referring to ethanol in most instances.

light factions, and low boiling materials are commonly used to describe the most volatile components in gasoline. These are the elements that boil and evaporate first. The behavior of gasoline in an engine cannot be predicted from the IBP alone. A better indicator is the temperature for 10 percent evaporation (T-10) and its Reid vapor pressure.

REVIEW QUESTIONS

(1) The fuel pressure required by a Demon carburetor when fueled with gasoline:

a: is 2-3 psi
b: is 6-8 psi
c: varies with engine design
d: is 45 psi

(2) A block-mounted diaphragm-style pump delivers fuel to the carburetor:

a: under full engine load
b: only when the needle valve is closed
c: during closed-throttle high-vacuum conditions
d: when the needle valve is open

(3) BG electric fuel pumps are of which design?

a: vane-and-rotor positive displacement
b: centrifugal
c: negative displacement
d: They vary by model and application

(4) A fuel pressure regulator is used:

a: when the fuel pump has no internal bypass
b: on a belt-driven-style pump only
c: when the fuel pump has an integral bypass
d: on alcohol engines only

(5) When installing an electric fuel pump, a relay should be used:

a: always
b: only if the pump is more than 10 feet from the battery
c: if the fuel pump draws more than 10 amps
d: on race cars

(6) A diaphragm bypass requires:

a: an electric fuel pump
b: the use of a fuel cell
c: a return line back to the fuel tank or cell
d: AN-style fittings

(7) The octane of gasoline represents its:

a: power potential
b: heat content measured in Btu
c: ability to resist ignition by heat or pressure
d: much spark advance the engine needs

(8) The density of gasoline is measured by:

a: either a specific or API gravity test
b: RON + MON/2
c: a distillation test
d: catalytic cracking

(9) When lead is added to fuel:

a: octane goes up
b: density decreases
c: octane goes down
d: RVP is altered

(10) All gasoline is considered:

a: legal for street use
b: the same composition
c: fungible
d: the same density

Answers: 1) B, 2) D, 3) A, 4) C, 5) A, 6) C, 7) C, 8) A, 9) A, 10) C

How to Tune & Win with DEMON CARBURETORS
Tuning for Street/Strip

Bolting on parts to an engine comes relatively easy for the majority of automotive enthusiasts, but the finesse of a fine tune evades most. For a person to be accomplished in this area, it takes a special understanding of engines and mechanical things. For this to occur, a synergy needs to be established between you and the complete vehicle. This is why a tuner can be compared to the conductor of an orchestra: He does not play any of the instruments, but under his guidance, music is made instead of noise.

The road to understanding is not a simple one, though, and often includes topics that many performance enthusiasts do not believe are important – even though they are. They become one-dimensional, not recognizing that an impressive engine is one that does many things well. Acknowledging this concept, let's discuss the tuning elements of the Demon carburetor for an engine that serves duty on the street, or dual purpose on both street and strip. Race-engine tuning will be covered in Chapter 10 and will use the fundamentals established here as a foundation.

THE HOW AND WHY OF SPARK ADVANCE

Throughout the development of the Demon carburetor line, it has been recognized that other aspects of the engine will ultimately affect the carburetor's performance. The same logic has been applied to this book and is the reasoning behind establishing a complete understanding of spark advance.

According to the Demon technical line, the most common mistake when tuning a carburetor is an incorrect amount of base timing. The theory of how ignition and fuel delivery work hand-in-hand is usually not recognized. The epitome of a dialed-in engine encompasses the proper carburetor jetting, air bleeds, and emulsion orifices, along with the correct rate of spark advance. All too often the requirements of the engine are oversimplified and a fixed amount of advance is set and never touched again.

Any conversation about spark timing is actually a discussion of the gas-exchange process and the theory of flame speeds and burn rates. During combustion, the spark travels slower than the piston, which is why it is necessary to give it a head start. Combustion in an engine depends on the ability of the flame front originating at the spark plug to travel into regions of unburned mixture. This occurs by means of conduction, diffusion, radiation, and then convection of heat. The unburned mixture is then heated and compressed, and it ignites. Conduction and diffusion of heat from the burned to unburned charge into the fresh charge, and vice versa, are of great importance during the expansion stroke.

Although it's not easy to determine the exact speed of the flame front during propagation, the consensus of most engineers is a rate of 10-25 meters/second. Many factors affect the speed of the flame, and thus the amount of spark advance the engine requires to produce the best power without entering abnormal combustion, more commonly known as detonation or ping. The spark plug firing is always referenced against the position of the crankshaft in rotational degrees. As an example, a total

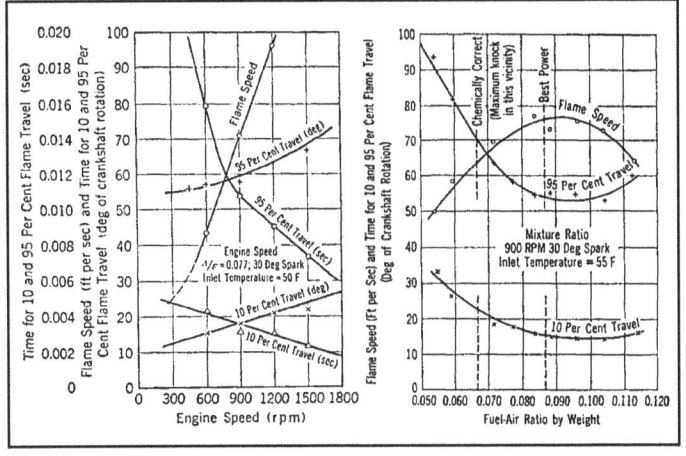

Many factors affect flame travel across the cylinder, including compression ratio, combustion chamber design, and mixture ratio. This chart uses fuel/air ratio instead of the more customary air/fuel ratio. Measured in this scale, 0.77 is approximately 13.0:1 air/fuel ratio.

Both the mixture ratio and spark curve need to be calibrated properly for the carburetor to perform as intended.

advance curve of 42 degrees BTDC translates to the arcing of the spark plug when the crankshaft is 42 rotational degrees before TDC. The purpose of spark timing is to control and utilize the greatest amount of energy from the fuel consumed by allowing the cylinder pressures to peak in as few rotational degrees of the crankshaft past TDC as possible. This will allow for the most energy to be imparted against the piston as the flame front expands, transferring more power to the crankshaft.

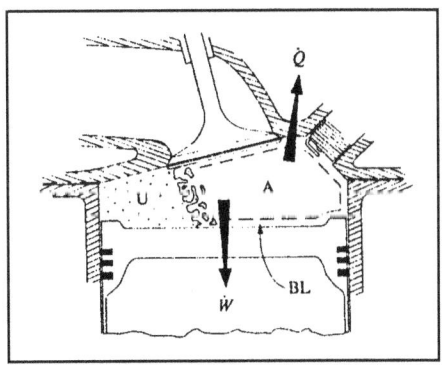

The air/fuel mixture supplied by the carburetor is ignited by the arcing of the spark plug. As the flame travels from burned to unburned regions, represented by Q and U, respectively, the expansion compresses the unburned fuel and raises the cylinder pressure and turbulence. During this time, both the cylinder pressure and turbulence are low, until an area known as the reaction zone is established.

The problem for the tuner is that the flame speed, identified as a median velocity, depends on a combination of burning speed, flow speed, and expansion speed, which are impacted by compression ratio, mixture ratio, charge motion, spark plug location, cylinder head material, and combustion chamber design. Additionally, the bore size and the flame termination process (when it reaches the cylinder wall) come into play.

The final stage of combustion is when the flame slows down as it approaches the far walls of the chamber. It is difficult to detect this exact point, so most travel is referenced to the 95-percent position. The quicker the mixture burns, the less head start the flame will require; conversely, the opposite applies. A good rule is, as the compression ratio increases or as the spark plug moves closer to the center of the bore, the amount of advance for maximum power goes down. On the OE level, the timing curve is usually referenced against the engine's ability to produce maximum brake torque, or MBT. Occasionally, this abbreviation may denote maximum best timing for torque.

During combustion, if the flame spreads out from the spark plug with no bias flow paths, the leading-edge burning layer takes the shape of a spherical shell, also known as a flame kernel. The edges of the sphere will be ragged due to convective currents in the highly turbulent mixture. Once the flame reaches the vicinity of the combustion chamber wall, it cools and slows down. During the beginning periods of combustion, the cylinder pressure rise is small because the amount of charge burned is extremely minute. At this point, the flame speed is usually slow due to minimal

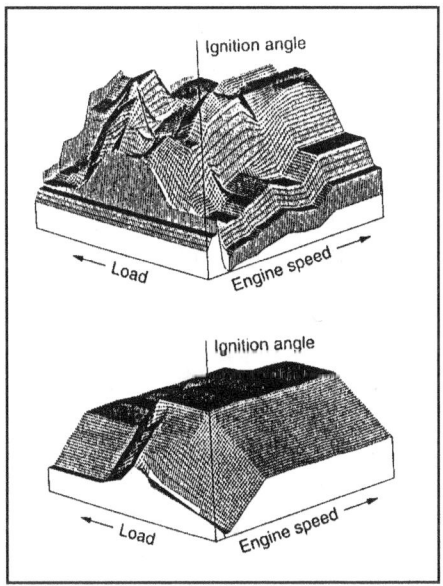

Spark advance rates are not a one-dimensional equation of RPM vs. advance. The top graph shows the advance rate that an engine would require for maximum power, accomplished through electronic controls. The lower graph is what a conventional vacuum/mechanical advance system delivers.

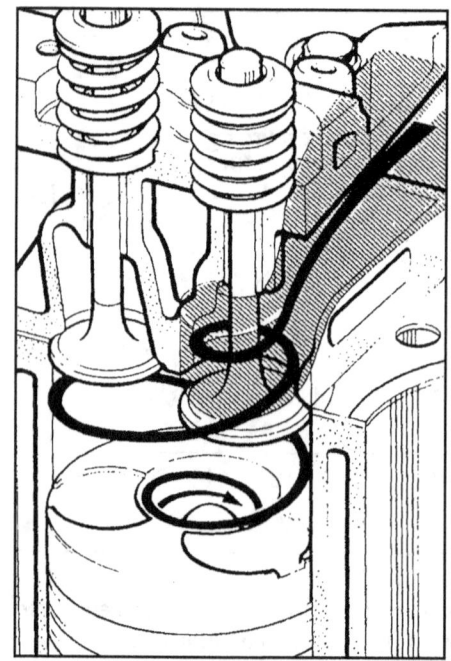

Externally-induced mixture motion that follows the bore of the cylinder is known as swirl. This motion creates turbulence and increases burn rates. As burn rates go up, the need for spark lead goes down.

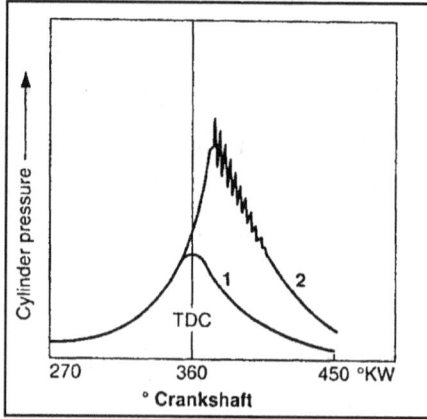

The uncontrolled release of the fuel's energy during abnormal combustion causes both the cylinder pressure and temperature to spike in a destructive manner.

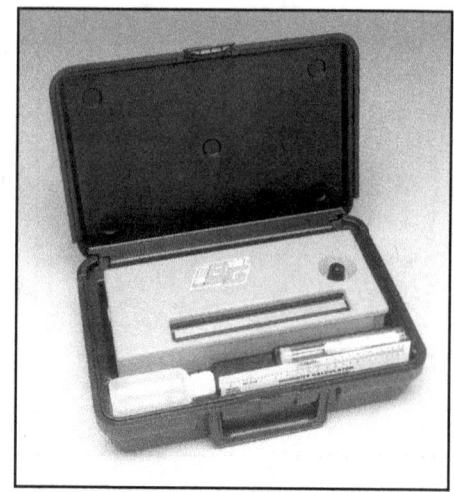

A psychrometer is a device that comprises two thermometers: one a dry bulb, the other a wet or wick-covered bulb. It's used to determine the moisture content or relative humidity in air. It may also be called a wet-and-dry-bulb thermometer. This BG electric version determines the temperature and humidity without the need for constant monitoring. A battery-powered fan provides constant airflow to the thermometer bulbs for greater accuracy than sling-style units.

turbulence, and because an area identified as a reaction zone needs to be established, where the heat will transfer from the burned to unburned mixture. The turbulence rises from the velocity of the incoming charge and impacts flame speeds likewise. Most spark plug locations, other than centralized in the bore, are in low-turbulence areas and require more lead time. If the timing of the spark is either advanced or retarded from the optimal position, the work transfer to the piston will decrease. Engineers are also concerned with the mass-burned fraction and the time to burn 10 and 95 percent of the fuel.

What does the engine really want?

It's difficult to believe, but if you are using any type of mechanical advance controls on a street engine, you're probably not even close to the ideal spark curve. This is best illustrated by the chart located near the end of this chapter. Looking at the ignition curve supplied by mechanical means, it is quite obvious that it varies drastically from what the same engine used to produce MBT, accomplished

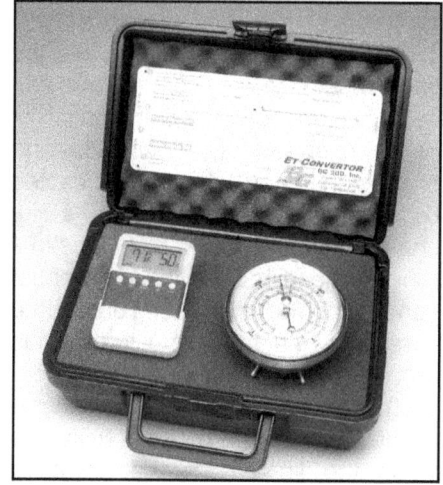

The BG Weather Factor kit is designed as an economic alternative to a complete weather station for 10- to 16-second bracket racers. It includes a weather factor slide rule, precision-grade barometer, digital Thermo-Hygrometer, and protective hard plastic case.

with electronic controls.

Mechanical advance systems work under the assumption that the spark demand is linear with engine RPM and then levels out, or in simpler terms, a total amount of advance by a given RPM. This is the byproduct of looking at engine vacuum and RPM only to determine an advance curve. Including the static position of the distributor, this allows for a 3-degrees-of-freedom (DOF) ignition curve while the vacuum signal is still being produced.

In contrast, electronic engine-controlled spark timing plots the spark

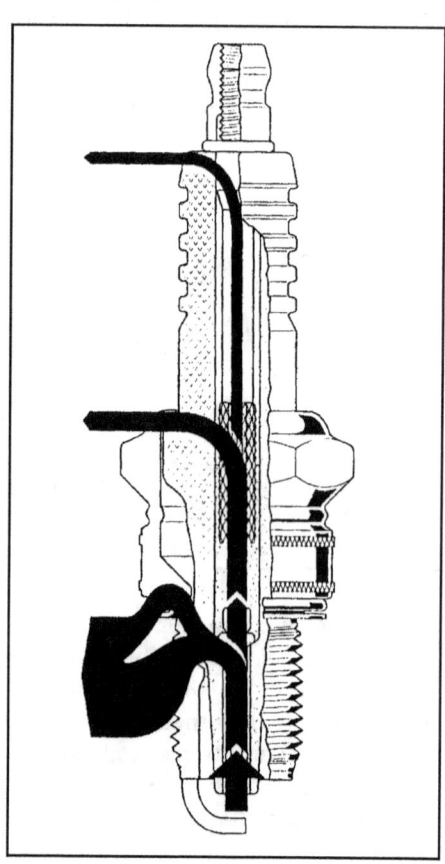

Some of the heat of combustion escapes through the spark plug as seen in this drawing.

108   *How to Tune and Win with Demon Carburetors*

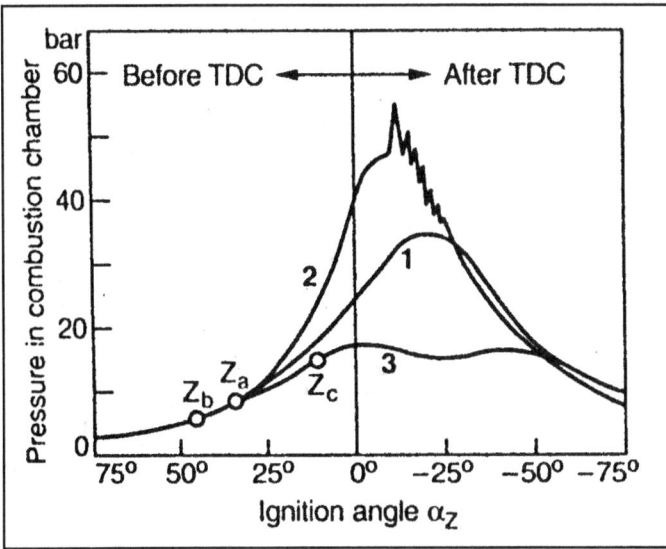

The ideal spark-advance curve will allow cylinder pressure to peak in as few rotational degrees of the crankshaft past TDC as possible. Plot 1 represents the proper advance rate for the subject engine, while plot 2 is abnormal combustion, and plot 3 retarded from MBT. Note that during abnormal combustion, the cylinder pressure is high while the piston is still coming up on TDC.

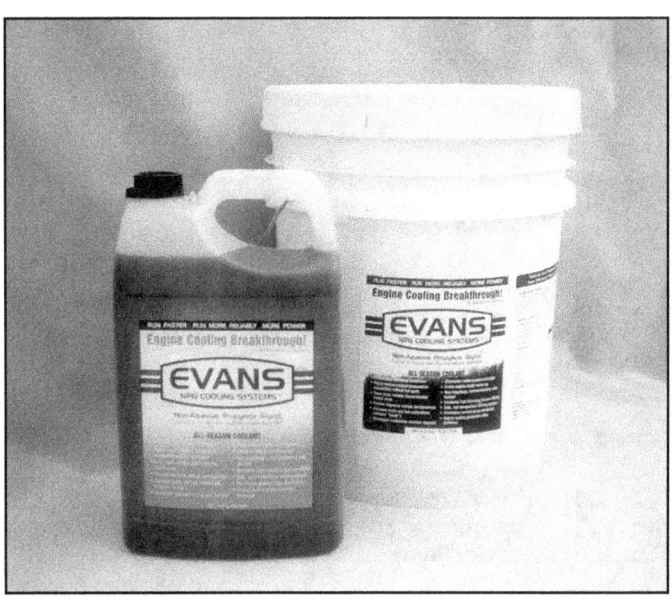

The cooling system is often neglected as a means to increase power and octane tolerance while lowering BSFC. The Evans NPG coolant replaces both water and conventional antifreeze. Since it boils at 369 F degrees with no pressure, it effectively quenches detonation and allows high compression ratios on lower octane fuel.

advance curve based on load, RPM, and coolant temperature at finite intervals, offering almost infinitely variable control. In practice, an engine requires a varied amount of spark advance as load and speed change, due to variations in volumetric efficiency, cylinder pressure and turbulence, air density, intake manifold tuning, EGR dilution, and coolant temperature. Unfortunately, even after gaining a thorough understanding, a successful spark table is usually determined by trial and error.

Although it would be nice to use a blanket figure for total advance for every engine of a particular make, that is not possible. The combustion chamber shape and spark plug location in relation to the bore center are the most significant factors in flame travel and the necessary spark lead. This would include the piston crown design, since even the slightest protrusion from a dome piston into the flame's path will slow it down. Combustion chamber types vary beyond the familiar open/closed and hemispherical classifications.

Today, it is more accurate to describe a cylinder head based on its ability to generate mixture motion, and then quantify it further into internal charge acceleration and externally induced motion. Other factors affecting the ignition curve are the efficiency of the engine coolant and the air/fuel ratio. Rich mixtures require less spark advance than lean ratios, and cooler cylinder head metal temperatures allow more advance before entering detonation.

Whenever the ignition timing is retarded beyond the optimal setting, exhaust gas temperatures rise since the burn is completed in the exhaust manifold or header during blow-down. Obviously, this is a waste of energy because it is not used to expand against the piston. Very early initiation of the spark creates excessive cylinder pressure as the piston is sweeping toward TDC, trying to force it back down prematurely. In extreme cases, it may bend the connecting rod.

Accepting the importance of the proper timing is all well and good, but for an accurate advance curve, you need two things to happen: accurate identification of TDC on the number 1 cylinder, and accurate primary switching or interrupts. Referencing from timing marks that have error due to a stack-up of tolerance will lead to incorrect amounts of spark advance, making the tuning job harder. Most engines trigger the primary ignition switching from the distributor that is connected to the crankshaft via a timing chain, which leads to error due to stretch and the meshing of the timing gears. It makes no sense to try to determine the crankshaft's position through these intermediate components and not from the crankshaft itself.

Recognizing this, aftermarket ignition companies such as ACCEL, MSD, Mallory, and Electromotive offer electronically programmable ignition systems referenced from a very accurate crankshaft-located sensor, elimi-

A car that hooks well and leaves hard like this Nova may require jet extensions at the track to keep the main jets covered with fuel. Never use jet extension on the street, as a rapid stop will starve the engine of fuel and cause it to

How to Tune and Win with Demon Carburetors

CNC cylinder heads of Pinellas Park, Florida, uses computer numerical control milling machines to port and contour combustion chambers for maximum flow and mixture motion.

nating this error. Wear in the distributor gear and shaft bushings adds play and timing error. This will vary the primary switching point on each cylinder, yielding different timing on each bore. For this reason it is advisable to check for cylinder timing variations using an ignition oscilloscope. A very high-RPM engine accentuates this problem, and a distributor with a very stiff shaft that is supported by bearings instead of bushings should be employed.

Before you tune a mechanical advance curve, the ignition and fuel system should be in satisfactory working order. The ignition needs to not only produce a high-voltage and high-ampere spark, but keep the plug arcing for as much of the crankshaft's rotation as possible. The advance mechanism should be clean and work smoothly, and the vacuum advance diaphragm should be checked for leakage with a vacuum pump. Clean the timing marks, and if possible, verify TDC. Use either a timing tape or a dial-back timing light. Starting with the static setting, the advance curve should be checked and recorded individually. Then add the base timing and mechanical and vacuum advance for the total timing. At WOT, the restriction of the throttle plate is no longer present, and manifold vacuum drops to near zero, eliminating any advance from the vacuum canister. When using an OE distributor, you will need an aftermarket advance kit. Some companies offer adjustable vacuum advance units; if possible, use one to dial in the part-throttle timing curve. Additionally, a vacuum gauge in parallel with the vacuum advance unit allows you to chart the amount of advance vs. vacuum signal.

UNDERSTANDING EMISSIONS

Considering that we all breathe air, the enthusiast must realize a responsible approach to exhaust emissions, accepting that power and exhaust cleanliness can coexist on a street car. Almost every state has implemented some style of emissions testing for licensed vehicles, and a lack of compliance can make your vehicle illegal to drive.

The byproduct of the combustion event in an engine is generally referred to as exhaust emissions. Creating a more powerful engine necessitates the input of more fuel while concurrently producing more residual end gases. So the enthusiast is caught in a catch-22 situation. Since the introduction of the Clean Air Act (1970), which was limited to a steady-state idle-emissions test, the requirements have progressed to the current inspection/maintenance (I/M) 240 drive-cycle procedure. With its stricter standards, the drive-cycle program examines an additional pollutant, oxides of nitrogen, which has been identified as a major contributor to ground-level ozone and photochemical smog.

THE OFFENDERS

The pollutants that we are concerned with are hydrocarbons, carbon monoxide, carbon dioxide, oxygen, and oxides of nitrogen. Each is the result of an inefficient combustion process that can be identified.

Hydrocarbons (HC)

Gasoline consists of hydrogen and carbon atoms, thus any level of hydrocarbon in the exhaust represents unburned fuel. Measured in parts per million (PPM), it is the emissions that

All of the technology in the world is meaningless if the machine work and engine-assembly procedures are of poor quality. Siglers' Machine Shop in Great Meadows, New Jersey, stresses quality and the use of Demon carburetors.

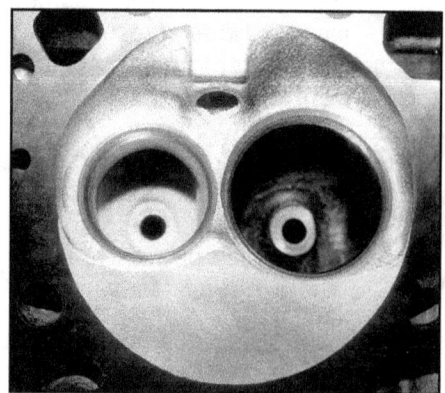

Swain Technologies of Scottsville, New York, uses ceramic metallic coatings in both the combustion chambers and exhaust ports to limit thermal losses. They allow more of the combustion heat to expand against the piston while increasing octane tolerance and supporting leaner mixtures. This coated Vortec cylinder head was used with a 650 Speed Demon carburetor to produce BSFC readings of .40 at MBT during a test conducted for *Corvette Fever* at the University of Northwestern Ohio.

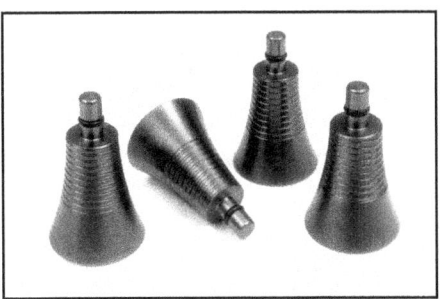

Whenever performing bench work on any carburetor, use some style of feet or stand. The BG part number 130045 feet snap quickly in place and protect the linkage and base-plate assembly.

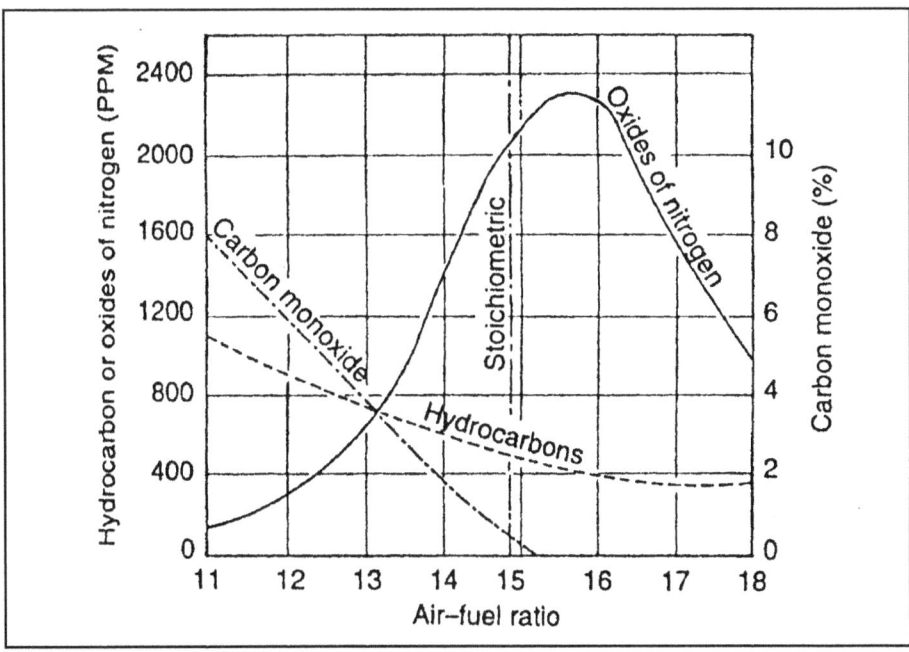

The mixture ratio has a profound effect on emissions output in any engine. Note the curve for NOx: as the mixture is leaned, the combustion temperature rises, creating more of this emission. At approximately 16.0:1, NOx starts to decline since there is not enough fuel to support proper combustion and the exhaust cools from the residual hydrocarbons.

make your eyes tear from the exhaust of a poor-running car or an engine with a large camshaft. Mistakenly thought of as a rich air/fuel ratio, HC is know as the misfire meter. HC levels escalate when the engine is not experiencing complete and efficient combustion. HC emissions are created by ignition problems, excessively lean mixtures, camshaft design, and excessive crevice volumes or carbon deposits in the combustion chamber.

Carbon Monoxide (CO)

Measured in percent, CO is partially burned fuel created by a lack of necessary oxygen to support combustion. Simply put, whenever CO readings are high, the mixture is overly rich. A failed CO test indicates a plugged air filter, poorly adjusted or calibrated carburetor, or fuel dilution in the crankcase.

Carbon Dioxide (CO_2)

As a byproduct of the bonding of the carbon and oxygen molecules during combustion, CO_2 demonstrates how efficient the engine is running. Measured in percent, the higher the reading, the greater the combustion efficiency.

Oxygen (O_2)

Defined as a colorless, odorless gas, oxygen is the most common element known to man. During an emissions test, high levels in the exhaust represent additional oxygen molecules that do not have a carbon element to bond with. Oxygen readings increase if the mixture is excessively lean and also during scenarios that would normally promote high HC. If the fuel is not being burned, neither is the oxygen. Usually inversely proportioned to CO_2, it is measured in percent.

Oxides of Nitrogen (NOx)

Measured in PPM, NOx is present during all phases of combustion but escalates dramatically when leading-edge flame-front temperatures exceed 2,500 F degrees. Requiring heat, cylinder pressure, and exposure time to be produced, detonation is a leading source of this pollutant. Since 1973, exhaust gas recirculation (EGR) valves have been used to cool combustion chamber temperatures by introducing inert exhaust gases. At first it may be hard to understand how hot exhaust gas can cool a combustion chamber, but it accomplishes this by consuming space in the bore, thus limiting the amount of combustible mixture that fills the cylinder. Since NOx

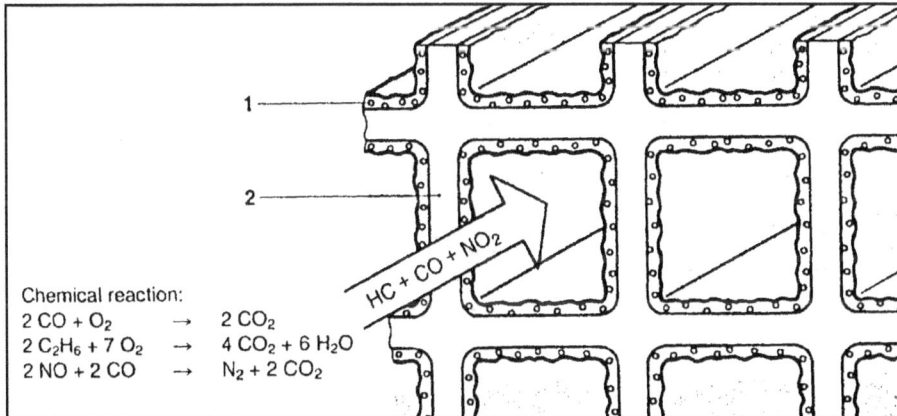

Early catalytic converters used pellets, but the current methodology incorporates a honeycomb structure to produce a greater surface area in a smaller envelope. All current catalytic converters work the most efficient when the engine out mixture ratio is 14.7:1.

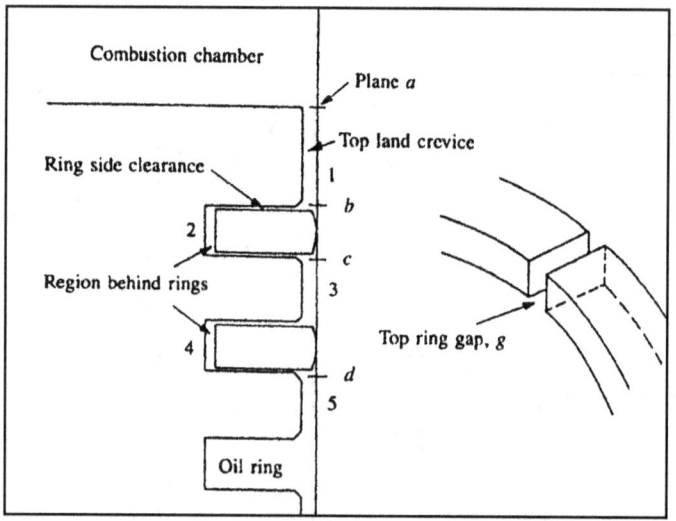

	cm³	%
Displaced volume per cylinder	632	
Clearance volume per cylinder	89	100
Volume above first ring	0.93	1.05
Volume behind first ring	0.47	0.52
Volume between rings	0.68	0.77
Volume behind second ring	0.47	0.52
Total ring crevice volume	2.55	2.9
Spark plug thread crevice	0.25	0.28
Head gasket crevice	0.3	0.34
Total crevice volume	3.1	3.5

The crevice region created by the ring-land area of the piston is the largest contributor to hydrocarbon emissions production. Current Detroit technology places the ring package nearer the piston crown to reduce this area.

Crevice regions are easily identified and even include the thread of the spark plug. These measurements were taken on a 231-cubic-inch V-6.

production is highest under part-throttle light load, when the air/fuel ratio is usually the leanest, NOx was the impetus for the I/M 240 test schedule.

THE CATALYTIC CONVERTER

Being geared toward the replacement and street-performance market, the Road Demon line will be the most likely candidate for use on an engine equipped with a catalytic converter. Anytime an emissions-control device is placed in the exhaust stream, it is an attempt to correct what could not be controlled in the combustion chamber.

By definition, a catalyst speeds up a chemical reaction without itself being consumed. Simply, a catalytic converter "scrubs" the exhaust. Early catalysts contained pellets made of 70 percent platinum and 30 percent palladium. The pellet-style converters were eventually replaced by a ceramic monolith of noble metals that exposed a larger surface area while maintaining smaller exterior dimensions. However, not all catalysts are effective on all emissions.

Application-specific catalysts are designed to neutralize certain elements. Oxidation catalysts convert CO and HC to CO_2 and water, and reduction catalysts treat NOx by converting it back to nitrogen and oxygen. Dual-bed designs are a melding of two different catalyst strategies and affect NOx in the first section and CO and HC in the rear section. Three-way catalytic converters simultaneously scrub all three gases in one unit.

For a catalyst to function properly, it must attain a minimum operating tem-

The mechanism for hydrocarbon emissions production is based upon crevice regions and the end of flame travel produced by the cylinder wall and the bulk quench factor.

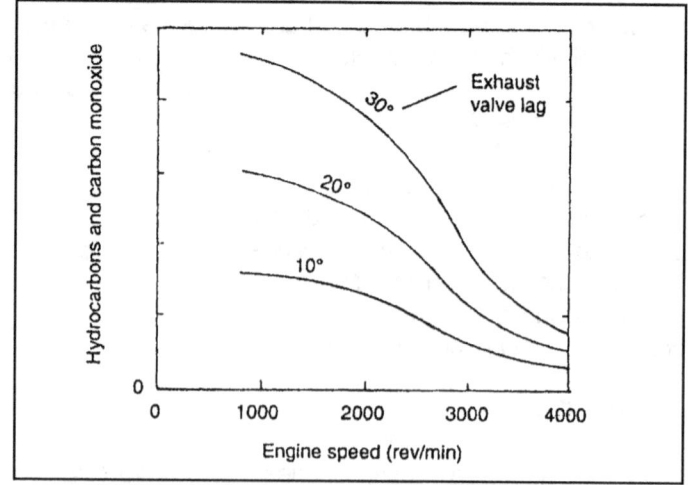

Camshaft overlap represented here as a delay in exhaust valve closing creates reversion into the bore, diluting the fresh charge and increasing emissions. As the engine speed increases, the effect is reduced since the throttle plate is opened further and the intake charge has more velocity and is experiencing a higher pressure.

Altitude affects the VE of an engine with lower atmospheric pressure and reduced oxygen content. The BG part number 130009 FAA-certified altimeter provides accurate readings for calculating density altitude and barometric pressure relative to altitude.

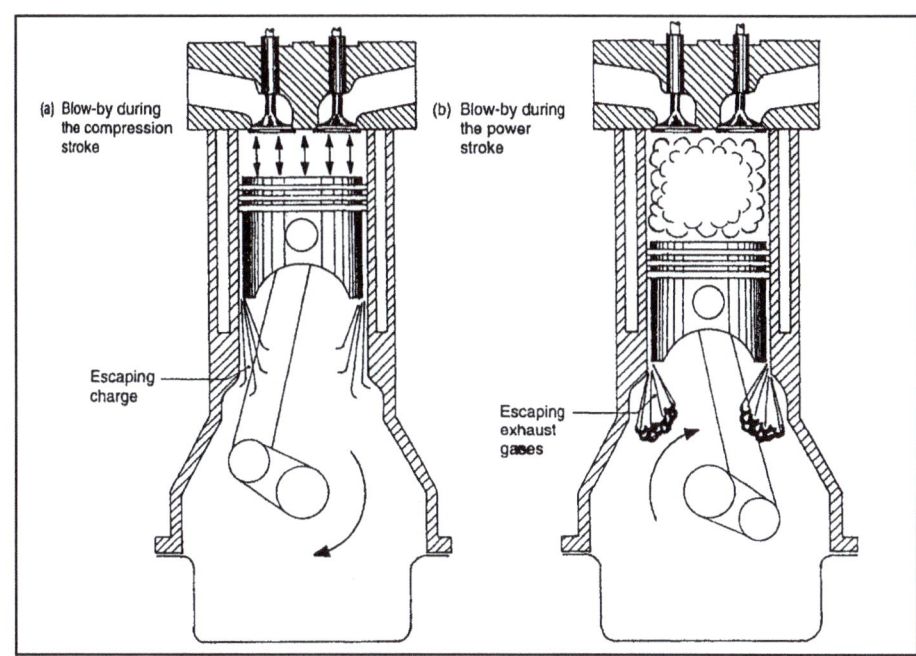

Proper piston-ring seal is critical for maximum power and the lowest emissions. Blow-by can occur during both compression and expansion strokes, as represented above.

perature of 600 F degrees, but during many driving scenarios they produce temperatures of 1400-1500 F degrees or more. When the conversion process begins, the converter is consider to be in "light-off." Converter efficiency is rated in percentage of conversion, with a minimum of 85 percent being the performance standard for today's vehicles. Due to the effects of thermal inertia, which requires a body to become saturated with heat before being able to transfer it, catalysts are placed as close to the exhaust port as possible. Though a definite flow restriction, a correctly sized and properly placed catalyst will impose only a small penalty on power but will have a dramatic effect on exhaust emissions when used with unleaded fuel. Contrary to popular belief, leaded fuels do not plug the converter but rather coat the catalytic material and insulate it from chemical conversion.

DESIGNING AN EMISSIONS-FRIENDLY, HIGH-OUTPUT ENGINE

When dealing with combustion efficiency and the gas exchange process, the most challenging emissions to eliminate are HC and NOx. These properties are inextricably linked to the means normally associated with increasing engine output: camshafts with excessive overlap and high compression ratios. Carbon monoxide can be easily controlled with air/fuel ratio adjustments, and O^2 is not a concern since it is only used as a diagnostic gas. Carbon dioxide is tested as an easy means to quantify the integrity of the exhaust system.

When trying to control HC production, the crevice volume or region becomes highly relevant. The crevice is an area in the combustion chamber that the flame front cannot access, but one that the A/F mixture will. The largest contributor to crevice volume is the area created by the piston and piston rings in relation to the cylinder wall. Other crevice areas are represented by the threads around the spark plug, the space around the spark plug center electrode, the space between the heads of the intake and exhaust valves and the cylinder head, as well as the head gasket cutout.

As the cylinder pressure rises during compression, the mixture is forced into these regions. During combustion, cylinder pressure rises even more, forcing more HC into the crevices. Since the flame travel cannot access these areas, the A/F mixture waits in the crevice until cylinder pressure is lower than the crevice gas pressure and flows out of the exhaust. For this reason, the trend in current production engines is to move the top ring as close to the crown of the piston as possible, thus curtailing the major contributor to crevice volume.

In an engine that is experiencing proper combustion, it has been determined that the ring package is responsible for 80 percent of the hydrocarbon production, the head gasket crevice 13 percent, and the spark plug threads 5 percent. All other sources contributed the rest. Besides being a major producer of HC emissions, crevice regions waste fuel, which is being used as a filler and not to add energy to the expansion cycle. How picky does it get? The Ford Motor Company has determined that the direction arrow stamped on the piston top was contributing to crevice area, so it was replaced with a mark on the underside of the piston.

A camshaft with excessive overlap reduces low-RPM engine efficiency, which in turn promotes poor burn rates and results in high HC output. Overlap should not be considered a completely bad contrivance, though. It can be used as an internal EGR function to pull spent gases from the exhaust port and introduce them to the cylinder. Finding a delicate balance of overlap is ideal but is beyond the realm of the enthusiast. It will remain the domain of the cam companies to acknowledge the emissions issues. Since success is

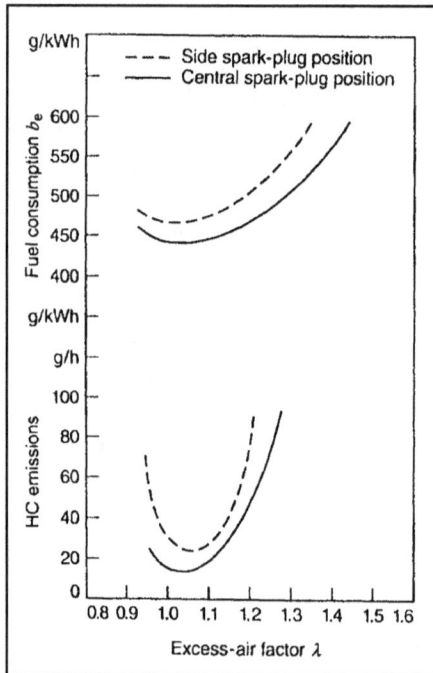

Spark plug location in the design of the combustion chamber affects both BSFC and HC emissions. The ideal placement is in the center of the bore. The excess-air factor can be converted to air/fuel ratio by multiplying the factor by 14.7.

An exhaust gas recirculation valve is used to cool the combustion chamber at light load by introducing inert exhaust gas.

linked directly to a systems approach, if crevice volumes are summarily reduced, then the engine would be more forgiving of overlap because HC emissions are not being stored.

Oxides of nitrogen emissions output is the most difficult to balance. Although there is a need for compression ratio for thermal efficiency and to increase burn rates, high cylinder pressure is what produces NOx. The easiest method for controlling NOx is to use a quick-burn-rate combustion chamber. Temperature, pressure, and exposure are necessary for the promotion of NOx, but if the design can speed up burn rates, exposure time would be limited, removing one element from the recipe.

In the 1970s, the domestic auto industry failed to realize that old, slow-burning combustion chambers would not work well enough to satisfy NOx standards, and it drastically reduced compression ratios instead. Rather than redesigning the combustion chamber, it took compression out and added nearly 30 percent EGR dilution. Although EGR is an effective, inexpensive means for controlling NOx, it disturbs burn cycles in the cylinder. The less EGR dilution, the better the driveability will be. EGR is administered during part-throttle, light-load conditions, so it will not affect idle quality or WOT performance. However, all of this is moot if the engine enters abnormal combustion known as detonation. NOx production goes off the scale during detonation due to the extreme temperature and pressure rise that an uncontrolled release of the end gas energy produces.

Many aftermarket cylinder head companies mimic the combustion chamber technology of the latest offerings from Detroit. Quick burn rates, internal charge acceleration by means of squish pads, and external mixture motion from swirl of the incoming charge will produce power and pay dividends toward compliance.

PUTTING IT TO THE TEST

The I/M 240 test got its name from the 240-second sampling time with the vehicle situated on a chassis dynamometer to simulate load. The engine runs at idle, is accelerated, and is then allowed to idle again. The tester then averages the results.

To certify a vehicle for sale in the United States, the EPA mandates Federal Test Procedure-75 (FTP-75). Divided into three segments, the total test time is 4500 seconds (75 minutes), and it is performed on an extremely sophisticated 48-inch roller chassis dynamometer with a load cycle designed to simulate morning commuter traffic in Los Angeles. Since 80-85 percent of engine emissions occur during the first two minutes of operation, an independent cold-start test is also performed with the vehicle placed in a room and chilled to 20 F degrees.

In another procedure called SHED, the vehicle is placed in a test cell that resembles a paint booth. The HC emitted while the engine is not running are measured for 24 hours. While state I/M programs measure readings in either percent or PPM, the FTP cycle weighs the tailpipe output and records grams of each pollutant per mile of operation. For this reason, smaller-displacement engines are easier to certify since they displace less air, and even if they are dirtier, they'll exhibit fewer recorded grams/mile. Some states will initially adopt a shorter version of I/M 240 called 5015. The difference is that it calculates 50 percent of the load while accelerating to 15 miles per hour.

TUNING TIPS

When tuning for the least emissions, access to an exhaust analyzer becomes essential. Many of the new I/M laws have made previous emissions analyzers invalid for the inspection procedure but are still excellent and affordable tuning devices for the hot-rodder. Units that had cost $5000 to $10,000 new are now around $500. It is essential to realize that these testers will not be able to read NOx but will measure at least CO, HC, and CO_2. It must be recognized that a catalytic converter will function effectively only when the air/fuel ratio is within two percent of 14.7:1. Wander beyond these values and the converter does little or nothing to clean the exhaust.

CARBURETOR ADJUSTMENT

For the sake of discussion, let's take a generic look at carburetor adjustment. Later in this chapter we'll include a full description of the proper Demon carburetor adjustment procedure.

When using an emissions analyzer, the best readings will be obtained by first gently seating the mixture screws and then turning each out the same number of rotations before beginning

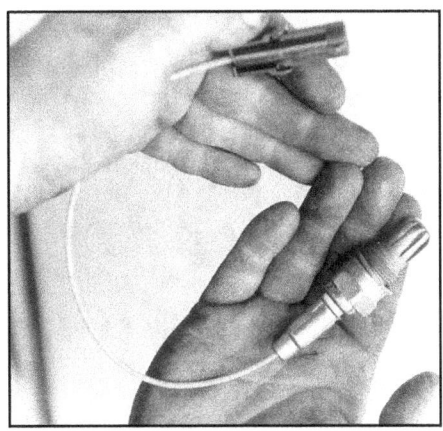

Single- and three-wire oxygen sensors can only accurately identify a mixture of 14.7:1, meaning inexpensive air/fuel ratio meters are not the best methods for tuning.

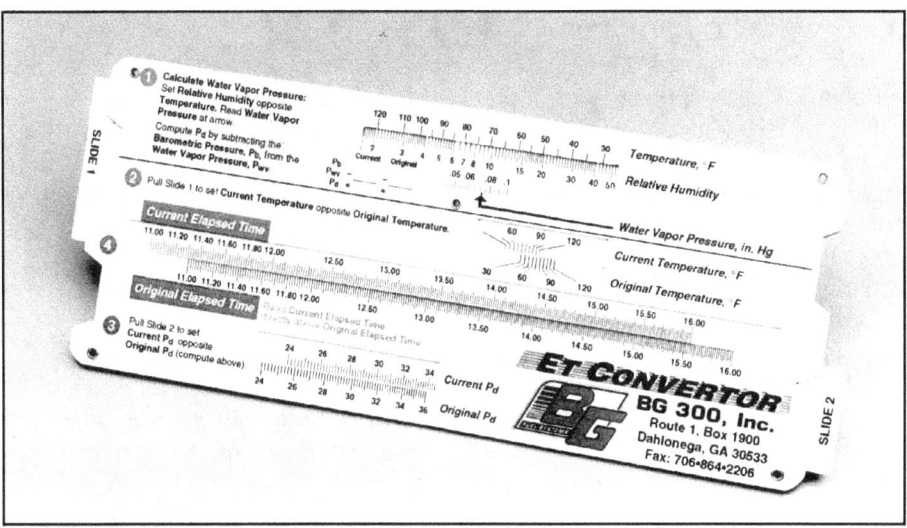

The BG ET Converter slide rule quickly determines your elapsed time based on weather conditions compared against previous runs.

the adjustments. Your goal is to have the lowest CO reading with the highest CO_2 reading. Achieve this and the engine will operate the most efficiently.

Remember, if the mixture is too lean, HC output will rise since there will be an insufficient amount of fuel in the combustion chamber for the flame front to propagate. Identified as a lean misfire, the flame extinguishes, and the residual fuel elevates the HC emissions. Early power valve actuation will raise light-load CO readings. On a carbureted fuel system, the CO will be the highest at idle since the throttle plate is closed, and RPM is low. If your readings are substantially richer at higher RPM than at idle, check float level, power valve setting, and air bleeds.

Ignition

Advanced ignition timing will raise HC emissions at idle and under light-load conditions. Retarding the spark will lower HC and, in many instances, the level of NOx, even if detonation is not present. Ignition timing has no direct effect on CO but can impact it by changing the amount of throttle angle in relation to the area of the transfer slot in the carburetor that is required to keep the engine running. A high-energy aftermarket capacitive-discharge-style ignition allows the spark plug to burn for more of the crankshaft's rotation, cleaning up the level of HC. Multiple-strike systems also have a positive impact on HC production. Spark advance curve tuning by means of adjustable vacuum advance units and spring kits is essential for any drive-cycle testing.

PCV

Remove the PCV valve while tracing the level of CO. If the analyzer reading drops more than one percent, then the engine oil is contaminated with fuel and is richening the mixture. It is best to perform an oil and filter change before an emissions test or any carburetor tuning.

EGR

A street car that will be subjected to a drive-cycle test will best be served by choosing an intake manifold that is equipped with an EGR passage as a means of limiting NOx. The installation should include a thermal vacuum switch connected to a ported vacuum source; then the EGR valve will function only when the engine is fully warmed and at part-throttle light load.

Air Pump

An air pump is an effective means for reducing the tailpipe HC and CO readings. It may cost 10 horsepower at 6000 rpm, but the additional oxygen in the header or exhaust manifold will burn residual exhaust gases.

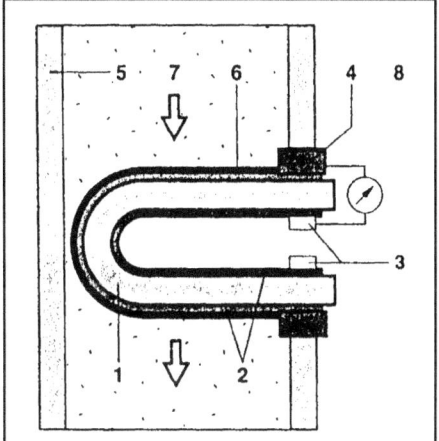

All oxygen sensors reference an exhaust sample against the atmosphere. The numbers represent the following: 1) sensor ceramic, 2) electrodes, 3) contact area, 4) housing contact, 5) exhaust pipe or header, 6) porous ceramic protective layer, 7) exhaust gas sample, 8) reference air from atmosphere.

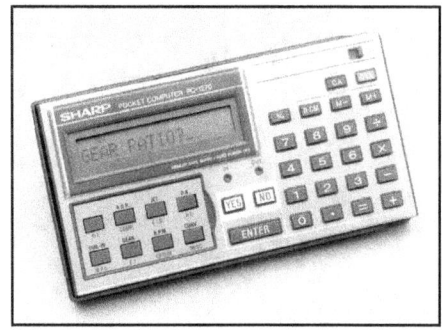

Both drag-race and oval-track version of the BG Professor II computer are available for the serious racer.

WHAT TO LOOK FOR

Begin by contacting your local motor vehicle department to obtain the standards for the year your vehicle was manufactured. Engine-out emissions numbers (which are readings taken prior to the catalytic converter) on vehicles equipped with catalytic converters will always be higher than the tailpipe reading if the converter accomplishes light off and is functioning. The I/M test is based on a tailpipe reading, so the sooner the converter starts to function, the lower the readings will be.

A modified street/strip engine will have higher engine-out emissions numbers and will require a more effective converter to scrub the exhaust. However, all converters are not created equal. Most aftermarket brands do not work nearly as well as an OE replacement. As an example, on a modified Speed Demon-equipped 383 Chevy small-block test vehicle, 607 PPM HC were registered without a catalyst. With an aftermarket catalytic converter installed, the reading dropped to 484 PPM HC. In contrast, when a GM catalytic converter was introduced, the tailpipe HC went down to 71 PPM HC. If your state conducts the idle-speed-only test, running the engine at 2000 rpm for two minutes before taking a reading will raise the converter temperature enough to bring it on line.

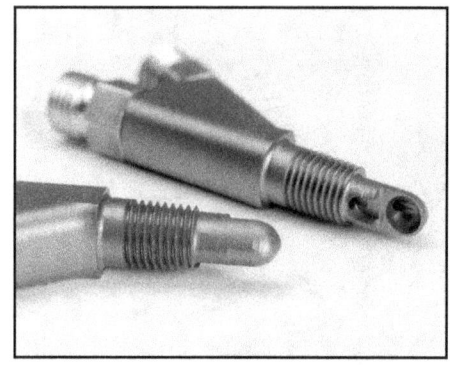

The patented NitrousWorks Power Wing nozzle offers the best atomization and mixing of the nitrous and fuel for the most horsepower and torque.

On non-catalyst-equipped vehicles with a mild-performance camshaft and little attention to crevice volume, readings of as much as 600 PPM HC, 0-1 percent CO, 8-11 percent CO_2, and 1200 PPM NOx are considered acceptable. Engines with a catalyst should reduce those values below 200 PPM HC, 9-12 percent CO_2, and less than 900 PPM NOx.

GENERAL TROUBLESHOOTING AND DIAGNOSING

The carburetor is usually assumed to be the culprit of every driveability issue, but more often than not it is an innocent bystander. Before attacking any problem, I like to apply the SAT logic: stop and think. From my many years of experience diagnosing performance and driveability problems, I have learned that time spent thinking and analyzing and not jumping to conclusions and arbitrarily replacing parts pays huge dividends. Ask yourself the following questions before putting a wrench to the engine:

1) Was any work or maintenance performed before the problem occurred?
2) Have you looked for cracked vacuum hoses, disconnected spark plug wires, etc.?
3) Have you identified the exact symptoms and the engine load or operating RPM at which it occurs?
4) Could the condition be the result of a mechanical failure or a poor choice of parts (too large a cam profile, incorrect carburetor application, etc.)?
5) Have you listened to the exhaust to determine if the problem is dedicated to one cylinder or common to all?

If the problem is still elusive, then you need to determine whether the cause is fuel, ignition, or mechanical. I found the quickest method to determine this is to add fuel, subtract fuel, advance timing, retard timing. If the air/fuel ratio is altered and the timing advanced and retarded to no avail, then the poor performance is caused

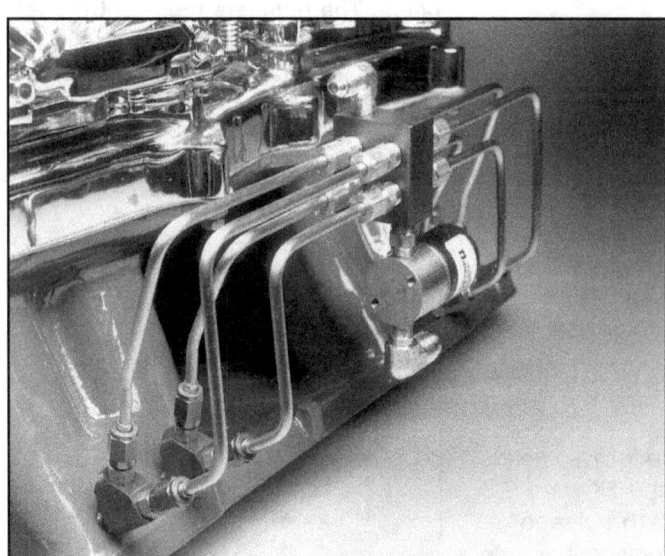

A direct-port nitrous system is the best method to guarantee even distribution to every cylinder. Though it appears complicated, it's a good choice for a street/strip car.

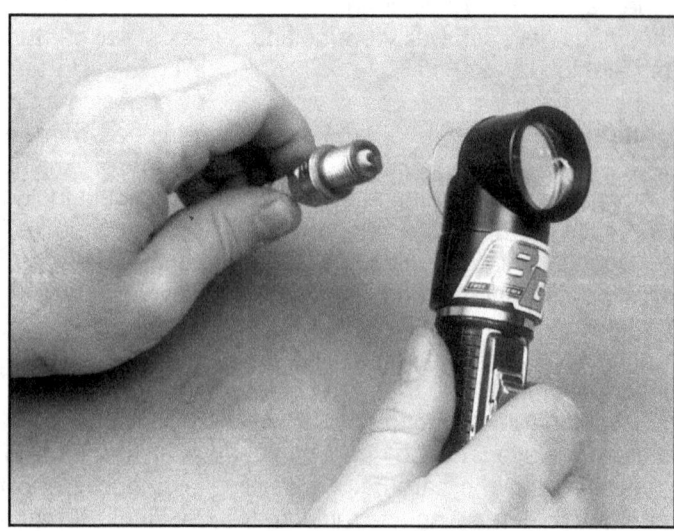

Close inspection of the spark plugs using a BG lighted magnifying glass will detect the precursor to detonation and is extremely important when tuning any engine, not just a nitrous-assisted one.

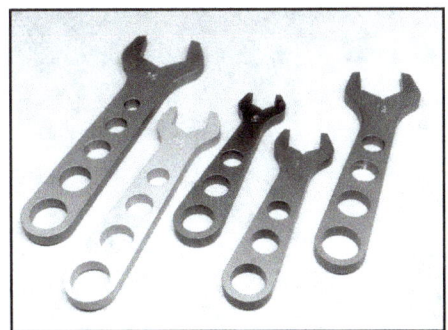

BG part number 130010 wrenches are made of anodized aluminum, which prevents damage to AN fittings and hose ends.

by something other than spark advance or fuel delivery. An ignition scope analysis, compression, leakdown, and power balance test is then in order. The best method to alter the fuel curve temporarily is to use the mixture screws or choke the carburetor with your hand. To lean out the mixture beyond the authority that the idle circuit allows, a small vacuum leak can be induced. Altering the phase of the distributor will confirm the engine's desire for spark advance.

A good preventative maintenance schedule is usually the best method to avoid problems. Regular oil changes, fuel filter and ignition component replacement, along with keeping the carburetor clean and tight to the intake manifold, goes a long way toward trouble-free motoring. Driving habits can also add longevity. If you limit the number of cold starts and idling time, and do not command full power until the engine oil and coolant are at operating temperature, less wear and tear will occur. Being astute and acknowledging any peculiar sounds or behavior from the engine will allow small problems to be remedied before they become major issues. A true engine aficionado is constantly listening and recognizing the performance of his vehicle.

TUNING THE DEMON CARBURETOR

The first step in extracting the most performance from your Demon carburetor is to choose the proper model and calibration for your use and application. If you have not yet made your purchase or are in doubt about the selection that was made, please call the Demon technical information line at (706) 864-4712 for a recommendation. As mentioned previously, a carburetor that is sized incorrectly will make your tuning job harder.

By virtue of its design and manufacturing process, the task of dialing in a Demon for street and strip is relatively easy. For those of you used to working with lesser brands of carburetors, the arduous tasks of drilling out air bleeds, emulsion holes, and the like will rarely be required. This is an important feature that at first may not be recognized. The Demon approach does not allow the tuner the opportunity to incorrectly modify the carburetor to such an extent that it will no longer function and a replacement will have to be purchased.

The emphasis of this discussion will be on the Road and Speed Demon lines since they are primarily used as dual-purpose carburetors. This is not to say that a Race or King Demon will not find its way onto a vehicle that is driven on the street. Unless the vehicle is a very radical Pro Street-style entry, the choice of a racing carburetor will be more for aesthetics than for functionality. Look to Chapter 10 for tuning tips using race carburetors.

Though it would be nice to have access to an emissions analyzer and chassis dyno for some of the tuning functions, other methods can be used. The essential equipment that is required are an accurate tune-up-style tachometer, dial-back timing light, and vacuum and fuel pressure gauges.

Using a building block approach the end result will be a carburetor tuned in all areas. Setting criteria for performance encompasses more than just horsepower or drag strip elapsed times, and should represent an engine that starts easily hot and cold, idles smoothly, accepts an idle load dump such as the transmission placed in drive or the air conditioner engaged, and exhibits vibrant tip-in throttle response while featuring smooth powerful acceleration and wide-open throttle performance. To add more factors into the juggling act, these requirements all need to be met while offering the best fuel economy and least emissions as possible.

Before you do any carburetor tuning, the engine should be checked for vacuum leaks. The best method is to fabricate a propane-enrichment tool by cutting the head from an old torch and attaching a few feet of rubber line with a steel tube end to direct the propane. Go around the intake manifold and EGR valve, if the car is equipped; any increase in engine RPM indicates a leak.

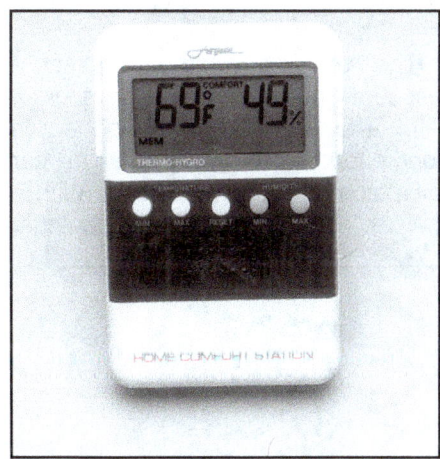

The BG digital Thermo-Hygrometer keeps both temperature and humidity percentages in constant view. A memory function records and stores the minimum and maximum readings for reference.

The prescribed method to accomplish this is to first have the engine idle properly, since the position of the idle mixture screws will impact the amount of fuel delivered to the transfer slot. If not, an improperly adjusted idle mix-

How to Tune and Win with Demon Carburetors **117**

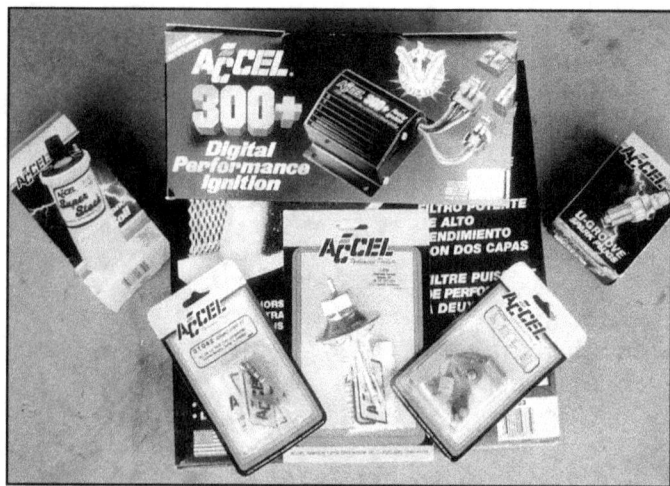

Your Demon carburetor needs a strong ignition system to perform up to standards. Trying to tune around a weak or defective ignition will be a waste of time, money, and effort.

Point ignition systems can integrate a CD ignition box such as the ACCEL 300+ for increased capacity while retaining a factory appearance.

ture will haunt you during transition as the throttle plates are opened and the main metering system is evoked. Qualifying where the carburetor tune-up currently exists is important, and the more data you collect, the easier and quicker the optimal performance will be obtained. In almost all instances the engine will run with the carburetor installed from the box and require only minor tweaking to the four mixture screws.

The next step would be to attach a vacuum gauge to a full-time source. Affix a feed line to the gauge that is long enough to be brought into the car or attached to the windshield. With a helper to document the readings, drive the vehicle while recording different road loads, conditions, and transmission gear selections. This information will be used later when tuning the power valve setting and if the carburetor is equipped with vacuum secondary operation. In most street engines, the vacuum readings may vary from 15 to 17 inches at idle, 8 to 10 inches under light load, and under hard deceleration or coast-down, up to 22 inches.

The areas of the carburetor that will be altered are the mixture screw position, jet size, air bleed dimension, float level, power valve vacuum setting, accelerator pump cam and squirter style, secondary throttle plate angle, idle speed, and choke setting. Though these are the common tuning areas, in some rare instances the idle feed restrictor and emulsion orifice dimension and locations may need attention.

CHECKING BASELINE ADJUSTMENTS

Since all Demon carburetors are subjected to a rigorous quality-control procedure and wet-flow bench calibration, they have set new standards for out-of-the-box use. It is always advisable to make sure that no damage has occurred during shipping, so prior to installing your carburetor, take a few moments to make the following checks.

Successful racers often use an air-density meter to compare the performance of their engines and jet settings against varying weather conditions.

Longtime tuner and fuel systems expert Bob Ida uses a sophisticated chassis dyno to accurately document and tune Demon carburetors and NitrousWorks power-adder kits. He logs horsepower, torque, rate of acceleration, and air/fuel ratio on a computer screen.

Part number 130015 fuel-flow tester measures the flow of the complete fuel system to determine the system's ability to feed the carburetor.

Throttle and Accelerator Pump Linkage

Check the travel of the throttle linkage for damage during shipping. The throttle plates and accelerator pump mechanism should work smoothly to wide open and return to their full closed position when released. At wide-open throttle, all butterflies should be parallel to each other at approximately a 90-degree angle to the base plate gasket surface.

When the throttle plates are closed simulating the curb-idle position, there should be no play in the adjustment of the accelerator pump arms. The pump levers should begin compressing the pump diaphragm(s) as soon as the linkage begins to move. Play in the pump arm linkage will delay the fuel discharge and result in a stumble or hesitation as the throttle plates are opened. At wide-open throttle, be sure that 0.015-0.020 inch travel remains in the accelerator pump linkage. If the pump diaphragms bottom out, premature wear or binding in the linkage will occur.

Slop in the linkage can be adjusted by either tightening or loosening the lock nut. This will control the length of the compressed spring. Slightly bend the cam follower to adjust for a linkage that bottoms out. In rare instances, it may take a balance of both cam follower and spring adjustments to get the system working best for your application. Different cam profiles are available that can alter the timing, volume, and duration of the pump shot. If the pump cams are changed, it may be necessary to readjust the linkage.

Closed Butterfly Position

The initial setting will be application-specific to the model carburetor, venturi size, and fuel type. Most gasoline applications will have the butterflies positioned to expose approximately 0.020 inch of the idle transfer fuel slot referenced from the intake manifold side of the throttle plates. Primary and secondary butterflies should be open equal amounts if the engine idles at or above 1000 rpm and never seated tightly against the throttle bores in the base plate. For engines that idle below 1000 rpm, the secondary butterfly should be closed to below the transfer slot. The position is adjusted using the idle-speed set screw in the base plate. Turn the screw clockwise to open the butterflies, counterclockwise to close. The most successful tuners keep detailed information in regard to all of the carburetor settings, along with performance and weather data.

Idle Mixture Screws

The idle mixture, also referred to as the curb-idle adjustment, is located on each side of both the primary and secondary metering blocks. These threaded needle valves control the amount of idle fuel that is discharged into the plenum from the idle passages located in the base plate. To check the initial settings, rotate each adjustment clockwise one-half turn at a time until it lightly bottoms out in the metering block. Then rotate the mixture screws counterclockwise to their original settings. For most applications, use 1.5 turns open as a baseline adjustment. All four mixture screws should be adjusted to the same position before starting the engine. Keep in mind that this adjustment is only a starting point and that additional fine tuning will most likely be required.

Bolting the Carburetor to the Intake Manifold

After the linkage and baseline settings have been checked, the carburetor is ready to be installed. Be sure to use a new gasket and clean the mounting pad on the manifold. If studs are used, the carburetor should slide easily over them. Do not force the carburetor if it gets caught on a stud as damage may occur that will not be covered under the warranty. If the carburetor will not fit easily over the studs, check for bent or improperly installed studs and replace as necessary.

Once the carburetor is sealed against the gasket, make sure it sits squarely on the mounting flange. It should not rock or be able to be moved diagonally. Rocking is indicative that the manifold or spacer is warped. This must be corrected before the fasteners are tightened. Once a square installation is accomplished, it will be safe to secure the fasteners. Use an alternating X-pattern, while tightening each fastener incrementally. A torque of five to seven lbs./ft. is all that is required. Once the fasteners are evenly torqued, check the carburetor linkage for smooth operation to wide open and then back to closed positions. Please note that any damage that occurs to the base plate during an improper installation procedure will not be covered by the warranty.

Connecting Throttle Linkage

For this part of the installation, a helper is required, who will sit in the vehicle and hold the accelerator pedal firmly against the floor board or stop. A rigid, positive stop is necessary. This is especially important in vehicles with fabricated sheet metal firewalls that can flex under pressure from the driver's foot. Do not rely on the base plate linkage as a stop! Failure to use a positive pedal stop can result in damage to the linkage that may cause the throttle to stick in the wide-open position.

With the pedal held firmly against the stop, pull the carburetor to its wide-open position. Adjust the linkage rod or cable to the proper length and attach it to the base plate linkage. The pedal should come against the positive stop just as the carburetor accomplishes wide-open throttle. With the linkage rod attached to the base plate, make sure the carburetor returns to closed position. Install the return springs and check again for smooth operation.

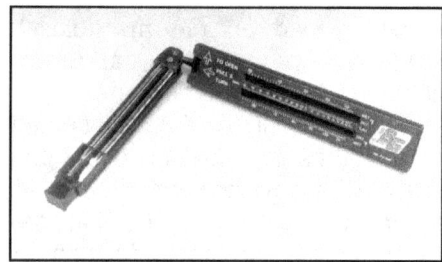

An entry-level psychrometer will serve the needs of most racers but will make your wrist a little tired from swinging it around.

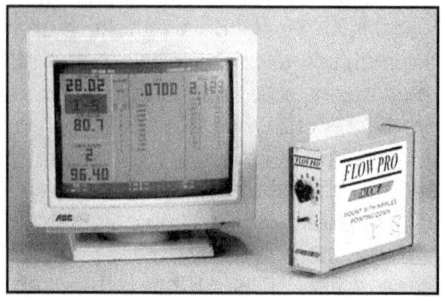

Audie Technologies offers a home-based cylinder-head flow-testing tool that is powered by a shop vacuum.

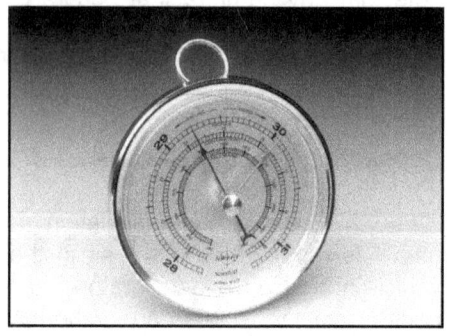

A premium-grade barometer like this BG part number 130019 unit offers more accurate readings and tuning decisions than a cheap hardware-store or home-center model.

Demon dealer Pro-Motion Engines of East Hanover, New Jersey, offers quality crankshafts, piston, and connecting rod kits. However, without a properly tuned carburetor, these parts cannot do their job.

Connecting Fuel Lines

Always use lines and fittings that are built for automotive use and are compatible with your type of fuel. Stainless-steel, braided, or push-lock-type reinforced hose with AN swivel connections are recommended at all fuel connections. Do not use thread locker, sealing compounds, or Teflon tape on AN fittings. When installing fuel bowl inlet fittings use only the sealing washers or O-rings provided with the fitting. In most instances, a drop of oil is a good measure to prevent thread galling. If a thread sealant is used on pipe fittings, use extreme caution to prevent any tape or compound from entering the internal flow area.

Check for leaks with the fuel system pressurized without the engine running. If a leak is detected, repair or replace the defective part or joint before proceeding. When installing new fuel lines, be sure to flush them clear of any residual debris from manufacturing or cutting procedures.

Connecting Vacuum Lines

All Road and Speed Demon carburetors have three vacuum sources available on the base plate that can be used for PCV, distributor vacuum advance, diagnostics, or any other vacuum accessory. The large fitting on the rear of the base plate and the second of the two smaller fittings on the side of the base plate are direct manifold vacuum sources. The front small fitting on the base plate opposite the throttle linkage is a ported or timed source. All vacuum outlets that are not being used need to be plugged or capped prior to starting the engine.

Priming the Carburetor

The prescribed method for priming an empty carburetor requires a fuel-compatible plastic squeeze bottle, such as BG part #130041. Fill the float bowls of the carburetor through the vent tubes until fuel is visible in the sight windows. Depress the accelerator pump levers until fuel is seen at the discharge nozzles. On vehicles equipped with an electric fuel pump, bump the pump switch on and off to fill the bowls in small increments. Avoid an abrupt surge of fuel into an empty carburetor since this can damage the float assembly and cause flooding.

Starting the Engine

If possible, it is best to have a helper around during the initial startup. An extra set of eyes to look for potential problems is invaluable. For most engines, the initial timing should be set 18-24 degrees BTDC to help the engine fire with the new carburetor. Before starting the engine, depress the throttle once or twice to the floor and then release. This will set the automatic choke if your Demon is equipped with one and will provide a shot of fuel from the accelerator pump. Then crank the engine. If it does not start after a reasonable crank time, repeat the above procedure. Every engine will require a slightly different starting procedure, so do not be alarmed if yours does not fire instantaneously.

Set the engine to fast idle during warmup by either allowing the fast idle cam on choke-equipped models to function or turning up the idle-speed screw on Demons without choke plates. If the curb idle screw is going to be used, record the number of turns so that it can be brought back to the same position. On most mild engines, a fast idle speed of 1300 to 1500 rpm is recommended. Once the engine is near operating temperature, lower the idle speed or disengage the fast idle cam before any tuning adjustments are made.

Preliminary Float Adjustment

Although the float levels are preset during the assembly process, it is recommended that they are rechecked each time the fuel bowls are removed or on initial startup. The sight window in later-model Demons will have three potential levels indicated, with the lowest setting identified for street use, the middle for street/strip, and the last and highest level for oval-track racing. Please note that these are only considered initial settings and may be altered to obtain the maximum performance from the carburetor.

Changes to the float level are accomplished by loosening the lock screw and rotating the adjuster nut on the top of the bowl. To prevent fuel leakage during an adjustment, loosen the locking screw only enough to allow rotation of the adjuster nut. Turning the adjuster nut clockwise will lower the float setting; conversely, rotating the adjuster nut counterclockwise will raise the setting. It is important to note that increased fuel levels are immediately visible in the sight glass, but lowered fuel levels are not. The excess fuel in the bowl must be consumed before stabilizing at the lower level. When lowering float levels, allow the engine to run for a few minutes, or gently raise the RPM until enough fuel is consumed to establish the new lower setting.

Curb Idle Speed and Mixture Adjustment

Fine-tuning of the idle speed and mixture must be done with the engine at operating temperature and the use of a tune-up-style tachometer. Any

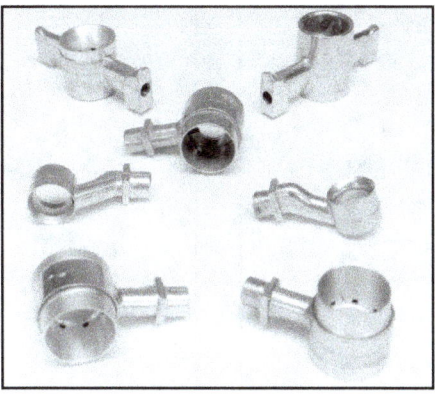

Boosters are not like socks; one size does not fit all. Demon offers a total of seven different designs, with each integrated into the calibration of the carburetor.

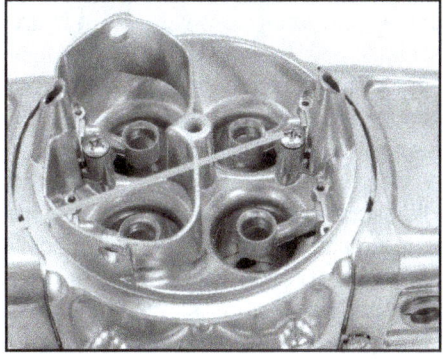

Dual-squirter carburetors have a mechanical secondary that requires the additional accelerator pump to compensate for the opening of the additional butterflies.

adjustments made with the engine cold usually result in a rich mixture when normal operating temperatures are reached. If the engine stalls when taken off fast idle, that is usually an indicator of a lean air/fuel ratio. Turn all four mixture screws out one-quarter to one-half turn from their current settings. If the engine still has difficulty running, more in-depth adjustments will be required.

To obtain the best idle quality and mixture adjustment, all changes should made with the air cleaner assembly in place and, if the vehicle is equipped with an automatic transmission, in drive with the wheels chocked and the brake applied by a helper. This will simulate the pressure drop across the venturi that the carburetor will see in actual use. Often adjustments are made with the transmission in park and the air filter assembly removed,

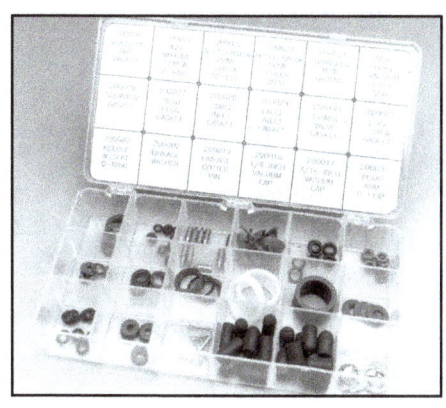

A small parts assortment kit includes all of the little items needed to service Demon carburetors housed in a durable, divided, clear plastic case.

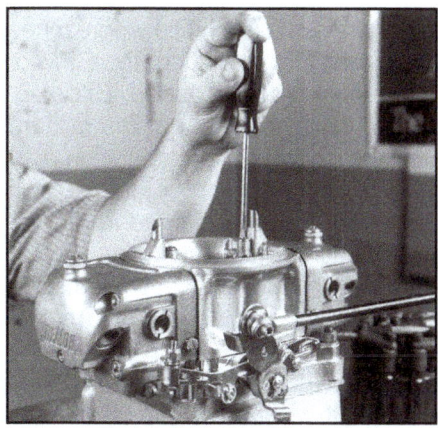

When servicing any part in the venturi area while the carburetor is still on the engine, stuff a rag or paper towel in the main body, just in case you drop something.

resulting in a degradation in idle quality and a change to the mixture when exposed to actual conditions.

Before making any adjustments, let the engine idle and check for fuel dripping from the boosters. If a discharge is present, the float level may be high, the butterflies too far open, or the fuel pressure excessive. Do not attempt to tune around this condition with the idle mixture screws; take the necessary corrective action before continuing.

The proper procedure will often require adjusting the mixture screws in two or three steps, bringing the calibration into line incrementally. Turning in the mixture screws leans the air/fuel ratio, and rotating them outward richens the mixture. Begin by turning each screw in one-eighth turn while watching the tune-up tachome-

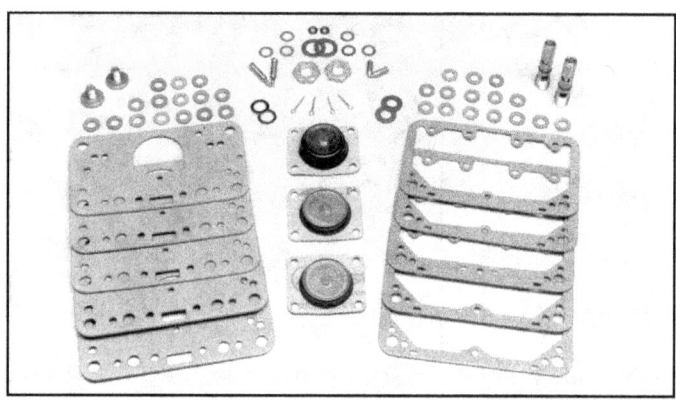

Demon prides itself on selling the proper carburetor the first time, but that doesn't mean a little fine-tuning by the end user cannot improve upon that. We suggest getting a gasket and power valve kit when you make your purchase.

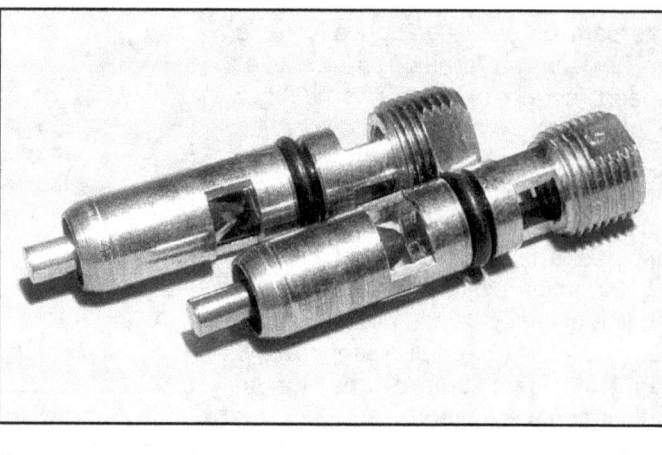

Developed for alcohol use, stainless-steel high-flow needle-valve assemblies possess an unrestricted opening at maximum float drop.

ter. As the mixture ratio approaches the most efficient setting, the RPM of the engine will increase in lock step. The theory is to lean out the mixture until the engine RPM drops, then start to turn each of the four mixture screws out (rich) in one-eighth-turn increments until the highest engine RPM is recorded. This process demands patience; the engine will take a few seconds to respond to the new setting because fuel is already in transit through the intake manifold runners. During this time, the idle speed will need to be kept in check, and it is common for the throttle plates to have to be closed slightly to maintain the desired idle speed as the optimum mixture ratio is reached.

If the end result places the mixture screws less than one full turn out from seated, an off-idle stumble may result. If the engine idles best with the mixture screws less than one turn from fully seated, this indicates an overly rich idle circuit calibration. Then the IFR (idle feed restrictor) orifice dimension should be decreased by 0.002 inch to lean the idle circuit and allow authority to return to the mixture screws. The correct carburetor calibration will yield a mixture screw adjustment of 1 to 2.5 full turns from seated. If the engine responds to turning the screws out more than 2.5 turns, it usually is an indication that your particular engine combination requires a richer idle circuit.

To correct this, you may first try decreasing the size of the idle air bleed by 0.003 to 0.004 inch at a time. If the idle air bleed is decreased by 0.006 to 0.008 inch and the mixture is still too lean, then the IFR in the metering block will need to be increased in 0.002-inch increments until the correct mixture screw orientation is achieved. The idle air bleed and IFR can be made larger by drilling and made smaller by the use of a press-in bleed that is available from Barry Grant, Inc. The IFR is located in the metering block below the main well for each idle circuit of the carburetor.

The goal to achieve the best idle quality and throttle response is to have the engine idle with the butterflies closed at the correct RPM, with the highest manifold vacuum, lowest CO, highest CO_2, and mixture screws between 1 and 2.5 turns from seated. The best transition from idle to main metering fuel will happen when the mixture screws are oriented one full turn from fully seated. During this process, remember that the desired result is a properly performing engine,

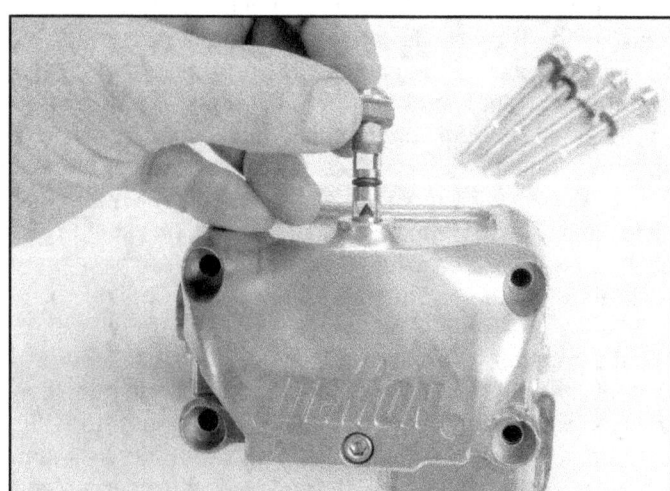

The needle-valve assembly is easily removed from the top of the float bowl.

Road Demons require the removal of the secondary vacuum pod from the main body to access the calibration spring.

regardless of mixture-screw position. If the engine exhibits an off-idle hesitation, the IFR must be made smaller.

Achieving a Smooth Idle

The best idle quality will be obtained when a balance between the air/fuel ratio and spark advance occurs. Due to the limited amount of VE an idling engine experiences, the turbulence created in the cylinder as the piston sweeps toward TDC is less than when the throttle plates are open. This limits the flame speed, and thus requires more spark lead.

As the engine RPM or the load is increased, or the throttle is opened further, the amount of spark advance required is usually diminished. You will need to determine an acceptable base setting between the throttle angle, initial timing, and mixture screw adjustment. Also consider the fact that an engine produces a minimal amount of its potential torque at idle, and accessory drive loads can consume as much as 40 percent of what is available.

Factors independent of the engine such as the torque converter stall speed will affect the change in engine RPM when selecting between neutral and drive. If your vehicle is equipped with air conditioning, you may consider integrating an older-style GM idle-up solenoid to increase the throttle angle when the air conditioner load is engaged.

Jet up or down?

The most common area of carburetor tuning is the jet change. Located in both the primary and secondary metering blocks, the orifice size will determine the air/fuel ratio. Remember that any modifications made to the jet dimension will affect the mixture throughout the RPM range. Applying common logic to this, if you step up two numbers in jet dimension, the mixture will be richer at all operating ranges, with the least impact at idle due to the IFR. However, the jet cannot be used as a one-dimensional tuning aid; it needs to work in unison with the air bleeds. An easy way to remember this is that jets alter the fuel curve at all points, while bleeds will change the shape of the fuel curve. For instance, if your engine was rich at 2500 rpm but in range at all other engine speeds, a bleed change would be in order to alter the mixture at that one point.

What is difficult about working with jets is not physically changing the part, but determining which way to go in size. Demon suggests that when making any changes in jets, always modify both the primary and secondary sides a like amount. The only time this theory would not apply is if a mixture distribution problem becomes apparent. Before any jet changes are made, it is advisable to qualify the air/fuel ratio. Different approaches can be used to determine this, all with varying levels of accuracy. The most desirable method is to use a linear air/fuel ratio meter that incorporates a fast-acting oxygen sensor.

During the development of the Demon carburetor, an ETAS-brand meter was used exclusively to tune the final calibration of the Road Demon and Speed Demon models. This style meter uses an advanced five-wire oxygen sensor and requires a threaded bung to be attached to the header collector or exhaust pipe near the manifold. Being of linear design, this oxygen sensor has the ability to accurately document the air/fuel ratio and display it on a digital readout. A instrument of this caliber will cost around $4000, so it is usually considered impractical for the enthusiast trying to dial in his carburetor.

Inexpensive, one-, two-, and three-wire oxygen-sensor-based meters are represented by their manufacturers as being able to identify the mixture ratio, but in truth have limited ability. Contrary to claims made, these meters use a Lambda = 1 sensor that can only accurately identify an air/fuel ratio of 14.7:1. Thus, the only factual statement that can be made when using this style of instrument is the mixture is richer, leaner, or at 14.7:1. A concern common to all oxygen-sensor-based meters is the inability to use leaded fuel. Gasoline of this composition will coat the shell of the sensor, insulating and corrupting its output.

Exhaust gas temperature (EGT) probes placed in the primary tubes of

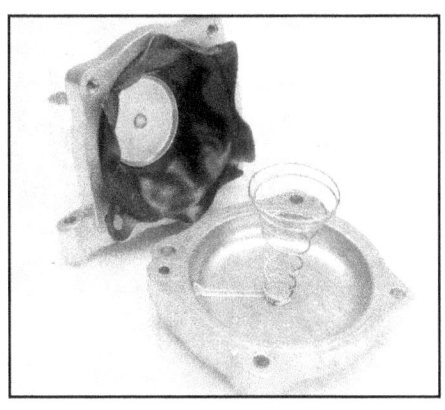

Once the vacuum pod cover is removed, the calibration spring and diaphragm are serviceable.

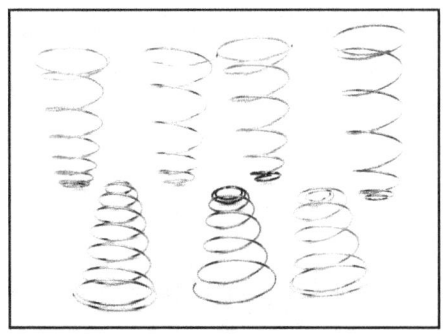

Seven different diaphragm springs are available. The stiffness of the spring determines the opening rate of the secondary butterflies.

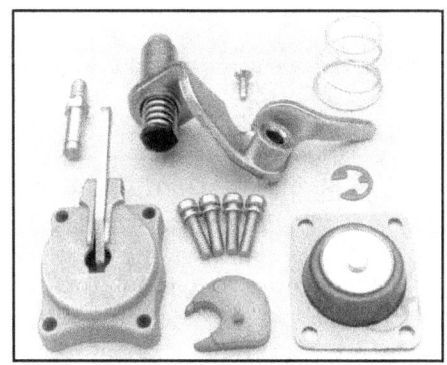

Road and Speed Demons come equipped with 30cc accelerator pumps. BG offers a huge 50cc kit for Race and King Demons.

the headers are another method to determine the air/fuel ratio. However, without any fuel consumption data, they become one-dimensional and inconclusive. Leaner mixtures produce higher EGTs, but so do slow combustion-chamber burn rates and brake torque ignition curves retarded from a maximum value. An engine

Many accelerator pump cams are available and are color-coded for ease of identification. However, with a street carburetor this circuit will hardly ever need to be tuned.

The 30cc accelerator pump kits are available as a service part from BG Fuel Systems.

dyno session that plots air/fuel ratio by measuring the fuel consumed in comparison to the air ingested by the engine would be required to establish a correlation of mixture ratio vs. EGT for this to be an accurate method.

This brings us back to the old standby: spark plug color. Though a very good indicator, the color of the spark plug is rather insensitive to minute changes to the mixture. As an example, it would be impossible to quantify visually a change in mixture of less than one-half of a ratio. Spark plug color is a valuable qualifier of distribution in the intake manifold though and, under very close examination, as a precursor to detonation.

Begin with the baseline calibration supplied by Demon, and always start your tuning by moving up in jet size first. This logic is prescribed because it is always safer to make an engine rich than lean, since you have no true idea of where the mixture currently is. If a chassis or engine dyno session is not in order, then the best place to tune is at the track, under full load and wide-open throttle. Continue to increase the jetting by two sizes until the vehicle begins to slow down or the ET suffers. Then back up one jet size, and this will usually be the optimal setting. As the weather changes or the vehicle is operated at different altitudes, the jetting will need to be altered. As the ambient temperature, humidity, or altitude increases, smaller jets will be required since the air will contain less oxygen. The converse will also hold true.

Demon research has found that if the humidity stays constant, only temperature fluctuations of around 30 F degrees or altitude differences of 1200 feet or greater will require jet tuning. As mentioned previously, only Barry Grant, Inc.-manufactured jets should be used to maintain the quality standard of your Demon carburetor. A good rule for jet sizing is that each step alters the fuel delivery rate one percent, which would then impact the total delivered mixture ratio by four percent if all four jets are altered. This is a factor of approximately one percent change for each of four jets.

The carburetor's ability to generate a booster signal is going to impact the complete calibration along with the jet size. A weak booster signal will not allow a sufficient amount of fuel to be pulled through the main metering circuit, so consequently, a larger main jet would be required. Those of you who are used to working with other brands of carburetors will find that the Demon line produces a very linear fuel curve, and due to improved atomization characteristics, will result in lower BSFC values. An overly rich calibration will cause the engine to act excessively sluggish compared to the same calibration on another brand of carburetor. Tuning for street and strip use is a much more daunting task then getting a race-only unit to function properly. For this reason, those who understand the workings of an engine are usually the most successful.

Air Bleeds

The concept of jet-orifice dimension to fuel-delivery rate follows common sense, but the air bleeds use reverse logic and work in two different areas simultaneously. As the dimension of the air bleed is enlarged, it will not only work to lean the mixture, but delay the discharge of fuel at the booster. Conversely, reducing the air bleed size richens the mixture and activates the main metering system earlier. For this reason, the air bleed has the ability to change the shape of the fuel curve.

A good example of when air bleed tuning needs to be used is during a burnout at the drag-strip. A well-tuned carburetor will have the ability to deliver the precise amount of fuel for all operating ranges, not sacrificing performance in one area to satisfy another. After wetting the tires, the burnout creates an especially unique set of cir-

Before any parts or internal tuning changes are made, the float level, throttle plates, and mixture screws need to be adjusted properly. Don't forget that the idle circuit functions throughout the operating range of the carburetor. Often the idle mixture will need to be adjusted to compensate for the changes in air density from summer to winter.

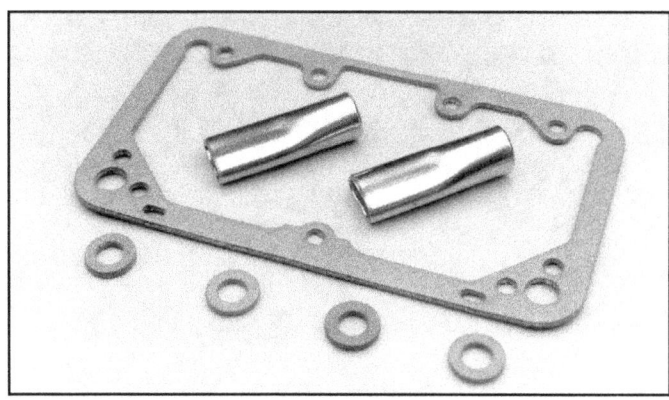

When a drag car leaves the line, the fuel in the secondary float bowl flows toward the rear, uncovering the main jets. These extensions maintain the intake flow path toward the rear of the bowl, keeping the jets covered at all times to prevent fuel starvation. Jet extensions can be installed at the track but should never be used on the street. A panic stop will drive the fuel away from the extension and cause the engine to stall.

cumstances. Let's define what's happening in the engine and carburetor.

Once the tires overcome their grip, the amount of load on the engine is minimal, which translates into a relatively small amount of throttle opening for the RPM produced. Thus, the amount of transfer slot area exposed is minimal, and the engine is running predominantly from the idle circuit with a weak signal produced in the booster. With this established, the low-speed air bleed dimension along with the mixture screw adjustment will determine the air/fuel ratio. As the engine RPM increases with a constant load, the amount of fuel required by the engine stays almost the same and will actually lean slightly due to less reversion from the overlap of the camshaft. The goal is to have an engine that comes up on the converter quickly and easily, and stays nice and clean and crisp during the burn out. This would be achieved by tuning the above-mentioned circuits.

Since most street engines fall prey to racer syndrome and are over-cammed, the need to alter the shape of the fuel curve through air-bleed orifice dimension becomes important. In most instances, if you ordered your Demon carburetor and chose the engine combination properly, then tuning in this area is usually not required.

Conditions may arise when the IFR will need to be enlarged using the logic of supplying more fuel instead of less air to richen the mixture. If any changes are made to the IFR circuit, then the air bleed should be returned to the original dimension before any additional tuning is done. Conversely, if the engine has a very elastic fuel demand, requiring large main jets, the IFR dimension may need to be decreased so that the mixture screws can then be oriented properly. The final air bleed dimension becomes a function of IFR dimension, position of the throttle plates, and the design of the idle transfer circuit.

As mentioned previously, if the mixture screw position is required to be

The accelerator pump diaphragm delivers fuel over a period of time, not all at once. This allows the engine to transition smoothly until the signal in the booster is strong enough to supply the needed fuel through the main metering circuit.

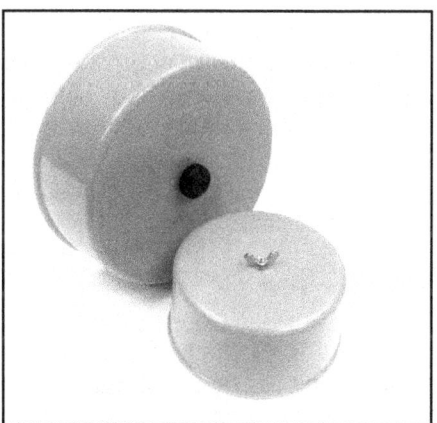

If the air-cleaner assembly or the carburetor is going to be removed, a plastic hat will keep it free from dust, dirt, and debris. Never leave a carburetor on a work bench unprotected.

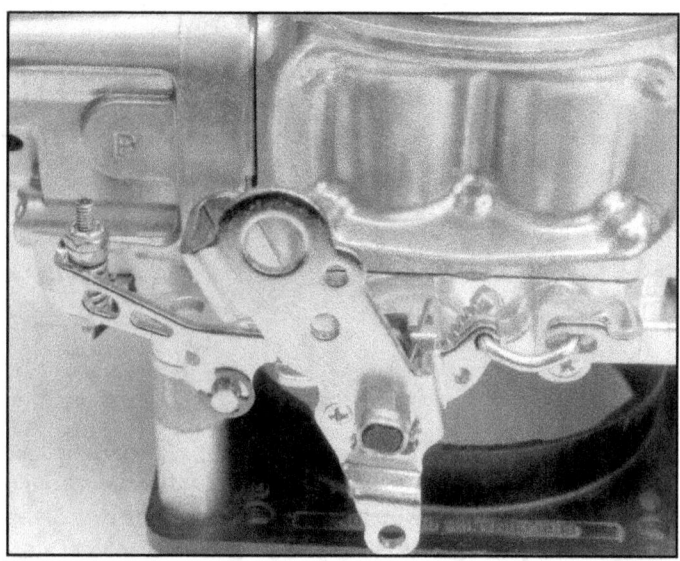

The proper amount of free play is required for the accelerator-pump arm and is detailed in this chapter.

Demon street carburetors are shipped with standard-style squirters, but those of tube design can be installed if desired. Usually tuning of this circuit on a street carburetor is the result of a problem elsewhere that is being covered up with huge amounts of accelerator pump stroke.

less than one full turn out from fully seated, the IFR should be altered instead of the idle air bleed. Many do not realize this and take the approach of introducing more air instead of less fuel. You need to remember that once the air bleed is altered, it will change the shape of the mixture curve while impacting the air/fuel ratio at a given point. Enlarging the air-bleed diameter leans the mixture and delays activation of fuel discharged at the booster. Conversely, reducing the air-bleed dimension richens the mixture and initiates fuel flow in the main metering circuit sooner. If a larger air bleed is used to achieve the proper mixture-screw orientation, the fuel curve will be leaner just off idle, which may affect performance, driveability, and emissions.

The air bleeds are located in the upper most portion of the main body between the wall and the venturi. There are eight bleeds in total, with the idle bleeds being closer to the outside and the high-speed bleeds nearer the center.

Emulsion Bleeds

There are six emulsion bleeds per metering block, three for each main well. These orifices play a part in controlling the density of the fuel in the block by metering the amount of air that is introduced into the main well. They work in conjunction with the air bleeds to shape the fuel curve. In almost all applications of a Road or Speed Demon carburetor, tuning to the emulsion bleeds will not be required, and only alterations to the idle and high-speed air bleeds are used to correct any tuning issues.

Float

Often the float level is not considered a tuning tool and other circuits are modified instead. Raising the float level would have a similar effect as a smaller air bleed: richening the mixture and activating the main metering system sooner. Lowering the float level would result in the opposite effect. Do not interpret this statement as saying that float level can be used in lieu of air bleed tuning; it works as an adjunct. Where air bleeds can shape the fuel curve, float level adjustment can only alter the required strength of the booster signal to pull fuel. The air bleed function will remain constant.

Power Valve

As important as the vacuum setting is, the power valve channel restrictor (PVCR) ultimately controls the amount of enrichment, with the vacuum signal only controlling the timing. The opening point of the power valve needs to be correlated with the needs of the vehicle. Carburetors used in a more aggressive street/strip application can alter the power valve setting to mask or cover holes in the fuel delivery. Since the function of the valve is keyed to engine vacuum, as the rating goes higher, the valve opens sooner. For this reason, it was suggested earlier in this chapter that the vacuum of the engine be documented during different driving ranges.

In many instances, early power valve activation wastes fuel and increases carbon monoxide emissions by introducing an excessive amount of fuel when the engine does not require it. The Road and Speed Demons come factory-equipped with 6.5-inch power valves and a 0.59-inch PVCR. Applications involving towing may consider earlier power valve activation as a means to quench the combustion chamber and limit the possibility of detonation. If the engine seems starved for fuel, then the PVCR would need to be enlarged.

Cam profiles that limit the amount of vacuum produced at idle require recognition of the power valve circuit. Many novices have gone to great lengths to try to lean out the mixture at idle and low speeds that was being enriched by an activated power valve. Selection of the power valve opening point should then be linked to the amount of engine vacuum present during normal operating conditions, and can only be determined by plotting the engine's load with a vacuum gauge.

Accelerator Pump

Being activated by a cam in lieu of a rod allows for fine tuning of this circuit.

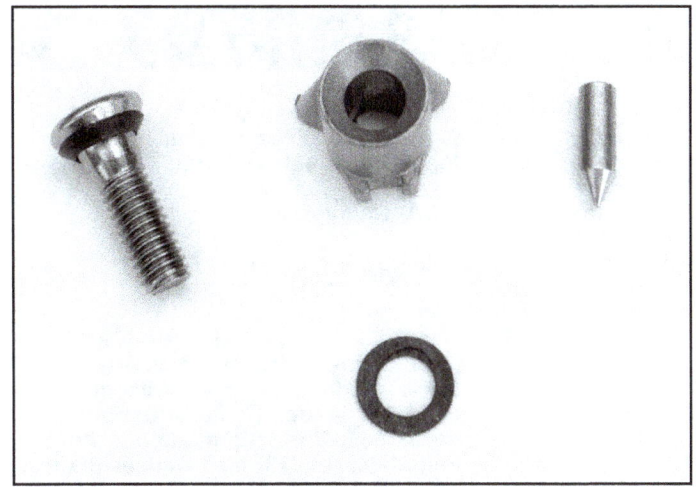

A standard-style squirter is used almost exclusively on Road and Speed Demon applications.

A good tuner's engine runs well during all operating ranges. Proper adjustment of the choke-spring tension will result in quick cold starts and excellent driveability during the intermediate period between a cold and fully-warmed engine.

The pump timing and discharge volume can be altered by varying the shape of the cam that activates the circuit. Cams are identified by a color code and are altered to change the amount of lift vs. degrees of rotation. Most Demon carburetors are factory equipped with a pink color-coded cam. On a street application, the cam should lift the plunger at a slow rate of gain relative to the throttle opening. The idea is to introduce just enough fuel to cover the lean spot, sometimes referred to as a hole in the fuel delivery, so the engine does not stumble. This needs to be a balanced effort since at greater butterfly openings, there still needs to be squirter activation left in reserve as the throttle is transitioned.

A borderline street/race application often requires a complete different logic applied to this circuit than a true street entry. A more aggressive engine would require a large amount of fuel at a specific throttle opening, and then have the requirement taper off. A drag car usually looks for help from the accelerator pump circuit when leaving the starting line when the throttle is opened very quickly. This is especially critical if the driving technique includes flashing the torque converter.

Road-racing demands usually include a constant modulation of the throttle and often mimic the squirter activation of a street car. Road and Speed Demons are factory equipped with 30cc pump covers and standard-style squirter nozzle. Barry Grant, Inc. offers two different styles of discharge squirters: standard and tube. In practice, the squirter or the accelerator pump cam profile rarely need to be altered from the factory issue. The standard squirter is a simple casting with two drilled discharge orifices; the other incorporates a small discharge extension that resembles a tube. Both styles are designed to discharge on the booster venturi to break the fuel apart. The tube design has the fuel exit closer to the booster for a more concentrated shot.

Vacuum Secondary

The operation of the secondary circuit can be timed by changing the tension of the internal spring. Prior to this, the performance of the vehicle should be documented at a drag strip or race facility. Often a calibration may feel better on the street but has actually slowed the car down. After documenting the performance, take note of any problem areas such as a stumble, hesitation, or lack of power under hard acceleration. Also make a mental note of the feel of the engine as the secondary opens.

What is nice about a vacuum-operated secondary is that it almost self-regulates the amount of air the engine ingests. It has the ability to make a carburetor that is too large act like a smaller one. Many enthusiasts want to feel a distinct kick when the secondary opens, but often this means that the engine is producing less than optimal performance. The additional butterfly should open slowly, meeting the airflow demands of the engine while the piston velocity builds. The operation should be analog and not digital in function. If the circuit is evoked prematurely, the sudden surge in power is actually after the air door has opened and the engine speed finally catches up to the available throttle area and creates a signal strong enough to pull fuel. Establishing a baseline is important and should be done with the air cleaner assembly in place because in many instances it will cause the secondary to open sooner.

If the carburetor seems to be working properly and there are no flat spots, select the next-lighter spring from the secondary tuning kit available from Barry Grant, Inc. Continue this process until you install a spring that causes the engine to bog or develop a flat spot. At this point your selection has become too aggressive and you need to return one step higher in spring tension.

Other functions of the carburetor tuning can also create a bog and must be corrected before doing any tuning in this area. A good rule is that an excessively slow-opening secondary will offer lazy engine performance, whereas a premature-opening will bog the engine in the 2000- to 3000-rpm range. As an example, if the flat spot occurs below this RPM, it usually is a function of an improperly tuned accelerator pump circuit.

AIR DENSITY AND ENGINE PERFORMANCE

If you are using your Demon carburetor on a street/strip application, the ability to tune for maximum performance in all weather conditions becomes an important element. To be proficient at this requires an understanding of what happens to air as its density changes, along with the proper tools to determine the condition of the air. The BG part number 130014 Air Density meter should be considered an essential part of your tool kit.

Fuel, oxygen, and a heat source are the three necessary components of combustion in any engine. In a spark-ignition engine, the heat source is established by the arcing of the spark plug, which in turn allows the mixture of fuel and air to burn. The amount of energy that expands against the piston is based on the amount of fuel that is burned, but burning the fuel requires oxygen. The amount of oxygen in the air is affected by the density or weight of the air.

Two factors that influence air density are temperature and barometric pressure. Higher temperatures cause lower air density, and higher barometric pressure increases air density. The opposite holds true for lower temperatures and barometric pressures. As the density of the air increases, the engine has the ability to burn more fuel, and thus produce higher power. Remember, an engine produces the most power when there is a sufficient amount of fuel to burn all of the oxygen in the bore, not the other way around. As the air density decreases, so does the ability to burn fuel, and the result is less power produced. Adjustments to the fuel mixture are also often necessary to maintain the correct air/fuel ratio at different air densities.

The hard part of this is that without an air-density instrument, you are only guessing at the tune-up. Containing metal components that expand and contract with changes in temperature and barometric pressure, the meter responds to differences in density. Reading the meter scale will indicate the density of the air. Racers and engine tuners can then monitor the changes in the air density and use this information to calculate the required carburetor jet changes. Understanding and using this information will give you a competitive edge over racers who do not use an air-density scale and only guess at tuning.

USING THE AIR-DENSITY METER

The meter must be removed completely from the padded case to allow free circulation of air through the vent holes on the sides of the meter body. The instrument should be kept in a shaded area away from any heating or cooling source that will cause inaccurate readings.

The first step is to establish a baseline tuning factor. On a given day, race or dyno the engine and perform jet changes to determine the best size for maximum performance on that day. Then record this information along with the readings from the air-density meter in a notebook. This will now become the baseline for all future tuning calculations. Each time you make a tuning change, it must be recorded along with the air density. After a short while you will establish a chart showing which jet works best with a given air density. If you are a drag racer, elapsed time for each density reading will provide a baseline for calculating your dial-in.

The number of steps in jet size required is equivalent to the amount of change in air density. To calculate the jet flow change according to the air density (A/D), use the following formula:

$$\text{A/D Change} = \frac{\text{Present A/D} - \text{Baseline A/D}}{\text{Baseline A/D}}$$

For example, if your baseline A/D number from your original test day is 92, and today the reading is 98, the following would hold true:

A/D Change =

$$\frac{98 - 92}{92} = \frac{6}{92} = 0.065 \text{ or } 6.5\%$$

In this instance the air became more dense, represented by a higher meter reading, so it will reflect the need to jet up. If the A/D number decreases, the percentage will be a negative, indicating smaller-than-baseline jet dimensions. To calculate the jet change required, you must first multiply the A/D change percentage by the area in square inches of your baseline jet. This amount must then be added or subtracted from the baseline jet area. The theoretical new jet dimension will be the one that is closest in area in square inches to the desired calculated area.

Let's consider the following scenario: Your baseline testing was done when the A/D meter reading was 92, and the engine performed best with #76 jets. The A/D meter now reads 98, as stated in the previous example. Using the jet change chart, it would be determined that a #76 jet has a drill size of 0.084 inch and an area of 0.005542 square inch. The required area change is equal to the area of the baseline jet multiplied by the decimal equivalent of the A/D change percentage. Adding or subtracting this will give you the total area required for the new jet. Remember, add the change as the air density increases, and subtract for lower densities.

Jet area change =
0.005542 X 0.065 = 0.000360

New jet area size =
0.005542 + 0.000360 = 0.005902

Use the jet chart on the following page to determine which jet size is closest to the calculated requirement.

It is recommended that the orifice hole found in the vacuum passage not be modified. It is designed to regulate the rate at which the secondary opens. It allows this to happen in a smooth, controlled manner. Modification to this component will cause premature secondary actuation and result in a severe engine bog under wide-open-throttle acceleration.

Make note of a few suggestions. Heavier cars generally require a stiffer spring. The more restrictive the air cleaner assembly, the stiffer the spring needs to be. Cracking the throttle with no load will not open the secondary. If it does open while doing this, the spring is too weak and will create a driveability issue. Clipping the spring to make it shorter will actually cause the secondary to function later. Though you reduce the preload on the spring, which in theory will cause the opening to start sooner, the spring becomes stiffer and will resist opening to full throttle until a higher RPM. Never operate your Demon carburetor without a secondary spring. This will ensure that the throttle will return to a constant idle speed when required. If you have installed the lightest spring in the diaphragm and the secondary still does not open and all other aspects of the carburetor are functioning properly, then the carburetor is too large for the engine. Any attempt to manually force the secondary open will lead to a reduction in the engine's performance.

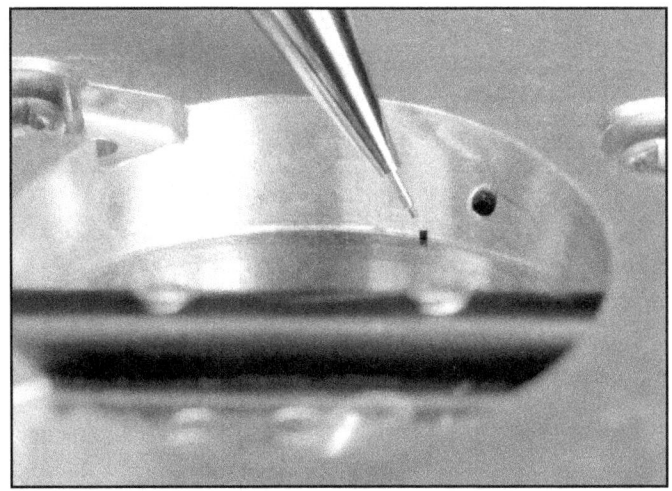

When the throttle plates are set properly, there will be approximately a 0.020-inch area of the transfer slot exposed.

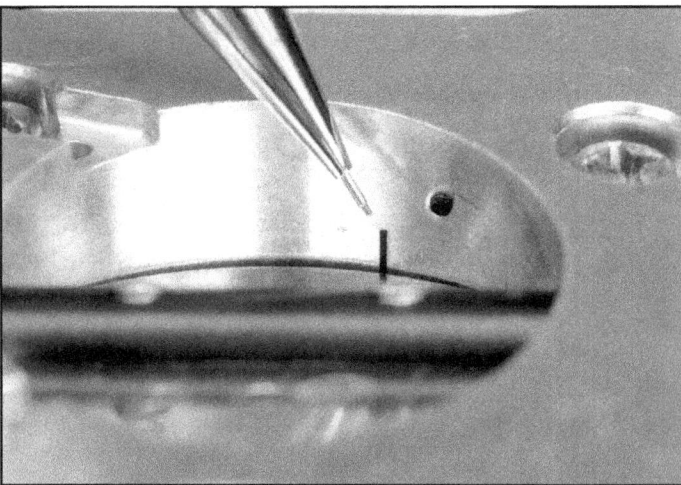

Engines that are over-cammed will require the throttle plates to be opened further to maintain an acceptable idle speed. This creates a problem since it exposes an excessive amount of the transfer slot area and can result in an off-idle stumble.

Spacers

Although they are not part of the carburetor, a properly designed and sized spacer can help dial in the engine for best performance. There are two types available: open and four-hole. The first is used to increase the intake manifold plenum area and enhance midrange to top-end power. A four-hole design increases air velocity rates through the carburetor and works to improve bottom-end to midrange torque. Spacer thickness also comes into play, and a good rule is that every inch will raise the power band 500 rpm. A side benefit of a phenolic spacer is its insulating properties that keep the carburetor body cooler. An aluminum spacer is easier to modify with a die grinder but offers little or no insulating qualities.

Hood Scoops, Cowls, and Air Pans

For a hood scoop or cowl induction to function properly, an air pan is required to seal the area between the carburetor and the underside of the hood. This will guarantee that the carburetor is fed with a supply of cool, fresh air. If this area is not sealed when the vehicle is moving at high speeds, the air velocity over the carburetor can create an area of low pressure, siphoning fuel from the carburetor. At speeds of over 100 mph, a well-designed and sealed scoop can create a positive pressure in the intake manifold, which will function as a mild supercharging effect.

BG designed a special anti-reversion spacer that has a seven-degree taper and special undercut that dampens reversion pulses before they reach the carburetor. This works to improve the signal and has the ability to increase power.

Open plenum spacers usually work best at higher RPM. A rule for all spacers is that every inch of thickness will raise the peak power of the engine 500 rpm.

JET AND NOZZLE SPECIFICATIONS

Jet Specifications

Jet No.	Drill Size	Jet No.	Drill Size	Jet No.	Drill Size	Jet No.	Drill Size	Jet No.	Drill Size	Jet No.	Drill Size
40	.040	51	.050	61	.060	71	.076	81	.093	91	.105
41	.041	52	.052	62	.061	72	.079	82	.093	92	.105
42	.042	53	.052	63	.062	73	.079	83	.094	93	.105
43	.043	54	.053	64	.064	74	.081	84	.099	94	.108
44	.044	55	.054	65	.065	75	.082	85	.100	95	.118
45	.045	56	.055	66	.066	76	.084	86	.101	96	.118
47	.047	57	.056	67	.068	77	.086	87	.103	97	.125
48	.048	58	.057	68	.069	78	.089	88	.104	98	.125
49	.048	59	.058	69	.070	79	.091	89	.104	99	.125
50	.049	60	.060	70	.073	80	.093	90	.104	100	.128

Jet Flow Chart

Jet No.	Flow	Jet No.	Flow	Jet No.	Flow	Jet No.	Flow	Jet No.	Flow	Jet No.	Flow
60	285	67	392	74	542	81	731	88	952	95	1320
61	298	68	411	75	566	82	765	89	987	96	1375
62	311	69	429	76	587	83	795	90	1014	97	1440
63	325	70	448	77	615	84	824	91	1080	98	1500
64	341	71	470	78	645	85	858	92	1150	99	1570
65	357	72	492	79	677	86	890	93	1200	100	1640
66	374	73	517	80	703	87	923	94	1260		

Areas of Nozzles and Jets

Jet Size Dia. (")	Jet Size Area (sq. ")	Jet Size Dia. (")	Jet Size Area (sq. ")	Jet Size Dia. (")	Jet Size Area (sq. ")	Jet Size Dia. (")	Jet Size Area (sq. ")	Jet Size Dia. (")	Jet Size Area (sq. ")	Jet Size Dia. (")	Jet Size Area
.020	.000314	.049	.001886	.078	.004778	.107	.008992	.136	.014527	.164	.021124
.021	.000346	.050	.001964	.079	.004902	.108	.009161	.137	.014741	.165	.021383
.022	.000380	.051	.002043	.080	.005027	.109	.009331	.138	.014957	.166	.021642
.023	.000415	.052	.002124	.081	.005153	.110	.009503	.139	.015175	.167	.021904
.024	.000452	.053	.002206	.082	.005281	.111	.009677	.140	.015394	.168	.022167
.025	.000491	.054	.002290	.083	.005411	.112	.009852	.141	.015615	.169	.022432
.026	.000531	.055	.002376	.084	.005542	.113	.010029	.142	.015837	.170	.022698
.027	.000573	.056	.002463	.085	.005675	.114	.010207	.143	.016061	.171	.022966
.028	.000616	.057	.002552	.086	.005809	.115	.010387	.144	.016277	.172	.023235
.029	.000661	.058	.002642	.087	.005945	.116	.010568	.145	.016513	.173	.023506
.030	.000707	.059	.002734	.088	.006082	.117	.010751	.146	.016742	.174	.023779
.031	.000755	.060	.002827	.089	.006221	.118	.010936	.147	.016972	.175	.024053
.032	.000804	.061	.002922	.090	.006362	.119	.011122	.148	.017203	.176	.024329
.033	.000855	.062	.003019	.091	.006504	.120	.011310	.149	.017437	.177	.024606
.034	.000908	.063	.003117	.092	.006648	.121	.011499	.150	.017672	.178	.024885
.035	.000962	.064	.003217	.093	.006793	.122	.011690	.151	.017908	.179	.025165
.036	.001018	.065	.003318	.094	.006940	.123	.011882	.152	.018146	.180	.025447
.037	.001075	.066	.003421	.095	.007088	.124	.012076	.153	.018385	.181	.025730
.038	.001134	.067	.003526	.096	.007238	.125	.012272	.154	.018627	.182	.026015
.039	.001195	.068	.003632	.097	.007390	.126	.012469	.155	.018869	.183	.026302
.040	.001257	.069	.003739	.098	.007543	.127	.012668	.156	.019113	.184	.026590
.041	.001321	.070	.003848	.099	.007698	.128	.012868	.157	.019359	.185	.026880
.042	.001385	.071	.003959	.100	.007854	.129	.013070	.158	.019607	.186	.027172
.043	.001452	.072	.004072	.101	.008012	.130	.013173	.159	.019856	.187	.027465
.044	.001521	.073	.004185	.102	.008171	.131	.013478	.160	.020106	.188	.027759
.045	.001590	.074	.004301	.103	.008332	.132	.013685	.161	.020358	.189	.028055
.046	.001662	.075	.004418	.104	.008459	.133	.013893	.162	.020612	.190	.028352
.047	.001735	.076	.004536	.105	.008659	.134	.014103	.163	.020867	.191	.028652
.048	.001810	.077	.004657	.106	.008825	.135	.014314				

CHOKE INSTALLATION AND TUNING

All Road Demons come factory equipped with a choke, but the Speed Demon line would require the end user to install the optional electric choke kit, part number 421440. It's a relatively straightforward installation requiring the following tools: small hammer, small drift punch, 3/32-inch Allen wrench, 9/64-inch Allen wrench, #2 Torx driver, 0.309-inch-diameter drill bit, deburring knife, needle-nose pliers, small flat-blade screwdriver, Philips-head screwdriver, and a small file.

Before attempting the choke installation, review this procedure. If you have any questions, call the Demon Tech Line at (706) 867-4712. The carburetor will need to be removed from the engine and all of the fuel drained to accomplish this task.

1) If your carburetor is equipped with a vacuum secondary, remove the diaphragm assembly prior to starting the choke installation. This can be accomplished by removing the three screws that attach the unit to the main body. Next the E-clip holding the diaphragm to the secondary throttle lever will be removed. Take special care not to lose the small rubber O-ring seal that attaches to the main body.

2) Turn the carburetor upside-down and with the secondary butterflies partially closed; note how much of the transfer slot is exposed. An alternative and more accurate method is to count the number of turns of the idle-speed screw for the secondary throttle plates to be fully closed. After removing the original idle-speed screw, use the 3/32-inch Allen wrench to return the butterflies to their closed positions.

3) Using a small hammer and drift punch, knock out the sealing slug located to the side of the choke horn. It will take only a few firm taps to dislodge it. It is essential that the oval-shaped hole be free from any debris; it may need to be deburred.

4) Slip the nylon sealing tab into the small slot below where the sealing slug is. The tab must be inserted with the hole chamfer facing toward the base plate of the carburetor. The sealing tab must be free to move front to back. The hole in the tab needs to move the complete length of the oval hole in the casting. Deburring on the main body or light sanding on the sealing tab may be necessary.

5) Insert the short end of the choke linkage through the nylon sealing tab. It will need to be worked through the hole; be careful not to bend the linkage. Orient the link so that the end is facing away from the choke horn.

6) Install the choke butterfly shaft into the choke horn. If it does not slide freely, you may need to deburr the two holes in the choke horn, or clean them out using a 0.309-inch drill bit. If any drilling or deburring is done, make sure the carburetor is upside-down so no shavings enter the main body. Once the shaft is installed, insert the choke linkage through the hole in the choke shaft end plate. Then slip one of the two small washers over the link and secure it with the included cotter pin.

7) Using the two Torx screws, install the butterfly. It is important that the butterfly does not drag on the sides of the choke horn or impede the ability of the shaft to rotate. Once it is in the proper position, remove and reinstall the Torx screws one at a time with a drop of blue Loctite.

8) Install the end plate/spring combination. The spring slides into the U-shaped end plate. The end plate with the double-D is then slid over the shaft. Note that it will intersect the first end plate along the flat area to the left of the shaft, and with the spring to the right of the shaft. It is usually easiest to attach the spring first. If the outer end plate will not slip on the flat area of the shaft, touch it up to achieve a good fit. Use the Phillips screw to secure the assembly.

9) Insert the long end of the choke linkage through the end plate of the choke pod. Use a washer and cotter pin to secure the assembly. Make sure that the fast-idle cam is in the proper location. It should be positioned above the link.

10) Now reinstall the secondary vacuum pod that was removed in step 1. Follow the removal procedure in reverse and do not forget the O-ring seal.

11) Pull the fast-idle cam down, which should open the butterfly, and position the fast-idle screw on the choke cam with it set to the deepest step.

12) Attach the choke pod to the main body using the long Allen screws and the 9/64-inch Allen wrench. Make sure the fast-idle cam does not catch on any of the stand-offs. If they do, loosen and reposition the pod.

13) Reinstall the carburetor on the engine. Locate a switched 12-volt positive source. Connect a wire from there to the terminal marked (+) on the choke housing. Connect a second wire from the choke housing terminal identified as (-) to a good ground.

Now it is important to make sure that the choke is adjusted properly. There are two primary adjustments: the fast idle and the choke spring tension. The choke fast-idle screw in conjunction with the fast-idle cam is responsible for a cold fast idle. The fast-idle speed is adjusted by the choke-idle-speed screw; turning it in will raise the fast-idle speed. It's important to note that when the choke is open completely, the fast-idle cam must be disengaged. Rotating the black pod cover controls the choke timing.

The timing of the choke is defined by the amount of preload that is induced into the thermostatic spring. Rotating the cover clockwise will decrease the amount of spring tension, and counterclockwise will increase tension. As the spring tension is increased, the choke will be evoked longer, taking more time to open. The amount of spring tension required will be the result of a combination of factors, including but not limited to the climate in which the vehicle will operate, the calibration of the carburetor, and the amount of heat travel into the intake manifold. For this reason, the only prescribed method is to start at the midpoint and tune from there. If the engine is balky during the warmup period then the spring tension needs to be increased slightly.

Occasionally, it may be necessary to dimple the air cleaner to allow the full range of travel for the choke shaft and butterfly. Failure to do so could result in an excessively high idle speed, which could make the vehicle hard to control or stop.

TUNING TIPS AND TROUBLE-SHOOTING FOR DEMON CARBURETORS

Symptom:	Remedy:
Fuel comes out of vent tube or runs out	A) Lower float level B) Decrease fuel pressure C) Remove, clean/replace needle-&-seat D) Inspect float to ensure it's moving freely
Backfires or pops through carburetor	A) Open idle-mixture screws B) Increase squirter size C) Increase jet size
Backfires or pops through exhaust	A) Lower float level B) Decrease fuel pressure C) Decrease jet size D) Readjust butterfly position, primary & secondary
Engine won't start	A) Prime carburetor with fuel B) Pump squirters to get fuel flowing C) Check ignition timing
Fuel leaks from throttle shafts	A) Lower float level B) Decrease fuel pressure C) Readjust butterfly position, primary & secondary
Is rich at idle	A) Increase initial timing B) Tighten mixture screws C) Readjust butterfly positions D) Lower float level E) Decrease fuel pressure
Stumbles under light acceleration	A) Open mixture screws B) Readjust butterfly positions C) Raise float level
Stumbles under hard acceleration	A) Readjust butterfly position B) Increase squirter size
Won't return to idle	A) Increase initial timing B) Readjust butterflies
Surges at part throttle	A) Open idle-mixture screws B) Open primary butterflies & close secondary C) Raise float level D) Increase jet size
Emits black smoke under hard acceleration	A) Lower float level B) Decrease fuel pressure C) Decrease jet size

IDLE-ENRICHMENT KIT FOR SPEED AND ROAD DEMON CARBURETORS

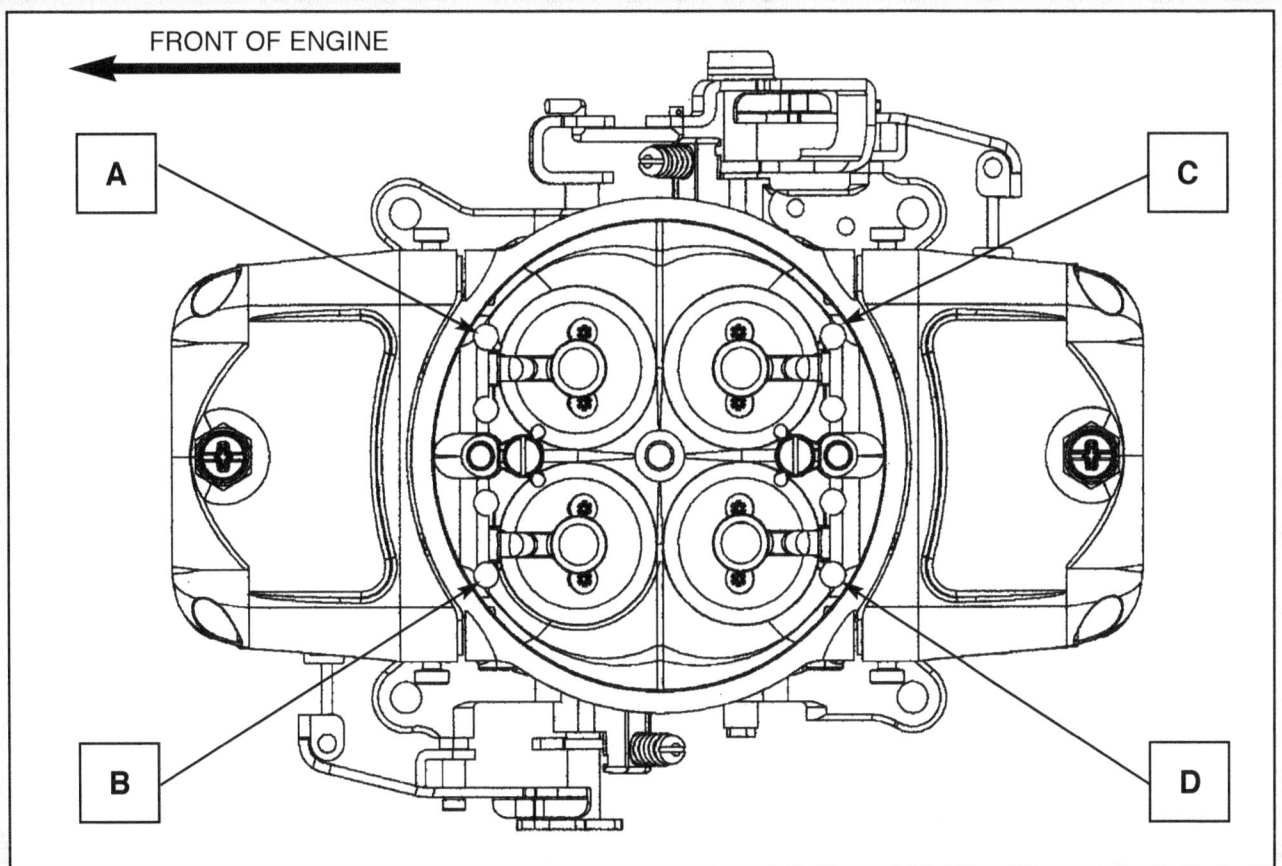

FRONT OF ENGINE

This kit is designed to overcome lean idle conditions. One or more of the following symptoms best identifies this condition:

1. The engine will not return directly to idle without hanging at a higher RPM.

2. The idle mixture screws, located in the metering blocks, need to be adjusted to a position of three (3) revolutions or more out from the seated position.

3. The engine has a stumble when the butterflies are opened slightly from the idle position.

If your engine suffers from any of the above-mentioned conditions, completion of the following steps should eliminate the problem.

1. Remove the carburetor from the engine.

2. Select one of the four bleeds from the attached bag and place in the hole marked "A".

3. Using a punch and hammer, tap the bleed into place.

4. Repeat the process for the hole marked "B".

5. Re-install the carburetor to the engine.

If the problems persist, repeat the above process for holes "C" and "D". It should be noted holes "A" and "B" are on the primary side of the carburetor, while "C" and "D" are on the secondary side. It is important to perform the modification in pairs. In other words, don't modify "A" without modifying "B".

All Demon carburetors produced after Spring 2001 will include an adjustable idle-air bypass. Using a calibrated orifice, additional air is introduced below the throttle plates so the transfer slot relationship can be maintained. This exclusive feature will eliminate drilling air bypass holes in the throttle plates and is tunable through a calibrated threaded orifice.

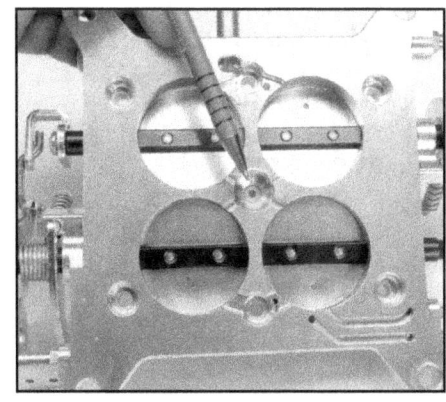

How to Tune and Win with Demon Carburetors

TUNING THE VACUUM SECONDARY

Though they function the same, there are two styles of vacuum-activated secondary mechanisms on Demon carburetors. The standard pod, identified as part number 421387, is attached to all Road Demons. All vacuum Speed Demon models are supplied with a quick-change pod cataloged under part number 421388. Due to differences in tuning procedures, each style pod will be discussed separately.

Tuning either design primarily involves changes to spring pressure to obtain the proper engine RPM opening and rate. This is achieved by using a tuning kit from Demon Carburetors, such as part number 420083. It includes an assortment of springs that will vary the amount of preload and spring rate to tune for the best performance.

STANDARD VACUUM POD
PART #42137, ROAD DEMON

1) In order to change the spring on this style, it is necessary to remove the pod from the carburetor. This may be accomplished by removing the E-clip that attaches the pod diaphragm to the secondary shaft end plate. Once the clip is removed, the three socket-head screws that attach the pod to the main body will need to be extracted. The pod will now be free for removal from the main body. Residing behind and between the pod and the main body is a small O-ring that isolates the vacuum signal from atmosphere. Make sure not to misplace or tear this seal, as installation with a damaged or missing seal will render the secondary inoperable.

2) On a work bench, remove the four socket-head cap screws that secure the top of the pod to the body and gently remove the top lid. The secondary spring will now be exposed. All Demon Carburetion secondary springs are color-coded. Use the chart to select the proper spring for your application.

3) Secure the new calibration spring in the pod lid and replace the assembly on the pod body. Reattach the fasteners and reinstall the pod to the carburetor main body, including the O-ring and E-clip removed previously.

QUICK-CHANGE VACUUM POD
PART #42138, SPEED DEMON

The Quick-Change pod allows for tuning without the need to remove the pod assembly from the carburetor main body.

1) Using a wide-blade screwdriver or a coin, remove the billet disk from the center of the pod lid. Lift the disk from the pod lid and remove the spring. Take care not to lose or tear the O-ring that seals the disk to the pod lid.

2) Choose the desired calibration spring and reverse the removal instructions for installation.

CARBURETOR CALIBRATION CHART

FROM:

MODEL#: _____

PART#: _____

VENTURI COLOR/ SIZE: _____

IDLE AIR BLEEDS: _____

H.S. AIR BLEEDS: _____

BOOSTER TYPE/ LEG: _____

SQUIRTER SIZE: _____

BASEPLATE COLOR/ SIZE: _____

B'FLY AIR HOLE SIZE: _____

PUMP CAM COLOR/ PART #: _____

M-BLOCK COLOR/ PART #: _____

SIPHON BREAK: _____

EMULSION HOLE #1: _____

EMULSION HOLE #2: _____

EMULSION HOLE #3: _____

EMULSION HOLE #4: _____

EMULSION HOLE #5: _____

TRANS. SLOT RESTRICTION: _____

P.V.C.R. SIZE: _____

I.F. RESTRICTOR SIZE: _____

MAIN JETS PRI: _____

MAIN JETS SEC: _____

POWER VALVE PRI: _____

POWER VALVE SEC: _____

N & S SIZE/ TYPE: _____

FROM:

MODEL#: _____

PART#: _____

VENTURI COLOR/ SIZE: _____

IDLE AIR BLEEDS: _____

H.S. AIR BLEEDS: _____

BOOSTER TYPE/ LEG: _____

SQUIRTER SIZE: _____

BASEPLATE COLOR/ SIZE: _____

B'FLY AIR HOLE SIZE: _____

PUMP CAM COLOR/ PART #: _____

M-BLOCK COLOR/ PART #: _____

SIPHON BREAK: _____

EMULSION HOLE #1: _____

EMULSION HOLE #2: _____

EMULSION HOLE #3: _____

EMULSION HOLE #4: _____

EMULSION HOLE #5: _____

TRANS. SLOT RESTRICTION: _____

P.V.C.R. SIZE: _____

I.F. RESTRICTOR SIZE: _____

MAIN JETS PRI: _____

MAIN JETS SEC: _____

POWER VALVE PRI: _____

POWER VALVE SEC: _____

N & S SIZE/ TYPE: _____

DON'T BE SQUARE

Over the years, there has been much controversy over the theory of square vs. staggered carburetor jetting. The former refers to using the same jet size in all four corners of the carburetor; the latter describes a calibration that has smaller primary than secondary jets.

The logic behind staggered jetting is due to the use of a power valve on the primary side of a Road or Speed Demon. These carburetors are calibrated at the factory with a PVCR that is eight jet sizes larger than the main jets. For example, a carburetor that is shipped with #70 jets in the primary will have #78s in the secondary side. Square jetting is then used as a common tuning theory on a race carburetor that has no power valve. Conversely, if a race-only unit is equipped with power-valve circuitry on both primary and secondary circuits, then square jetting may be employed, but for the opposite reason.

One may come to the conclusion that there is no need for a power valve; just remove and plug the passage in the metering block and square jet the carburetor. Even though the engine will run, the air/fuel ratio will be extremely rich and the fuel economy and driveability will suffer accordingly. The original concept for a load-based enrichment circuit was named an economizer valve instead of a power valve. This may seem like a paradox since the valve increases fuel flow substantially, but its use allows a weaker mixture strength during normal operation. For this reason, all Road and Speed Demon should retain their power valve function and be tuned with the primary jets eight numbers smaller than the secondary jets. This will ensure even fuel distribution to all the cylinders.

REVIEW QUESTIONS

(1) An engine usually requires more spark advance at idle than under load because:

a: the piston is traveling slower than at maximum power
b: the vacuum advance unit will not work
c: the VE is limited, which impacts the amount of turbulence created in the bore as the piston sweeps toward TDC
d: the mixture is leaner than under load

(2) High hydrocarbon emissions are usually indicative of:

a: a rich mixture
b: too large a jet in the carburetor
c: retarded ignition timing
d: a misfire

(3) High carbon monoxide emissions are the byproduct of:

a: a lean mixture
b: a rich mixture
c: advanced ignition timing
d: excessive camshaft overlap

(4) A catalytic converter works most efficiently:

a: when the engine out air/fuel ratio is within two percent of 14.7:1
b: with leaded fuel
c: with very lean mixtures
d: when the spark advance curve is very aggressive

(5) The term crevice volume or area is used to describe:

a: a region where the incoming charge will travel to but the flame front cannot access
b: the valve relief in a piston
c: the capacity of the accelerator pump cover measured in cc
d: the area of the plenum of the intake manifold

(6) On a street engine, the manifold vacuum signal will:

a: decrease as the throttle plate of the carburetor is opened and load is applied to the engine
b: stay the same with a Demon carburetor since it is a constant-vacuum design
c: be highest at wide-open throttle
d: a performance engine has no vacuum

(7) When preparing your Demon carburetor for installation, one of the steps includes:

a: checking the jet size in the old carburetor
b: adjusting the throttle plates so that approximately 0.020 inch of the idle transfer slot is exposed
c: measuring the throttle bore diameter with a vernier caliper
d: lubricating the throttle linkage

(8) Before starting the engine, you should position all of the mixture screws:

a: four turns from fully seated
b: fully seated
c: 1.5 turns out from fully seated
d: it makes no difference since the engine will be fast idling

(9) Jet changes alter the air/fuel ratio:

a: at idle only
b: at wide-open throttle only
c: throughout the operating range
d: they have no effect at all

(10) The float level should:

a: be set at different levels in primary and secondary bowls since gravity will pull the fuel backward
b: be set at the lower scribe mark for a street engine
c: automatically set itself according to atmospheric pressure
d: only be adjusted if the air bleeds will not solve the problem

Answers: 1) C, 2) D, 3) B, 4) A, 5) A, 6) A, 7) B, 8) C, 9) C, 10) B

How to Tune & Win with DEMON CARBURETORS
Race Track Preparation

The first step in preparing your Demon carburetor for a competition engine is purchasing the proper carburetor and calibration. This is extremely important, so the Demon technical line should always be consulted due to the number of minute but important changes that define each calibration. This chapter will focus on both the Race and King Demon series since they are designed to meet the requirements of a high-performance engine. As mentioned previously, certain elements of tuning that pertain to both street/strip and competition carburetors were covered in Chapter 9. To avoid redundancy, please reference that chapter for this information.

In almost every racing venue, the use of a large camshaft in a normally aspirated engine becomes the major stumbling block to tuning and efficient carburetor operation. As camshaft overlap is increased to improve cylinder filling and emptying at high engine speeds, the velocity through the intake manifold, and thus the strength of the signal created by the booster, is diminished during low-speed operation. This also creates an excessive amount of reversion that dilutes the incoming charge, but the carburetor is still required to provide the proper-mixture ratio despite these conditions. Compounding this is the high idle speed that is usually necessary to balance out these concerns.

For this reason, the use of throttle plate air holes is common in race-series carburetors. They allow the relationship of the throttle plate to the amount of exposed transfer slot area to be maintained while allowing for a higher idle speed. Thus, most tuning will be done with air and emulsion bleeds and not the main jets, shaping the fuel curve once the proper jetting dimensions have been determined. Other concerns are addressed inside the float bowl with application-specific floats, fuel dams, and jet extensions.

A unique feature of the Race and King Demons is that they do not need to be modified to work on a competition engine. Before their introduction, it was the practice with lesser carburetors to remove and grind off the air horn choke extension to unshroud the intake path, machine surfaces for flatness, switch or substitute base plates, modify the idle circuits through drilling, and thin the throttle plates, along with other processes. With a competition-series Demon, none of this is necessary; at most a simple thread-in bleed will need to be changed. Due to the excellent design that has gone into the complete Demon line, this chapter will concentrate on the theory of when and what to modify instead of the actual process itself.

AIR DELIVERY

For maximum horsepower, the coolest, most dense air possible should be fed to the carburetor inlet. The theory should be based on minimizing any restriction in the airflow path, and if possible, even pressurizing the air before entry into the air horn assembly. The air density has a direct impact on the engine's ability to produce power since it will afford the opportunity to supply the engine with more fuel.

It must be remembered that any engine will produce the most power when there is a sufficient amount of fuel present to burn all of the oxygen in the bore, not the other way around. If the type of racing that you are involved with allows a hood scoop or an outside air intake, they are highly recommended. In contrast, it is very undesirable to have the carburetor breathe underhood air. This environment is heated by the engine, and since air is elastic, it expands when heated and contracts when cooled. Thus, underhood air becomes less dense than outside air. This relationship has been documented and will produce an effect on power of one percent for every 10 F degrees the air temperature is altered.

When a scoop is used, it becomes critical to maintain a minimum of four inches of clearance between the top of the venturi and the scoop itself. If an air filter assembly is used, the tallest possible filter is preferred with a minimum height of four inches. For the best result with a hood scoop or external air intake system, it needs to be sealed to the carburetor. If this is not done, the air will flow across the top of the carburetor and away from the air-horn assembly. If the air is forced past the carburetor, it can cause a siphoning of fuel, making tuning very difficult. Windshield snorkels are especially notorious for this unless the forward-facing section is sealed. Air-pan kits for sealing the carburetor to the scoop are commercially available or can be home-fabricated from sheet metal and foam. In all cases, an air bell or radiused inlet should be used whenever possible to create a lamina path into the air horn of the carburetor.

If a drag-race car sees no improvement in performance when a scoop is installed and sealed off, the scoop itself is too short or the fuel delivery system is inadequate. Depending on the circumstances, a performance improvement of up to 3/10 second and an increase in trap speed by as much as 7 mph is possible with a properly functioning and sealed hood scoop over a flat hood. Likewise, oval-track entries will typically improve lap times by 1/10 to 1/2 second once the air-intake system is optimized.

FLOAT ADJUSTMENT

On race carburetors, the float level should be set to the highest mark on the bowl assembly as a starting point. This will provide the greatest amount of fuel in reserve and will initiate flow through the main metering circuit sooner than lower levels. At times the fuel level may need to be adjusted slightly, especially in a drag car that launches very hard. As a rule, never set the float level below the lowest line, and use this adjustment to help achieve the best possible all-around engine performance.

IDLE MIXTURE SCREWS

The engine should be at operating temperature when adjusting the idle. Gently seat the four idle mixture screws, and then back them out 1.5 turns each to establish a starting point. With the engine idling at operating temperature, slowly turn the screws in or out as needed to establish the best idle quality. You usually need to do this twice to find the best idle. The first time is a coarse adjustment; the second is a fine or final tune. If the idle quality cannot be adjusted satisfactorily, or the mixture screws cannot be backed out far enough to obtain the smoothest idle, it may be necessary to rework the IFR

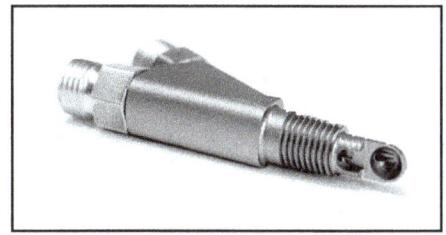

The NitrousWorks division of Barry Grant, Inc. features its patented Power Wing nozzle for the ultimate in fuel and nitrous gas delivery.

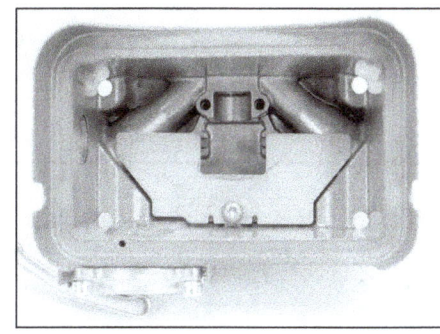

A fuel dam can be installed to control the fuel-delivery process and reduce foaming when using a very high-volume fuel system.

circuit. A common cause is the camshaft profile not creating enough vacuum below the throttle plates to pull fuel from the idle circuit.

Another reason for a lack of adjustment through the mixture screws is that the butterflies are excessively open and initiating fuel flow through the transfer slot. Remember, as flow is started in the transfer slot, that fuel is stolen from the idle circuit. The sec-

No matter what type of racing you do, Demon has the carburetor to make your engine perform the best.

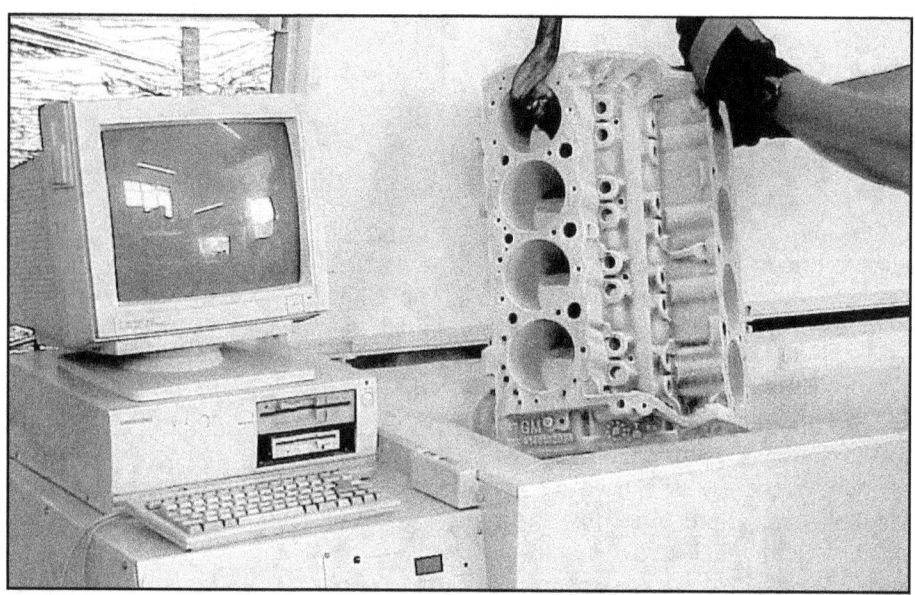

What good is power that doesn't last? 300 Below Inc. of Decatur, Illinois, cryogenically processes engine and driveline parts at -300 F degrees for stability and long life.

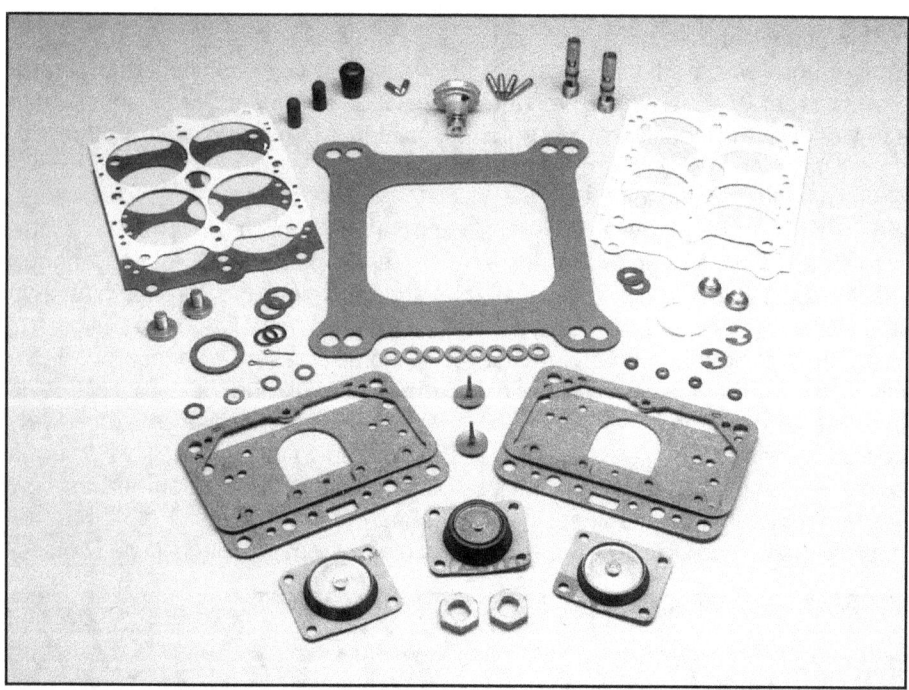

A Demon carburetor used in competition should be rebuilt once each season, more often if operated in a dirty environment.

ondary throttle plates should be just slightly open at idle. Sometimes it is necessary to open or close the throttle adjustment due to camshaft profile. Even though this ultimately is a trial-and-error procedure, the Demon exclusive air-bleed holes make this task much easier. When setting the idle speed, it is important to have the butterfly opening adjusted equally on both the primary and secondary sides, while keeping an area that is equal to approximately 0.020 inch of the transfer slot exposed.

JETTING

If ordered properly, the factory jetting issued by Demon should be very close to the requirements of the engine. When altering jet size for maximum performance, jet up by two steps, but jet down one step at a time. This logic is used to allow you to reach the desired fuel curve more quickly while sneaking back down on the proper tune-up once you go overly rich. As long as the engine's performance is increasing, continue your tuning until the power levels off or performance drops. At some point the elapsed or lap times will start to fall off. This would indicate that you have moved past the optimal air/fuel ratio. It is advisable to jet for performance and not spark plug color, though the color should be acknowledged.

Most high-energy ignition systems will leave very little residue on the spark plugs, making an accurate reading hard to obtain. With a dragracer, spark plugs can often remain bone white, so trying to read the color in these circumstances becomes an exercise in futility. An oval or road racer will eventually color the spark plugs due to their extended running time, but incremental jet changes will be very hard to read. If the engine appears to run excessively hot, then the carburetor jetting can be used to cool the combustion chamber. In most instances a jet change one to two steps richer will alleviate this problem with little impact on power. If the engine seems to require an unusually large jet size, then either the carburetor venturi dimensions are too large for the application or the fuel system is flow limited.

In general, an engine will usually offer a telltale sign by popping, missing, or surging if it is excessively lean, although an extremely rich condition can create the same symptoms. As a rule, cool, dense air requires larger jets, and hot, thin air would want smaller jets. If a carburetor spacer is added or removed, or any other change is made to the engine, such as a cylinder head or camshaft swap, the tuning procedure will need to begin over again.

A stumbling can occur on a drag-race vehicle if the fuel is moved away from the secondary main jets during a hard launch. Often the accelerator pump circuit is falsely identified as the culprit, but no amount of tuning in this area will alleviate the problem. This condition occurs when a car leaves the starting line so hard that the fuel in

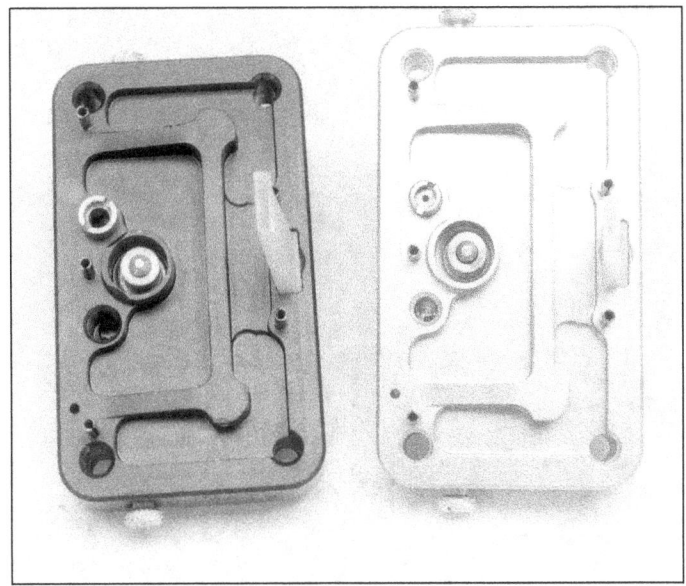

Alcohol requires much larger jets and fuel passages than gasoline.

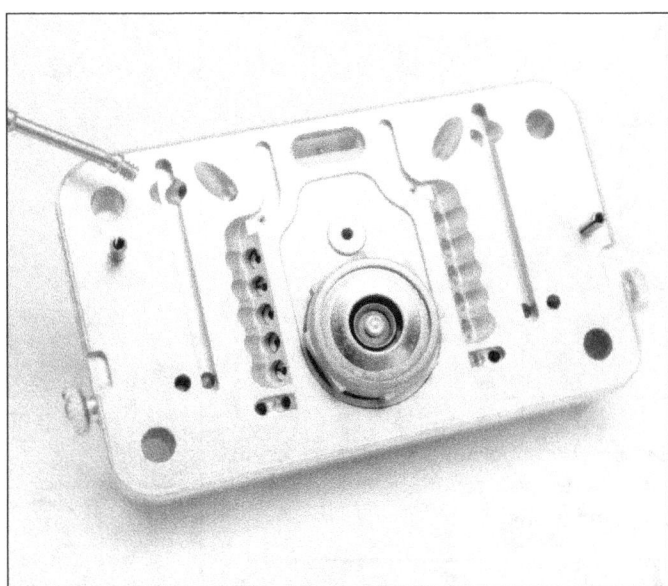

Race and King Demons use threaded air bleeds for tuning ease, but all Demon carburetors can be tuned for maximum performance.

the secondary bowl is pushed up against the rear wall, uncovering the jets. Jet extensions are used to eliminate this and need to be installed in the secondary side of the carburetor. Whenever jet extensions are used in a carburetor equipped with a secondary power valve, it must be removed and the hole plugged. In addition, the jetting must be stepped up eight sizes to compensate for the enrichment delivered through the PVCR circuit.

ACCELERATOR PUMP

Even when the jetting and power valve circuit tuning are correct, the performance of the engine during throttle transition will be poor if the accelerator pump squirter diameter is incorrect. Sluggish performance during initial acceleration, a puff of black smoke leaving the line with a drag car, or coming off a corner with an oval or road-race entry indicates a squirter diameter that is too large. Often this condition can be created by another problem independent of the accelerator pump: the spilling of fuel from the bowl vent tubes. A bowl vent problem can be cured by attaching a rubber hose connecting the primary and secondary side vents. It is important to cut a slot at the top of the hose to allow atmosphere pressure to be introduced to the fuel bowls.

The process to determine the best squirter diameter is usually accomplished by trial and error. Adjust the

The accelerator pump and secondary linkage are often neglected in tuning but reap big rewards in performance.

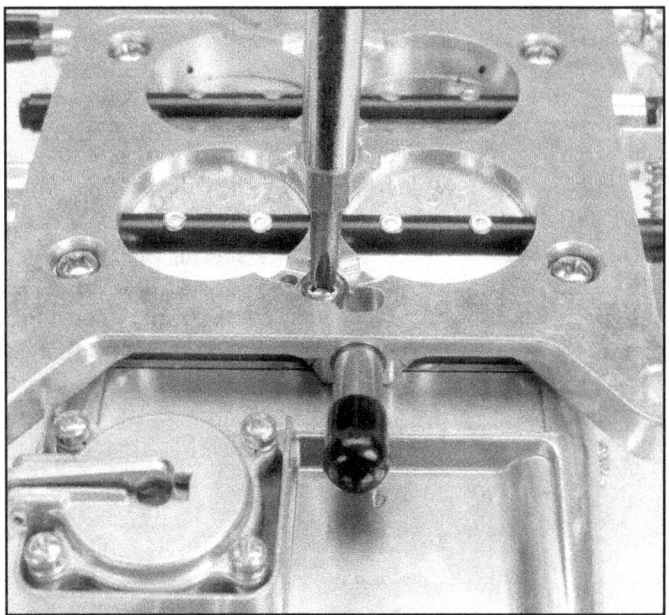

Always make sure all fasteners are secure to eliminate air leaks and keep your Demon carburetor performing at its maximum.

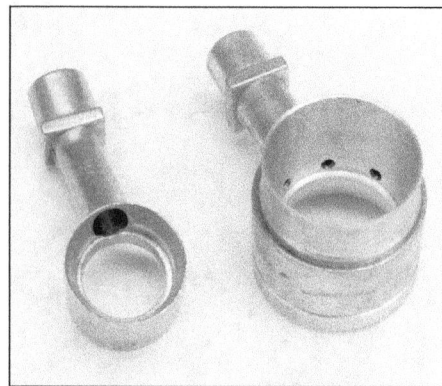

Before changing booster designs, consult the Demon technical line for recommendations.

A dyno session is the quickest and least expensive way to tune any competition engine.

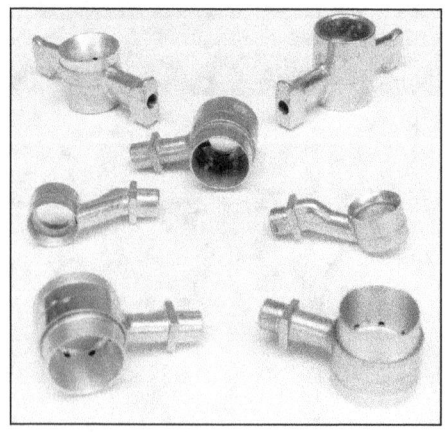

Using the wrong booster design can decrease power and throttle response, making tuning very difficult.

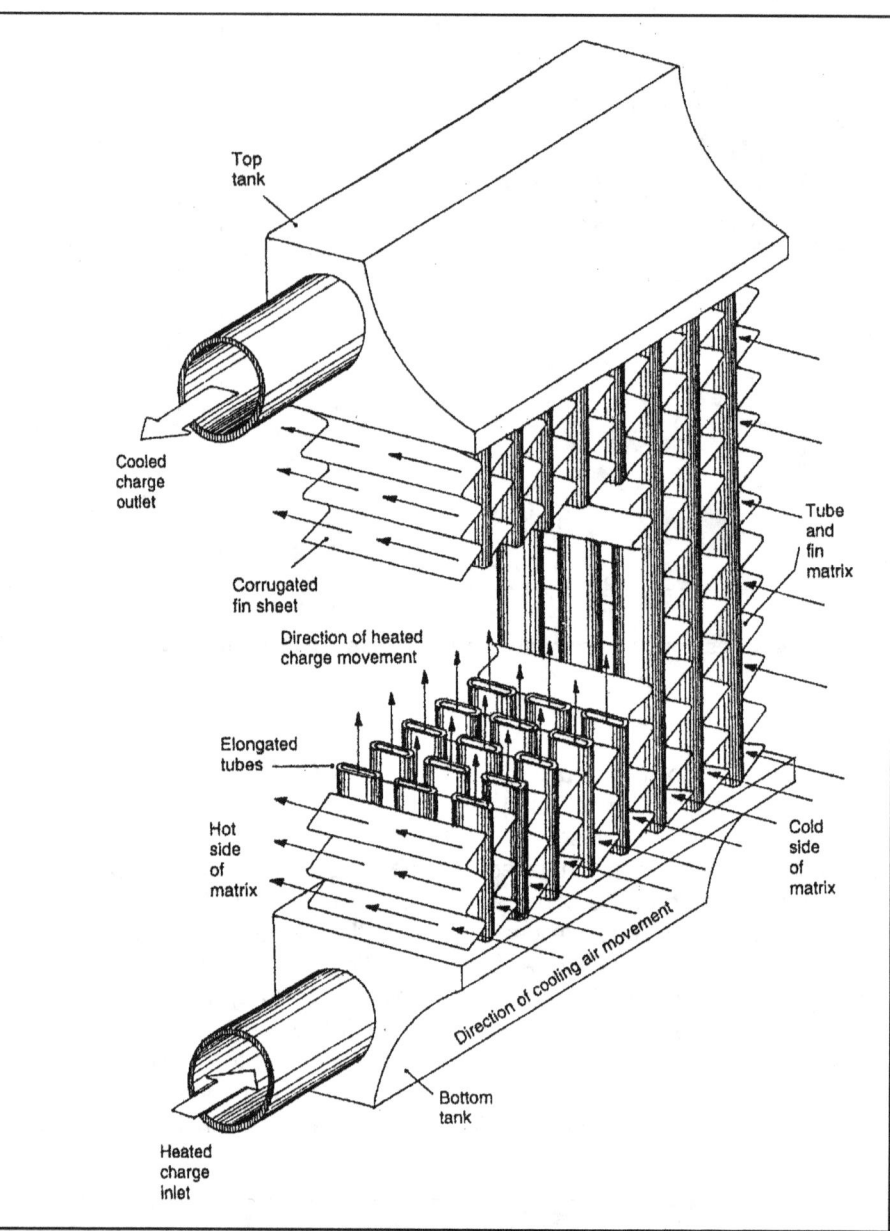

Whenever using forced induction, try to incorporate an intercooler for maximum air density.

size up or down to achieve the best throttle response and engine rate of acceleration. An additional area of tuning beyond the orifice dimension is the pump-lever adjustment. For oval-track use, the lever should be adjusted so that there is no play in the pump linkage when the throttle is closed. This will ensure that there will be no lean stumble when the carburetor is brought off idle. Achieving the maximum performance coming out of a corner frequently involves reducing, rather than increasing, pump volume and discharge rate. Drag racing demands a slightly different approach though.

For the strongest starting-line launch with a foot brake, the accelerator pump lever override spring should be adjusted so that at any throttle movement, fuel starts to discharge through the nozzle. The key is to have no backlash in the accelerator pump system at the starting-line RPM so the pump shot does not become used up before that engine speed. Adjusting the accelerator pump as described will create an excessive amount of looseness in the linkage at idle and low speeds and may produce a stumble when driving the car through the pits, but on the track it will perform better. Vehicles equipped with a transmission brake or manual transmission

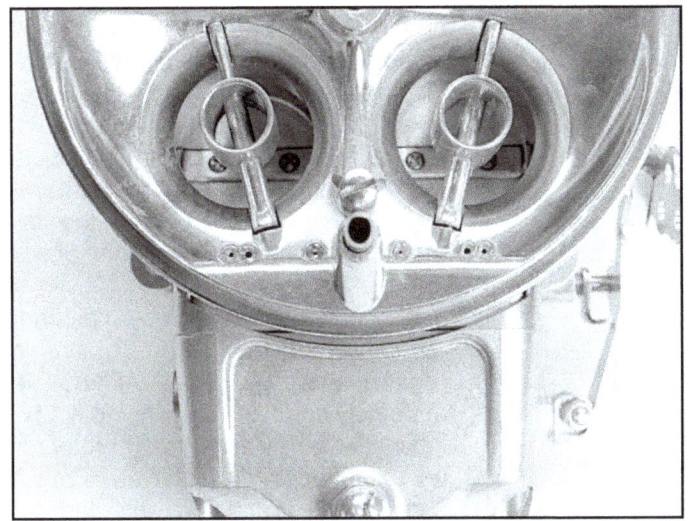
When tuning bleeds, think about how the carburetor functions to determine the direction of your changes.

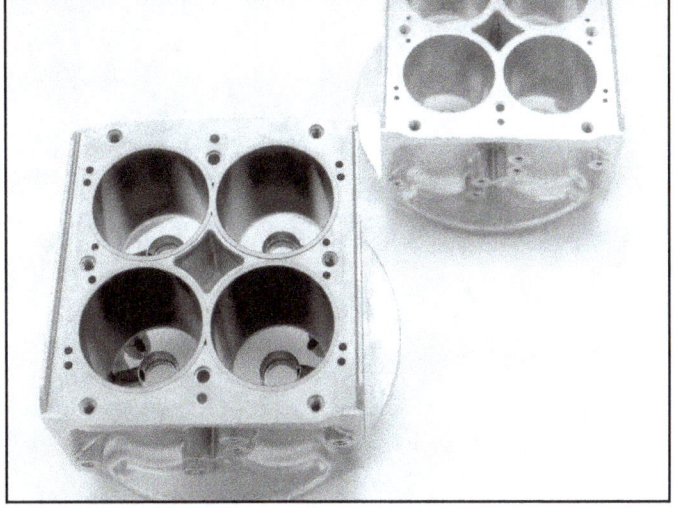
An RS-model carburetor is a good choice since it can be fine-tuned as your engine package changes.

where the launch procedure is accomplished with the throttle wide open should set the pump linkage the same as an oval-track entry.

It is important to realize that an excessively lean squirter will create a tip-in hesitation and, in extreme cases, a backfire through the carburetor; or it may actually cause the engine to flame out during a rapid throttle movement. Always consider at which rate the manifold vacuum drops off since it would be undesirable to have the squirter tuned too lean because of an early-opening power valve.

POWER VALVE

The power valve's function is to supply extra fuel through the main metering circuit for wide-open throttle and high load conditions. When the manifold vacuum falls below the number stamped on the power valve, it opens and enriches the mixture the equivalent of eight jet sizes. This will occur under high engine loads such as full-throttle acceleration. The setting of the power valve should be approximately 1.5-2 inches of mercury below the vacuum produced by the engine at idle.

As an example, if your engine has 8-9 inches of mercury at idle, a 6.5 power valve would be a good starting point. As the power valve rating goes lower, the circuit operation becomes delayed and may cause a temporary lean condition. However, on an oval-track car with a restricted carburetor, the use of a lower-rated power valve may sometimes improve performance exiting the corners. Any drag car with a secondary power valve must have the carburetor oriented sideways to avoid fuel starvation. The power valve is placed higher on the metering block than the jets and is the first to be uncovered as the fuel is pushed to the rear of the float bowl. Since there is no way to attach an extension to the power valve, the carburetor must be positioned perpendicular to the engine to perform properly.

THROTTLE LINKAGE

The best performance from the engine cannot be obtained unless the carburetor butterflies are opening fully when the accelerator pedal is pushed completely down. Consequently, the throttle opening should be checked regularly, as well as immediately following any major changes or alterations to the engine compartment. Likewise, if the throttle blades are pulled past the wide-open position, the engine will be starved for air as they become a restriction. For this reason, and as a safety feature, all Demon carbs require a positive stop to prevent the carburetor linkage from over-traveling and binding open. The throttle linkage must always operate smoothly with no binding and should be free of obstructions that may cause the throttle to stick and not return to a closed position when released. An

There is no one better than a racer to design a racing carburetor.

auxiliary spring must always be installed to ensure that the throttle closes positively.

TUNING FOR CHANGING WEATHER CONDITIONS

Shifts in air density due to changes in temperature, barometric pressure, and humidity will have a direct impact on engine performance. As the air density changes, adjustments to the fuel mixture are often necessary through jetting. These factors can be different from afternoon to evening. As the air cools down, it carries more oxygen per cubic foot and has the ability to support more fuel. The weather conditions may not differ enough during the course of the day to require tuning, but as the seasons come and go, the tune-up of the car-

How to Tune and Win with Demon Carburetors

The ultimate race carburetor.

buretor will need to be altered. Traveling to race events at different altitudes and climates will require jet tuning if the maximum performance is to be obtained from the engine.

SPACERS AND PLENUM DIVIDERS

Spacers and plenum dividers provide an easy way to change the configuration of the intake tract and the relationship it has with the carburetor. Adding a divider to an open-plenum manifold will help keep the left-to-right fuel distribution balanced for oval or road-race applications when going around a turn. This is especially helpful on engines that use alcohol as a fuel. Dividers usually do not have any measurable effect on power or torque and are used more for fuel management in the plenum.

Spacers between the carburetor and intake manifold can produce dramatic power gains and results. The use of a four-hole spacer can improve the low end and midrange by helping the carburetor draw and atomize fuel. An open-center spacer increases the plenum area and can benefit the midrange and upper-RPM power. It is not uncommon to see combinations of spacers being used with results that vary greatly from the established norm. The impact of any spacer can only be measured during a testing-and-tuning session either on a dyno or at the race track.

CARBURETOR AND FUEL-SYSTEM MAINTENANCE

For consistent performance and a long useful life, your Demon carburetor needs to be kept clean. Spraying the air bleeds with a carburetor cleaner should become a habit before entering any competition. Air bleeds can become clogged from atmosphere-borne dirt particles and from the dye used in racing fuel. When this happens, a stumble or high-speed misfire can occur. If the engine is going to sit dormant for a period of time, a light spray of WD-40 or an equivalent product down the venturi while turning the engine over with the ignition system disabled will protect the valve seats and cylinders from rust. A Demon carburetor that is used in competition should be disassembled and rebuilt once a year, more frequently if it's operated in a dirty environment. Before storing a race vehicle for the winter, always run the carburetor out of gasoline to prevent the formation of varnish in the float bowls and fuel passages.

Applications that use alcohol require a more complex maintenance regime than gasoline. Alcohol is extremely corrosive and should not be left in the fuel system or carburetor for an extended period of time. Proper care includes draining and flushing the entire fuel system, usually with gasoline. The most common method is to drain the system and add gasoline to the fuel cell or tank, allowing the fuel pump to draw the gasoline through the lines and into the carburetor. Alcohol carburetors use much larger jets and orifices than gasoline, so when the engine stalls when idling, the system is well flushed. During the racing season, always use an approved fuel-system additive for lubrication.

TUNING EMULSION BLEEDS

Race Demons have five-hole emulsion blocks, and King Demons use four-position versions. As shipped from the factory, most calibrations do not use all holes. In almost every instance the position and orifice dimension designed by the Demon engineers will not need to be altered, but in some rare occasions tuning in this area will be required. This will usually be the result of an engine combination that requires an extremely different fuel curve. Since the emulsion holes are used to mix air with the gasoline in the main well, they cannot be tuned randomly; before any changes are made, documented data is required.

The first step before changing an emulsion orifice or dimension is to talk with the Demon technical line. In most instances, fuel-curve adjustments can be made by altering the low- and high-speed air bleeds. King Demon models offer a third tuning choice with the intermediate circuit bleeds before any work needs to be done on the emulsion holes. A good rule is that the inter-

CAMSHAFT TERMS

Understanding camshaft terms will allow you to pick the grind that will work best for your application. The following is a brief description of cam lobe and design terminology.

Ramp. The portion of the cam-lobe event from zero lift (base circle) to the defined opening or closing point.

Base-circle radius. The portion of the cam contour at zero lift (valves closed).

Flank. The section of the cam lobe between the ramp and the nose radius.

Nose radius. The radius that is tangent to the flank and the maximum lift point. Also the instantaneous radius at the maximum lift point on the nose of the cam.

Inflection point. The point on the lift curve where acceleration (of the lifter) changes from positive or negative, or vice versa.

Main event. *The portion of the cam-lobe profile from the ramp to the nose.* There are two main events, one each for the opening and closing halves of the profile.

Velocity. The rate at which position changes. In most instances, it is expressed in terms of distance vs. time (MPH, feet per second, etc.). When dealing with camshafts, time is replaced by degrees of camshaft rotation. This allows the study of camshaft profiles to be independent of the engine speed.

Acceleration. The rate at which velocity changes. It is expressed in cam logic as inch/degree or thousandths/degree.

Jerk. How fast the acceleration changes, expressed in units of inch/degree.

Duration. The amount of time in crankshaft rotational degrees that it takes for the lifter to travel from a specified lift point on the opening side of the lobe to the same lift point on the closing side.

Lobe centerline. This represents an imaginary line, referenced from the true center of the base circle out to the end of each lobe, expressed in crankshaft rotational degrees. Intake centerline values are found in the crankshafts rotation ATDC, while exhaust centerlines are found at travel BTDC. Lobe centerlines are commonly thought to be the actual midpoint of the flank and are usually close to that, but different ramps on the opening and closing sides may change that reading.

Lobe separation angle. LSA is measured in camshaft degrees and refers to the amount of rotation it takes to travel from the intake centerline to the exhaust centerline. As this number increases, the distance between the centerlines is spread out. LSA is often considered an indicator of overlap, or the period of time both valves are open on the same cylinder. Because it is a partial function of LSA, overlap can be calculated with fair accuracy using duration and LSA values.

ROD-TO-STROKE RATIO: HERE WE GO AGAIN

The more you seem to understand this concept of engine building, the more confused you become. It is my opinion that rod/stroke ratio is something you need to look at with a defined goal in mind. There is no denying that lower numerical ratios create more frictional losses through the engine and create higher piston side loads, while increasing thrust-side bore wear. However, what is hardly discussed is the fact that the instantaneous piston velocity is greater with what is defined as poor ratios. This allows the engine to effectively pump more air and promote a greater VE.

The opposing camp then chimes in that the longer the piston dwells at TDC, the longer the quench area remains small as the flame front starts to expand. When it's finally allowed to turn the crankshaft, more force from the same amount of fuel is realized. As an example, a standard Ford 302 engine enjoys a ratio of 1.69, which is one of the best among current domestic V-8 engines, whereas a 347 has a value of 1.58. At 3000 rpm, the 302 and 347 would have mean piston velocities of 3000 fps and 3400 fps, respectively. This is not an apples-to-apples comparison, since the displacement, stroke, and rod-length combinations are different. However, referencing airflow-to-piston velocity only, the stroker would in theory be able to pump more air.

There are too many variables to make a blanket assessment as to which ratio is best. It appears, though, that an engine equipped with cylinder head intake port runner volume that is too great would benefit from a poorer numerical ratio due to the higher instantaneous piston velocities. A properly sized port would better respond to the longer quench time and reduced motoring friction. If longevity becomes a major concern, then higher numerical ratios are the only way to go. Conversely, race engines that experience high RPM continuously would suffer greater losses from motoring friction than the gains realized from the higher instantaneous piston velocity.

---

mediate circuit on a King Demon has the ability to alter the fuel-delivery rate approximately six percent. The only time changes should be made to the emulsion hole position or dimension is when the engine is fully instrumented on a dyno. A tuning mistake in this area can create a dangerously lean condition that can ruin an engine. To accurately tune this circuit, a plot of BSFC values for every RPM point on the dyno sheet needs to be available. By watching the fuel curve in relation to consumption, any rich or lean spots in the power curve become readily apparent. Without this information, it is best to leave the emulsion holes and positions as shipped from Demon. Horsepower alone is not a valid enough indicator for emulsion changes and can result in a costly mistake.

THE BENEFIT OF DYNO TESTING

As unusual as it may seem, many racers do not see the benefit of using a dyno to tune their carburetors and engine combinations. They believe that the best place to tune a car is at the track. Though track testing is the final element of any tuning procedure, the process is a multiple-dimensional equation. A well-instrumented engine dyno session will reveal important data beyond horsepower and torque curves. Information such as fuel consumption, RPM potential, rate of acceleration, mixture distribution through EGT readings, and air/fuel ratio are all of the elements required for the best performance from an engine. This data can then be used to determine carburetor jetting, air bleed size, fuel pump delivery volume, torque converter stall speed, final drive gear ratio, transmission ratio, etc.

The next logical step is to invest in a chassis dyno session once the engine is installed in the vehicle. This will document the amount of power actually getting to the rear wheels. By comparing the flywheel power to the output at the tires, the driveline losses can be minimized. Also, the VE of the engine changes when installed in most car bodies due to an increase in heat transfer and differences in breathing and the fuel-delivery system. The last step is to do the final tuning at the race track. If the previous two tuning sessions are executed properly, a minimal amount of track tuning will be required.

Often the up-front cost of engine and chassis dyno tuning scares racers away; they think that they can save money by skipping these steps and going right to the race track. Applying numbers to this one can quickly demonstrate that dyno tuning sessions are very cost-effective and work out more economically in the long run. The average engine dyno session is $500-$600 for a day. Chassis dyno tuning will usually cost $100-$200 for a two- to four-hour session. That means a maximum of $800 would be invested for both dyno sessions. Consider that in most parts of the country a day at the race track, including tow vehicle expenses, race fuel, meals, and entrance fees, will run around $250. Using a drag-strip scenario with the average of two or three time trials, and assuming that you lose in the first round of eliminations, it can take you all season and more than $1000 in expenses, and you would still be guessing at the proper engine and carburetor settings.

REVIEW QUESTIONS

1) A large amount of overlap ground into a camshaft affects the:

   a: signal produced in the booster and the amount of engine vacuum
   b: size of the accelerator pump cover
   c: float level
   d: PVCR dimension

2) Both Race and King Demons offer use-specific:

   a: secondary metering circuits
   b: floats
   c: accelerator pumps
   d: main body castings

3) To produce the most power, an engine requires:

   a: hot intake air
   b: damp air
   c: cool dry air
   d: air temperature makes no difference because of the latent heat of vaporization

4) The float level on a Race or King Demon should be set:

   a: to the lowest line on the float bowl
   b: to the middle line on the float bowl
   c: to the top line of the float bowl
   d: wherever the engine runs best

5) Jet extension should be installed only:

   a: in the primary float bowl
   b: when using alcohol as a fuel
   c: on tunnel-ram applications
   d: in the secondary float bowl

6) For a drag-race application, the accelerator pump override spring should be set:

   a: with any throttle movement
   b: to 300 rpm above the launch RPM
   c: just as the secondary butterflies open
   d: when WOT is reached

7) When a power valve is removed, the main jet size needs to:

   a: be decreased eight steps
   b: stay the same
   c: be increased eight steps
   d: be increased two steps

8) As the ambient air temperature increases, the jet size:

   a: increases
   b: stays the same
   c: decreases
   d: is varied on the primary bores

9) Four hole spacers:

   a: help increase top-end power
   b: help decrease low- to midrange power
   c: are used for fuel distribution in the intake manifold
   d: improve the signal in the booster and increase low- to midrange fuel atomization

10) Emulsion bleeds should only be altered:

    a: at the race track
    b: for a street engine
    c: after air bleed tuning and by using a dyno with BSFC data
    d: by seat-of-the-pants feel

Answers: 1) A, 2) B, 3) C, 4) C, 5) D, 6) A, 7) C, 8) C, 9) D, 10) C

How to Tune & Win with DEMON CARBURETORS
Glossary of Terms

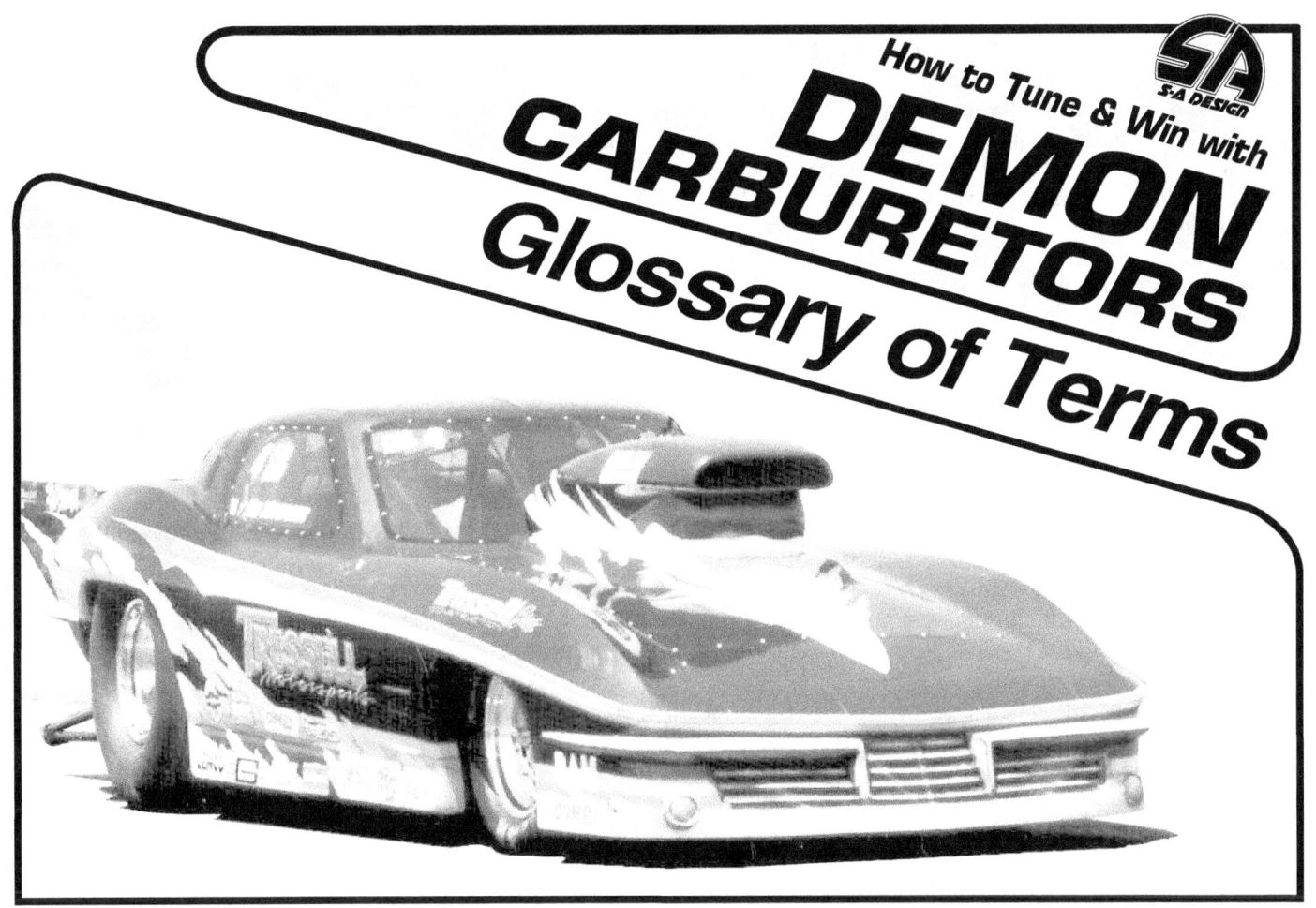

accelerator. Pedal that controls fuel flow and airflow to the engine. Depression of the pedal causes vehicle to accelerate.

accelerator pump. Circuit of the carburetor that provides fuel enrichment to offset leaning of the mixture when the throttle plates are opened rapidly.

advanced ignition. The timing event in a spark ignition engine that occurs before the optimal setting.

aftercooler. Heat exchanger that cools the induction air before it enters the cylinders of an engine. Often incorrectly called an intercooler.

air-bleed passage. Jet or passage in a carburetor with a branch to atmosphere through which air is drawn and introduced into the fuel flow.

air cell. A small chamber in the cylinder head of an indirect-injection engine in which combustion is initiated.

air-check valve. One-way check valve in an emissions control airpump system that prevents return of exhaust gases to the intake system.

air cleaner. Any device, such as porous paper, wire mesh, or oil bath filter, that prevents airborne particles from entering the air inlet of an engine.

air/fuel delivery ratio. The mass ratio of air to fuel inducted by an engine.

air injection. The addition of an air stream under pressure, but particularly to an exhaust system to promote combustion of unburned hydrocarbons and the conversion of carbon monoxide to carbon dioxide.

air scoop. Normally a forward-facing raised aperture on the vehicle's hood that acts as an air intake for ramming air into the induction track of the engine.

air silencer. Device placed at the entry to an induction system to attenuate the noise of induction.

alcohol. Organic compound containing a hydroxide group, the basis of many synthetic solvents, and ethyl alcohol.

aliphatic. Hydrocarbon compound with open carbon chains rather than a ring structure.

alternative fuel. General term for any automotive fuel other than gasoline or diesel fuel.

aluminum. Soft ductile element of high electrical conductivity. For engineering structural purposes, it is

How to Tune and Win with Demon Carburetors

used in alloy form, with copper, manganese, zinc, silicon, and other elements depending on the properties required. Resistance to atmospheric corrosion varies with alloy composition. Available in wrought, cast, and extruded forms.

anaerobic. Without air, in the sense of a process that takes place with the exclusion of air.

antibackfire valve. Valve that allows air to flow from an air pump into an induction system on deceleration to prevent backfiring.

antiknock. Counteracting a propensity for abnormal combustion in an engine. Can refer to fuel or combustion-chamber design.

antiknock index. Specifications of the antiknock properties of gasoline in North America. Defined as one-half the sum of the research and motor octane numbers of gasoline.

anti-run-on valve. Valve that prevents running on or dieseling of a spark-ignition engine when the ignition is switched off.

antipercolator. Tube and orifice in a carburetor through which fuel vapor can escape from the main jet tube to prevent over-enrichment due to vapor pressure.

aromatics. Unsaturated hydrocarbon additives containing at least one benzene ring, such as toluene, xylene, and elated hydrocarbons, which may be added, as appropriate, to fuels or lubricants.

ash. Non-combustible residue, or a fuel after combustion.

aspiration. Breathing or induction process of an engine. Non-pressure-charged engines are referred to as naturally or normally aspirated.

ATDC. The amount of crankshaft rotational degrees prior to the piston reaching its furthest point in travel upward.

atomization. Conversion of a liquid into very fine particles.

automatic choke. Thermostatically operated choke valve in a carburetor inlet track that closes when cold and opens gradually as the engine temperature rises.

average piston speed. See mean piston speed.

backpressure. Pressure resisting the flow of gas in an exhaust pipe.

backfire. An explosion of unburned or partially-burned fuel in an exhaust or inlet system.

balance pipe. Pipe or tube joining the venturis of twin carburetors.

ballast resistor. Electrical resistor used to regulate ignition coil output at higher engine speeds and to increase spark voltage during starting.

banjo. Hose fitting that connects a hose at right angles to the axis of a pipe. The circular body with one radial pipe connector gives the appearance of the musical instrument from which it takes its name.

barrel. Main air passage of a carburetor in which air and vaporized fuel are mixed. Also the traditional unit to measure petroleum, which is equivalent to 159 liters or 41.34 gallons.

base blend. Primary liquid contents of a fuel to which additives are added.

base stock. Primary liquid constitute of a lubricant to which additives are added.

Bavery compound jet. Submerged carburetor compensating jet through which the flow is determined by the ratio of throat pressure to atmospheric pressure.

BDC. Bottom dead center of a crankshaft's arc of rotation. The point of piston travel when the piston is nearest to the axis of the crankshaft. The lowest point of travel for the piston in the bore.

bench test. Operating test carried out on an engine or other major components removed from the vehicle and mounted to instrumentation.

benzene. Organic chemical consisting of a hexagonal ring of carbon atoms with a hydrogen atom attached to each. Compounds containing one or more benzene rings are called aromatics and are an important part of petroleum.

benzole. Mainly aromatic hydrocarbon fuel additive or solvent.

blowback. Sudden reversal of airflow through a carburetor, often caused by incorrect ignition or valve timing.

blow-by. Unwanted leakage past piston rings of an engine.

blow-through. A forced-induction system for an engine that has the compressor blow directly into the carburetor, thus having the carburetor operate under a positive pressure.

blower. Supercharger or turbocharger.

boost. The additional pressure above atmospheric that a blower creates.

boost gauge. Instrument for measuring positive pressure in the intake manifold.

boost control. Automatic control of boost pressure.

bore. The internal diameter of the cylinder of an engine.

bore/stroke ratio. Ratio of the engine's bore to the stroke. A ratio of 1:1 is considered a square engine.

bottom dead center. See BDC.

brake. The device of an engine dynamometer that absorbs the power output of the engine.

brake mean effective pressure (BMEP). Engine cylinder pressure, derived by calculation, that would give the measured brake horsepower. It is the product of indicated mean effective pressure (IMEP) and mechanical efficiency.

brake power. Power developed by an engine as measured at the crankshaft by a dynamometer brake.

brass. Alloy of copper and zinc, often with other elements and proportions of zinc up to 40 percent. Grades exist with good electrical and thermal conductivity and moderate strength.

breather. A vent to an enclosed container or case, for example, a fuel tank or engine crankcase.

breeches pipe. Y-configuration exhaust pipe forming a connection of two exhaust manifolds to one exhaust pipe.

bronze. Alloy of copper and tin, often with other elements of generally high strength, good thermal conductivity, and corrosion resistance.

BTDC. The amount of crankshaft rotational degrees before the piston reaches TDC and is heading toward the bottom of the bore.

butterfly valve. Disk valve pivoted about its diameter and acting as a throttle in a pipe or chamber. Used as a carburetor term to describe throttle plates but is a misnomer. An actual butterfly valve consists of two half-hinged disks, opening and closing like the wings of a butterfly.

bypass. Passage or line through which gas or a liquid may flow instead of or in addition to its main channel. Sometimes used to refer to the transition system between the idle and main metering circuits of a carburetor.

bypass valve. A valve for redirecting flow through a bypass.

cam. A shaped or profiled component that produces linear or angular motion or lift of a follower while rotating.

cam follower. The part of a cam mechanism that rides on the contour surface of a cam.

cam profile. The shape of the periphery of a cam. The contour determines the stroke and linear action of the follower.

cam roller. Cam follower in the form of a rotating wheel.

camshaft. Shaft on which suitably phased cams are mounted.

carbon. Chemical element that can exist on its own in several forms, such as amorphous carbon, graphite, diamond, and coal. It is present in all organic compounds and, when combined chemically with hydrogen, forms hydrocarbons. Also the principal deposit, but not the only deposit, found on the piston crown, combustion chamber, and valves of an engine.

carbon monoxide. Gaseous product of incomplete combustion of a hydrocarbon-based fuel.

carburetor. Device for vaporizing liquid fuel and mixing it in appropriate proportions with a stream of air prior to combustion in an engine.

catalytic converter. Emissions-control device placed in the exhaust system of an internal-combustion engine. The catalytic converter reduces the toxicity of combustion by recombination.

cetane. Paraffinic hydrocarbon and primary reference fuel to determine the ignition quality of diesel fuel.

Cooperative Fuel Research (CFR) engine. Variable-compression test engine developed to determine the antiknock properties of gasoline.

charge air cooling. Cooling of the air charge downstream of a blower.

charcoal canister. Trap containing charcoal granules to store fuel vapors and prevent them from entering the atmosphere.

charge. The quantity or mass of the fuel and air entering the cylinder of an engine.

charge cooling. Removal of heat from the induction track of an engine to increase the density of the charge.

chassis dynamometer. Test equipment fitted with rollers for the wheels of one or both axles of a complete vehicle, capable of providing drive input and measuring output parameters such as power and torque at the wheels.

choke. Valve that restricts the amount of air entering an engine on the induction stroke, thereby enriching the air/fuel ratio for ease of starting and running when cold.

choke stove. Heat-exchange chamber on the exhaust manifold to speed the operation of an automatic choke.

choke valve. Valve that restricts the flow of a gas or liquid. Sometimes referred to as a choke plate.

choked. An engine running with the choke in operation.

chromium. Silvery white, relatively soft metal with high resistance to atmospheric surface degradation. Used as a decorative plating on mainly steel components, though process exists for facilitating plating onto plastics.

CI engine. A compression-ignition engine commonly known as a diesel.

city cycle. Any standard vehicle test cycle that simulates urban driving, with frequent gear shifts and driving predominantly in lower gears.

clearance volume. Volume remaining above the piston of an engine when it reaches top dead center.

climatic wind tunnel. Wind tunnel with facilities for simulating climatic influences such as temperature and humidity, and for assessing heating, cooling, and air conditioning systems.

closed-loop engine-control system. Automatic control of engine parameters through direct feedback of data, as from electronic sensors.

closed-loop fuel system. Electronically controlled carburetor or fuel injection system in which the air/fuel ratio is adjusted by a feedback signal from the monitoring of exhaust gas composition.

cocktail effect. Environmental effect in which a mix of pollutants may have a more serious effect on health than the individual pollutants by themselves.

coke. Carbon deposits in an engine.

cold cranking rating. Current drain of a battery when the starter motor is turning a cold engine for a specific time.

cold plug. Spark plug that operates at a low temperature in relation to the combustion temperature, having a relatively high heat conductivity.

cold-start device. Any device, such as a choke or additional fuel injector, that temporarily enriches the flow of fuel to an engine to facilitate starting when cold.

cold sticking. The sticking of a piston ring in the groove when the engine is cold. Normally the ring will become free when the engine warms up.

combined fuel economy. Standard measure of fuel economy derived from a stipulated proportion of urban and highway cycle driving.

combustion chamber. The part of an engine in which combustion takes place, normally the volume of the cylinder between the piston crown and the cylinder head casting.

combustion chamber surface-to-volume ratio. Ratio of surface area of the combustion chamber to its volume at a stated stroke of the piston. The ratio influences the quenching effect of the cylinder walls and the local formation of hydrocarbon emissions.

common rail. A fuel-injection system that has the fuel supplied to each injector from one high-pressure source.

compensating jet. Jet or passage in a carburetor with a branch to atmosphere through which air is drawn and introduced into the fuel at high-flow rates, thus preventing an overly rich mixture.

compound carburetor. Carburetor with more than one choke or mixing chamber per inlet port.

compression. The increase of pressure in an engine cylinder as the piston travels toward top dead center.

compression-ignition engine. Reciprocating engine in which the fuel charge is ignited spontaneously by the heat of combustion. A diesel engine.

compression ratio. The ratio of cylinder combustion chamber volume at the bottom of the stroke to the value at the top of the stroke. Compression ratio is a volumetric ratio and not a pressure ratio.

compression ring. The uppermost piston ring.

compression stroke. The stroke of a reciprocating engine in which the air or air/fuel charge is compressed prior to ignition.

connecting rod. Linkage that connects the crank to the piston in an engine or other reciprocating machine.

constant-depression carburetor. Carburetor with a variable-section venturi. Also known as a variable-choke or constant-vacuum carburetor.

continuous sampling. Taking of samples continuously, as for exhaust emissions analysis.

control ring. The oil scrapper ring of a piston.

coolant. Usually a liquid, such as water or water/glycol mixture, used in a cooling system of an engine, compressor, or other machine that requires cooling during operation.

copper. A metal that, in its purest form, is used for its high electrical conductivity, particularly as wire or strip. Also available in alloy forms, notably with the addition of zinc (as brass) and with tin (as bronze).

cracking. The breaking down of large molecules into smaller molecules in an oil-refining process.

crankcase. Part of the structure of an engine that contains and supports the crankshaft and main bearings.

crankcase compression. Induction process in some smaller two-stroke engines, when the mixture charge is compressed in a sealed crankcase by the descending piston prior to passing the combustion chamber by way of a transfer port.

cranking enrichment. Additional fuel for starting a fuel-injected engine.

cranking speed. Rotational speed at which an engine is turned for starting.

crankshaft. The main powershaft of a reciprocating engine, comprising the crank (which imparts reciprocating motion to the pistons by way of their crank throw or offset from the shaft axis) as well as the journals (whereby it is located and supported by the crankcase main bearings).

critical speed. Speed at which some phenomenon, usually unwanted, manifests itself.

cross flow. A cylinder head having the intake and exhaust manifolds on opposite sides, creating a flow path across the cylinder head.

crude oil. Natural oil prior to refining.

cylinder. Tubular chamber in which the piston of a reciprocating engine or pump reciprocates.

cylinder block. The part of an engine containing the cylinders.

cylinder head. The part of a reciprocating engine that seals or closes the upper ends of the cylinder.

cylinder liner. Thin-walled hard metal cylinder inserted into a cylinder block in which the piston rides.

damper. Device for dissipating energy of vibrations, and hence for reducing vibration.

damping. Dissipation of energy in a vibrating system.

dead center. The location of the piston of a reciprocating engine when at either extreme of its stroke.

decarbonize. To remove carbon deposits from the cylinders of an engine.

deceleration valve. Valve that allows extra air to flow into an intake manifold on deceleration to prevent backfiring.

deep cycling. Repeated total discharging and recharging of an electrical storage battery.

delivered air/fuel ratio. The ratio of the mass of air to the mass of fuel, delivered to, but not necessarily combusted within, the cylinder.

demerit rating. System of rating engine deposits from combustion and lubrication, typically on a scale of 0-10, with 0 being complete cleanliness.

desmodronic valve. Inlet or exhaust valve that opens and closes under positive cam action, sometimes with spring-assisted final setting.

desorption. Loss or release of absorbed material from a substrate.

detergent. Lubricant or fuel additive that reduces formation of carbon deposits and other deposits in an engine's fuel system.

detonation. Rapid and uncontrolled combustion. Detonation can occur in the cylinder of a spark ignition engine when operating on a fuel of inadequate octane rating, or with ignition timing too far advanced. Also referred to as pinging, knock, and abnormal combustion.

diaphragm carburetor. Floatless carburetor incorporating one or two diaphragms and capable of operating at any angle and normally unaffected by vibration and acceleration.

diesel engine. A reciprocating engine that operates on compression ignition.

dilution air. Used in exhaust emissions testing, ambient air that is passed through filters to stabilize the hydrocarbon concentration and dilute the vehicle's emissions.

DIN rating. Standard for measurement of engine performance specified by the Deutsche Institut fur Normung (DIN).

direct injection. Diesel engine injection system in which the fuel is injected directly into the engine cylinder and not a pre-combustion chamber.

director plate. Multiple orifice plate fitted to a gasoline fuel injector to aid in spray formation.

discharge tube. Tube by which an emulsified air/fuel mixture enters the venturi of a fixed-choke carburetor.

dished. A cylindrical form with an integral depression, such as a piston.

displacement. The product of stroke and the cylinder bore multiplied by the number of cylinders.

domed. Raised contour of a piston crown.

double-barrel carburetor. Carburetor in which two barrels share the same float chamber.

downdraft. A carburetor through which the intake air flows vertically downward into the manifold.

drag. air resistance.

drag coefficient. The aerodynamic drag of a vehicle per unit cross-sectional area, as a non-dimensional quantity.

driveability. An engine's or vehicle's ease of control, particularly referring to engine response and control of torque at low operating speeds.

dual-fuel engine. An engine capable of running on two distinct types of fuel.

dual overhead camshafts. Arrangement of two camshafts per cylinder bank that resides over the valves and is fixed to the cylinder head.

economizer. Device that regulates the fuel flow of a carburetor under high-load conditions. More commonly referred to as a power valve.

emulsion. Mixture of fine droplets of one fluid dispersed in another fluid. Also, partially vaporized and heavily enriched air/fuel mixture prior to entering the main venturi of a carburetor.

emulsion tube. Combined main and compensating jet tubes in a carburetor with provision for drawing air into the fuel flow to create an emulsion at higher engine speeds.

engine map. Three-dimensional graphic representation of engine control parameters, for example, angle of ignition advance plotted against functions of throttle opening and engine speeds.

enrichment. An increase in the amount of fuel to a fixed amount of air in a carburetor.

ethanol. Ethyl alcohol as an alternative fuel or as a composite of gasoline.

evaporative emissions. Fuel vapors that escape to atmosphere by evaporation.

excess air factor. Factor by which the air/fuel ratio of an inducted mixture exceeds that of stoichiometric (excessively lean).

exhaust analysis. Quantitative measurement and presentation of the constituents of an engine's exhaust gases, vapors, and particulates.

exhaust backpressure. Resistance that impedes the flow of the exhaust gases from the engine to atmosphere.

exhaust calorimeter. Device for measuring the heat content of an engine's exhaust.

exhaust-gas recirculation. Mixing of exhaust gas with intake air to decrease the potential specific heat of the charge and the formation of NOx.

exhaust stroke. Motion of the piston in an internal-combustion engine that expels spent gases from the cylinder. Also identified as the pumping loop.

fast idle. The high-speed idle used on a choked engine.

filter. Porous material, or device containing such material, for removing suspended particle matter from a fluid.

firing order. The numbered sequence in which the cylinders of a multi-cylinder engine fire.

fixed-choke carburetor. A carburetor with a constant-size venturi, with airflow controlled by a throttle plate.

flash point. The lowest temperature at which the vapors of a flammable liquid product will ignite, though not necessarily remain under continuous combustion.

flat out. Operating at full throttle or at maximum speed.

flat spot. A transient reduction in torque of an engine on acceleration, often called a hesitation.

flexible. An engine that exhibits good torque characteristics throughout its speed range, particularly the ability to pull at low speeds.

float. A buoyant part of a fluid-metering system.

float bowl. Main fuel reservoir in a carburetor.

float needle. Needle valve actuated by a float in a carburetor.

flooding. Condition that prevents starting of an engine when more fuel is drawn in than can be ignited.

follower. Part of a mechanism that is directly driven by a cam and imparts motion to the working components of that mechanism.

four-stroke cycle. Thermodynamic cycle of an engine that requires four strokes of the piston to be completed.

friction drag. Aerodynamic drag resulting from friction between the moving air and the surface of the vehicle.

friction horsepower. The part of the total power of combustion of an engine that is spent on overcoming mechanical friction.

front-end octane. Research octane quality of the lower-boiling-point components of gasoline.

fuel. A combustible form of energy for an engine, usually in liquid form.

fuel cell. Device that converts gasoline or liquid fuel into electrical energy through electrochemical rather than mechanical forces.

fuel consumption. Rate of consumption of fuel by an engine expressed in units, such as miles per gallon.

fuel injector. Device whereby fuel is injected in metered quantities into an engine.

fuel-pressure regulator. Pressure-actuated diaphragm valve that maintains the pressure in a fuel system to a preset value above manifold pressure.

fuel pump. Mechanical or electrical device that draws fuel from a tank to provide the fuel supply to the carburetor or fuel-injection system.

full-flow filter. Filter through which the total flow of fluid passes, as opposed to the bypass filter, which filters only part of the flow.

gas chromatography. System of analysis of gases or vaporized liquids, such as exhaust gas, using a chromatograph, which separates and identifies individual components of a mixture according to their tendency to be absorbed in a column or a capillary tube.

gasohol. Automotive fuel normally consisting of nine parts gasoline to one part alcohol.

gasoline. Light hydrocarbon fuel used in spark-ignition engines.

gauze carburetor. Early form of carburetor in which induction air gathered fuel vapor from gauze over which gasoline flowed. Also known as a wick carburetor.

geometric displacement. Displacement or capacity of a Wankel engine.

gross power. The measured power output of an engine operating without any power-absorbing accessories such as an alternator, generator, pumps, or induction silencers.

gulp valve. Valve to introduce extra air to induction track on acceleration to prevent an overly rich air/fuel ratio.

harmonic balancer. Rotating or oscillating counterbalance that counteracts the out-of-balance forces and/or couples in a reciprocating engine.

harmonic-induction engine. Induction system in which the length of the inlet track is chosen to improve volumetric efficiency over a narrow operating speed.

heat aging. The effect of long-term exposure to heat on the mechanical and physical properties of a material.

heat-control valve. Valve that regulates the flow of exhaust gas so that some of its heat content is passed to the intake manifold, thereby helping to vaporize the fuel mixture in a cold engine.

heat engine. Engine deriving energy from the heat of combustion of a fuel, whether burned internally or externally.

heat range. Range of temperature for optimum operation of a spark plug.

heat-range index. Standard range of operating temperature of a spark plug.

heated intake. System whereby the induced air or air/fuel mixture in an engine is heated to reduce emissions on starting to allow operation in the cold.

Helmholtz resonator. Acoustic device, shaped like a jug or bottle, which resonates at predetermined frequencies.

horsepower. The customary non-metric unit of power, equivalent to 0.7457 kilowatt, defined by a working rate of 33,000 lbs./ft. per minute.

hot-soak losses. Fuel vapors emitted during a specific period beginning immediately after the engine is turned off.

hot spot. Point of contact between intake and exhaust manifolds to transfer heat to the mixture, and thereby promote vaporization. Also an overheated point of a piston or combustion chamber.

hot-start enrichment. Enrichment of the fuel mixture for starting a hot engine, usually applicable only to gasoline engines.

hot sticking. Adhesion of a piston ring to the groove caused by the formation of deposits at higher temperatures.

hunting. Variation of speed of an engine at a constant fuel setting.

hybrid engine. Engine combining two principal modes of operation, such as that of a diesel engine and spark-ignition engine.

hydraulic lifter. Small hydraulic actuator that operates the intake and exhaust valves of an engine.

hydrocarbon emissions. Unburned hydrocarbon-based fuel emissions from an internal-combustion engine.

hydrogen. An elementary gas with components of water and hydrocarbons. Hydrogen has potential as an alternative fuel for an internal-combustion engine.

idle speed. Rotational speed of an engine during a no-load or minimal throttle setting.

idle system. Arrangement of jets and tubes in a carburetor to enrich the fuel supply when the engine is idling.

idling jet. Slow-running jet.

ignition. Initiation of combustion.

ignition coil. Induction coil or voltage transformer that provides the high-tension voltage for the spark in a spark-ignition engine.

ignition delay. Time interval between the spark and the initial release of heat of combustion in a spark-ignition engine.

ignition timing. The timing of the spark relative to the piston top dead center in a spark-ignition engine.

IHP. Indicated horsepower.

indicated power. Engine power calculated from an indicator diagram. Power developed in the cylinders rather than the output shaft of the engine.

indicated thermal efficiency. Ratio of indicated work available at the piston to the ideal work available from combustion. The thermal efficiency assuming zero friction and pumping losses.

indicator. Instrument for visually recording engine cylinder pressure during a working cycle.

induction. Drawing air or an air/fuel charge into an engine.

induction air. Air drawn into an engine before the introduction of fuel.

induction stroke. The stroke of the piston in which the working fluid is drawn into the cylinder.

inductive kick. Phenomenon that augments the secondary voltage in an ignition system by interrupting the current after the points have been opened.

infrared gas analyzer. Instrument for quantitative measurement of exhaust emissions.

instantaneous piston velocity. Piston speed at any specific point in its stroke or crankshaft angle.

intake depression. Mean reduction in static pressure below atmospheric in an engine air-intake system.

internal-combustion engine. Engine in which energy is provided by combustion within a working chamber, causing direct mechanical action on a piston, turbine, rotor, or other mechanical element.

iso-octane. Hydrocarbon used as a primary reference fuel in determining the octane of fuels, having assigned values of research and motor octane.

jackshaft. Small shaft within a machine for transmitting rotary motion, for example, in an ignition distributor.

jet. An accurately drilled hole through which liquid can pass at a controlled rate, as in a carburetor.

How to Tune and Win with Demon Carburetors

judder. A low-frequency vibration.

Kadenacy effect. In two-stroke motors, the creation of a partial vacuum by the sudden release of exhaust gases through exhaust ports.

Kettering ignition system. Commonly used inductive-ignition system comprising an ignition coil, breaker, capacitor, and battery pioneered by Charles Kettering.

knock. Noise resulting from the spontaneous ignition of a portion of the air/fuel mixture in an engine cylinder and occurring ahead of the normal spark-initiated advancing flame front.

knock rating. Octane rating.

knock sensor. Instrument that detects the onset of detonation in an internal-combustion engine.

lambda sensor. Electrochemical sensor that relays data on oxygen content of exhaust gases to an electronic engine-management system or laboratory equipment.

lean-burn engine. Engine capable of running on a fuel/air mixture significantly lower than stoichiometric.

lean mixture. Inducted air/fuel mixture containing an excess of air.

light-off. Coming into operation of a catalytic converter when operating temperature is reached.

light-off time. Time from engine start to operating temperature of an exhaust catalytic converter.

liquefied natural gas. Natural gas as an automotive fuel, principally consisting of methane.

liquefied petroleum gas. An automotive alternative fuel consisting mainly of propane, sometimes with the addition of butane, which can be stored at relatively low pressure. Also known as LPG.

liquid-cooled. Cooled by conduction and convection to the passage of a liquid, such as water.

lobe. Part of a cam profile that extends beyond the base circle and brings about the lift of a follower or tappet.

loop-scavenging. Scavenging of a two-stroke engine by vertical circulation within the cylinder and to the exhaust port of unburned gases ahead of the incoming charge.

main jet. Principal jet in a carburetor through which the greater proportion of fuel flows in normal steady-state operation.

main metering system. Pertaining to a carburetor float chamber, main discharge tube, jet, or venturi as a complete functional unit.

manifold. System of ducts or pipes that divides flow and conducts it to more than one point of delivery, or that unites a flow from a number of sources for delivery at one point.

manifold absolute pressure. The mean gas absolute static pressure in an engine-induction manifold, usually measured by a mercury scale.

manifold depression. Difference between the mean static pressure within the engine induction manifold and the ambient pressure. Although the difference is usually negative in a naturally aspirated engine, it will be positive in a supercharged engine.

map. Electronic data bank from which signals controlling one or more parameters can be outputted in consequence of one or more signals.

maximum brake power. Maximum measured power of an IC engine measured on a dynamometer.

mean effective pressure. The mean pressure in an engine cylinder during the working or power stroke.

mean piston speed. Effective distance traveled by a piston per unit time as a function of crankshaft RPM.

metering rod. Valve consisting of variable-section rod and orifice by which flow of a fluid can be metered.

methane. Hydrocarbon constituent of natural gas, also produced by sludge digestion.

methanol-methyl. Alcohol as an alternative fuel source.

methyl tertiary butyl ether. Oxygen-bearing antiknock fuel blend component known as MTBE.

misfire. Failure of a fuel charge to fire or ignite in the proper way.

mixing chamber. The barrel of a carburetor.

molybdenum disulfide. Black powdery solid sometimes added to lubricants to reduce friction.

MON. Motor octane number.

mono-block construction. A reciprocating engine that has the cylinder cast in a single block through which cooling water can flow continuously. Also refers to an engine in which the cylinder block and crankcase are one unit.

monolith. Originally a large block of stone, but used to describe a catalytic converter that is made of a ceramic honeycomb-shaped element.

Morse test. Engine test for multicylinder engines in which each cylinder of the running engine is stopped in turn so that its contribution to the total output can be measured.

motor method. A standard test for fuel octane.

motor octane number. A guide to the antiknock performance of a fuel under relatively severe driving conditions, such as full throttle with elevated engine coolant temperatures.

motoring test. Method of testing an engine without combustion present while being turned over by an electric motor to determine frictional and pumping losses.

multi-point fuel injection. A fuel-injection system in which fuel is administered to each cylinder by a separate fuel injector.

multi-spark ignition. A primary ignition event initiated by a rapid sequence of sparks rather than a single spark.

multi-throw crankshaft. Shaft with cranks set at equal angles of less than 180 degrees.

mushroom valve. A valve with a narrow stem surrounded by a disk, like a head with a concave face.

NACA duct. Aerodynamically profiled shallow duct, developed by the United States National Advisory Committee for Aeronautics.

narrow V-engine. Engine of V-configuration with cylinder axis less than 60 degrees to each other, and in some cases at an angle so narrow that the cylinders are staggered to avoid interference.

needle bearing. Rolling-element bearing in which the rollers are small-diameter needle-like elements.

needle valve. Valve by which fluid flow rate is controlled by the degree of insertion of a tapered needle into a fixed-diameter orifice.

neoprene. Chlorophene polymer synthetic rubber, with a range of mechanical properties, noted for its resistance to oil solvents at moderate temperatures.

net power. Brake power of a fully-equipped engine.

nitrile rubber. Synthetic rubber polymer of butane and acrylonitrile, noted for its oil, fuel, and temperature resistance, and therefore often used in shaft seals.

nitromethane. Organic liquid, sometimes used as a fuel, with the addition of methyl alcohol.

nitrobenzene. An organic fuel additive that is highly poisonous.

nitrogen oxides. Compounds of nitrogen and oxygen produced during combustion and conforming to the general formula NOx.

normally aspirated. An engine that breathes air at atmospheric pressure.

octane number. Measure of the antiknock properties of a fuel, particularly gasoline, derived from comparative testing using a standard variable-compression engine. The antiknock properties of the fuel under test are compared with those of a fuel containing iso-octane (given an arbitrary rating of 100) and heptane (rated at zero). The volumetric percentage of iso-octane is taken as the octane rating of the fuel under test. Three values exist: motor, research, and front-end octane.

oil-control ring. Piston ring that removes excess oil from the cylinder walls of an engine and returns it via oil passages in the piston to the oil pan. It is the ring that resides the farthest from the crown.

open-cycle turbine. A gas turbine operating cycle in which air enters from the atmosphere and is discharged to the atmosphere along with the byproducts of combustion.

open-loop engine control. Control of engine parameters such as ignition timing and fuel mixture by preset, often mechanical controls.

opposed cylinder engine. Reciprocating engine in which pairs of pistons operate in each cylinder, the combustion chambers being formed between the piston crowns. Also known as a deltic engine.

organic compound. Substance containing carbon and hydrogen, possibly with other elements. Not all organic compounds are necessarily of natural derivation, like coal and natural gas. Some are synthetically produced.

O-ring. A toroidal elastometric static seal.

Otto cycle. The four-stroke spark-ignition engine cycle patented in 1876.

outer dead center. The equivalent of top dead center in a horizontally or vertically opposed engine.

oval piston. Engine piston manufactured to slightly elliptical cross-section to counteract the effects of thermal distortion.

overrun. The motoring of an engine by way of the inertia of a vehicle in motion with the throttle closed.

over-square engine. Engine having a cylinder bore larger than its stroke.

oxygenates. Alcohol-based fuels or fuel additives.

parasitic drag. Aerodynamic drag caused by the projection of objects into the airflow, such as a hood scoop.

particulate. Solid particle content of the exhaust products, mainly in the form of carbon (soot) and partially burned hydrocarbons.

peak brake power. Highest power developed within the speed range of the engine.

peak torque speed. Engine speed at which peak torque occurs.

peaky. An engine that develops its effective power over a very narrow speed range.

pentane. Light and volatile paraffinic constituent of gasoline that aids in starting.

pentroof. Shallow-angled wedge or cone, particularly of a piston crown. Often used to describe the shape of a four-valve combustion chamber.

phenolics. Thermosetting plastics of many forms and based on phenolic resin, to which are usually added fillers and colorants. Phenolics are generally strong and dimensionally stable, with good electrical insulating properties. Often used as a material for a carburetor spacer.

pilot jet. Carburetor jet that admits fuel downstream of the throttle for starting.

piston. Component, usually in the form of a cylinder closed at one end, that converts pressure into mechanical motion.

piston boss. Sturdy, reinforced area that is bored to accept the wrist pin.

piston crown. The top or closed end of the piston.

piston ring. A ring generally of hard, springy material, set in a groove machined into the piston and to act as a seal or scraper.

piston skirt. Nominally parallel-sided cylindrical walls of the piston extending beneath the piston crown.

piston slap. Noise made by contact between a loose or worn piston and the cylinder wall of the engine.

piston speed. Linear velocity of a piston in its reciprocating motion within a cylinder.

pitting and piling. Erosion of one ignition contact breaker and deposit of metal on the other resulting from high-temperature vaporization and incorrect condenser capacity.

plenum chamber. Any chamber at which air or gas is held at higher than ambient pressure. This term is modified when dealing with an intake manifold, described as a chamber that connects the runners of an intake manifold and is under a vacuum on a normally aspirated engine.

poisoning. The degradation or rendering ineffective of a catalytic converter by exposure to lead in the exhaust.

pollutant. A substance released into the environment that represents a hazard to man or nature.

poppet valve. Disk-shaped valve, with the disk attached to a stem, the reciprocating movement of which causes the valve to open and close.

popping back. Premature ignition of the air/fuel mixture in the intake manifold.

positive crankcase ventilation. Emissions-control device that prevents crankcase gases from entering the atmosphere, usually by drawing the gases from the crankcase and feeding them to the engine to be burned.

positive-displacement pump. A pump that delivers a fixed or metered amount of liquid per stroke or cycle.

post-ignition. Ignition emanating from hot spots within the engine cylinder and occurring after the initiated ignition.

power stroke. Stroke of a reciprocating engine during which the piston moves under the effect of combustion pressure.

prechamber. A small chamber in which combustion is initiated prior to delivery by way of a narrow port into the main combustion chamber of an engine.

preheated catalyst. Exhaust catalytic converter that heats up on or before starting of the engine, and is not therefore delayed in operation by the need to absorb heat from the engine exhaust. Usually electrically preheated.

pre-ignition. Ignition of the air/fuel mixture in a spark ignition engine before the timed spark, caused by a hot glowing surface.

pressure drag. Aerodynamic drag resulting from differences between pressures acting on forward- and rearward-facing surfaces.

pressure-wave supercharging. Increasing engine intake pressure by tuning the intake duct to resonate at a particular operating speed.

pressurized cooling system. Sealed engine cooling system that uses the vapor pressure of the hot coolant to create an above-ambient pressure in the system and thus raise the boiling point of the coolant.

propane. Hydrocarbon gas fuel stored in a liquid state under pressure.

proportional control. Closed-loop engine-control system in which the feedback signal is proportional to the output of the measured parameter.

pulse air injection. System that uses exhaust-pressure pulsations to force air into an exhaust system to oxidize exhaust pollutants.

pump. Mechanical device that causes liquids, gases, or vapors to flow by means of a pressure differential or positive displacement.

pumping losses. Part of the total or indicated power that is expended on the induction of the fuel and air charge into an engine, and expelling the gases on the completion of combustion.

quarter wavelength resonator. Acoustic device of cylindrical form with a preset or adjustable resonant frequency determined by length.

quench. The cooling of a portion of the cylinder head gases during combustion in an IC engine, usually by minimizing the clearance between the piston crown and cylinder head. The high surface-to-volume ratio effects rapid heat loss and suppresses detonation, though at the expense of higher hydrocarbon emissions.

quiescent chamber. Type of combustion chamber of a direct-injection diesel engine in which the mixing of the charge is predominantly non-turbulent or quiescent.

quiescent combustion. Non-turbulent combustion, particularly in a lower-speed diesel engine and normally employing a multi-nozzle injector.

quieting ramp. Section of an engine valvetrain cam profile that reduces acceleration and so limits the generation of mechanical noise.

radial. Disposed at right angles.

radial engine. Multi-cylinder engine in which the cylinders radiate from one single-throw crankshaft.

ram air. Air in orderly rapid motion relative to the vehicle and therefore possessing kinetic energy, particularly in context of air required to charge an air-breathing device such as a cooling or engine-induction system.

Ram-air induction. Pressure charging created by the momentum of the induction air in an intake pipe of tuned length.

ram duct. In an engine with two inlet valves of specific function, the part of the inlet tract that provides ram air, usually without intentional swirl.

reach. The significant length or extent of a component. For example, the reach of a spark plug is the length required to locate the electrode correctly in the combustion chamber.

reciprocating engine. An engine in which a piston is constrained to move in a cylinder by a crankshaft and a connecting rod.

reformulated gasoline. Gasoline formulated to minimize exhaust emissions, having, for example, low vapor pressure and low aromatic and sulfur content, with the addition of oxygenates to reduce emissions of carbon monoxide and hydrocarbons.

relative wind. The velocity and direction of ambient airflow experienced by a moving vehicle, consisting of the components of vehicle and wind velocity and direction.

relay. Electrical switch magnetically operated by the flow of current through a coil, used prior to electronic systems for voltage and current controllers.

research octane number. A guide to antiknock performance of a fuel under mild driving conditions. It is derived from one of the standard comparative tests using the Cooperative Fuel Research engine.

resonator. Acoustic chamber, generally of fixed volume, with specific resonant frequency.

retarded ignition. Timing of the ignition spark to occur later than the optimum timing for fuel of a specified octane rating.

Ricardo engine. A standard variable-compression engine used for test or research purposes.

Ricardo head. A high-squish, high-turbulence combustion chamber.

rich mixture. Fuel/air mixture in which the proportion of fuel exceeds that necessary for the theoretically complete or stoichiometric combustion.

ring expander. Annular spring within a piston ring to enhance sealing action of the lower rings in worn cylinders.

ring gap. Gap in the annular shape of a piston ring, enabling the ring to be opened out for installation, and to accommodate thermal expansion.

ring groove. Annular slot or recess in piston into which a piston ring fits.

road octane number. Usually the octane number of primary reference fuel that just gives trace knock in a vehicle on the road or on a chassis dynamometer under specified conditions.

rocker arm. Centrally pivoted beam that transmits a linear displacement at one end to a linear displacement at the other.

roller chain. Chain in which the fastening pins carry rollers, permitting high speeds of operation with reduced wear and noise.

roller lifter. Cam follower, tappet, or lifter incorporating a small roller wheel that is in contact with the cam.

RON. Research octane number.

roots blower. Mechanical-induction pressure charger in which air pressure is provided by contiguous rotation of two- or three-lobed rotors or pistons.

runaway knock. Engine knock that becomes progressively worse under steady speed and load conditions.

runaway surface ignition. Improper ignition within engine cylinders emanating from hot engine components (not from carbon deposits), becoming more pronounced as engine temperatures increase.

run-out. Eccentricity of a shaft, bearing, or any other rotating component.

SAE rating. The standard for engine horsepower measurement for an engine with no parasitic components attached, such as an alternator, power steering pump, or any other ancillary.

SAE viscosity. The viscosity of motor oil per the standard of the Society of Automotive Engineers.

scattershield. A protective safety cover over any item that has the potential to explode or come apart, such as a clutch assembly.

scavenger. Halogens present in a lead antiknock compound that prevent the buildup of lead oxides and sulfates in an engine's combustion chamber by rendering lead compounds formed during combustion volatile so that they may pass through the exhaust.

scavenging. The removal of exhaust gases from an engine cylinder, particularly by an induced flow of gas.

scavenging efficiency. The ratio of the mass of working gas retained in an engine cylinder at completion of the exhaust cycle to the total charge mass supplied.

Schrader valve. A type of pneumatic non-return valve used especially for tire inflation. Depression of a central spigot opens the valve to facilitate inflation and the measurement of tire pressure. This style valve is also used in other applications.

scoop. A cowled aperture to gather and direct ambient air.

scraper ring. Piston ring that removes excess oil from a cylinder bore and returns it to the lubricating circuit.

scuffing. Abrasive or adhesive damage to surfaces in relative motion resulting in scraping or scratching.

secondary. When pertaining to engine balance, an event that occurs at twice engine speed.

secondary couple. The out-of-balance disturbance in an engine that causes rocking about a horizontal or vertical axis at right angles to the crankshaft and at twice the engine speed.

secondary venturi. A small venturi mounted coaxially within the main venturi of a carburetor. More commonly known as a booster venturi.

sensitivity. When pertaining to gasoline, the difference between the research and motor octane ratings.

sensor. Device in a control system that provides information from an input. An example would be an oxygen sensor's reading of oxygen content in an engine's exhaust.

siamesed. Joined or paired.

side branch resonator. Acoustic resonator fitted as a dead-end branch to a relevant tract, such as an inlet or exhaust, with no flow through the resonator.

side-draft carburetor. Carburetor with a horizontal barrel.

single-acting engine. Engine in which the working pressure of combustion gases is applied to one side of the piston only, as in a normal automobile engine.

slide-operated carburetor. Carburetor in which the volume flow of air is regulated by a simple slide valve in the inlet track. Commonly found on motorcycles and light-industrial engines.

slipper-skirt piston. Piston with skirt cutaway beneath the piston pin axis to provide crankshaft clearance and reduce friction. Also known as a partial-skirt piston.

slotted piston. Piston in which the skirt is slotted to counteract the effects of thermal distortion.

slow-running jet. A carburetor jet that compensates for the natural reduction in mixture strength at low engine speed by supplying excess fuel.

soak. In the context of heat, the stabilizing of temperature throughout a body, such as an engine that has been running for a short period, whereby a part farthest from the cylinder reaches the same temperature.

sonic throttling. Increasing the flow velocity of a gas or vapor in a pipe, tube, or orifice to sonic speeds by throttling, as applied to carburetion or engine-induction airflow.

spark knock. Detonation within an engine cylinder caused by excessively advanced ignition timing rather than surface ignition.

specific fuel consumption. Fuel consumed per unit of power output, usually expressed as mass or volume per unit power, per unit time, for example, pounds per brake horsepower hour.

square engine. Engine in which the cylinder bore diameter is equal to the piston stroke.

squish. The squeezing of the air/fuel mixture in an engine's combustion chamber away from the end-gas region at the top of the compression stroke. Also the area of the engine combustion chamber with minimal clearance between the piston crown and cylinder head at top dead center.

squish lip. Bowl-in-piston combustion chamber featuring squish with reentrant bowl and hard-edged entrance from the bowl to the crown.

squish motor. Engine in which squish is a prominent feature of the combustion chamber configuration.

stoichiometric ratio. Ratio, usually of mass, between air and a flammable gas or vapor, at which complete combustion or chemical combination takes place. Often referred to as the chemically correct mixture.

stratified charge. Reciprocating engine-combustion system in which combustion is initiated in a layer of relatively fuel-rich mixture, and then spreads to a much weaker mixture elsewhere in the combustion chamber to increase fuel economy.

stroke/bore ratio. Ratio of stroke to cylinder diameter in an engine.

supercharge. Artificial increase in pressure of induction air or gases achieved by pressure charging from a mechanical pump.

surface carburetor. Early form of carburetor in which the induction air is passed over an exposed surface of fuel.

surface ignition. Ignition emanating from hot spots within an engine cylinder rather than from a timed spark.

surface/volume ratio. Numerical ratio of surface area to volume, specifically in the combustion chamber of an engine.

surfactant additive. Organic fuel additive that forms a coating on metals or other surfaces, which it protects, acting also as a detergent or dispersant by making deposits partially soluble.

swept volume. In a reciprocating engine, the volume of the cylinder formed by the bore diameter and the stroke of the piston.

swirl. Orderly rotation of combustion

gases in an engine cylinder to improve mixing and heat transfer.

swirl chamber. Small chamber or cavity formed in a cylinder head of an engine to promote swirl.

T-head engine. Side-valve engine with the inlet valves and exhaust valves on opposite sides of the cylinder block, producing a combustion chamber that resembles the shape of the letter T.

tailpipe emissions. Emissions from an engine's tailpipe, as opposed to evaporative and other emissions.

TAME. Tertiary amyl methyl ether. Oxygenate used as a gasoline blend component.

tappet. Cylindrical reciprocating cam follower that converts cam lift into linear reciprocating movement, which transmits directly to the valve.

TDC. Top dead center of a crankshaft's arc of rotation.

test cycle. Laboratory or highway test procedure that follows a strictly controlled sequence of operating parameters, usually to simulate driving under realistic conditions and to assess performance in respect to emissions, fuel consumption, etc.

thermal efficiency. Ratio of useful work performed by an engine to the total energy content of the fuel consumed. A measure of efficiency of the combustion process.

thermal loading. Total effect of heat and temperature on mechanical and structural components, particularly of an engine.

thermodynamic cycle. Idealized sequence of operating stages of an engine or other heat machine, often illustrated by a diagram showing pressure plotted against displacement volume. Actual engine cycles of operation differ considerably from their ideals.

throat. Narrow end of a tapered aperture or venturi of a carburetor.

throttle. A butterfly valve for controlling the flow of fuel and air through a carburetor.

top dead center. Uppermost point of movement of piston in a cylinder, or the point farthest from the crankshaft axis.

tuned intake pressure charging. Increasing the mass of the inducted fuel mixture by matching the acoustic resonance of the induction system to engine speed.

unburned hydrocarbons. Unburned or incompletely burned products of engine combustion released into the atmosphere as an exhaust emission.

undercrown. The underside of a piston crown.

under-square engine. Engine with a larger stroke than cylinder bore.

unleaded gasoline. Gasoline that has no added lead alkyls as octane improvers, but may nevertheless contain a specified very low maximum amount of lead.

updraft carburetor. Carburetor in which the inducted air flows upward past a jet, usually located in a central venturi.

urban cycle. Driving test cycle that simulates driving conditions in a typical urban area.

V-engine. Engine in which the cylinders are set at an angle to each other so that the axis forms the letter V.

vacuum advance. Mechanical-pneumatic system for advancing ignition timing, using carburetor throat depression as a source of vacuum.

vacuum carburetor. Carburetor in which the air slide is controlled by suction or depression from the inlet tract.

valve. Any device for controlling, restricting, or interrupting the flow of a fluid.

valve bounce. Bouncing of a poppet valve on its seat when closing, usually as a result of spring resonance or over-speeding.

valve gear. The mechanism that actuates a valve, in particular the mechanical parts of the valve mechanism from cam to valve.

valve face. The beveled mating surface of a poppet valve.

valve guide. Tubular insert in an engine cylinder head that constraints the concentricity of the valve stem and the seating of the valve.

valve head. The disk end that performs the sealing operation of a poppet valve.

valve overlap. Period, usually expressed in degrees of crankshaft rotation, between the opening of the intake valve and the closing of the exhaust valve.

valve lifter. Valvetrain component that bears directly on the cam. Also known as a tappet or follower.

valve recession. Accelerated wear and erosion of an engine valve seat, particularly of an engine designed to run on leaded gasoline when unleaded fuel is used.

valve rotator. Mechanism for rotating a poppet valve while the engine is running.

valve timing. Geometric positions in relation to the crankshaft rotation or other reference at which valves open and close.

valvetrain. The total mechanism from the camshaft to poppet valve of an engine that actuates the lifting and closing of a valve.

vapor-lock. Interruption of flow in a piped fluid system resulting from vaporization of the fluid or entrapment of air.

vapor-lock index. Index that combines the reed vapor pressure and the percentage evaporated at a specified temperature of a gasoline. It measures the fuel's propensity for vapor-locking.

variable-compression engine. Usually a standard engine for laboratory or research use in which the compression ratio can be varied, particularly while the engine is operating.

varnish. A lacquer-like deposit composed of products of combustion and lubricant breakdown, often occurring on piston skirts.

venturi. Convergent-divergent nozzle that accelerates and lowers static pressure in gases or vapors flowing through it. In a carburetor, the venturi provides the depression in the airflow pressure that causes fuel to be drawn from its bowl or chamber into the air stream.

volumetric efficiency. The amount that the cylinder of an engine is filled by the incoming charge following an exhaust stroke. A measure of the ability of an engine to breathe freely. Volumetric efficiency is a ratio of masses, not volumes. The original definition was the ratio of the volume of induced charge at the inlet valve temperature and pressure to the engine's swept volume.

warmup. The period of engine operation between starting and reaching a stable operating temperature.

wastegate. Valve that diverts exhaust gases away from a turbocharger turbine when charge pressure has reached the requisite figure.

water injection. Injection of water mist directly or indirectly into a cylinder of an IC engine to cool the incoming charge and limit detonation.

weak mixture. A lean air/fuel mixture.

wedge combustion chamber. Tapering combustion chamber of an overhead valve engine intended to reduce the tendency for detonation.

wick carburetor. Early form of carburetor in which induction air gathered fuel vapors from an exposed wick.

Racing demands the best components if you want to win. GPT 300 Inc. can supply all of your fuel system needs.

wind tunnel. Aerodynamic test facility in which air is blown in orderly fashion over an object such as a vehicle or scale model to determine elements of aerodynamics.

Y-pipe. Two-branch exhaust manifold connecting the exhausts of a V-engine to form a single exhaust pipe.

zinc. Metal used mainly in alloy form for intricate castings where strength is not a prime consideration, and as a protective coating for steel.

A smoky burnout sounds powerful, but depending on the throttle angle, the engine may be running mostly on the idle and main-metering circuit.

NOTES

More great titles available from CarTech®...

S-A DESIGN

Super Tuning & Modifying Holley Carburetors — Perf, street and off-road applications. *(SA08)*

Custom Painting — Gives you an overview of the broad spectrum of custom painting types and techniques. *(SA10)*

Street Supercharging, A Complete Guide to — Bolt-on buying, installing and tuning blowers. *(SA17)*

Engine Blueprinting — Using tools, block selection & prep, crank mods, pistons, heads, cams & more! *(SA21)*

David Vizard's How to Build Horsepower — Building horsepower in any engine. *(SA24)*

Chevrolet Small-Block Parts Interchange Manual — Selecting & swapping high-perf. small-block parts. *(SA55)*

High-Performance Ford Engine Parts Interchange — Selecting & swapping big- and small-block Ford parts. *(SA56)*

How To Build Max Perf Chevy Small-Blocks on a Budget — Would you believe 600 hp for $3000? *(SA57)*

How To Build Max Performance Ford V-8s on a Budget — Dyno-tested engine builds for big- & small-blocks. *(SA69)*

How To Build Max-Perf Pontiac V8s — Mild perf apps to all-out performance build-ups. *(SA78)*

How To Build High-Performance Ignition Systems — Guide to understanding auto ignition systems. *(SA79)*

How To Build Max Perf 4.6 Liter Ford Engines — Building & modifying Ford's 2- & 4-valve 4.6/5.4 liter engines. *(SA82)*

How To Build Big-Inch Ford Small-Blocks — Add cubic inches without the hassle of switching to a big-block. *(SA85)*

How To Build High-Perf Chevy LS1/LS6 Engines — Modifying and tuning Gen-III engines for GM cars and trucks. *(SA86)*

How To Build Big-Inch Chevy Small-Blocks — Get the additional torque & horsepower of a big-block. *(SA87)*

Honda Engine Swaps — Step-by-step instructions for all major tasks involved in engine swapping. *(SA93)*

How To Build High-Performance Chevy Small — Block Cams/Valvetrains — Camshaft & valvetrain function, selection, performance, and design. *(SA105)*

High-Performance Jeep Cherokee XJ Builder's Guide 1984-2001 — Build a useful, Cherokee for mountains, the mud, the desert, the street, and more. *(SA109)*

How to Build and Rebuild Rochester Quadrajet Carburetors — Selecting, rebuilding, and modifying the Quadrajet Carburetors. *(SA113)*

Rebuilding the Small-Block Chevy: Step-by-Step Videobook — 160-pg book plus 2-hour DVD show you how to build a street or racing small-block Chevy. *(SA116)*

How to Paint Your Car on a Budget — Everything you need to know to get a great-looking coat of paint and save money. *(SA117)*

How to Drift: The Art of Oversteer — This comprehensive guide to drifting covers both driving techniques and car setup. *(SA118)*

Turbo: Real World High-Performance Turbocharger Systems —*Turbo* is the most practical book for enthusiasts who want to make more horsepower. Foreword by Gale Banks. *(SA123)*

High-Performance Chevy Small-Block Cylinder Heads — Learn how to make the most power with this popular modification on your small-block Chevy. *(SA125)*

High Performance Brake Systems — Design, selection, and installation of brake systems for Musclecars, Hot Rods, Imports, Modern Era cars and more. *(SA126)*

High Performance C5 Corvette Builder's Guide — Improve the looks, handling and performance of your Corvette C5. *(SA127)*

High Performance Diesel Builder's Guide — The definitive guide to getting maximum performance out of your diesel engine. *(SA129)*

How to Rebuild & Modify Carter/Edelbrock Carbs — The only source for information on rebuilding and tuning these popular carburetors. *(SA130)*

Building Honda K-Series Engine Performance — The first book on the market dedicated exclusively to the Honda K series engine. *(SA134)*

Engine Management-Advanced Tuning — Take your fuel injection and tuning knowledge to the next level. *(SA135)*

How to Drag Race — Car setup, beginning and advanced techniques for bracket racing and pro classes, and racing science and math, and more. *(SA136)*

4x4 Suspension Handbook — Includes suspension basics & theory, advanced/high-performance suspension and lift systems, axles, how-to installations, and more. *(SA137)*

GM Automatic Overdrive Transmission Builder's and Swapper's Guide — Learn to build a bulletproof tranny and how to swap it into an older chassis as well. *(SA140)*

High-Performance Subaru Builder's Guide — Subarus are the hottest compacts on the street. Make yours even hotter. *(SA141)*

How to Build Max-Performance Mitsubishi 4G63t Engines — Covers every system and component of the engine, including a complete history. *(SA148)*

How to Swap GM LS-Series Engines Into Almost Anything — Includes a historical review and detailed information so you can select and fit the best LS engine. *(SA156)*

How to Autocross — Covers basic to more advanced modifications that go beyond the stock classes. *(SA158)*

Designing & Tuning High-Performance Fuel Injection Systems — Complete guide to tuning aftermarket stand-alone systems. *(SA161)*

Design & Install In Car Entertainment Systems — The latest and greatest electronic systems, both audio and video. *(SA163)*

How to Build Max-Performance Hemi Engines — Build the biggest baddest vintage Hemi. *(SA164)*

How to Digitally Photograph Cars — Learn all the modern techniques and post processing too. *(SA168)*

High-Performance Differentials, Axles, & Drivelines — Must have book for anyone thinking about setting up a performance differential. *(SA170)*

How To Build Max-Performance Mopar Big Blocks — Build the baddest wedge Mopar on the block. *(SA171)*

How to Build Max-Performance Oldsmobile V-8s — Make your Oldsmobile keep up with the pack. *(SA172)*

How to Make Your Muscle Car Handle — Upgrade your musclecar suspension to modern standards. *(SA175)*

Full-Size Fords 1955-1970 — A complete color history of full sized fords. *(SA176)*

Rebuilding Any Automotive Engine: Step-by-Step Videobook — Rebuild any engine with this book DVD combo. DVD is over 3 hours long! *(SA179)*

How to Supercharge & Turbocharge GM LS-Series Engines — Boost the power of todays most popular engine. *(SA180)*

The New MINI Performance Handbook — All the performance tricks for your new MINI. *(SA182)*

How to Build Max-Performance Ford FE Engines — Finally, performance tricks for the FE junkie. *(SA183)*

How to Build Altered Wheelbase Cars — Build a wild altered car. Complete history too! *(SA189)*

How to Build Period Correct Hot Rods — Build a hot rod true to your favorite period. *(SA192)*

How to Rebuild and Modify AMC V-8 Engine — Build an AMC beast! *(SA193)*

Automotive Sheet Metal Forming & Fabrication — Create and fabricate your own metalwork. *(SA196)*

How to Build Max-Performance Chevy Big Block on a Budget — Great new Big Block from the master, David Vizard. *(SA198)*

Chevy/GMC Pickup Performance Projects 1967-72 — Great new projects for Chevy's most popular truck. *(SA201)*

Performance Automotive Engine Math — All the formulas and facts you will ever need. *(SA204)*

S-A DESIGN RESTORATION SERIES

How to Restore Your Mustang 1964 1/2-1973 — Step by step restoration for your classic Mustang. *(SA165)*

Muscle Car Interior Restoration Guide — Make your interior look and smell new again. Includes dash restoration. *(SA167)*

How to Restore Your Camaro 1967-1969 — Step by step restoration of your 1st gen Camaro. *(SA178)*

S-A DESIGN WORKBENCH® SERIES

Workbench® Series books feature step by step instruction with hundreds of color photos for stock rebuilds and automotive repair.

How To Rebuild the Small-Block Chevrolet — *(SA26)*
How to Rebuild the Small-Block Ford — *(SA102)*
How to Rebuild & Modify High-Performance Manual Transmissions — *(SA103)*
How to Rebuild the Big-Block Chevrolet — *(SA142)*
How to Rebuild the Small-Block Mopar — *(SA143)*
How to Rebuild GM LS-Series Engines — *(SA147)*
How to Rebuild Any Automotive Engine — *(SA151)*
How to Rebuild Honda B-Series Engines — *(SA154)*
How to Rebuild the 4.6/5.4 Liter Ford — *(SA155)*
Automotive Welding: A Practical Guide — *(SA159)*
Automotive Wiring and Electrical Systems — *(SA160)*
How to Rebuild Big-Block Ford Engines — *(SA162)*
Automotive Bodywork & Rust Repair — *(SA166)*
How to Rebuild Pontiac V-8s — *(SA200)*

HISTORIES AND PERSONALITIES

Quarter-Mile Chaos — Rare & stunning photos of terrifying fires, explosions, and crashes in drag racing's golden age. *(CT425)*

Fuelies: Fuel Injected Corvettes 1957-1965 — The first Corvette book to focus specifically on the fuel injected cars, which are among the most collectible. *(CT452)*

Slingshot Spectacular: Front-Engine Dragster Era — Relive the golden age of front engine dragsters in this photo packed trip down memory lane. *(CT464)*

Chrysler Concept Cars 1940-1970 — Fascinating look at the concept cars created by Chrysler during this golden age of the automotive industry. *(CT470)*

Fuel Altereds Forever — Includes more than 250 photos of the most popular drivers and racecars from the Fuel Altered class. *(CT475)*

Yenko — Complete and thorough of the man, his business and his legendary cars. *(CT485)*

Lost Hot Rods — Great Hot Rods from the past rediscovered. *(CT487)*

Grumpy's Toys — A collection of Grumpy's greats. *(CT489)*

Woodward Avenue: Cruising the Legendary — Revisit the glory days of Woodward! *(CT491)*

Rusted Muscle — A collection of junkyard muscle cars. *(CT492)*

America's Coolest Station Wagons — Wagons are cooler than they ever have been. *(CT493)*

Super Stock — A paperback version of a classic best seller. *(CT495)*

Jerry Heasley's Rare Finds — Great collection of Heasley's best finds. *(CT497)*

Ed 'Big Daddy' Roth — Paperback reprint of a classic best seller. *(CT500)*

Visit us online at www.cartechbooks.com for more info!

www.ingramcontent.com/pod-product-compliance
Lightning Source LLC
Chambersburg PA
CBHW051409070526
44584CB00023B/3359